Waging War, Planning Peace

A VOLUME IN THE SERIES

Cornell Studies in Security Affairs

edited by Robert J. Art, Robert Jervis, and Stephen M. Walt

A list of titles in this series is available at www.cornellpress.cornell.edu

Waging War, Planning Peace

U.S. Noncombat Operations and Major Wars

AARON RAPPORT

Cornell University Press

Ithaca and London

First published 2015 by Cornell University Press

First printing, Cornell Paperbacks, 2015

Printed in the United States of America

Library of Congress Cataloging-in-Publication Data

Rapport, Aaron, author.
  Waging war, planning peace : U.S. noncombat operations and major wars/ Aaron Rapport.
        pages cm. — (Cornell studies in security affairs)
  Includes bibliographical references and index.
  ISBN 978-0-8014-5358-8 (cloth : alk. paper)—
  ISBN 978-0-8014-5661-9 (pbk. : alk. paper)
  1. United States—Armed Forces—Operations other than war—History—20th century.   2. United States—Armed Forces—Operations other than war—History— 21st century.   3. United States—Armed Forces—Operations other than war—Case studies.   4. United States—History, Military—20th century—Case studies. 5. United States—History, Military—21st century—Case studies.   I. Title.
  UH723.R37 2015
  355.4—dc23

                                                            2014026587

Cloth printing   10 9 8 7 6 5 4 3 2 1
Paperback printing   10 9 8 7 6 5 4 3 2 1

For Joyce

Contents

Acknowledgments

Seeing this book through to publication has been the most rewarding part of my career to date. As with any research project that has consumed the better part of a decade, the author of this one owes a debt of gratitude to numerous individuals and organizations. It is fitting that for a study of security and psychology so many people were willing to intervene on behalf of my physical and mental well-being when I reached critical junctures.

Several organizations helped to make my research possible. At the University of Minnesota, Ron Krebs, Martin Sampson, John Sullivan, and Gene Borgida oversaw the earliest phases of my work. Ron and Martin were particularly encouraging in the very beginning when I was not yet sure whether the project had any legs to stand on. Ron has been enmeshed in each turn my argument has taken, and has a knack for pointing out faulty logic and evidence in my writing with scalpel-like precision. Without him I'm not sure how I could have refined and improved the weaker elements of my work without "killing the patient," so to speak, which is something all researchers are tempted to do at certain points. I am less intellectually intimidated now than when I started this book, so either I'm getting smarter or Ron is using shorter words. I like to think it is the former.

My research also took shape at Minnesota in informal working groups. Logan Dancey, Chris Galdieri, Dana Griffin, Henriet Hendriks, Serena Laws, Jenny Lobasz, Kjersten Nelson, Jon Peterson, Eve Ringsmuth, and Lauren Wilcox all helped me with their perspectives and advice, even (especially?) those whose research interests were quite different from my own.

The Miller Center at the University of Virginia, and Brian Balogh, director of the center's fellowship program, made my time as a fellow a highly enjoyable and productive one even while I was working from afar. If it had not been for the Miller Center I would not have had the great privilege of working with Jack Levy, who agreed to mentor me even though he had never met me nor likely even heard my name before. Jack's knowledge of politics, psychology, and history has helped me immensely in my work, often proving invaluable. I was simultaneously ensconced at the Belfer Center for Science and International Affairs at Harvard University, where Steven Miller and Stephen Walt head the International Security Program. My officemate there, Ilai Saltzman, provided me with helpful feedback on my work and even free donuts from time to time. Other Belfer colleagues whose insights were especially important for my study of the Iraq War include Philip Bleek, Jennifer Dixon, Brendan Green, Jacqueline Hazelton, Jennifer Keister, Negeen Pegahi, and Melissa Willard-Foster.

I am grateful to have had a terrific group of colleagues in the Political Science Department at Georgia State University as the book was taking shape. Materially, Georgia State supported me with a research grant that enabled me to spend weeks visiting three presidential libraries. My use of archival materials was facilitated by the able staff at the Franklin D. Roosevelt Library in Hyde Park, New York; the Harry S. Truman Library in Independence, Missouri; and the LBJ Library in Austin, Texas. My proximity to the University of Georgia also allowed me to be one of the first visitors to the new Richard B. Russell Library, whose staff helped me navigate Dean Rusk's personal papers. Sayan Banerjee, Jason Levitt, Gulcan Saglam, and Alexandra Wishart also provided research assistance during my time at Georgia State. My new colleagues at the University of Cambridge helped me get accommodated to a new department, not to mention new country, as I was making the final revisions to the manuscript.

James McAllister deserves special credit for reading the entire manuscript and providing excellent comments, particularly on the studies of Germany and Vietnam. Jonathan Mercer, whose work at the intersection of psychology and international relations continues to influence my thinking, read and provided valuable comments on some early drafts. Dominic Tierney, whose own research on U.S. military operations and psychology gave me plenty to think about while writing the book, also provided me with helpful advice on some of my case studies. I was also fortunate to meet Larry Berman while working in Atlanta; his expertise on the Vietnam War and familiarity with its historiography substantially improved my understanding of the Johnson administration's actions in 1964–1965.

I entered the academy entirely unfamiliar with the process by which a book manuscript gets published. Roger Haydon at Cornell University Press was very helpful at guiding me every step of the way, answering every question I had as punctually as could be desired. I am grateful to have had him as an editor, especially on my first book.

My family members' support throughout has known no bounds. Adam, my younger brother, would give me encouraging words over the phone, first from college in Philadelphia, and later as a working man in New York. My parents, Phil and Becky, have seen me through all my low and high points over the years, and should know that all the low points came despite what they did, and all the highs due in no small part to their efforts. I love the three of you a whole bunch.

Finally, I am inestimably lucky to have my wife Joyce. She is my best friend and love of my life. In the five years we have been married my work has taken us to live in three different cities in two different countries, twice driving hundreds of miles with an angry hyperventilating cat in the backseat. I have no idea how I would have done it all without her, and marvel at her ability to make good things seem great and bad things seem manageable. For all this and more, I dedicate this book to her.

Abbreviations

ARVN	Army of the Republic of Vietnam
CCF	Chinese Communist Forces
CCS	Combined Chiefs of Staff
CENTCOM	U.S. Central Command
CFLCC	Combined Forces Land Component Command
CINCFE	Commander in chief, Far East
CLT	construal level theory
CORDS	Civil Operations and Revolutionary Development Support
CPA	Coalition Provisional Authority
DPRK	Democratic People's Republic of Korea
DRV	Democratic Republic of Vietnam
DT	domino theory
EAC	European Advisory Commission
ECA	Economic Cooperation Administration
ECOSOC	Economic and Social Council
FEA	Foreign Economic Administration
GVN	Government of Vietnam
IIA	Iraqi Interim Authority
JCS	Joint Chiefs of Staff
JIC	Joint Intelligence Committee
JTF	Joint Task Force
KMAG	Korean Military Advisory Group
KPA	Korean People's Army
MACV	Military Assistance Command in Vietnam
NATO	North Atlantic Treaty Organization
NSAM	National Security Action Memorandum

NSPD	National Security Presidential Directive
OIF	Operation Iraqi Freedom
ORHA	Office of Reconstruction and Humanitarian Assistance
PPS	Policy Planning Staff
ROK	Republic of Korea
RVN	Republic of Vietnam
SHAEF	Supreme Headquarters Allied Expeditionary Force
SIGIR	Special Inspector General for Iraq Reconstruction
UNC	United Nations Command
UNCURK	United Nations Commission for the Unification and Rehabilitation of Korea
UNKRA	United Nations Korean Reconstruction Agency
WSC	Working Security Committee

Introduction

Ambitious Aims and Meager Plans

In the course of World War II the U.S. military conducted substantial civil affairs operations in countries liberated from Nazi occupation and partook in an occupation of its own in Italy. These experiences highlighted significant challenges facing military units administering foreign territory, especially those units serving in North Africa and former Axis countries.[1] Meanwhile, officials in Washington were preparing for larger occupations to come in Germany and Japan. American wartime propaganda had portrayed the Japanese as subhuman sadists, but the U.S. government nevertheless planned to democratize Japan and radically alter its society. The historian John Dower describes this endeavor as "an audacious undertaking" with "no legal or historical precedent."[2] Given America's wartime experiences with military government, combined with prevailing images of the defeated enemy and the enormity and unfamiliarity of the tasks that lay ahead, one might expect considerable apprehension among U.S. officials pondering Japan's occupation. Instead, they significantly underestimated the costs involved. The common view in 1945 was that an occupation would last no longer than three years, when in fact it extended into 1952.[3] Unrealistic optimism would mark future occupations as well. One commentator has argued that the U.S. government in general has been remarkably blasé about military operations related to "governance" after combat, as it "entered virtually all of its wars with the assumption that the government of the opposing regime would change or that the political situation would shift to favor U.S. interests."[4]

U.S. policymakers have often ambitiously sought to alter the regimes of former enemies after war, but analysts have observed that the only reliable thing about U.S. military operations meant to secure postwar goals is that they are usually improvised and underresourced.[5] James Dobbins, who served as President George W. Bush's special envoy to Afghanistan, remarked of the U.S. government that "every time they do a post-war occupation, they do it like it's the first time, and they also do it like it's the last time they'll ever have to do it."[6] This book's purpose is to explain this alleged regularity by examining the main factors that shape American political leaders' assessments of noncombat military operations, placing the judgments of top officials—presidents and their principal advisers—at the center of its explanatory framework. Noncombat operations are defined here as activities carried out by personnel in a theater of combat in which the use or threatened use of force is *not* the primary means by which objectives are secured. They are typified by activities such as the provision of humanitarian assistance; civil affairs operations, up to and including the administration of an occupied territory; the reconstruction of infrastructure; and the reform, restoration, or creation of political institutions. They are also sometimes misleadingly referred to as "postconflict" or "postcombat" operations, but as the 2003 intervention in Iraq demonstrated, the assumption that such activities will take place in a peaceful environment is highly suspect.

The ways in which officials gather, process, and act on information do not arise in a vacuum. A host of existing institutional dynamics and power relationships shape the process by which military plans are made and carried out. But even though these factors structure the informational environment in which officials operate, a closer examination of the psychological mechanisms affecting leaders' assessments is necessary to explain apparent disconnects between means and ends in strategy. Take the 2003 Iraq War as an example: many top officials, including President George W. Bush, stated in public and private that the political transformation of the country and the Middle East was a major objective of the intervention. Paradoxically, an administration devoted to transformation paid little attention to the process by which this transformation would take place. It is further necessary to examine leaders' assessments of noncombat operations in multiple cases to see whether decision making prior to the Iraq War was unusual or if a general causal process can account for variation in assessments across different military interventions.

The primary argument in this book is that findings from a body of psychological research based on "construal level theory" (CLT) can account for much of how U.S. officials' have assessed noncombat operations in the midst of fighting or preparing to fight major wars.[7] Drawing on CLT, I argue that military operations that policymakers believe will take place in the more distant future will be evaluated largely on the *desirability of the goals* they are meant to achieve, whereas assessments of operations in the near future will be based more on *how feasibly they can be executed*. As desirability becomes more salient, decision makers are prone to underestimate the costs and risks of future actions; as feasibility rises to the fore, they become less prone to examine whether immediate costs are justified by overarching objectives. Abstract thinking becomes increasingly dominant in the decision-making process as actions and events are perceived to become further removed in time.

Why Study Assessments of Noncombat Operations?

American assessments of the costs and risks involved with noncombat operations are of interest due to the frequency with which the United States has undertaken these tasks. In 2004 the Defense Science Board reported that the country had become involved in a new set of stability or reconstruction operations every eighteen to twenty-four months since the end of the Cold War. It further observed that these operations had been costly in lives and dollars and that they usually lasted between five and eight years.[8] Such undertakings were not uncommon in more distant U.S. history. The U.S. military took on governance and other noncombat tasks repeatedly in the nineteenth century, including operations within the country's own borders during post–Civil War Reconstruction. Such operations began anew in Latin America and the Pacific after the Spanish–American War. Soldiers acted as administrators while overseeing the creation of new governments, the formation of which commonly overlapped with combat of a vicious intensity.[9] U.S. soldiers then occupied the Rhineland after World War I, foreshadowing the more intensive occupation of Germany after World War II.

The ramifications of poor performance in noncombat operations can be severe. On one hand states may find foreign-imposed regime change a useful tool for preventing future threats. On the other hand forcible regime change increases the likelihood of civil war within the targeted state, and weakly democratic governments imposed by outside powers can make life worse for targeted countries and their neighbors.[10] Given the difficulty of installing governments via force and the propensity of civil wars to draw in regional states, it is distressing that the United States, as the country responsible for the largest number of forced regime changes in the past half century, has apparently not developed a deeper appreciation of the challenges that face such endeavors.[11] Of course, policymakers need not seek regime change for noncombat operations to be crucial for success. Attempts to prop up existing regimes may also hinge on influencing an ally's governance during war, as U.S. experiences from Korea to Afghanistan have demonstrated.

Following the 2003 invasion of Iraq, one might have thought a new American approach to war was afoot. In November 2005 the Defense Department issued a directive asserting that stability and reconstruction activities were no longer secondary to combat operations, stating "they shall be given priority comparable to combat operations and be explicitly addressed and integrated across all DOD activities including doctrine, organizations, training, education, exercises, materiel, leadership, personnel, facilities, and planning." General William B. Caldwell, writing in the preface to the U.S. Army's new field manual on stability operations, declared that the document qualified as "a milestone in Army doctrine."[12] The military's policy moves were preceded by similar steps by civilian departments. The State Department created a new Office of Reconstruction and Stabilization, which President

3

Bush directed to coordinate the planning and implementation of reconstruction and stabilization missions. State's new office was accompanied by an Interagency Management System designed to "integrate military and civilian planning at the Washington, Combatant Command, and Embassy/Joint Task Force Levels."[13] Likewise, academic research on state and nation building proliferated. Directed at policymakers as much as scholars, this work stresses a somewhat standard set of activities that must be executed if conflict-torn states are to be strengthened, especially the provision of population security and construction of institutions necessary for governance and peaceful political competition.[14]

Beyond the question of what (and how) noncombat operations should be implemented on the ground, one must also consider how political leaders assess such tasks in the first place. It should not be taken for granted that, once in place, new organizations and doctrines will have a considerable impact on the assessments of political leaders. Addressing the Iraq War, one prominent scholar of international relations noted that neither policy advisers nor theorists had a strong grasp on how the assessment of postconflict costs affect the initiation or execution of military campaigns.[15] Do political and military leaders evaluate the risks, costs, and goals associated with noncombat or postconflict operations the same way they assess those of major combat activities, or are there systematic differences between the two? Will they be receptive to the advice offered by the military and new executive organizations, never mind the academic literatures, or will officials' intervention goals discourage them from engaging with or accepting such counsel? There are reasons to suspect the answer to be negative, for as Fred Iklé states succinctly, "war plans tend to cover only the first act."[16]

Iklé's contention carries major implications. The activities scholars and policy experts have recommended for securing peace after conflict—from the relatively simple task of providing humanitarian assistance to the highly ambitious aim of erecting new legal and political institutions—are unlikely to materialize without some forethought and support from top decision makers. More importantly, the decision to initiate a military intervention should depend on the potential difficulties that could arise in *all* types of operations and stages of a campaign. Just as leaders may reconsider military action after revising estimates of the opposing side's strength, they may reconsider intervention if military victory means having to administer an ungovernable territory. Whether or not government reorganization can compel top decision makers to pay greater heed to such factors remains to be seen.

Existing Analyses: Culture, Organizations, and Their Shortcomings

Unjustified confidence with respect to noncombat operations is not likely limited to the United States. Overconfidence in war is not an uncommon occurrence.[17] Overconfidence toward military occupation and civil administration thus might be expected. David Edelstein, in one of the most systematic accountings of military occupations to date, estimates these types of campaigns have succeeded in attaining occupiers' objectives less than a third of the time since 1815. Despite this dismal record, Edelstein documents a three-stage "occupation dilemma" that begins with occupying powers underestimating the difficulty of the tasks in front of them.[18] The juxtaposition of repeated failure in the aggregate and overconfidence on a case-by-case basis is puzzling.

Still, given the prominence of the United States in such endeavors, it is tempting to discern the origins of this pattern in some particular aspect of U.S. or liberal political culture. Between 1945 and 2003, the United States engaged in at least six interventions whose primary purpose was to forcibly remove the government of another state, or almost half of all such campaigns conducted by the permanent members of the United Nations Security Council in that period.[19] This type of objective frequently requires some type of military administration, reconstruction, or stabilization activities after hostilities. Furthermore, the United States either led or was involved in ten of the sixteen occupations recorded by Edelstein in the same time frame. With this historical backdrop, Colin Dueck argued that the difficulties facing the Bush administration during the Iraq War were not isolated from previous events but rather the result of liberal assumptions inherited from "Woodrow Wilson through Franklin Roosevelt and Harry Truman to William Jefferson Clinton." According to Jonathan Monten, "the widely recognized inadequacy in postwar planning in Iraq is evidence of an underlying Progressive faith in progress and liberal rationality." Similarly, Dominic Tierney argues that "cultural forces" cause Americans to view militarily imposed regime change in the name of democracy as "glorious" but "nation-building in places like Vietnam and Afghanistan as a wearying trial," thus accounting for a measure of exuberance at the start of such ventures that quickly dissolves.[20]

The primary shortcoming of political-cultural explanations of U.S. performance in noncombat operations is that a constant cannot explain variation between cases. If liberal assumptions made U.S. officials underestimate the cost of occupying Iraq in 2003, why did they not have the same effect on George H. W. Bush and his administration when considering an occupation of Iraq in 1991? The idea was rejected, according to Bush and his National Security adviser Brent Scowcroft, because the United States "would have incurred incalculable human and political costs."[21] Bush and Scowcroft might be argued to be more "realist" than most American political leaders, but according to Dueck American realists retain some commitment to liberalism while exhibiting a greater willingness to expand U.S. liabilities than other policymakers.[22] Relatedly, political culture cannot explain differences in individuals over time, or between individuals in specific cases. Why did Richard Cheney oppose attacking and occupying Baghdad as secretary of defense during the Gulf War, only to become one of the most vociferous proponents of such a campaign a decade later as vice president?[23] Why did Secretary of State Colin Powell challenge Cheney's and others' optimistic assessments of what an occupation of Iraq would entail? Societal-level variables like political culture do not carry us far in addressing these questions.

The values and practices of the U.S. military have also featured in scholarly explanations of noncombat performance. It has been argued that U.S. failures during noncombat operations are due to a host of values and biases within the U.S. armed forces. These may be epitomized by General William Westmoreland's simple response to the question of what would defeat the communist insurgency in South Vietnam: "firepower."[24] Even in post–World War II occupied Germany, commonly regarded as a successful case of U.S. troops facilitating a democratic political transition, there have been strident critiques of military efforts by those with firsthand knowledge of the occupation's preparation and execution.[25] One officer reviewing the history of the country's performance in nation building summarized the U.S. Army's attitude thusly: "train for war, adapt for peace, with just enough and just in time!"[26]

If the U.S. military, as the organization responsible for conducting stabilization and reconstruction activities, does not value expertise in these types of tasks nor invests in training and doctrine to improve its performance in noncombat operations, these missions may be neglected, misunderstood, or denigrated. Officers should not then be expected to forcefully advocate the importance of noncombat activities in deliberations with political leaders, instead focusing on the use of firepower and maneuver to defeat the enemy. If the only tool you have is a hammer, everything starts to look like a nail. However, it would be a gross simplification to assert that the hammer is the only tool in the U.S. armed forces' toolbox. While institutional practices stressing importance of "military operations other than war" have waxed and waned over time, they have never disappeared. Additionally, the military's ability and inclination to inform civilian leaders' assessments of noncombat operations are affected by more than organizational practices and values. Though military personnel have some leeway in how they achieve campaign objectives, the amount of autonomy they enjoy is contingent.[27] They might expect to be especially constrained in the area of noncombat operations. Because of their "political" nature, these operations appear closer to stereotypical bastions of civilian authority than do combat actions. What is more, if the political balance of power in government tilts too far toward either civilians or the military, effective collaboration may be blocked.[28] If the military does not have the opportunity to significantly impact leaders' assessments of noncombat operations, one arrives back at political-cultural explanations, the shortcomings of which have been outlined.

Overview of the Argument: The Challenges of "Thinking Ahead"

As already noted, it is important not to conflate noncombat and postconflict operations, as military units may be simultaneously engaged in combat and noncombat activities. However, while different types of military operations will overlap, it is often true that combat operations will commence before activities related to the administration of an occupied territory. This sequencing encourages the use of the "postconflict" label for noncombat operations. It also likely reinforces Alexander George's observation that presidents and top officials evaluate risks in the sequence with which they are projected to arise, as well as contentions that officials tend to think of war as being divided into distinct stages.[29] It is not surprising that individuals think of events sequentially, nor does it elicit shock to suggest that undesired consequences arise when the actual order of events does not turn out as predicted. However, it is less intuitive that a person's belief about when an event or action will take place in a sequence—whether one expects something will occur in the near or more distant future relative to other events—can fundamentally affect the cognitive process that person uses to assess the event or action in question. This nonobvious assertion is the core of CLT and this book's argument regarding leaders' assessments of noncombat operations.

In the 1970s, Daniel Kahneman and Amos Tversky began documenting a host of psychological biases and mental shortcuts people employ when processing information and making decisions, including one bias dubbed the "planning fallacy."[30] They found that people systematically underestimated how long it would take them to complete a task, even when they had completed similar tasks in the past. This was true of people one might expect to be least susceptible to such biases, such as scientists and engineers. To use a military analogy, people appeared to neglect the potential for "friction," or unexpected events that could hinder the completion of a project as it moved forward. Individuals were also overconfident about the precision of their estimates. If a task typically took six months to complete, plus or minus one month, someone succumbing to the planning fallacy might expect it to take four months, plus or minus one week. Kahneman and Tversky reasoned that people contemplating a project's completion necessarily had to focus on the future, which in turn led them to neglect the variability of their past experiences. However, other researchers have found that even if people do attend to previous instances in which unexpected setbacks increased the challenge of completing a task, they do not necessarily incorporate this information into their new predictions about similar projects.[31] Furthermore, the tendency to downplay the risks and costs associated with a plan of action appears to become more pronounced the farther into the future a task is to be completed or undertaken.[32]

As research on the planning fallacy progressed, Robin Vallacher and Daniel Wegner were examining how people understood and interpreted their own actions. According to their "action identification" theory of behavior, people either think about actions primarily in terms of their purpose and consequences, or focus on the specific details of how a given action is carried out.[33] The former represents an abstract "high level" mode of thinking, while the latter is concrete and "low level." An abstract representation of an action emphasizes its ends, while a concrete representation highlights means. People normally think about actions with which they are familiar in abstract, high-level terms, whereas novel actions often necessitate more concrete low-level forms of thought. For example, an experienced driver is likely to think about a car trip in terms of the purpose of their journey, rather than carefully focusing on applying the gas or signaling turns. Conversely, a novice driver might need to think very carefully about the specific steps necessary to safely operate their vehicle, rather than concentrate on their ultimate destination. Vallacher and Wegner observe that high-level cognition is something of a "mixed blessing." While high-level representations of an action help us to understand the fundamental "essence" or purpose of that behavior, it can also promote inattention to detail.[34]

CLT integrates the insights behind research on the planning fallacy and action identification theory, treating the temporal distance of an action or event as a crucial feature of the decision-making environment. According to the CLT framework, the overconfidence that Kahneman and Tversky documented when people think about their future plans occurs because of a shift in their level of action identification. This theoretical approach was pioneered by Yaacov Trope and Nira Liberman, and has become increasingly prominent in the field of psychology.[35] Theirs and others' research has shown that framing an activity as something that comes first or last alters the cognitive style individuals apply to its analysis. When people assess actions they presume will come early in a sequence of events they tend to engage in a more concrete style of analysis then when they evaluate those that will occur in the more distant future. Again, "low-level" concrete thought is detail-oriented and concerned with *how* an action or event will occur. A concrete thinker is attuned to contextual details that may hinder or facilitate an action's completion. Alternatively, people considering a task's ultimate completion have a more distal temporal focus, and are disposed to engage in abstract high-level thinking focused on the reasons *why* a particular action will be carried out. This means they will be less attentive to contextual details relevant to the action's implementation. Ask an author writing a book manuscript what they will be working on next week and they will likely give you concrete details, such as the method they are using to analyze data or track down sources. Ask the same author to think about what they will be doing once the manuscript nears completion, however, and you are likely to get a more abstract description of their primary research goals, and the contribution they anticipate the book will make to existing knowledge. Furthermore, the author's high-level goals are likely to remain relatively constant, even if events force her to alter the means by which she goes about writing it.

It is not hard to understand why someone considering the more distant future might be more likely to think about the goals they are trying to achieve rather than the concrete steps necessary to attain those goals. Concrete thinking demands an awareness of the particular conditions that can constrain or enable one's actions. It is easier to acquire meaningful, reliable details about the context in which an action will be carried out when it will happen in the near-future. Conversely, concrete thinking is more difficult the further removed in time an action or event becomes. Furthermore, as a specific event is presumed to come later and later in a sequence, the context in which it will occur becomes more dependent on preceding events, some of which will likely be unaccounted for in a strategic plan. However, because the overarching goals that a series of actions and events are supposed to achieve are fairly context-independent, these can continue to factor into individuals' assessments without much cognitive strain.

Normative rationality dictates that when someone is choosing between different courses of action, they should jointly consider the value of the objective they are trying to obtain and the probability that a given action will lead to that outcome. Findings from the construal-level paradigm, however, depart from this normative model. All else being equal, people should assign lower probabilities to the success of actions later in a sequence. Temporal distance increases the dependence of ultimate results on earlier outcomes, as well as allowing more random events to intervene and upset plans. Instead, studies have shown that people cope with the cognitive strain of considering the feasibility of future actions together with the more certain desirability of future goals by discounting the former in favor of the latter. As an action becomes further removed in time, details of how it will be carried out, along with the likelihood of its success, become increasingly less important criteria for decision making relative to the magnitude of the goals to be achieved.[36] Details regarding how an objective will be obtained are neglected, but decision-makers remain fixated on the value of the goal itself.

This thought pattern indicates that reliance on abstract thinking is a heuristic device, or cognitive shortcut, used to simplify decision making and reinforce dedication to the attainment of distant goals. In some scenarios this heuristic could be "functional" in the sense that it might lead to the achievement of valued objectives while minimizing cognitive stress. If people did not reason this way, perhaps we would rarely commit ourselves to important but costly long-term goals, and the world would be a poorer place for it. However, neglecting the feasibility of one's means will also lead decision makers to be overly optimistic about the likelihood of ultimate success. It is quite risky to commit to an endeavor because one covets the reward at the end without seriously considering whether that reward can be had, or whether it will be worth the effort. Injecting a measure of concreteness into one's thinking can help prevent poorly thought-out decisions, as considerations of feasibility are considered jointly with those related to desirability. Still, it would be incorrect to assert that a cognitive style that is concrete is invariably preferable to those that are abstract. If strategy is fundamentally an exercise in selecting appropriate means to achieve one's ends, it is clear that a balance between abstract and concrete thought is necessary for effective strategizing. Decision makers who rely on highly concrete construal can grasp the potential challenges involved with each discrete step required to carry out a specific task but may also endorse courses of action that can be feasibly executed but do not necessarily advance overarching goals. Concrete thinkers may treat their means, which are merely tools for achieving objectives, as ends in and of themselves.

This book proposes that the challenges of thinking about the future should affect the decision making of officials considering military action just as it affects construal of other complex tasks. CLT proposes that leaders preparing to embark on a military intervention will focus more attention on the details of near-term combat operations in a campaign than on plans for securing peace after victory, even if early combat operations are more likely to succeed than the operations that follow. The feasibility of noncombat operations and tasks that tend to be executed in the late or "postwar" phases of a campaign will pale in comparison to the desirability of the goals these tasks are meant to achieve. As a result, decision makers may commit themselves to an intervention they would not have had they given greater weight to the feasibility of future tasks. In some cases, they will seek the political transformation of a targeted state, if that is an end they value, but not devote much attention or resources to preparations for noncombat operations meant to achieve this aim. Rigorous assessment need not accompany a sincere desire to achieve long-term change. Noncombat operations are not doomed to neglect, however. Senior officials will be more likely to engage with the concrete details regarding their execution if it is believed these activities will occur concurrently with, or precede, conventional combat activities. However, if officials' cognitive style becomes overly concrete, a disconnect will emerge between strategic goals and operational plans, and the latter will develop in isolation from the former.

Accurate assessment and rigorous preparation for noncombat operations are not sufficient to ensure that officials will achieve their primary objectives, just as such preparation cannot guarantee success when combat activities are in question. Factors that are largely resistant to policymakers' planning may be extremely important in determining whether a military campaign succeeds or fails. Accurate strategic assessment is still important, however; it may lead to an alteration of political goals, or the abandonment of military plans altogether. The difference in cost between two "successful" campaigns—one of which involves years of violence between intervening forces and an occupied population, the other in which an occupation is short and violence rare—is clear.

Temporal Construal in a Political Realm

Theories of the relationship between temporal distance and human cognition are often tested and refined using controlled experiments in which researchers carefully manipulate participants' perceptions of time. Outside of the experimental setting, factors beyond the researcher's control govern these perceptions. One feature of noncombat operations is that they often begin later than major combat by necessity and are thus framed as postconflict. However, additional variables will affect perception of these operations as well.

First, this study hypothesizes that the goals the president and senior officials establish in a military campaign will significantly affect cognitive style and thus problem construal. In some instances, policymakers primarily seek to maintain or return to the recent status quo. These are categorized as *maintenance* objectives. They include attempts to preserve a foreign regime or put a recently deposed regime back in power, safeguard regional balances of power, or restore peace after an outbreak of violence. Alternatively, *transformative* objectives seek to alter the status quo, not maintain or restore a former state of affairs. Examples include campaigns to depose regimes, create new political institutions in targeted states, or significantly alter the intervening state's security environment. It is assumed that, on average, political leaders with transformative objectives will have longer "time horizons" than leaders with maintenance goals. The latter are expected to have short time horizons because they are focused on maintaining their present situation, or restoring conditions that existed in the recent past. They are expected to highly discount the value of events as they become further removed in time. Conversely, leaders with transformative aims will likely focus on near-term military operations, but their goals will also lead them to be concerned with some future, unrealized state of affairs. They will adopt the more distant future as a focal point, rather than the status quo. Though leaders with short time horizons are more prevalent in maintenance interventions and those with long time horizons more prevalent in transformative ones, there is also a "mix" of individuals within each intervention type, making for fruitful within-case comparisons.

This discussion of transformative and maintenance objectives leads back to the paradox of U.S. foreign policy laid out above: leaders set ambitious transformative goals but neglect the means necessary to achieve them. Ironically, CLT predicts that officials with shorter time horizons will be most inclined to think about the details and feasibility of operations needed to achieve long-term objectives, even though they do not value those goals as much as their "farsighted" counterparts. Transformative goals, and the positive expectations associated with them, will overshadow more concrete details regarding how temporally distant operations meant to achieve said goals will be carried out. This is less likely to be the case for individuals pursuing maintenance objectives, who have shorter time horizons. Their goals encourage a less distal focus, and thus more concrete thinking. Additionally, the lack of longer-term objectives lessens the chance that construal of future actions and events will be infused with optimistic feelings. Though it is no simple matter to measure how much value government officials' assign to future goals, there are methods by which officials can be placed in a rough order based on their time horizons. An individual's policy jurisdiction, her publicly and privately stated values before and during a military campaign, and the congruence between public and private statements can all be used as indicators of time horizon length. These techniques will be detailed more fully in following chapters.

Aside from an intervention's goals, the balance of forces in a military conflict will also affect leaders' time horizons. The more this balance is perceived to favor the intervening state, the more attention individuals can afford to give to future actions rather than near-term or ongoing operations. Larger military advantages should increase officials' confidence that initial military operations will be successful, allowing them to focus more on the future. Furthermore, a favorable shift in the balance of forces reduces the opportunity costs of saving resources, rather than employing them for short-term gains on the battlefield. This is equivalent to increasing the subjective value of the future relative to the present.

Leaders' beliefs about noncombat operations will also be shaped by how the information they receive prior to and during a military intervention impacts expectations of success. If military actors and the intelligence community disseminate information indicating that noncombat operations will take place in a secure environment among a population willing to comply with policy goals, one might expect political leaders to be optimistic about their prospects for success and feel less compelled to engage with the details of military plans. Conversely, if leaders receive uncertain or conflicting reports, or intelligence that asserts that noncombat operations will have to clear major hurdles to achieve their goals, it could be expected that officials would feel the need to devote more attention and resources to these operations, or reevaluate their objectives.[37] CLT qualifies these expectations by drawing attention to conditions under which people are more or less receptive to specific types of information. As laid out more fully in the next chapter, individuals are more likely to attend to information that complements their existing frame of mind. People who are disposed to think abstractly will be more receptive to information regarding the desirability of proposed goals than the feasibility of actions meant to achieve those goals; the reverse will be true of those inclined toward concrete analysis.

Strategic Assessment and Noncombat Operations

Factors such as the balance of power between opposing forces, the information available to decision makers, and the structure of organizations charged with providing leaders information may all shape officials' evaluations of military operations. While acknowledging the role these variables play, this book advances a psychological explanation of variation in assessments and, by doing so, embraces the assertion that political leaders are crucial in determining policy outcomes. Analyses of the role leaders play in foreign policy have often pivoted on particular leadership "styles." Some decision makers have been found to be more driven by personal goals and less sensitive to the demands of particular situations, whereas others appear more sensitive to context, political constraints, and incoming information.[1] While some leaders are undoubtedly more sensitive to context and some more motivated by personal priorities, the basic argument of construal level theory (CLT) is that the relative salience of context-dependent constraints and personally valued goals will depend on how temporally distant policymakers perceive future actions and events to be.

This chapter first defines the universe of cases addressed by the argument presented here. It then proceeds to define the concept of strategic assessment and lay out explanations of variations in assessment based on CLT. After setting forth hypotheses derived from the theory and explaining their rationale, it then discusses alternative explanations gathered from existing international relations literatures. It concludes with a discussion of cases and methodology used to test the CLT hypotheses as well as those based on alternative explanatory frameworks.

The Scope of the Argument: Noncombat Operations within Wars

The objective of this book is to analyze assessments of the costs and risks associated with noncombat activities that coincide with large-scale combat operations. Three principal types of noncombat tasks are covered: the administration, stabilization, and reconstruction activities involved in state building; ancillary noncombat activities that often support state building, such as the provision of basic humanitarian assistance; and pacification. These operations will more often than not be associated with the "postconflict" phase of military campaigns, though this will not always be the case.

The Introduction defined noncombat operations as those in which the use of force is not the primary means by which a military campaign's objectives are secured. A mission constitutes a combat operation if the majority of that mission's personnel are tasked with forcibly defeating, seizing, or destroying enemy armed forces, population, or territory, or are directly supporting personnel engaged in these tasks.[2] Some military activities that have been categorized as "peace operations" in the scholarly literature are combat rather than noncombat activities within this definition. For example, Paul Diehl and colleagues categorize collective enforcement, protective services, and interventions in support of democracy as types of peace operations, and all three revolve mainly around the use of force.[3]

This book primarily deals with state building, which involves the creation or restoration of a government capable of exercising sovereign control over a defined territory, as well as the construction of infrastructure which facilitates the activities of the state and civil society. The U.S. Army lays out the specific tasks of state building: "Rebuild host-nation institutions, including various types of security forces, correctional facilities, and judicial systems necessary to secure and stabilize the environment; revive or build the private sector, including encouraging citizen-driven, bottom-up economic activity and constructing necessary infrastructure; develop representative government institutions." If existing institutions of government are absent or largely ineffectual, military personnel may establish and run a transitional government in which they control the functions normally associated with a sovereign state.[4] State building need not involve the construction of liberal political and economic institutions. Intervening military forces may seek to create a variety of different institutions in the polities they target, including those policymakers believe will facilitate imperial domination. Adolf Hitler's Nazi regime was intent on constructing institutions in occupied Europe to solidify the German Reich, for example.[5]

A large undertaking like state building will also encapsulate many other activities that would by themselves fall outside the purview of this study. For instance, "traditional" peacekeeping missions sanctioned under chapter VI of the United Nations (UN) Charter are typically not accompanied by combat operations. Instead, peacekeepers act as mediators who serve as buffers, monitors, and nominally neutral conduits of information between two or more belligerents, or as election monitors after periods of civil war.[6] They may also provide humanitarian assistance to civilians affected by a conflict. Because interveners in these missions are supposed to be impartial secondary actors, their presence in a host state or territory typically depends on belligerents' consent. These missions fall outside the scope of this book unless they coincide with major military interventions in which combat is undertaken.

Pacification represents a mix of both combat and noncombat activities, and thus it is nested within both of these categories. Pacification includes combat operations such as defeating local armed groups and the forcible separation of belligerents; it also involves using nonviolent methods to quell civil disturbances and maintain law and order.[7] Unlike state building, the noncombat aspects of pacification are more geographically and politically confined. Pacification missions attempt to create, reconstruct, and stabilize economic and political conditions in a local area within a country, rather than target the central political and economic institutions of a state as a whole.

What Is Strategic Assessment?

Strategic assessment is the process by which decision makers evaluate and select political goals and the military strategies meant to achieve them. It refers both to the measures decision makers take to structure their analysis of a problem and the actual substance of policymakers' assessments. To make strategic assessments, actors establish rules and norms for gathering, distributing, and deliberating over information. The substance of actors' assessments includes their conceptualization of desired goals and specific courses of action, the anticipated costs and benefits of those plans, and perceptions of whether chosen courses of action are working as predicted.[8] The way decision makers structure the assessment process will determine the substance of their assessments; however, actors' prior beliefs will also affect how they structure the assessment process. If decision makers believe a goal should be easily achievable, they may select different procedures for gathering information or choosing policy than if they had initially thought said goal would require them to surmount many taxing problems.

While researchers have sought to explain variation in the success of strategic assessment across cases, less attention has been given to how policymakers' assessments vary across different lines of operation within military campaigns. Likewise, academic work does not prominently feature strategic assessment in accounts of how noncombat military operations unfold. Take, for example, work on military occupations, which often include the transformation of a targeted state's political institutions. Studies have attributed the success or failure of occupations to the nationalism of the occupied population; the coercive capacity of the occupying force; whether an occupied state has been decimated by war; the presence or absence of a threat shared by the occupiers and occupied; and the ability of the occupier to make credible commitments.[9] These factors are resistant to manipulation by policymakers, and thus do not leave much of a role for strategic assessment. Others have found that an occupation's success relates to the strategies and tactics adopted by the occupier, which in turn implies the importance of strategic assessment, but these arguments remain implicit.[10]

Strategic Assessment, Operation Sequence, and CLT

While there are significant differences between major theories of international relations, it is difficult to think of a perspective which would challenge the assertion that caring about the future encourages preparations for it. Although this contention may seem mundane, it actually contains a major assumption: people think about objectives in the more distant future much the same way they think about similarly valued objectives in the short term. They are assumed to be just as attendant to probability considerations and the risks and potential costs of plans to attain future objectives as they are when considering how to attain their goals in the present. However, there is a significant body of literature in the field of psychology on the effects of time delay on cognition and choice which challenges this premise. Much recent research on how people think about the future is based on CLT.

THE CLT PARADIGM

CLT starts from the basic premise that it is more mentally challenging to ascertain reliable details about the context in which actions will be carried out the more temporally distant that context is. It is always difficult to envision how the distant future will be shaped by one's present actions in combination with unexpected events. Choosing from many possible commonplace examples, this can be illustrated by considering preparations for a trip to visit friends in another town. Among the relevant pieces of information one might want to consider when planning a trip are the monetary costs of different forms of transportation; how weather might affect arrival and departure times, as well as what clothing is appropriate to bring; how long of an absence can be allowed for given demands at one's workplace; and so on. All of this contextual information will be easier to obtain if one's trip is in three weeks rather than three months, let alone a year or more. Even if people do take multiple contingencies into account, individuals tend to be poor predictors of how they will react to future events.[11]

Normatively rational models of choice assume that people engage in compensatory decision making: each dimension of one's possible options is assigned a value which is summed with the values of the other dimensions associated with that option. This aggregated value is then weighed against the values of all the alternative options to arrive at a ranked set of preferences. Using the example of taking a trip, the monetary cost of flying may be compensated for by the short amount of time that air travel takes, allowing for more time at the final destination. Such a decision-making strategy, though utility-maximizing, is also cognitively demanding. Is the value of time saved commensurable with that of money? How many relevant dimensions of each alternative are there, and how liable are the values one assigns to these dimensions to change? Given these demands, one may try to limit the criteria that are evaluated when making a choice by instead using noncompensatory heuristics, or "mental shortcuts." Heuristics serve to limit the number of criteria individuals must consider when making a decision.[12]

To cope with the complexities of evaluating choices having to do with temporally distant outcomes, CLT holds that people simplify the decision-making process by focusing on criteria that are less context-dependent. One such heuristic is to focus on the desirability of one's ultimate goals, or the reasons *why* an action is being taken, instead of the feasibility of one's goals, which relates to *how* a goal will be obtained. In other words, abstract construal emphasizes ends, while concrete construal highlights means.[13] In the terms of CLT, focusing on desirability, or "why" criteria, is an abstract "high level" construal: one's actions are thought of in terms of their ultimate purposes and consequences, while feasibility considerations are placed at the periphery of one's thoughts. High-level considerations are relatively independent of contextual constraints, and they thus require less mental effort than low-level considerations, particularly when assessing more distant actions. The purpose of a specific trip, whether business or pleasure, can stay relatively fixed regardless of the means of transportation one takes.

Besides being relatively independent of contextual constraints, abstract considerations involve deductive reasoning from simple, preexisting beliefs or theories of the way the world works. If it is difficult to picture how possible constraints will affect the completion of a specific task, one is likely to focus on the "prototypical" example of that task instead. Returning to the example of taking a trip, someone might refer to the prototypical components of a "family vacation" or "business travel," and make deductions from these ideal-type categories to fill in any blanks. The prototypical example of a "vacation trip" may differ quite a bit from person to person. However, one thing people's prototypical categories have in common is that they emphasize what each person sees as the most fundamental and constant dimensions of an activity or event. Variations between specific examples of the broader category are obscured. This aspect of deductive thinking is crucial to Daniel Kahneman and Amos Tversky's explanation for the "planning fallacy" discussed in the Introduction.[14] When people brush aside variations in their previous experiences completing a task, they downplay the potential for unexpected events to interfere with the completion of the task the next time around. Table 1.1 lists the features of high-level, abstract construal and low-level, concrete construal.

Given that it is difficult to predict how future conditions will constrain one's actions, one might expect that people would tend to be ambivalent or pessimistic when evaluating plans to attain long-range objectives. However,

Table 1.1 Features of abstract and concrete construal

Abstract Construal	Concrete Construal
Favored when actions/events are temporally distant	Favored when actions/events are temporally near
Simple, general, decontextualized	Complex, detailed, context-dependent
Deductive, theory-based reasoning	Inductive reasoning
Focus on "why" (ends)	Focus on "how" (means)

combine people's tendency to neglect unexpected events with a focus on the desirability of one's future goals, and you have a recipe for overconfident assessment. This is not the same as motivated reasoning, in which overly optimistic perceptions are driven by a need to ignore or downplay emotionally upsetting information.[15] Rather than being prompted by anxiety or other unpleasant feelings, a reliance on abstraction is a simplifying mechanism that helps a decision maker to evaluate complex and uncertain actions. Furthermore, one would expect individuals engaged in motivated reasoning to exhibit overconfidence regardless of whether they were considering near or distant future actions, whereas CLT expects overconfidence to be more prominent as temporal distance increases.

CLT does not expect that abstract thinking and the desirability of one's goals will always hinder assessment of the potential difficulties of accomplishing a task. Instead, abstract and high-level considerations will become more prominent when people consider goals that are temporally distant, because this type of construal facilitates decision making when contextual information is scarce.[16] Concrete, low-level construal becomes more common as an action or event becomes closer in time, even if the ultimate end one seeks is very attractive, because it is not as difficult to envision possible difficulties that will impact a task's implementation. Concrete construal involves inductive reasoning about the details of a specific case, rather than general deductive reasoning about the category in which that case fits.

CLT'S CAUSAL MECHANISMS AT WORK

To reiterate, the primary mechanism identified by CLT which affects strategic assessment is a temporally induced preference for *privileging desirability or feasibility* during decision making. Temporal distance also affects whether individuals rely on *deductive or inductive reasoning*. The third mechanism which reinforces the first two is changes in an individual's *communication fluency*, or receptivity to abstract and concrete information.

Desirability vs. Feasibility. Because it is difficult to envision the concrete details surrounding distant future actions, decision makers focus intently on their goals, which are less context-dependent, when making evaluations. Focusing on goals—the "why" of a task—draws attention to the desirability of one's anticipated payoffs.[17] This occurs to the detriment of a concern with the feasibility of the means to attain desired goals; because important details necessary for such evaluations are "out of sight," they are also "out of mind." Overreliance on abstract thinking results in a failure to consider whether one's goals are reasonable or not. A failure to consider the specific steps in a policy can translate into an inability to consider unintended outcomes.[18] This leads to overconfidence that is akin to risk blindness. This is not equivalent to risk acceptance, however, which is quite compatible with rational modes of decision. Risk-acceptant actors recognize that their probability estimates of different outcomes might be flawed.[19] Rather than accounting for the potential pitfalls a course of action might entail, "risk blind" decision makers sally forth in ignorance of what might be lurking around the bend, failing to take into account relevant information that would lead to more accurate assessments. Counterintuitively, then, *the planning for a long-term goal may be neglected even though an individual does not discount the value of the goal itself.*

This phenomenon is observable in studies of lotteries. Consider someone facing two alternatives with the same expected values. Both options carry immediate consequences (a gain, loss, or no change) once selected. Individuals whose choices yield immediate outcomes tend to prefer options with small payoffs but a high probability of winning to those that are low-probability, high-payoff gambles. When the outcomes of these same two choices are delayed, however, this preference is reversed: high-risk, high-reward gambles become more appealing. Prospect theory, among the most prominent psychological theories to be applied to security studies, explains risky gain-seeking behavior in part by positing that people overweight low probabilities.[20] However, studies have found that as the temporal distance of a potential payoff grows, people pay less attention to probability and focus instead on the size of the possible gains.[21] In other words, people do not overemphasize probability considerations, but instead overlook them.

As implied by this finding, the amount individuals are willing to wager is more dependent on the magnitude of a payoff when outcomes are temporally distant, whereas wagers on near-term outcomes are more influenced by the probability of winning. Similarly, people find lotteries increasingly attractive as the chances of winning increase, but delaying a lottery's outcome by just two months substantially lowers the effect of improving its odds. Other studies have found that manipulating the likelihood of a negative event's occurrence in the more distant future has no effect on how threatening people judge the event. Research has also shown that as outcomes of actions become further removed and abstract construal is induced, people exhibit similar confidence in the likelihood of a positive outcome regardless of whether success depends on skill or chance, demonstrating the increasing irrelevance of one's means as evaluation criteria.[22] In short, desirability tends to trump feasibility in the long-term.

As concrete procedural matters become less salient relative to a goal's desirability, people are less mindful of the costs associated with obtaining their aims, and thus are more prone to underestimate resources such as time and effort that must be expended to reach their ends. Even if actors expect negative events to arise in the distant future, CLT predicts they will be optimistic about whether their own actions will effectively deal with these events. People typically feel positively about the goals they set, and these positive feelings become more pronounced as their ultimate objectives become increasingly salient relative to other considerations.[23] If the ultimate goal of some policy is viewed more positively than the steps which must be taken to attain that goal, then the policy will be evaluated more positively when the time to realization or implementation is further away, because its abstract components will be more salient. As the date of the hypothetical policy's enactment approaches, however, its concrete elements will be given more weight, and its overall appeal may decline. Relatedly, numerous studies have found that positive feelings (or "affect") promote overconfidence and more simplistic reasoning, while neutral or negative feelings produce more accurate assessments and conservatism.[24] Accordingly, as the length of time until an opportunity to act grows, people fear errors of omission more than errors of commission. This means they believe they would have greater regrets if something undesirable happened because they did *not* act than if something undesirable happened because they did act.[25] People are more disposed to endorse bold action when considering distant opportunities because they are mentally associated with desirable consequences and positive feelings, whereas potentially costly errors become more salient in the near term.

Communication Fluency. CLT further predicts strategic assessments will be affected via shifting "communication fluency," or receptivity to different types of information. It is easier for people to comprehend information that is congruent with their mental state. When people engage in abstract construal they become more receptive to information about the desirability of their goals and less receptive to concrete information about how proposed actions meant to achieve their goals might transpire. The opposite pattern holds when someone is in a low-level, concrete state of mind. People are mentally "primed" to receive information for which their mind-set is already encouraging them to search, and accordingly they weight abstract or concrete information more heavily in their judgments when considering the distant or near future, respectively.[26] One example of communication fluency involves how people evaluate candidates for political office. When participants in an experiment were presented with information about fictional candidates in an election, they found campaign messages which revolved around how policy should be implemented significantly more appealing when they were told the election was one week away, as opposed to six months in the future. Conversely, abstract messages about values and ideals concerning why policies should be pursued were more appealing when the election was six months away.[27]

Aside from being primed to receive high-level information more readily than low-level information, or vice versa, people also mistakenly attribute their comprehension of a message (or lack thereof) to the quality of the message being sent, rather than how congruent it is with their mind-set. People have trouble distinguishing between the thoughts and feelings promoted by their preexisting mental state and those induced by the message they are receiving. Thus, they may attribute negative evaluations of incoming information to its content and organization rather than their own transient predispositions. This misattribution effect has been shown to be present in people's evaluations of messages regarding public policy.[28]

Deductive vs. Inductive Reasoning. Given the messiness of reality and constraints on information availability, it is unavoidable that people form general, abstract theories of how the world works. Information constraints will normally be greater when people try to evaluate how temporally distant events will unfold. This encourages greater reliance on deductive reasoning, leading people to anticipate outcomes based on preexisting beliefs about a general class of actions or events rather than concrete, observed information about a specific case.[29] Conceptions of distant future actions and events will be less complex and more prototypical than will those which are immediate or impending.

A decision maker assessing temporally distant actions may need to draw from preexisting knowledge and beliefs about similar situations or policy domains to form a basis for plans, or else be stymied in their attempts to acquire important but obscure context-specific information. Nevertheless, simple, deductive reasoning can obscure how the case at hand departs from the more general set of phenomena to which it is related. It can thus increase confidence in preexisting theories, which will nevertheless be less accurate when it comes to evaluating a particular case rather than a broad set. Moreover, because conceptions of the future are simpler, information that decision makers focused on the present might have seen as ambiguous is instead more readily assimilated and interpreted as consistent with existing mental categories, reinforcing confidence in preexisting theories.[30] Furthermore, altering decision makers' reliance on deductive or inductive reasoning also contributes to shifting communication fluency. Following a Bayesian logic, as reliance on preexisting theories (prior beliefs) declines, the subjective impact of new information increases. Of course, individuals are not pure Bayesians. People's conformity to normatively rational modes of learning will be contingent on numerous factors.[31] On the whole, however, CLT suggests that people will be less apt to revise preexisting beliefs when they consider more temporally distant events. Conversely, near-term actions and events will be viewed as more unique. Predictions about likely outcomes will be based on available contextual information rather than deduced from prior knowledge and beliefs, and less weight will be placed on ambiguous information which does not necessarily support any conclusion (see Figure 1.1).

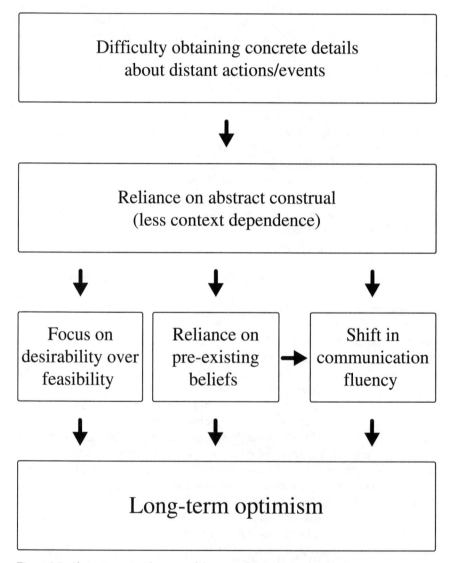

Figure 1.1. Abstract construal, overconfidence, and intervening mechanisms

CLT AND LONG-RANGE GOALS

Although the temporal distance of an action is a crucial aspect of CLT, it is not the only important variable to consider. The value that people place on long-term objectives must also be taken into account. Together, these elements help to determine an individual's "time horizon," a metaphor for how people think about future events.[32] As already discussed, time horizons are partly a function of the temporal distance of future time periods policymakers consider when making assessments. CLT addresses this aspect of time horizon length by highlighting the greater difficulty of ascertaining concrete information about actions falling later in a sequence, as temporal distance obscures contextual details. The second component of time horizons is the subjective value of long-term goals relative to ongoing or short-term actions. CLT encompasses this aspect of time horizons by differentiating between a goal's ultimate desirability and the feasibility of the intervening steps necessary to obtain that objective. Both abstract, high-level thought and concrete, low-level construal deal with goals, but the latter deals with subordinate aims that must be accomplished if one's superordinate goals are to be realized. The less superordinate goals matter compared to intervening subordinate goals, the shorter a policymaker's time horizons. The last component of time horizons is an actor's discount factor. Some individuals may have stronger positive time preferences than others, which in colloquial terms means they have less patience—they strongly prefer immediate over delayed rewards. Altering someone's discount factor alters the weight they put on the future. Together, these components are necessary and sufficient to estimate time horizon length, though none by itself is sufficient.

The three primary mechanisms CLT expects to promote overconfidence are contingent on policymakers' thinking about distant operations *and* having valued long-term goals—in short, having long time horizons. Somebody who is attentive to the late stages of a sequence of actions but places little weight on future objectives cannot be said to have long time horizons, just as someone with valued future aims cannot be said to have long time horizons if present demands do not allow them to think very far ahead. Ironically, policymakers who put the most value on the ultimate ends of a military campaign will have *more* trouble making accurate predictions about distant events and long-term costs than those who primarily value short-term, subordinate objectives. Consider first the tendency for individuals to favor criteria relevant to desirability over those regarding feasibility as they evaluate actions in the more distant future. This promotes overconfidence by obscuring potential risks and costs of actions which are salient during concrete construal of how an operation is to be carried out. Instead, policymakers focus on the magnitude of possible outcomes associated with higher-level goals, which also promotes positive feelings. But what about policymakers who do not attach much weight to the ultimate objectives of a military campaign?

Even if it is still difficult for them to envision the contextual details impinging on distant actions, desirability criteria are less likely to overwhelm other considerations when they occupy a marginal place in an official's judgments. When the desirability of an operation's ultimate objectives are diminished, decision makers' considerations of the future will also be emotionally "neutral." Neutral or negative emotions lead to greater conservatism and often more accurate assessments than do good feelings.

Next, consider the mechanism of communication fluency. Officials who care a great deal about a campaign's ultimate goals are mentally primed to think abstractly when considering the more distant future, focusing on desirability criteria (the "why" of a campaign) that are relatively constant regardless of lower-level contextual considerations. Thus, arguments in which such general, abstract criteria are central are more appealing to them. Conversely, officials who place less weight on long-term objectives are not primed to think in terms of abstract desirability. Arguments about an operation's feasibility are thus more likely to resonate with them than their more "farsighted" colleagues. What is more, officials with short time horizons may be less motivated to think about the distant future, instead spending the bulk of their time concentrating on operations that are impending or ongoing. This will further prime them to be receptive to arguments about operations' feasibility, rather than the desirability of the goals that operations are meant to achieve. Lastly, those focused on near-term operations will have to rely less on deductive reasoning from prior knowledge about general sets of phenomena because contextual, concrete information is more readily available as temporal distance shrinks. This has the effect of making actions under consideration appear unique, rather than cases of a broader set of similar operations. Once again, this primes a concrete mind-set, and thus officials with short time horizons will be less persuaded by arguments which frame a military campaign or its constituent elements as part of a larger class instead of a particular case.

In short, having valued long-term aims augments the tendency for abstraction and overconfidence to accompany long-range assessment. Individuals with less attachment to the long-range goals of a military campaign are more likely to think critically about the details of postconflict plans than those policymakers heavily invested in the long-term outcomes of an intervention. On average, however, they will also be less likely than those with long time horizons to consider ultimate objectives in the early phases of a military intervention. Still, when prompted to do so by events in the field or requests for input, they will be more likely to consider subordinate goals and emphasize the (in)feasibility of political plans. Put another way, those with short time horizons will be less motivated to consider distant future events, and less "mentally prepared" to enter a high-level frame of mind when considering the future because their attention will have been focused primarily on the short term.

Table 1.2 Construal based on personal time horizon and temporal distance of events

	Initial Operations	Postconflict Operations
Individuals with Short Time Horizons	**Construal most tilted toward the concrete**	Construal tilted toward concrete; motivation to consider distant events may be low
Individuals with Long Time Horizons	Construal tilted toward the concrete	**Construal most tilted toward the abstract**

Because the mechanisms by which temporal distance promotes overconfidence are largely inoperative for those with short time horizons, another implication of CLT is that there will be little variation in these policymakers' strategic assessments depending on the phase of a military campaign they are evaluating. They should be prone to construe both impending/ongoing and postconflict operations concretely. Actors with long time horizons, however, will be prone to abstract construal when considering postconflict operations, but will be disposed to concrete construal when considering earlier operations that are perceived to be impending, because the subjective difficulty of ascertaining context-dependent details will not be as great (see Table 1.2).

CLT AND THE NATURE OF POLITICAL GOALS

Political leaders may have numerous different goals they hope to obtain via military operations. This raises the question of how to estimate how much weight leaders place on ultimate, superordinate objectives versus intervening subordinate tasks. To address this issue, I categorize certain types of goals as "maintenance" objectives, and others as "transformative" objectives. I argue that leaders who pursue maintenance goals will have relatively shorter time horizons than those who adopt transformative aims. Furthermore, campaigns in which maintenance goals predominate will also be directed largely by actors with short time horizons, while campaigns in which transformative objectives are more prevalent will be led by officials with long time horizons. Thus, according to CLT, there will be less overconfidence among political leaders as a group when they pursue maintenance goals, regardless of the type of military operation under consideration.

Military actions with maintenance objectives are meant to preserve or return to the recent status quo. Maintenance goals include the preservation a foreign regime; putting a recently deposed foreign regime back in power; safeguarding regional balances of power; or restoring peace after an outbreak of violence. Alternatively, military actions with transformative objectives seek to alter the status quo, not maintain or restore a former state of affairs. Transformative goals range from attempts to coerce a target to change its policies to the alteration of another state's leadership and domestic institutions to improve on—not just maintain—an intervening state's existing security situation. It is important to stress the difference between transformative goals, on the one hand, and transformative means, on the other. Other authors have used similar terms when describing military interventions, but have used these categories to describe how politicians frame military goals for the public, or to characterize the operations conducted during an intervention rather than the ends sought.[33] Transformative ends and means may be positively correlated, but are not equivalent. For example, John F. Kennedy and Lyndon Johnson both primarily sought to keep South Vietnam from falling to the communist North—that is, maintain the status quo—but some have argued Kennedy used more transformative means to achieve this maintenance objective, by seeking to alter the political environment within South Vietnam.[34]

Policymakers pursuing maintenance objectives will have relatively short time horizons because the current or recent status quo serves as their focal point as opposed to the achievement of some yet unrealized state of affairs. As a result, they will tend to be more concerned with the concrete elements of an intervention. Such policymakers will be attendant to the risks and feasibility of various operations throughout a military conflict, including noncombat operations falling in the "postconflict" stage. This is contingent on three conditions. First, the farther in time a state is removed from an event that has upset the status quo, the less likely leaders are to use their current political environment as a reference point. When Argentinean leaders tried to take control of the Falklands from Great Britain in 1982, the regime in power had never actually exercised sovereignty over the islands, and Argentina had not possessed the disputed territory for decades. It would thus be more correct to say that the Argentinean government was trying to realize a new set of political objectives rather than maintain or restore the status quo, even if leaders thought of their mission as protecting their country's sovereignty.

Second, maintenance goals are more likely to be accompanied by concrete construal the less amount of time a military campaign has been ongoing. This is because combat provides belligerents with information which can be used to revise their estimates of their status vis-à-vis their opponents. If leaders interpret incoming information to mean they are stronger than they previously believed, they may revise their expectations of what they can obtain through conflict, and expand their initial war aims—perhaps adopting the future time period in which these gains will take place as their cognitive reference point. However, it takes time for intelligence on how fighting has unfolded to be gathered, disseminated, and deliberated over. If a military action achieves success very soon after it commences, there may not be enough time for this process to take place. Likewise, if leaders gradually learn that they are weaker than they initially presumed, they may also become focused on the future, considering how they can salvage their political fortunes in a future settlement. Thus, it is in the early periods of campaigns to maintain or restore the status quo, when combat is impending or just initiated, that the future should be least salient.

Third, leaders pursuing maintenance objectives may be primarily worried about the effects a military defeat would have on their state's long-term reputation. Officials might believe the failure to protect a political client or retain a valued security asset will invite future challenges to their state's security interests. Even works that doubt state reputations are relevant to actors' strategic assessments in military conflicts agree that leaders often worry about whether their country has a reputation for resolve.[35] If policymakers are seriously motivated by long-term reputational considerations, and events do not create so much time pressure as to force them to focus only on immediate military operations, then abstract construal of noncombat operations very well might accompany campaigns with maintenance goals. One would still expect the biases associated with abstract construal to be checked somewhat in such cases, however. Although officials pursuing maintenance goals may sometimes be concerned with preventing future losses (e.g., a loss of credibility), such goals also indicate that actors are heavily invested in protecting current arrangements.

In contrast with maintenance objectives, transformative goals indicate that state actors are more focused on long-term gains that will enhance their interests in the future, rather than being invested in current arrangements. Leaders adopt as their reference point some future, unrealized state of affairs rather than the status quo.[36] This is to say that leaders will have longer time horizons in transformative campaigns than in maintenance interventions, and as such the payoffs of the transformative project will be more salient than the probability of its success. State leaders will still be mindful of the feasibility of an intervention's initial operations, but this will not be the case for postconflict operations meant to solidify gains made, as leaders will be accustomed to an abstract mind-set when considering the future. While planning for initial combat operations may be intense, later operations will be thought of in high-level terms. Policymakers will tend to presume that conditions favorable to the consolidation and maintenance of their long-term objectives will be present in the targeted country, and be unreceptive to arguments relating to the feasibility of postconflict operations. Ironically, then, state leaders will on average exhibit less concern about the long-term risks of highly ambitious transformative projects than when they adopt more conservative maintenance objectives.

HYPOTHESES ON STRATEGIC ASSESSMENT

In summary, whether individuals traffic in abstractions or concrete details—whether they engage in high-level or low-level construal—affects decision-making processes and outcomes. Temporal distance encourages people to downplay or even ignore the feasibility of their long-term objectives while nevertheless remaining fixated on the desirability of those goals. At greater levels of abstraction actors will be more sensitive to *possible* than *probable* utility, focusing on the maximum payoffs an operation could achieve rather than its chances of success.

This book derives several major premises from CLT. Assessments of military operations will be more prone to abstraction and, in turn, overconfidence when evaluating military operations that are temporally distant, as opposed to operations that are immediate or impending. This is contingent on leaders having valued long-term aims, which will most often be the case when they adopt transformative rather than maintenance objectives. Overconfidence translates into underestimating the amount of lives, time, and money an operation will cost, as well as overestimating its likelihood of success given available information. This overconfidence will be disproportionately directed toward noncombat operations, which more often occur after major combat in military campaigns. Even though the goals of postconflict operations are valued, policymakers will not necessarily attend to the actual content of postconflict plans. On the procedural side of strategic assessment, leaders will have difficulty setting up, managing, and guiding subordinate institutional bodies responsible for postconflict operations meant to achieve those goals, as this entails investment in consideration of means and calculations of feasibility. Conversely, the details and feasibility of initial military operations will be salient, and thus policymakers will be more conscientious in developing and estimating the potential costs of noncombat plans when they occur early in a sequence of operations, rather than after combat.

Furthermore, the type of information political leaders will find persuasive depends on the phase of military operations they are considering. Variation in officials' communication fluency may significantly affect civil–military relations. To the extent that military organizations instill officers with specialized, concrete knowledge regarding how operations can be implemented under constraints of risk and cost, officers will tend to provide military information that senior officials will find more persuasive when considering initial, near-term actions. When focused on immediate or impending operations, leaders will be more open to concrete information challenging their assessments. Alternatively, when postconflict operations that typically involve noncombat tasks are considered, leaders will be less receptive to concrete information about how tasks will be carried out and more attentive to abstract arguments about why the end goals of an operation are desirable and important. The sum effect of these hypotheses is that officers will be most able to sway their civilian superiors' initial beliefs when the earliest stages of military action are being considered. Abstract thinkers will likewise be reliant on simple, preexisting theories and general beliefs. They will also be less likely to become "bogged down" in lower-level details of how operations will be conducted. In combination with having fewer fears of making errors of commission, this will encourage them to act more assertively than concrete thinkers once they are presented with a plan that suits their goals and preconceptions.

Charles Kupchan has documented the preceding dynamics in his research on military intervention. He finds that senior policymakers considering military interventions typically predict that the initial costs of intervention will be substantial and that a significant amount of military resources will be required. However, state leaders often make erroneous, overly optimistic assumptions when anticipating the extraction of their forces. Specifically, Kupchan notes that policymakers wrongly assume that the military conflict will be short, that local political allies will be reliable, and that the intervention will not alter the political landscape of the targeted state except in the ways intended. Though skeptical of arguments relying on psychological biases, he admits that "given the consistency of assessment failures across cases . . . random miscalculation is somewhat unsatisfying" as an explanation for this pattern.[37]

Kupchan defines his universe of cases as "protracted foreign military interventions," so it might be expected that the policymakers under examination were overly optimistic; if they had foreseen a protracted conflict, they may not have authorized the use of military force in the first place. Still, a general tendency toward overconfidence cannot explain why policymakers' optimism appears to vary depending on the phase of an intervention under consideration. Dominic D. P. Johnson helps explain this variation by noting that "positive illusions" are likely to arise when people assess a "very general notion, such as one's intentions or future plans," and thus optimism is more prevalent in "abstract long-term plans" than in "day-to-day plans on the battlefield."[38] Johnson attributes the human tendency toward overconfidence to evolutionary mechanisms that are difficult to verify. By clearly specifying and tracing causal mechanisms CLT predicts will lead to overconfidence, one can be more certain in the validity of previous findings.

While individuals with short time horizons are less liable to overconfidence, it would be incorrect to say that thorough and accurate strategic assessment depends on whether decision makers thinking concretely rather than abstractly, or vice versa. Any hypothetical foreign policy endeavor will be defined by both means and ends. If state leaders thought only in concrete terms, they could not clearly articulate their policy goals. Policymakers prone to abstract construal will be better able to articulate and prioritize their long-term objectives than those primed to think concretely. Being overly concerned with concrete details may also obscure the need to evaluate how immediate or impending operations relate to final outcomes, as well as hinder leaders' ability to articulate ultimate goals and priorities.

Short-sighted individuals will also be more apt to endorse a course of action if it appears it can be feasibly executed, even if it does not advance the broader purposes of a military campaign. Concrete thinkers engage in "decomposition," a process by which an overall goal is broken down into smaller, more manageable subordinate goals.[39] Though decomposition may encourage greater considerations of feasibility, it is not a flawless approximation of rational assessment. Actors concerned with short-range problems will attend to the costs and feasibility of subordinate goals, but may treat subgoals as ends in and of themselves, compartmentalizing them rather than considering their connection to more abstract, high-level political objectives. This may produce confusion and disagreement as to what ends are being sought, as well as how to judge the ultimate success of a campaign. These outcomes are no less problematic than pursuing a goal without attending to the requisite sacrifices that must be made to obtain it.

CLT Hypotheses:
1. Noncombat operations projected to occur postconflict will be assessed abstractly, promoting overconfidence about their costs and risks.
2. Hypothesis 1 is contingent on leaders having valued long-term goals.
3. Noncombat operations preceding combat will be assessed concretely, reducing overconfidence but obscuring operations' connection to high-level goals.

SEQUENCE AND THE SUBJECTIVE NATURE OF TIME

It is pertinent to ask just how distant some object of assessment must be for individuals with valued long-term goals to become biased toward abstract construal. Research based on CLT has shown that even short time delays in which an event is pushed back two months can significantly alter the criteria people use when making decisions.[40] However, one cannot safely assert that perceptions of temporal distance can be based entirely on objective measures of time. Two months may seem like a blink of an eye or a veritable eternity depending on the matter at hand, and these subjective perceptions of a fixed period of time are important according to CLT. Research has shown that merely framing an event as more distant will encourage more abstract construal, even if the amount of concrete information available about the event is held constant, and that people primed to think abstractly or concretely about one set of actions or events are more likely to construe other stimuli abstractly/concretely as well.[41]

A period of several months may seem insignificant when planning a grand strategy. It is doubtful that U.S. policymakers in the Truman or Eisenhower administrations crafting doctrines for containment of the Soviet Union saw the Cold War as a momentary interlude disrupting normal international relations. In the context of a military campaign, however, several months may represent a significant portion of the endeavor as a whole. Following World War II, the median length of military interventions by the permanent members of the UN Security Council was six and a half months.[42] Thus, it is not unlikely that a period of just a few months will be seen as a "long time" when policymakers undertake military action to achieve their aims.

More important is the question of how placing an operation in a certain position within a sequence of actions affects whether it is seen as occurring in the "near" or "long" term. Actions which come later in a sequence will necessarily be more distant, but what if both initial combat operations and postconflict operations are anticipated to be many months away? Would this erase the temporal distinction between combat and noncombat operations? Not necessarily. Placing an operation later in a sequence in a military campaign serves to frame it as more temporally distant, regardless of the objective amount of time between its anticipated start date and the present.[43] Sequentially dividing operations, even if such a separation is artificial, gives temporal precedence to the activities presumed to occur first. In regards to military assessments, practitioners and historians have observed that instead of seeing combat and noncombat activities as overlapping tasks, U.S. policymakers have thought of them of them as occurring at different times in a given chronological order. Anthony Cordesman refers to this as the "rebuilding-effort-begins-after-the-war-ends syndrome," or the belief that military conflicts can be neatly divided into independent phases.[44] This belief makes it easier to picture the context in which initial combat operations will be carried out. The context of subsequent actions perceived to come "after" will depend on the degree of success initial activities enjoy, and thus require planners to account for numerous contingencies. Policymakers may be loath to make concrete plans to achieve long-term objectives in light of such uncertainty. Although such reluctance is arguably pragmatic, CLT expects it will allow the desirability of ultimate goals to overshadow their feasibility.

Rather than being overly concerned with precisely how many units of time need to pass before something shifts from "near-term" to "long-term," then, it is important to note that the types of noncombat operations discussed here are normally assumed to fall in the postconflict phase of a military campaign, after major combat operations have concluded. Although there may be little time separating the initiation of combat and postconflict operations, a period of just a few months may appear long relative to the projected length of a campaign. Even when combat and noncombat tasks overlap in time, combat will often be viewed as clearly preceding and separate from the postconflict environment. When an operation is seen as distinct and presumed to come later in a sequence, the task of obtaining concrete, contextual details becomes subjectively harder: details are increasingly seen as dependent on the unpredictable outcomes of preceding operations and events, rather than occurring within the same context. This will further bias decision makers toward construing the later operation abstractly. Not only does abstract construal increase as a function of temporal distance, then, it increases the more policymakers see "combat" and "postconflict" as distinct phases.

31

CLT AND INDIVIDUAL TRAITS

Just like other traits, the tendency to think about actions more in terms of their ends or their means varies within the population.[45] It is unclear whether situational factors or individual predispositions most strongly influence construal, or whether there is an interactive effect between individual predispositions and the decision-making environment. It may be that policymakers' predispositions toward abstract or concrete thought will confound the expectations of CLT the farther a policymaker is from the population norm.

Individuals also differ in their tendency to focus on the future. Interestingly, pessimists have been found to generally have a more distal focus than optimists, perhaps because the former are motivated to avoid future failures. Once again, it is unclear how strongly pessimistic or optimistic dispositions affect people's assessments of the future compared to environmental influences. If anything, the finding that pessimists are more likely to focus on the future makes it more likely that researchers would underestimate the association of long time horizons with overconfidence. It has also been shown that individuals can be more pessimistic in some contexts and optimistic in others.[46] Thus, a leader who is normally pessimistic about her ability to achieve political goals in the realm of fiscal policy may be more of an optimist when it comes to foreign policy or national security. Election cycles might also predispose political leaders in democracies such as the United States to think in more compressed time frames than in nondemocratic states, but it has also been argued that authoritarian dictatorships are more likely to produce leaders prone to short time horizons.[47]

Given the indeterminacy of the preceding paragraphs, this book asserts no firm hypotheses regarding how individual traits affect strategic assessments. It is difficult to draw conclusions about the relative size of the impact of personal characteristics versus environmental factors or interaction effects that may arise between the two. The task of deriving hypotheses is further complicated by the fact that personal tendencies may vary depending on the policy realm under consideration. Nonetheless, it is important to acknowledge that individual differences may matter, and that specific political leaders' assessments and behavior may not conform to the predictions of CLT due to their individual characteristics.

Alternative Explanations of Strategic Assessment

To determine how well CLT can account for political leaders' strategic assessments of noncombat operations, it is useful to compare the theory to alternative explanations derived from the scholarly literature on international relations. Doing so allows the researcher to identify factors and causal mechanisms that CLT does not highlight so as to guard against drawing spurious inferences.

THE OPPORTUNITY COSTS OF ASSESSMENT

Since resources are scarce, trade-offs are ubiquitous when crafting policy. In the realm of security, policymakers must decide not only how to allocate resources between guns and butter, but guns and allies or intelligence.[48] Fred Iklé's observation that "war plans tend to cover only the first act" summarizes his argument that military considerations related to combat normally trump whatever long-term concerns leaders have about conflict termination. This is in part because of the opportunity costs of devoting resources to prepare for temporally distant contingencies instead of using them to plan combat operations meant to obtain more immediate objectives. Accordingly, Iklé and other scholars have asserted that leaders will be most capable of thinking ahead and considering how to end their wars the more confident they are from the outset that an enemy can be overpowered.[49] In other words, the lower the perceived costs of initial or ongoing operations, the more resources can be invested in preparing for future tasks, including noncombat operations.

The proposition that security and military advantages encourage longer time horizons is commonplace in international relations theory. Stephen Krasner holds that the United States' power relative to other countries after World War II allowed it to pursue its vision of a properly ordered international society rather than focus simply on immediate security and economic concerns, while Kenneth Waltz believes that unipolarity has likewise allowed the United States to aggressively pursue more long-term aspirations.[50] According to offensive structural realism, the greatest concern of the most powerful states— regional hegemons—is not protecting their survival in the short run, but checking the rise of other regional hegemons which could threaten their security in the indefinite future.[51] G. John Ikenberry, in a reformulation of hegemonic stability theory, also presumes that states with a preponderance of power value continuous gains in future time periods more than small short-term gains when there are trade-offs between the two.[52] Time horizons are a central concept in Sarah Kreps's explanation of whether or not states pursue multilateral cooperation in their military interventions. The greater the immediacy and magnitude of a threat, according to Kreps, the shorter a state's time horizons become.[53]

The balance of military power between a state and its opponents can be measured using material factors such as troop numbers in a theater of operations, as well as less tangible factors such as force employment.[54] When a state's military capabilities strongly outweigh those of its opponent, policymakers will perceive fewer opportunity costs of diverting resources to prepare for noncombat rather than combat operations. Furthermore, one would expect this to be the case whether noncombat operations begin before or after the start of major combat. In the latter situation, if a state's forces are balanced with or at a disadvantage to an enemy's, the opportunity costs of saving resources rather than employing them for immediate gains will be great. Withholding resources may result in expensive setbacks and defeats on the battlefield, and postconflict plans will become moot. The likelihood of suffering these immediate costs decreases as a state's power advantages become more pronounced, which is equivalent to increasing the subjective value of the future relative to the present. The greater one's advantage over an opposing state, the more likely initial military operations will be successful, meaning there is a greater probability a state's forces will have to conduct operations in the later stages of a campaign. Investing resources in preparations for postconflict operations should then become more attractive. If leaders' policy goals allow it, they can try to avoid postconflict operations inside the defeated state altogether. If not, however, there will be incentives to plan for multiple contingencies so as to maximize the likelihood of achieving political objectives.

Now turn to a situation in which noncombat operations take place before a state's personnel engage in major combat. This was the case in U.S. interventions in Vietnam and, though combat was not sustained, in Somalia. Here too, an opportunity costs framework leads to the expectation that state leaders will focus on noncombat activities when their forces dominate potential opponents. Though the conclusion is the same as in situations in which noncombat tasks occur postconflict, the logic is different. The noncombat activities which are the primary focus here, state building and pacification, involve the provision of governmental services, infrastructure reconstruction, and the promotion of economic and institutional development. A secure environment in which an intervening power and its allies hold a monopoly on the legitimate use of force is a prerequisite for these activities. If a shifting balance of forces leads security to decay, more attention and resources will have to be invested in combat operations meant to correct the situation.

This assertion finds support in both military doctrine and practice. The success of stability operations depends on security. As the level of violence in a theater of operations increases, combat operations receive more emphasis relative to noncombat tasks.[55] When senior U.S. officials perceived the military situation turning against them in South Vietnam in late 1964, they argued that U.S. forces would have to move from advising and assisting in pacification efforts to executing sustained air and ground offensives in much larger numbers.[56] Likewise, when the first iteration of UN peace operations in Somalia (UNOSOM I) failed due to the resistance of local warlords, the UN Security Council authorized a U.S.-led force to use "all necessary means to establish . . . a secure environment for humanitarian relief operations in Somalia" under chapter VII of the UN Charter.[57]

The opportunity costs explanation yields two main hypotheses:

Opportunity Costs Hypotheses:
1. The greater a state's military advantage over its opponent(s), the longer its leaders' time horizons.
2. The greater a state's military advantage over its opponent(s), the more resources are devoted to strategic assessment of noncombat operations, resulting in more accurate estimates of their risks and costs.

THE "FOG OF WAR" AND THE NATURE OF THE OPERATION

If the opportunity costs of assessment hinge largely on the balance of forces in a theater of operations, one must ask how this balance is ascertained. Even if state leaders act rationally in their attempts to account and plan for military campaigns, the costs and challenges of military action will not be divined with perfect certitude. Decision makers must gauge the risks of dispatching and supporting large numbers of personnel and equipment, a force which will then be expected to communicate through a vast command chain to implement and adapt preestablished plans as necessary. The chance for Clausewitzian "friction" to impinge on operations is present at every turn.[58] Opposing forces' capabilities and resolve will not be known with certainty, political support for the intervention will wax and wane as events unfold, and so on ad infinitum. Errors in strategic assessment thus occur not only because policymakers act irrationally, but also because of imperfect information. It may only be by committing to battle that actors can obtain needed information about an opponent's strength.[59] Within the "fog of war," no plan survives first contact with the enemy.

Within this framework, which from here on is referred to as the fog-of-war theory of strategic assessment, leaders' assessments are only as good as available intelligence. Leaders' assessments of the future will be a function of the precision and level of agreement among information sources they are privy to, not cognitive biases associated with temporal construal. The less precision and agreement among the intelligence community's estimates of the costs and risks of a given operation, the less confident political leaders will be to endorse any particular course of action. Conversely, if intelligence estimates reliably agree and are couched in reasonably precise terms, policymakers will act more confidently in accordance with the projected future conditions in which an operation will take place.

There is also reason to believe that the nature of different military operations has a major impact on the quality of intelligence and thus the assessments state actors make. Thomas Schelling's classic differentiation between coercion and "brute force" illustrates how this is so. A strategy reliant on brute force aims to annihilate an opponent's capability to make war. This requires decision makers to assess an opponent's military capabilities, which are relatively simple to observe and quantify. Conversely, coercive strategies require a target to comply with the coercer's wishes for fear of something worse, rather than be forced to submit because its capacity to resist has been destroyed. To judge the likelihood that coercive strategies will be successful decision makers must not only to attend to an opponent's military capabilities, but also more opaque, intangible factors such as a target's resolve.[60] Compared to the assessment of an opponent's material capabilities, assessing resolve is particularly difficult for the military organizations charged with providing policymakers with intelligence.[61] By adding another, more elusive dimension for officials to evaluate, coercion theoretically increases the difficulty of strategic assessment. Empirical tests have been consistent with Schelling's conclusions. Interventions which require greater degrees of target compliance with an intervener are less likely to succeed than interventions which hinge on brute force.[62]

Stability and reconstruction activities inherently rely on the cooperation (or at least acquiescence) of local populations to be effective—in other words, they require estimates of the population's willingness to resist. This increases the challenge of estimating these operations' costs. From existing theory and empirical work, then, the fog-of-war theory expects strategic assessment to result in poorer predictions regarding the outcomes of noncombat operations relative to operations meant to annihilate opposing forces. The range of intelligence estimates are expected to vary more widely in comparison to estimates regarding combat operations and be less precise, even presuming officials expend the same amount of effort structuring the decision-making process for each type of operation. Thus, one would expect to see worse intelligence for noncombat compared to combat operations and, consequently, for policymakers to express more uncertainty and pessimism about the likely outcomes of noncombat operations. This will especially be true when noncombat operations fall later in a campaign. As noted, this is because it is harder to ascertain information about temporally distant events, especially when the context in which later operations occur depends on preceding outcomes.

Like the opportunity costs framework, the fog-of-war explanation expects policymakers to expend more effort and resources to structure decisions about temporally distant noncombat operations when their time horizons are long. The tasks of gathering and evaluating information about noncombat operations are expected to be especially onerous since the variance of these operations' costs is anticipated to be greater than those of combat operations. The more value actors attach to future outcomes relative to those in the present, they more willing they will be to cover these costs. Besides establishing mechanisms for gathering and distributing information about noncombat operations, policymakers with long time horizons will spend more time deliberating over this information. If estimates of noncombat operations' costs and feasibility are sensitive to assumptions about the environment in which those operations will be conducted, policymakers with longer time horizons will expend more effort critically analyzing these assumptions than those more focused on the present. Finally, policymakers with long time horizons will carefully weigh the expected utility of different courses of action against one another.

Fog-of-War Hypotheses:
1. Leaders' strategic assessments of military operations depend on the accuracy and consistency of information provided by intelligence estimates, both of which will be better for combat than noncombat operations.
2. Leaders will express more ambivalence and/or pessimism about noncombat operations relative to combat operations.
3. Leaders will invest more resources into strategic assessment of temporally distant noncombat operations when they have long time horizons.

ORGANIZATIONAL AND CIVIL–MILITARY EXPLANATIONS OF ASSESSMENT

Because they are executed and partially planned by military officers, the knowledge, values, and experiences of these personnel may be key to understanding how noncombat operations are assessed. A general set of propositions about the content of military officers' assessment can be derived by studying the organizations in which they are embedded. The doctrine, training, and incentive structure within military organizations may lead their members to privilege certain tasks over others. In the U.S. context there is reason to believe that, compared to combat operations, noncombat activities are neglected, misunderstood, and sometimes denigrated by military officers. This, in turn, will adversely affect the military's capacity to prepare for such operations, or advise civilian leaders on their likely costs.

The term "organization" describes the set of rules, norms, and principles used by a group of social actors to make decisions and carry out collective action, action facilitated by the adoption of stable "standard operating procedures."[63] The structure of organizations will affect how their members relate to their environment, formulate goals, and implement policies to achieve them. Organization principles will be reflected in norms and rules of promotion, thus incentivizing investment and specialization in certain tasks over others. Over time, members of an organization may take the importance of some tasks and the insignificance of others for granted. Decision rules for action in various contingencies may privilege certain environmental signals over others, thus influencing what is seen as important or trivial information.[64]

The organizational structure of the U.S. armed forces has been said to produce what Russell Weigley calls a particular "American way of war," a set of doctrine and practices which promote the overwhelming use of firepower to annihilate the enemy and achieve victory.[65] If this characterization is accurate, and political leaders partially rely on the military for information, it should reinforce the prior hypothesis that states have more reliable information about combat rather than noncombat operations. The American way of war has been alleged to be poorly suited to campaigns whose political objectives require an emphasis on state building and pacification. Andrew Krepinevich, echoing Weigley's thesis, attributes poor military performance in the Vietnam War to an "Army Concept" that evolved from an organizational culture promoting "high volumes of firepower to minimize casualties." Krepinevich and others adopted this argument several decades later to explain why U.S. military action in Iraq was faring poorly.[66] The usefulness of organizational theory in explaining the outcome of the Vietnam War, as well as the validity of the concept of an American way of war, have been hotly debated.[67] However, the critics have not questioned the fundamental assertion that U.S. commanders and military organizations have historically privileged combat operations over other types of missions when preparing for war.

Along with variations in leaders' communication fluency highlighted by CLT, the importance of organizational factors for leaders' strategic assessments should be contingent on the military's autonomy and political influence. Since civilian agencies are likely to have different knowledge and preferences than the military, altering the relative influence of each set of actors will affect the assessments made in a given campaign. Given the alleged military bias toward combat operations, increasing the influence of civilian groups relative to the military should bolster the resources invested in the assessment of noncombat activities, or at least not cause investments in these operations to decline. It might be that civilian leaders do not put much stock in the military's ability to plan and execute noncombat operations, which are somewhat "political" in nature, relative to combat missions. For instance, President Franklin Roosevelt was quite skeptical of the military's capacity to run governments in occupied territories.[68] Nevertheless, given the vastness of the U.S. military's budget and personnel, civilian officials may find they have no choice but to relinquish a great deal of responsibility for the planning and conduct of noncombat operations to the armed forces. The relative prestige of civilian officials and military officers will also vary over time. The Truman administration had to contend with the popularity of General Douglas MacArthur for much of the first year of the Korean War. Though MacArthur was ultimately relieved of his command, civilians in Washington were loath to challenge him even when his actions and statements bordered on insubordination.[69] The relationship between President Johnson and the Joint Chiefs of Staff in 1964–1965 is an example of the political balance leaning the other way: Johnson's dominance over the chiefs reduced their influence and led them to alter their policy recommendations regarding military actions in Vietnam.[70]

According to organizational theory, the opportunity costs of investing in noncombat operations will appear especially high to military officers. Officers are not necessarily more likely than civilians to advocate the use of force when a military intervention is being considered.[71] However, once an intervention is initiated, the decision-making logic changes. Members of a military organization should be conditioned to focus on combat activities once hostilities have commenced. Even though top U.S. military officers have rarely been relieved of command if they fail to achieve desired results on the battlefield, officers who fail to secure campaign objectives may lose opportunities to further their careers.[72] The military also cultivates and retains political power through various domestic constituencies via its large budget and the production it generates, as well as less tangible factors such as the armed forces' perceived prestige, legitimacy, and expertise. Officers should be reluctant to withdraw from a conflict once committed, as this might jeopardize or weaken domestic sources of support by calling into question the effectiveness of the military as a policy tool. In cases where noncombat operations constitute the initial part of a military campaign, commanders should thus be first to stress the utility of escalation to combat operations when the security situation in a theater appears to be deteriorating. If noncombat activities follow major combat operations, officers should have an incentive to avoid these activities, leaving them to other government agencies, if the hypothesized organizational disinclination toward noncombat operations exists.

Organizational Hypotheses:
1. The U.S. military will invest fewer resources and produce less accurate assessments for noncombat rather than combat operations.
2. The importance of organizational factors will be contingent on the military's political power and autonomy relative to civilian leaders.
3. Military actors will advocate for escalation to combat operations prior to civilian officials when the security environment in which noncombat operations are being conducted deteriorates.

Methodology and Case Selection

To evaluate the hypotheses derived from CLT, case studies must first establish whether noncombat operations were perceived as occurring "postwar," preceding, or overlapping with combat operations. Next, policymakers must be ordered according to the length of their time horizons. Figure 1.2 represents the systematized concept of time horizons.[73] Again, the length of a policymaker's time horizon is the determined by three components. The first is the temporal distance of future time periods they consider when making assessments. This component is in turn measured (not caused) by three

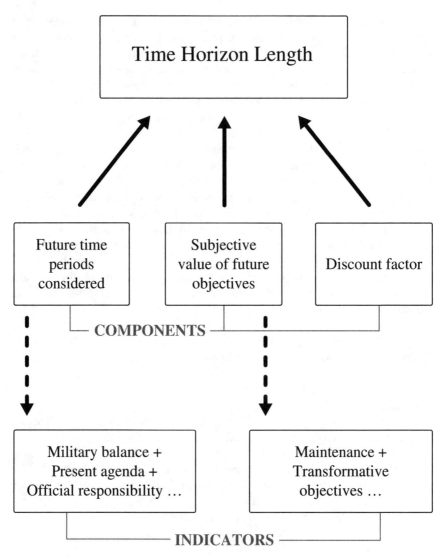

Figure 1.2. Systematized time horizon concept

primary indicators, as indicated by the dashed arrows directed toward the variables along the bottom level. The more favorable the military balance leaders perceive, the more future time periods they should have the freedom to consider. The smaller the number of pressing items on policymakers' present political agendas, the further into the future they are able to look. Lastly, officials' responsibilities, or policy jurisdictions, will indicate whether they are mostly focused on the immediate or more distant future. Being assigned a task involving postconflict policy should lead an individual to think further into the future than someone tasked with managing daily combat operations, for instance. The "+" symbol means that each one of these indicators are by themselves sufficient to gauge the number of future time periods officials consider. However, it is better to have some measure of all a component's indicators, as it is possible that one will indicate that distant future time periods are under consideration while another will indicate the opposite. It is also worth noting that the indicators used to measure each component of time horizons shown in Figure 1.2 may not be exhaustive, hence the ellipses.

The second component of time horizons is the subjective value of leaders' future objectives relative to the ongoing military campaign. These are primarily indicated by the goals policymakers seek, transformative or maintenance, though the opportunity costs framework predicts that the military balance will also affect the subjective value of the future. The key variables in question are ascertained using different officials' public statements and private correspondence. When public and private sentiments contradict one another, precedence is given to the latter. Even private communications may be used to manipulate other officials rather than express true beliefs, however. It is thus necessary to produce evidence that the substance of an actor's expressed goals remains consistent in different contexts and can be found in multiple sources. Officials' actions can also provide valuable information about how much they value different goals. If a policymaker is willing to incur immediate costs to secure long-term objectives, that is an indicator of long time horizons. If officials are willing to secure their immediate interests by adopting policies they believe will invite future harm, or damage the viability of long-term goals, they likely have short time horizons.

The last component of time horizons is an actor's discount factor. This component cannot be as easily measured as the first two. However, the subjective value actors appear to attach to future goals can be used as a proxy. Even individuals with a tendency to highly discount the future may have long time horizons if they value future objectives enough.

Once the status of these components is established, the studies use within-case comparisons to evaluate officials' assessments of near and distant military operations. By using within-case comparisons, the political actors involved, as well as other crucial factors, are "held constant" while only the phase of the war plan under consideration varies, approximating Mill's method of difference.[74] To increase confidence in the validity of causal inferences, differences in assessment between multiple actors faced with the same decisions and privy to roughly the same information are examined over time within a case.[75] Government actors' strategic assessments will be affected by where they sit within the government hierarchy. Upper-level officials will have access to different, and likely greater, information than their subordinates. They also have broader responsibilities than their subordinates, and likely less time to focus on any given piece of information. Top officials are also charged with considering the "big picture," which entails more abstract thought. Conversely, lower-level officials may be formally precluded from recommending policy ends and spend more time analyzing the concrete details of the narrow range of information to which they have access.[76] These differences mean that it is sounder to gauge the effects predicted by CLT by comparing the assessments of individuals within, rather than across, levels of hierarchy.

Within-case comparison does not eliminate the possibility of faulty causal inferences. As in many research designs, endogeneity is a problem which needs to be addressed. CLT states that a long time horizon leads to abstract construal, resulting in overconfidence regarding noncombat operations which typically fall near the end of a conflict. However, the causal arrow may also run the other way: intuitively, an optimistic outlook will lead one to place greater value on future outcomes. Thus, the analysis also uses process-tracing to show that the three "intermediate" mechanisms of CLT link the independent variables with strategic assessment, the dependent variable, as predicted by the theory.[77] Officials with long time horizons are predicted to exhibit overconfidence in regards to postconflict noncombat operations that is absent when they assess operations in the more immediate future. This will be due to abstract construal, manifested primarily as an emphasis on the desirability of ends rather than feasibility of operational means as decision-making criteria. CLT is unpersuasive as an explanation if actors with long time horizons seem highly focused on the feasibility of future operations and/or confidence arises due to their efforts at concrete planning. Two additional intermediate mechanisms are predicted to reinforce overconfidence in distant operations: deductive reasoning from general, preexisting beliefs, and a lack of receptiveness to messages containing concrete information. Endogeneity problems are also mitigated if the officials under study developed relatively stable long-term objectives prior to using military force to achieve those objectives. If this is the case, one can be more certain their time horizons developed independently of their strategic assessments of a specific campaign.

It would still be specious to conclude that the mechanisms specified by CLT are affecting strategic assessment of noncombat operations if potential confounding variables are not considered. "Competitive testing" of different explanations is one way to try to account for the effects of factors outside the CLT framework.[78] Three alternatives to CLT, the opportunity costs, fog-of-war, and organizational explanations, have been put forth. The CLT explanation holds that, while greater military advantages may allow officials longer time horizons, this may actually result in less accurate assessments of temporally distant noncombat operations. If it does not, the opportunity costs framework gains strength relative to the psychological theory. Likewise, if the bulk of information collected and disseminated to key decision makers indicates that noncombat operations that occur postconflict will be easy in comparison to operations in the near term, it would be difficult to attribute overconfidence to the mechanisms specified by CLT.

Aside from examining the congruence of the preceding explanations with the evidence in each case, there will be additional idiosyncratic factors present across cases that may affect assessment. For example, Franklin Roosevelt's health was failing in the late days of World War II. His physical ailments may have significantly affected his assessments of military operations.[79] When distinctive factors such as this have been advanced in the scholarly literature as relevant to strategic assessment in a particular case, they are taken seriously by the studies conducted here.

CASE SELECTION

A U.S.-centered study is merited given the country's military might and the liberal missionary zeal which it has often exhibited in its foreign policy.[80] While other countries have the capacity to project power abroad, the military strength of the United States, and thus its ability to intervene, will likely be unparalleled for years to come. Furthermore, since the mid-twentieth century the U.S. government has stood out not just for its attempts to topple or prop up existing regimes, but its efforts to fundamentally remake the political character of targeted states. Such transformations cannot be achieved by brute force alone, and thus policymakers' beliefs about noncombat operations, as well as the procedures used to structure the planning of such operations, are critical.

To evaluate the arguments regarding strategic assessment of noncombat operations, this book uses structured, focused case studies of four U.S. wars from 1941 onward: preparations for the occupation of Germany during World War II; assessment of the never-realized occupation of North Korea during the first year of the Korean War; evaluation of noncombat operations during escalation of the conflict in Vietnam, 1964–1965; and the 2003 invasion of Iraq. For each of the four cases, the evidence for CLT and the three alternative explanations of strategic assessment is gathered from primary and secondary sources of information. The amount and quality of attention given to combat versus noncombat operations (state building, pacification, and supporting activities) is ascertained, and the "fit" of available evidence to candidate explanations is assessed. The empirical studies primarily utilize within-case comparisons to make causal inferences about the strategic assessment of noncombat operations.

The characteristics of the chosen cases should not be biased to favor CLT. Although researchers may be tempted to select secondary sources that conform to their theoretical suppositions, CLT has been developed completely outside the domain of politics and military operations, limiting the problem of biased source selection.[81] Furthermore, leaders in major wars can be expected to be highly invested in the decision-making processes related to all military operations given the stakes involved. Despite their differing goals, the presidential administrations in each of the selected cases believed the United States had significant strategic interests at stake and committed a large number of military personnel and materiel to battle. The cases occurred after the United States had built up a large security establishment, meaning the president and his advisers in the executive branch had access to a wealth of relevant information and were well situated to influence the course of each military campaign.[82] Since the organizational culture of the U.S. military—like the political culture of the United States generally—has been portrayed elsewhere as consistently prejudiced against noncombat operations, organizational biases might be expected to have an impact on assessment in each of the studies.

The cases that follow also differ on the important variables highlighted in this chapter, allowing for a range of tests of the hypotheses derived from CLT and its alternatives. In two of the cases—Germany after World War II and Iraq in 2003—the president and the bulk of senior officials optimistically expected that postconflict noncombat operations could secure their political objectives at a minimal cost to the United States. In Korea and especially Vietnam, alternatively, officials' beliefs about noncombat operations were much less sanguine. While policymakers contemplating Vietnam were almost uniformly pessimistic, there were significant minorities in the other three administrations who disagreed with the majority views. Germany and Iraq were instances in which officials largely had transformative aims, and sought to comprehensively remake the political structure of the targeted countries. In Vietnam the United States primarily desired to maintain its security position by preventing the fall of the government in Saigon. Leaders entered the Korean intervention with maintenance goals, but gradually adopted more ambitious aims. In three cases it was anticipated that noncombat operations would occur in a postconflict environment, whereas noncombat operations preceded large-scale U.S. involvement in Vietnam.

Perceptions of the United States' military advantage relative to opponents vary across cases as well. In the years prior to the occupation of Germany, the U.S. government saw a gradual but inevitable shift of the balance of power in favor of the allies. This also describes officials' view during the fighting in Korea from June to late November 1950. Conversely, perceptions of the military balance in the Vietnam and Iraq cases are polar opposites of one another. There were significant concerns within the Johnson administration that the troop requirements in South Vietnam would be prohibitively costly, even among alleged war "hawks."[83] In Iraq, even officials who harbored major doubts about the feasibility of intervention goals had no doubt that the balance of military forces decisively favored the United States.

The empirical analysis of the cases is consistent with CLT's predictions on strategic assessment (Table 1.3). In cases in which leaders had primarily transformative objectives, the assessments of presidents and senior policymakers were more abstract when they evaluated noncombat operations, which were presumed to occur after major combat had ceased. The desirability of policy goals became more salient than the feasibility of late-stage operations, and correspondingly officials were optimistic that their aims would be realized while downplaying or ignoring potential obstacles. This was not the case when leaders adopted maintenance objectives: leaders' assessments of noncombat operations in Vietnam and Korea were found to be more concrete, and optimism was largely absent. Although there was a substantial difference in leaders' assessments of combat versus noncombat operations in transformative interventions, this was not so in maintenance interventions. CLT would expect assessments of different phases of a conflict to be more similar in maintenance interventions; even though concrete details about distant operations are harder to ascertain, the lesser value officials assign to future goals means desirability criteria are less likely to overwhelm feasibility considerations.

Aside from these findings, it also appeared that individual actors' cognitive style was affected by their personal time horizons: those who placed more value on long-term goals adopted a more abstract cognitive style when thinking about the postconflict stage of a campaign than those who did not give

Table 1.3 Intervention cases and leader assessments

Intervention	Policy Goals	Leaders' Cognitive Style (Construal Level)	Assessment of Noncombat Operations
Germany	Transformative	Primarily abstract; varies with phase of war considered. Conditional upon actors' personal time horizons.	**Postwar phase predicted to be easy though most estimates indicate otherwise.**
Korea	Largely maintenance, briefly transformative	Primarily concrete; modest variation depending on phase of war considered. Conditional upon actors' personal time horizons (effects of long time horizons less certain).	**Postwar phase expected to be difficult, in line with most estimates.**
Vietnam	Maintenance	Primarily concrete; no observable variation depending on phase of war considered. Actors overwhelmingly adopt short time horizons.	**Growing pessimism leading to escalation of U.S. combat involvement.**
Iraq	Transformative	Primarily abstract; varies with phase of war considered. Conditional upon actors' personal time horizons.	**Postwar phase predicted to be easy though most estimates indicate otherwise.**

as much weight to future objectives. This difference between individuals produced behavior which was quite ironic from a normative perspective. Those seeking transformation were not liable to pay attention to the details of noncombat operations meant to achieve it. Those who cared less about transformation could make apt assessments of the details and assumptions of post-conflict plans, but were not necessarily able to relate these plans to higher-level aims or judge whether these aims justified the costs and risks being entertained. However, in some cases there were notable examples of one or more officials whose assessments and behavior were not explicable via CLT.

The Occupation of Germany

The United States' occupation of Germany at the end of World War II culminated with a democratic West German state that was both an "economic miracle" and a member of the North Atlantic Treaty Organization (NATO). Early evaluations of the planning process for the occupation were less than charitable, however. Professor Carl J. Friedrich, an adviser to occupation forces in Germany, lamented that U.S. policy had produced unnecessary suffering and actually impeded the stated goal of democratization. Writing in the same volume as Friedrich, Dale Clark argued that there was essentially no coherent occupation plan when Germany surrendered.[1] General Lucius Clay, the American military governor in Germany, recalled that he had been given very little direction on U.S. policy, and did not know what kind of new government his civilian superiors intended to set up. Clay's adviser Lewis Douglas thought the occupation plan had been devised by "economic idiots."[2]

This chapter traces the creation of U.S. policy regarding noncombat operations in postwar Germany. It proceeds by providing a brief overview of the preparations made for postwar operations. It then analyzes different hypotheses which might explain the strategic assessments of leading government figures. This chapter focuses on President Franklin Roosevelt to a great extent, as he exercised a substantial amount of control over policy. As a result, the candidate explanations for strategic assessments of postwar operations are discussed largely from Roosevelt's perspective. Because of the president's relatively high level of control over the policymaking process, this chapter also includes an examination of factors idiosyncratic to Roosevelt to see if these attributes account for the quality of his assessments.

As predicted by construal level theory (CLT), Roosevelt and other members of the executive branch with long time horizons tended to think about the future in abstract rather than concrete terms. This tendency produced long-term assessments which centered on ultimate objectives while discounting feasibility concerns. Roosevelt and others' lack of receptivity to concrete information about occupation plans is also consistent with CLT's predictions regarding communication fluency. Analysis of the evidence shows that opportunity costs and organizational theory are useful, but insufficient, explanations for American preparations for the occupation. U.S. gains in relative power translated into longer time horizons, as evidenced by Roosevelt's growing attention to postwar issues. Relatedly, one of Roosevelt's top priorities was to maintain unity among Allied forces during the war. He expressed concern that attempts to reach diplomatic consensus among the U.S., British, and Soviet governments on postwar policy could harm Allied cohesion and disrupt the war effort. Lastly, in terms of organizational theory, the U.S. Army had prior experience occupying German soil, experience that was then translated into doctrine and training for civil affairs officers. This allowed soldiers to effectively implement short-term objectives in the early stages of the occupation.

Despite the contributions of the alternative explanations, however, they are not sufficient to account for the shape of U.S. policy toward Germany. Without the insights of the psychological theory, the actions of Roosevelt and his close advisers seem inexplicable. Despite the centrality of Germany to Roosevelt's long-term aims, and growing pressures to attend to the details of occupation plans, many major decisions were made in an ad hoc manner as Allied forces were nearing German soil. While initial aspects of the occupation constituted a tactical success, the overall strategy had to be significantly reworked. Gains in relative power shifted attention to the future, but did not lead Roosevelt to devote more attention or resources to assessment of noncombat operations specifically. Roosevelt and Secretary of State Cordell Hull gave little attention to their subordinates in State, where much of the work on postwar policy for Germany took place. Work done by military planners was likewise ignored until 1944, when it was strongly opposed by the president and Secretary of the Treasury Henry Morgenthau despite the fact that neither of them had given much thought to how an occupation would be executed up to that point.

Roosevelt's concerns about Allied unity were inconsistent with his hasty commitment to an alternative plan for Germany's occupation produced by the Treasury Department. The Treasury plan contradicted both British and Soviet expectations of how Germany would be managed after the war, and infringed on both countries' interests. U.S. delays in contributing to a more detailed occupation plan up to that point increased tensions with the Soviet leader Joseph Stalin, who was quite suspicious of Anglo-American intentions vis-à-vis Germany. Not only did Roosevelt's abrupt adoption of Morgenthau's plan after months of delay lead to friction with his allies during the war, it clearly risked harming Allied unity and cooperation after the war. Roosevelt's rapid adoption of the Morgenthau plan, and the poor job he did managing the U.S. public's reaction to the plan's details, also contradict his complaints to that point that he could not limit his political flexibility by setting concrete policy for Germany's occupation. The lack of attention Roosevelt gave to the upcoming occupation is also puzzling given favorable intelligence on the progress of the Allied offensive in 1943–1944. Thus, fog-of-war hypotheses are largely inconsistent with the evidence.

Planning for Occupation

U.S. officials began developing plans for the occupation of Germany well in advance of the landing at Normandy in 1944. Despite the time spent crafting postwar policy, two signs of poor long-term strategic assessment are apparent in the overview that follows. First, the operatives in charge of setting the fine details of U.S. occupation policy and executing it on the ground could not obtain needed direction from their superiors. Clay and others observed that, although the guidance they received about the occupation articulated some clear objectives, it largely lacked substantive directions on policy execution. Desirability, not feasibility considerations, dominated the concerns of senior policymakers. The second sign of poor assessment was that the initial framework for the occupation of Germany was largely disparaged by operatives in the country as unworkable because it was detached from actual conditions there. This prognosis eventually gained sway in Washington as well.

Before the United States officially entered World War II, Secretary Hull had given the Council on Foreign Relations his approval to organize study groups to analyze various aspects of the postwar world. Under Secretary of State Sumner Welles had urged Hull that it was important to avoid the mistakes of World War I, where little forethought had been given to the postwar environment. Groups of experts on economic, security, and territorial issues worked together in the Advisory Committee on Problems of Foreign Relations until 1940.[3] The State Department's Advisory Committee on Post-War Foreign Policy was created shortly thereafter and remained in operation until July of 1943. Studies conducted by its subcommittees on security, economics, and migration and settlement were especially pertinent in regard to Germany. These committees were succeeded by the Interdivisional Country Committee on Germany, which focused on providing policy guidance to Ambassador John G. Winant to use in his efforts to coordinate Allied policy through the European Advisory Commission (EAC).[4]

Despite the work being done at State, senior members of the Roosevelt administration paid little attention to the department's plans regarding Germany. Hull appears to have made little effort to become familiar with his department's recommendations.[5] His knowledge of his subordinates' work may not have mattered, given Hull's meager access to the president and Allied heads of government. The secretary was either absent from the meetings of the "Big Three"—Roosevelt, Stalin, and Winston Churchill—or allowed little input.[6] Some have suggested that Roosevelt placed postwar foreign policy in the hands of State to ensure his own control over the matter. Consistent with this hypothesis, Roosevelt instructed Hull and Winant to prevent the EAC from exercising much authority over postwar affairs.[7]

Military planning for the occupation of Germany began in earnest in 1943. Plans went through three main iterations. The British Chiefs of Staff first issued a directive which initiated planning for Operation Rankin. The plan focused on controlling strategic points inside Germany after an unconditional surrender. Rankin was significant for its omissions, namely a lack of any directions on the treatment of surrendered German forces; the disposal of war materiel; public order and care for displaced persons; the recovery of prisoners of war; or the establishment of military government.[8] The military began to take steps along these lines in early 1944, when the American and British Combined Civil Affairs Committee issued Combined Chiefs of Staff (CCS) Document 551, "Directive for Military Government in Germany Prior to Defeat or Surrender."[9] Among other things, CCS 551 directed that there be foundational principles for military government in Germany, the handling of German political, financial, and security institutions, and the maintenance of public order and welfare. On the whole, however, the document was intended to serve as general guidance for Allied forces that had entered Germany prior to the country's surrender. It was not a plan to accomplish specific tasks, but rather a statement of Anglo-American intentions.[10]

CCS 551 laid the groundwork for Rankin's successor, Operation Talisman. Talisman did not initially incorporate many elements of the CCS's guidance, but would be gradually augmented as 1944 wore on. Talisman was accompanied by a "tactical" civil affairs manual for U.S. occupation troops in the field and in military government, the *Handbook for Military Government in Germany*.[11] The codeword for Germany's occupation was changed from Talisman to Eclipse in November of 1944. Eclipse was labeled "the military continuation of Operation Overlord," referring to the Normandy landing. Military planners enumerated more than a dozen key objectives to be accomplished during the early stages of the occupation, and in this regard Eclipse was more extensive than either Rankin or Talisman. Its scope was still narrower than that of CCS 551, however. One reason was that the officers focused on posthostilities did not envision Eclipse being more than the first step of the occupation. The operation would be a complex yet short-term venture to secure Germany while facilitating the continued prosecution of the war against Japan.[12]

Another reason for Eclipse's narrow scope was the lack of policy guidance military planners received from their civilian superiors. The most consistent complaint of military planners was the inscrutable nature of their own government's intentions. In September 1945 Clay stated that one of the most frequent reports from military government detachments was that they still "lacked an understanding of the basic purposes and direction of the occupation."[13] As the war in Europe drew closer to an end, officers faced the conundrum of needing to formulate procedures for their units in Germany while still avoiding any contradiction of their superiors' (unknown) objectives. Roosevelt nevertheless asserted in February 1944 that the United States was "unquestionably better prepared" than the British regarding postwar questions. Conversely, in April the assistant chief of staff of the Army's subsection on postconflict operations insisted that his staff could make little progress "until political directives are received or improvised." As a result, many of the studies undertaken by the Army prior to CCS 551 were characterized as mere "window-dressing."[14]

On September 1, 1944, the first meeting of the Cabinet Committee on Germany convened in Washington, organized at the bequest of Secretary of War Henry Stimson to provide guidance to military officers in the field. Though Roosevelt initially opted for Morgenthau's plan for Germany with little regard for the positions of others in his cabinet, public and press disapproval of the harsh policies therein (described below) forced the president to abandon the Treasury proposal after its contents were leaked. Roosevelt, facing reelection in 1944, quickly distanced himself from Morgenthau, insisting he never approved of the secretary's most extreme measures while swearing to "catch and chastise" the source of the leak.[15] Afterward, Cabinet Committee meetings led to the American Joint Chiefs of Staff (JCS) Document 1067. The directive was a compromise between the competing recommendations of the State, War, and Treasury Departments. Allied policy on Germany was further developed, though by no means finalized, at the Big Three meeting at Yalta in February 1945. Preliminary decisions were made on the issues of German reparations, the handling of war crimes, and zones of occupation. Publicly, state leaders declared they had agreed to demilitarize Germany, eliminate the Nazi Party, and place the country in the "comity of nations."[16] Following the conference, Roosevelt told his new secretary of state Edward Stettinius to draft a directive to implement Allied policy within the framework of JCS 1067.

After a year and a half, the United States would abandon JCS 1067 and begin to embrace the stabilization policy being advocated by its top military governor in Germany. The Roosevelt administration had not planned on transitioning JCS 1067 to its successor, JCS 1779. While the first document aimed to keep Germany permanently enfeebled, the latter coincided with the Marshall Plan's tenets that Europe required German productivity for its order and prosperity. Though JCS 1779 could be interpreted as a response to the United States' emerging Cold War strategy of containment, it in fact accorded with the earlier views of those who had protested that JCS 1067 could not be practically administered, an argument that had little to do with any perceived Soviet threat. In fact, U.S. administrators responsible for the occupation interpreted JCS 1067 as liberally as possible to make their task workable.

They quickly realized that policy for Germany did not accord with reality. Assistant Secretary of War John J. McCloy's recollection was that JCS 1067 was a "do-nothing" plan. Army civil affairs officers viewed it as inadequate at best and counterproductive at worst, observing that their government's policies exacerbated the wide-ranging institutional and economic collapse they dealt with on a daily basis.[17] After Roosevelt backed away from his initial decision, the State and War Departments would use their new-found influence to revise occupation policy. JCS 1067 was vague enough that, despite remaining elements injected by Morgenthau, a clever administrator could exploit its loopholes. Clay interpreted his orders as requiring "what is manifestly necessary, a realistic and firm attitude toward Germany. [JCS 1067] does not . . . prevent the holding out always [sic] of a ray of hope to the German people."[18] Any of the economic substance of Morgenthau's plan that was not purged outright would soon be abandoned as overly burdensome to the U.S. occupation.

The Army had initially intended to keep German officials in their posts for a length of time to help administer the country, but the Roosevelt administration had considered such a proposal as anathema to its objective of de-Nazification. While it was desirable to rid the country of the scourge of National Socialism, it was not pragmatic to do so to at the pace which the White House insisted on. This was especially so given the destruction in the country, and the fact that German civil servants had to be Nazi Party members regardless of their actual devotion to Nazi ideology. In the words of one of the foremost historians of the occupation, Earl F. Ziemke, de-Nazification was "probably the least satisfactory of all military government undertakings. Before the end of 1945, de-Nazification on the terms originally envisioned had been proven impractical; and in the long run, if less had been attempted, more might have been accomplished."[19]

A CLT Explanation for Occupation Preparations

Criticism of the Roosevelt administration's assessments and planning for Germany's occupation may seem unfair given the immensity of the task that lay in front of them. However, it appears that Roosevelt and many American planners were not merely uncertain of the challenges that would face occupation forces, but also consistently downplayed the complexities that an occupation of Germany would entail and failed to provide clear guidance to operatives in the field. The historical record also shows that there was variation among executive-level officials in their attention to detail and confidence when pondering noncombat operations in Germany after the war. By incorporating insights from CLT the differences between government actors can be better understood. Members of the Roosevelt administration with long time horizons took a consistently abstract approach when evaluating policy choices and assumptions pertaining to Germany's future, and attached little weight to feasibility concerns. Those with shorter time horizons, by contrast, based their strategic assessment on concrete information that lacked the positive overtones attached to long-term objectives.

This section proceeds by establishing the transformative goals the president and senior officials in the State Department had for Germany and Europe, and the relatively short-term focus of their colleagues in the War Department. It then shows that the former individuals were more likely to underestimate the costs of the occupation of Germany, while the latter group was more attuned to the difficulties Clay and others brought to light once a military government had been put in place. Though the Treasury Department became heavily involved in the plans for Germany, this did not occur until late summer of 1944. Secretary Morgenthau's plan for Germany has been characterized by its unworkability and vengefulness, a characterization that is not disputed here. However, it cannot be said the plan did not account for the means by which Germany would be dismantled—unsurprising from a CLT perspective, since Morgenthau became involved in occupation policy late in the war, just a month before Roosevelt adopted his plan at the second Quebec Conference. What is notable is how quickly the president embraced such a plan without considering its feasibility.

TIME HORIZONS: POSTWAR OBJECTIVES

Of the members of Roosevelt's administration, the president himself and the top officials at the State Department placed the most weight on world order after the war. While they disagreed on the question of rebuilding the German economy and maintaining a unified German state, Roosevelt and State officials adopted transformative objectives they believed were crucial for postwar international security. Not only did officials at State possess valued long-term political goals, it has also been seen that they began planning postwar policy at the outset of the conflict. This was at Roosevelt's direction and, although the president was primarily concerned with ongoing military operations throughout 1942, his attention noticeably began to shift to the postwar world by 1943. Thus, Roosevelt and State officials exhibited both of the components necessary and sufficient for long time horizons: valued long-range goals and attention to distant time periods. Conversely, military officers and top officials at the War Department either lacked transformative objectives or were fixated on immediate combat operations, if not both. Their considerations of Germany's occupation revolved around the theme of "military necessity," meaning that the principal objective of noncombat operations was to facilitate the ongoing Allied offensive. Despite their different attitudes toward Germany, and as shown in the remainder of the chapter,

Roosevelt and State officials with long time horizons were prone to ignore the feasibility of their occupation plans, something which was not true of officials with short time horizons.

Editors of the wartime letters between Roosevelt and Churchill note that the president showed a tendency to "think globally and in idealistic and futuristic terms."[20] Roosevelt was determined that "something 'big'" would come out of the war, "a new heaven and a new earth."[21] Though Roosevelt sincerely desired to advance liberal political principles after the war, such as those articulated in the Atlantic Charter, his postwar aims extended beyond Wilsonian idealism. The president was mindful of the role military power and national interests play in international politics, and one of his top long-term priorities was to have the Soviet Union, Britain, and other great powers provide regional security after the war. Roosevelt's transformative ends thus relied both on appealing to the interests of regional powers to achieve postwar peace, as well as the promotion of political ideals via new international institutions.

A year before the attack on Pearl Harbor, Roosevelt spoke about the "four freedoms" of speech and worship, and from want and fear, in his State of the Union address. In regard to the latter two, he referred to the "failure of the democracies to deal with problems of world reconstruction" following World War I and concluded that the world's future would be founded on "economic understandings which will secure to every nation a healthy peacetime life for its inhabitants—everywhere in the world . . . [and] a world-wide reduction of armaments to such a point and in such a thorough fashion that no nation will be in a position to commit an act of physical aggression against any neighbor—anywhere in the world. That is no vision of a distant millennium. It is a definite basis for a kind of world attainable in our own time and generation."[22]

Harry Hopkins, one of the president's chief advisers during the war, stated privately that "you can see the real Roosevelt when he comes out with something like the four freedoms. He believes them!"[23] Roosevelt's words were matched by previous actions he had taken. In February 1940 he dispatched Sumner Welles to Europe to gauge the belligerent parties' attitudes toward a peace settlement. Among other matters, Welles was to discuss the possibility of strengthening global trade and establishing arms control regimes. That same month, Roosevelt authorized the State Department to contact more than forty neutral countries to discuss the same issues of economics and disarmament.[24] The Atlantic Charter, issued with Great Britain before the United States entered the war, further emphasized these priorities.

Not only had Roosevelt broached the four freedoms early in the war, he was willing to incur real costs to protect his long-term aims once the United States had joined the fighting. A prime example of such a sacrifice is the president's handling of Soviet territorial demands. Welles, who was quite devoted to the establishment of a liberal postwar order, angrily informed the British that they could not make territorial concessions in Eastern Europe to Stalin. He argued that "no healthy and lasting world order" could be built if the principles of the Atlantic Charter were ignored.[25] Two months later, in April of 1942, the president proposed to open a second front in Europe to ease the Soviet war burden. Roosevelt thought an early cross-channel invasion of Europe "might be the turning point which would save Russia this year" and insisted to his commanders that "you should strongly urge immediate all-out preparations for it, that it be pushed with utmost vigor, and that it be executed whether or not Russian collapse becomes imminent."[26] There were obvious immediate military reasons why a Soviet collapse would be disastrous for the war effort, but many historians believe that Roosevelt's costly pledge was also intended to appease Stalin and convince the Soviet leader to relinquish his territorial demands, thus protecting Roosevelt's postwar goals. Roosevelt's insistence on such a plan "whether or not" the USSR was on the verge of defeat lends credence to such assertions. Even more meager compromises of the charter were rejected: when Lord Halifax proposed granting the Soviets postwar basing rights in lieu of territorial concessions, both Roosevelt and Welles protested that the offer was contrary to the Atlantic Charter and public opinion.[27] Even though Welles's committee on postwar political problems recognized in 1942 that "Russia will claim certain territories for herself" after the war, it also insisted that Soviet security needs be balanced with the principle of self-determination and proposed that "individual liberties should be pledged to the peoples in the territories retained by Russia."[28]

The president's postwar aims were not confined to the realm of liberal Wilsonianism, and some have rejected the argument that Roosevelt's early military proposals vis-à-vis the Soviets were motivated by the principles of the Atlantic Charter.[29] It is less debatable that they served to shore up his vision for postwar security, however, in which amicable relations with Moscow would be crucial. Meeting with Churchill in the fall of 1941, the president broached the idea of an international security body and opined that the United States and Britain would have to police the world to prevent interstate war from recurring.[30] These ideas would evolve into Roosevelt's "four policemen" strategy for preserving the peace, which called for the United States, Britain, the USSR, and China to quash regional disputes before they grew into armed conflicts. This strategy was a key plank of Roosevelt's postwar foreign policy, and he thus worried that Stalin, whose forces bore the brunt of fighting against Germany, thought the Americans and British were bleeding his country for their own postwar advantage. The president's idea for an early Anglo-American invasion of France was meant to assuage such fears. At international meetings of the Allies, Roosevelt especially concentrated on gaining and maintaining Stalin's trust. Even after the war turned in the Allies' favor, Roosevelt worried about Soviet intentions in the conflict.[31]

Germany's future was crucial in Roosevelt's long-term thinking. If the United States and other great powers were to maintain security in their respective regions after the war, Roosevelt felt that sweeping changes would have to take place there. As Warren Kimball writes, "the intensity of that belief on Roosevelt's part is hard to overestimate." Writing to Stettinius in February of 1944, Roosevelt asserted that the "principal object" of U.S. policy was "to take part in eliminating Germany at a possible and even probable cost of a third world war."[32] Early in the war the president had differentiated between the German people and the Nazi leadership, but this changed when intelligence indicated that the mass public largely supported the regime. By the time of the Tehran conference in 1943 Roosevelt seemed sure that the German nation was innately aggressive.[33] The hardening of the president's views was coupled with optimism that there was a great opportunity, in the words of historian Steven Casey, to transform "a prostrate nation, a clean slate on which the Allies could write whatever they wished." Similarly, a JCS memorandum on conditions in occupied Europe reported that "it is believed that we desire a *tabula rasa* after the collapse of Germany on which to build a peace after a considerable period of trial during a prolonged armistice."[34] Of particular importance to Roosevelt was how Germany would relate to its neighbors, and especially how these relations would affect America's future ties with the USSR. He insisted that the "nature of the security which should rightly be accorded to the Soviet Union would depend upon the type of Germany which would be established at the end of the war."[35]

In regard to the internal politics and economics of Germany, Roosevelt saw the need for drastic, long-term transformation. He believed that no simple "decree, law, or military order" would be sufficient to alter what he saw as the country's militaristic culture. Roosevelt proposed that "the change in German philosophy must be evolutionary and may take two generations." On a separate occasion he declared his determination that the United States "must not allow the seeds of the evils we shall have crushed to germinate and reproduce themselves in the future."[36] The answer to these questions relied on the negative measures of de-Nazification, demilitarization, and deindustrialization and on the positive measure of democratization, which was linked to a just peace. Roosevelt was intent not just on eliminating the German threat, but initiating a Jeffersonian reformation of the collective German character. The idea that farmers could be "the backbone of a peaceful, perhaps a democratic nation," as Secretary Morgenthau would put it, was well received by the president.[37]

Roosevelt embraced Morgenthau's plan for Germany, which specified that the country would be disarmed and its industry removed to provide reparations to Europe. The Ruhr and Saar areas, on which the country's coal-based economy depended, would be internationalized and given to France, respectively. Germany would be further partitioned along its East–West axis. Military governors would be forbidden from rehabilitating the German economy in any way, and there would be tight restrictions on the country's trade and imports for "at least twenty years" to prevent any growth of industry.[38] The remnants of Germany were, in essence, to be made agricultural. While Roosevelt professed he did not want the German people to "starve to death" after the war, they did have to comprehend that they were "a defeated nation, collectively and individually," and thus could make do with soup from U.S. Army kitchens.[39]

Though top officials at the State Department never adopted the same harsh views of the German nation as the president, they did share Roosevelt's global perspective on the long-term political objectives to be achieved in the war's aftermath. Hull and Welles were firmly committed to a liberal international order. Both men had taken the lead in setting up bodies to study long-term U.S. foreign policy prior to America's entrance into the war. The key planks of State's postwar program were the development of international institutions to support open trade and collective security.[40] State's policy on postwar Germany was as transformative as Roosevelt's, though it was of a decidedly different tone. Like Roosevelt, State planners sought to make over the country so as to bar it from future aggression, which would involve disarmament and demilitarization. Early on, groups which Welles presided over stressed that "international security is considered the basic objective in determining the disposition of Germany," a consistent theme in State meetings.[41] But while Welles favored partitioning Germany into a loose confederation after the war, the majority of State planners focused on Germany intended to leave the country's productive capacity largely in place.[42] They opposed partitioning the country for fear of the economic damage that could result, and envisaged a Germany that would be integrated into the European economic system.

Hull strongly believed that free trade and peace went hand in hand, asserting in 1938 that "rearmament takes place when the political and economic health are lacking [sic] . . . political and economic agreement is the horse; limitation and reduction of armaments is the cart." This attitude was prevalent in State, and the department would generally uphold this position after Stettinius became the new secretary during the war.[43] The department sought to create a pluralistic democracy with an open economy in the place where totalitarianism had resided.[44] Conversely, rehabilitating the German economy was anathema to the president. Isador Lubin, one of Roosevelt's close economic advisers, composed a memo to Hopkins saying he was disturbed that State was "making for a prosperous Germany in the long-run interests of the United States."[45] This communication occurred at the same time the president was at the Second Quebec Conference with Churchill discussing Germany's future as planned by Morgenthau, illustrating the State Department's lack of influence on high-level policy in the White House.

Like the State Department, the U.S. military preferred Germany to be economically rehabilitated. Instead of arising from the belief that trade, democracy, and diplomatic engagement would produce a long and stable peace, however, the War Department's and the military's policies were driven by concerns about the short-term prosecution of combat operations. In the years between the world wars, Colonel Irwin Hunt spearheaded a movement for change in Army training and doctrine with reports on the inadequacy of preparations for occupying Germany in World War I. Hunt's reports were used to create *Field Manual 27-5*, published in 1940. Rather than emphasizing how noncombat operations were crucial for securing the ultimate political objectives of a campaign, the manual highlighted the support of ongoing combat operations as the primary task of military government. Immediate threats to security and stability were the military's predominant concern. Officers would be expected to restore local economies while taking steps to prevent disease and unrest from spreading among the occupied population.[46] The Anglo-American Combined Civil Affairs Committee's directive for military government in Germany instructed officers that "military occupation is intended: to aid military operations; to destroy Nazism-Fascism and the Nazi Hierarchy; to maintain and preserve law and order; and to restore normal conditions among the civilian population as soon as possible, in so far as such conditions will not interfere with military operations." Likewise, in the limited instructions on occupation policy General Dwight Eisenhower received in August 1944, the CCS instructed the supreme allied commander to focus on doing "the minimum required to prevent disease and unrest."[47] As was his response to State proposals, Roosevelt objected to military policy premised on "a reconstituting of a German state which," he noted with sarcasm, "would give active cooperation apparently at once to peace in Europe." Whereas the JCS had presupposed the unity of the country would be maintained, Roosevelt added that he was unwilling to announce "that we do not intend to destroy the German nation."[48]

Secretary of War Stimson was in some ways much like his colleagues at State in that he also believed an enduring peace would depend on liberal political principles and global economic prosperity. This had been his position during his own tenure as secretary of state under President Herbert Hoover.[49] Although Stimson had placed considerable weight on the long-term transformation of international politics in a more pacific direction, he did not focus on the postwar world to nearly the same extent as Roosevelt or top State officials during World War II. Although neither Roosevelt nor Stimson devoted much attention to the details of Germany's occupation early in the war, the president had been engaged in the establishment of long-term postwar policy as early as 1943. Despite his previous foreign policy experiences, which might have disposed him to be concerned with building a durable future peace, Stimson found himself to be too taxed by the day-to-day management of the war. This prevented him from turning his attention to postwar issues until the end of the conflict was near.[50] When approached by McCloy in March 1944 about future plans for Europe, Stimson replied he could not afford to get "churned up" over such ideas because there was still a war to win, adding he was unwilling to "set myself up as a sort of a master mind in this madhouse of Washington," a task to which he did not feel equal. Later that spring Stimson told Army Chief of Staff George C. Marshall that the idea of working on postwar military policies felt "artificial" to him. One biographer asserts Stimson had "the kind of mind that worked on one thing at a time and he was working on the winning of the war. Furthermore, by his calculations, the terminal boundaries of the conflict coincided almost exactly with the foreseeable limits of his own life, so he would leave the matter to those who would have some future to live in."[51] Stimson's involvement in higher-level postwar policy did not seem to have been spurred by forward thinking. Instead, it came as a result of his belated realization that directives were not emerging quickly enough given the pace of the Allied advance, and as a reaction to plans for Germany emerging from the Treasury Department in the late summer of 1944.

Stimson was also an early proponent of military government and shared uniformed officers' evaluations of the importance of military necessity, which saw the occupier's primary task as the ongoing prosecution of the war, not a fundamental transformation of the occupied country.[52] Accordingly, officials at the War Department were mainly preoccupied with how the Army would maintain law and order within an occupied territory without hindering military operations elsewhere. Stimson also described his primary objective in a peace settlement as maintaining America's friendly association with Britain—in other words, preserving the quality of prewar relationships. He told Hull in 1943 that the top priority in postwar planning must be the continuation of "the same controls as have saved us during the war, namely the close association between the English speaking countries."[53] These positions were a far cry from Roosevelt's and State officials' transformative objectives for Europe and Germany, and further indicated Stimson had much shorter time horizons than others in the administration.

GERMANY'S POLITICAL AND ECONOMIC FUTURE

The primary way CLT predicts that long time horizons promote overconfidence about distant military operations is by encouraging a focus on the desirability of the goals operations are meant to achieve, rather than the feasibility of the operations themselves. While Roosevelt and those in the State Department had very different transformative objectives for Germany, both assumed their plans could be easily enacted. The president's desire to create a prostrate, deindustrialized country blinded him to the complications such an endeavor would create for occupation forces. Roosevelt did not account for how chaotic conditions in postwar Germany could strain U.S. personnel. State's plans called for a democratic and economically rehabilitated Germany, and presumed a state and society that would be largely intact after the war to facilitate such plans. While the possibility of a German collapse had been considered, it was an axiom at State that it was both preventable and unlikely. From the perspective of CLT, it is unsurprising that those responsible for considering Germany's future did not adopt the collapse of its economy as a premise in their planning efforts. While this possibility would impact the means by which the occupation of Germany was implemented, it was not central to the transformative goals sought and thus was not salient in the abstract strategic assessments being made by Roosevelt or State officials.

When top officials in the War Department learned Roosevelt was seriously considering Morgenthau's proposed measures for Germany they were taken aback. They objected not only because the Treasury plan conflicted with their own policy preferences, but also because the project struck them as unrealistic. Stimson argued that Morgenthau's plan would greatly complicate efforts to secure postwar peace, and deprive Europe of needed resources after the war. Furthermore, he found the proposition that the Ruhr and Saar areas be "totally transformed" to be one he could not conceive "either possible or effective." He expanded on this theme a few days later, explaining that while all officials in the administration shared the objective of preserving the peace after war, his problem was with the "method" now under consideration. Stimson's assertion that the president's preferred policies were infeasible was independently supported by the major professional engineering associations in the United States.[54] McCloy condemned the Treasury plan for similar reasons, writing to Eisenhower that those behind it were "utterly innocent of any realization of the extent and complexity" of what they were proposing.[55] Though Hull and those at State generally shared Stimson's foreign policy views, they were not nearly as vocal or astute critics of the details and assumptions of Morgenthau's plan. If one is to attribute the character of Stimson's critiques to his preexisting beliefs and preferences, one must also explain that Hull and other State officials were not similarly critical. The CLT prediction that those with shorter time horizons will attend more closely to future plans' feasibility makes sense of this disparity.

Stimson's and McCloy's analyses were backed by the Foreign Economic Administration (FEA), formed in 1943 to deal with economic aspects of the war effort. In July 1944 the FEA pointed out that, after the war, coal production in Europe outside Germany would likely be well below prewar levels, while at the same time there would be excess demand wrought by the need for reconstruction. Damage to European infrastructure would stall the pace at which coal from the United States and Britain could make up the resulting deficits, and delays would be exacerbated if the war in the Pacific did not conclude quickly.[56] Morgenthau's proposal did not address these obstacles, instead presuming coal production and demand would be at prewar levels following Germany's defeat. Troubling discrepancies over such details did not factor into the president's judgments, however. Further, those charged with executing the Morgenthau plan asserted they would not be likely to succeed. The Supreme Headquarters of the Allied Expeditionary Force

(SHAEF) criticized the feasibility of the proposals emerging from Washington in September 1944 in no uncertain terms. To fulfill the tasks with which it had been charged, "this headquarters would have to be prepared, through the authorities of five liberated nations and despite conditions in Germany, to control the commodities in short supply required by 150 million people." Such an undertaking "would require personnel in numbers and with training not available to this headquarters and would result in political difficulties." SHAEF concluded that "the conditions and period of this headquarters responsibility in Germany are such that it appears impracticable for it to attempt any systematic reorientation of German industry."[57]

Ironically, available intelligence on the destruction being wrought in Germany should have minimized fears about its future economic capacity. From 1943 onward the Allies made the destruction of the German economy a top priority. Though information on the economic impact Allied attacks had on Germany was not entirely clear during the war, Alfred Mierzejewski correctly asserts that intelligence estimates mostly "emphasized that the German economy was stressed to the limit, and that no reallocation of resources in it or expansion of armaments output was possible. They repeatedly predicted its collapse and consistently exaggerated the effects of strategic bombing."[58] The U.S. Joint Intelligence Committee (JIC) held in August 1943 that, while only a third of German industry had been under "really heavy attack," and that for only three months, the "industrial centers of the Ruhr and Rhineland have been so devastated by bombing that they are openly regarded as front line zones whose essential activities must somehow be kept going."[59]

In the spring of 1944 Anglo-American intelligence services began to realize they had underestimated the capacity of the German economy. The JIC recognized that the Nazi regime had not been "finally geared to totalitarian war until the end of 1943."[60] Still, although 75 to 80 percent of Germany's physical industry remained intact after the war, the German economy and transportation system had been destroyed. Once Berlin was occupied, Clay observed that "there is a tremendous difference between the physical state of Germany's industrial facilities and the German economy. The latter has disappeared."[61] Two studies conducted by the United States shortly after the occupation began concluded that policies meant to prevent economic rejuvenation could not effectively pay the costs of occupation or allow the average German a minimum standard of living. Mass starvation and disease would be unavoidable if U.S. policies were not altered.[62] Ambassador Robert Murphy, one of Clay's top advisers, wrote that he and his associates were of the opinion that the destruction wrought by military operations was "so staggering that the obligation resting on the Allied organization to prevent disease and unrest and disorder" had become the "keynote" of occupation administrators.[63]

Roosevelt's desire to make Germany economically impotent had obscured the reality of conditions in the country and distracted his attention from whether or not his preferred policies could be feasibly pursued. It is not surprising Roosevelt accepted Morgenthau's plan given that it closely matched his policy preferences; however, his communication fluency also explains why Roosevelt failed to consider the plan's feasibility. CLT predicts that Roosevelt, whose long time horizons promoted abstract thinking, would have been most receptive to information about the desirability of his ends rather than concrete, context-dependent information about the necessary means for achieving his goals. His seeming inability or unwillingness to incorporate intelligence on bombing into his long-term assessments is consistent with a lack of communication fluency. Likewise, several scholars have echoed the view of Steven Casey that the president "was easily convinced" by Morgenthau's arguments.[64] Not only did Morgenthau's plan reflect Roosevelt's economic and political objectives for Germany, it appealed to his desire that U.S. troops would quickly leave Europe after the war. Point 14 of Morgenthau's plan stated that the "primary responsibility" for occupying and administering Germany should fall to European powers. "Under this program," stated the Treasury memorandum to the president, "United States troops could be withdrawn within a relatively short time."[65] Roosevelt quickly latched on to this assumption, which fit with his long-standing goals. In November 1943, Roosevelt had informed General Marshall that Americans would need to occupy Germany for "at least one year, maybe two," and told Stettinius a few months later that the British would have "plenty of time" to arrange for their future security vis-à-vis Germany, continuing that the United States "by that time will be only too glad to retire all their military forces from Europe."[66]

Roosevelt reiterated his expectations for the length of the U.S. presence in Germany to Churchill in November 1944, alarming the prime minister. "If after Germany's collapse you 'must bring American troops home as rapidly as transportation problems will permit,'" Churchill asked, citing Roosevelt's own words, "and if the French are to have no equipped postwar army or time to make one . . . how will it be possible to hold down Western Germany beyond the present Russian occupation line?" Roosevelt replied that "there should be no difficulty" equipping the French with arms taken from the Wehrmacht "when it surrenders or is destroyed."[67] This statement is somewhat astounding, not only because the president felt the process of arming the French would be simple, but also because of his expressed reliance on the resources of a German army that he acknowledged might be smashed. It contained none of the foreboding of Eisenhower's warning in August of that year that it was possible the German army "will never actually surrender and that we shall enter the country finding no central German authority in control, with the situation chaotic, probably guerilla fighting and possibly even civil war in certain districts."[68] Instead, Roosevelt's statement reflected his unexamined belief that the British would have plenty of time to figure out how to handle the occupation of Germany without U.S. assistance. Given the toll the war had taken on Britain's own military and economic power, Churchill was understandably less sanguine regarding prospects of such a venture. The prime minister had remarked that Britain could not afford to be chained to Germany's "dead body" after the war, and no reanimation of the German corpse was likely under the Morgenthau plan. Churchill's sudden acceptance of the plan at Quebec likely resulted from Britain's urgent need of further Lend-Lease aid; Morgenthau recorded that Churchill wept with relief after additional loans were secured at the conference.[69]

It can be argued that Roosevelt had legitimate reasons for believing U.S. soldiers would have to return home as soon as possible. Most notably, the president argued American public opinion would not permit a prolonged occupation. He told Stettinius that "political considerations in the United States" made his decision to withdraw U.S. forces "conclusive."[70] But even if the public was adamantly opposed to a long occupation, Roosevelt had not adequately addressed Churchill's security concerns. Indeed, the president's expressed belief was out of line with even the more optimistic elements of his own administration. At a time when the State Department still presumed a German economic collapse to be preventable, its planners foresaw the possibility of a decade-long occupation.[71]

Further, Roosevelt's perception of public opinion appeared to be based more on his own personal beliefs than evidence, again reflecting a lack of receptiveness to concrete information. A Washington intelligence office rightly noted that there was "no assurance" that any proposal regarding the postwar world would receive public support, but this was true of all of the Roosevelt administration's policies, not just those related to Germany.[72] Polls prepared for the White House in early 1943 indicated three-fourths of Americans were willing to accept the vague commitment "to have part of our Army stay overseas" after the war. In July 1944 Gallup produced more precise questions which showed that 43 percent of respondents believed U.S. forces would occupy Germany three years or longer, equal to the proportion who thought the occupation would last two years or less; a full quarter of respondents believed the occupation would last ten years or more.[73] In fact, when it came to postwar issues Roosevelt was surprisingly insensitive to public opinion, an aberration from his normally astute grasp of the domestic ramifications of foreign policy decisions.[74] He took no steps to try to prevent the Morgenthau plan from leaking to the public, and his considerations of policy toward Germany at Quebec omitted considerations of domestic opinion, a blind spot which seemed inexplicable given the ongoing presidential campaign in 1944. The only plausible explanation, Casey posits, is that Roosevelt was "remarkably optimistic" that he could keep postwar plans under wraps.[75] Once again, the president was ignoring how low-level constraints could impinge on his transformative objectives for Germany.

State officials did not share Roosevelt's goals, but were also overconfident that their plans for Germany could be implemented. Assertions that this was due to the idealistic nature of State Department planners' values and beliefs are too simplistic. Rampant uncertainty made the task of planning for Germany's political and economic future prior to the war's conclusion a demanding one. However, as predicted by CLT, planners in State coped with these demands by focusing on their desired policy ends more than the means by which these objectives would be achieved. As a member of Welles's Advisory Committee stated before America had entered the war, "the future is so uncertain, the course of the war so problematical, and the atmosphere in which peace negotiations may take place so unknown, that a specific approach seems to me untenable. Hence I feel driven to put down the things that to us *would seem desirable* only in the most *general* way."[76] This was a reasonable conclusion in 1940, but State planners likely did not appreciate how such an approach could lead to overconfident assessments of postwar outcomes.

Shortly after the United States entered the war, State's Advisory Committee tried to make the Atlantic Charter declarations more concrete or at least asked questions about the implications of such objectives, which implied some concern for feasibility. Among these early questions were those of whether enemy powers should be territorially broken up; if punishment should be imposed on enemy states and how; and whether enemy states should be reconstructed so as to constitute viable social and political units. Many of these questions revolved around the larger issue of the limits that could be placed on enemy self-determination in light of the Atlantic Charter principles.[77] However, rather than questioning how the war would affect the capacity of Germany to absorb the transformative changes being considered in the department, State planners assumed that the German state and economy would be in a position to facilitate the enactment of the policy objectives being proposed. Planners held that "fundamentally the same course as taken in 1918 should be taken again: insistence on assurance that representative government existed at the time of armistice. It was believed that the situation would be more favorable at the end of this war in view of the provision of the Weimar Constitution for a President and the fact that Hitler has not abolished the Constitution or the Presidency." Welles and others acknowledged uncertainty regarding what form of government would "exist behind the German military commanders" at the war's end, but presumed that the German state would be intact.[78]

State planners also envisioned that a customs union would be erected within something akin to a German confederacy, recommending against any partition that would complicate the country's economic viability or distract from establishing "a society of peace and security, in which education and intellectual freedom might flourish."[79] Reviewing such statements and assumptions, Carolyn Eisenberg comments that "there was an air of unreality" to the State Department's agenda and characterizes planners there as "insulated from the realm of practical decision making."[80] The premise that political and economic conditions in Germany would be conducive to State plans was not seriously reevaluated until the middle of 1944. In June the FEA raised several objections to the assumptions being made at State. The FEA, charged principally with matters of economic warfare, had given more consideration to the day-to-day status of the German economy than had most State planners. From its perspective State had done little to test its assumptions against the developing situation behind enemy lines. As a result, many concrete problems that could face occupation forces were not being taken into account.[81]

Paul Hammond, author of one of the most thorough accounts of the evolution of U.S. occupation policy, characterizes those in State as overly confident in their plans for Germany, but contends that military planners likewise assumed that occupying forces would find the German economy intact.[82] This is borne out by Eisenhower's evaluations of postwar plans, evaluations made as his forces were bearing down on German territory. Talisman, which had been based on CCS 551, placed much faith in the resiliency of German society. It thus seemed utopian to the supreme commander, whose experience after the Normandy landing suggested that much of Europe had become a shell of its former self. On August 23 he dispatched his views to Washington, pointing out that if the worst-case scenario he laid out came to pass he would not possess adequate guidance or resources to secure Germany. If conditions in the country were going to be as bad as SHAEF had projected, it would "be utterly impossible effectively to *control or to save* the economic structure of the country. That structure will inevitably collapse, and we feel that we should not assume the responsibility for its support and control."[83] In other words, neither Roosevelt and Morgenthau's harsh plans to reorient the Germany economy nor State's "soft" plans for economic rehabilitation would be feasible.

While the military planners behind CCS 551 and Talisman made optimistic assumptions about future conditions in Germany, it does not appear that the value planners' attached to long-term goals of the coming occupation had much to do with these assessments. First, Hammond's criticism of civil affairs officers' postwar plans is accompanied by the observation that Roosevelt and State planners encouraged those in the War Department to believe that a political and economic collapse in Germany was unlikely.[84] Furthermore, like the EAC, the military's Combined Civil Affairs Committee was given little authority by leaders in Washington, and thus it could not advance specific or novel proposals on its own. Needing to issue some set of directives to Eisenhower and other commanders in the field, they turned to the guidance provided by the field manual on military government inspired by Irwin Hunt.[85] As is the nature of field manuals, *FM 27-5* was not designed to be context-specific, but rather a set of general guidelines, and thus did not offer exacting descriptions of the environment in which military officers would operate. Indeed, the broad nature of the manual likely appealed to military civil affairs planners who were aware they had little authority to create precise instructions to send to Eisenhower. The resulting generality of CCS 551 obscured how the particular case of post–World War II Germany would depart from the broader class of phenomena—militarily occupied countries—in which it fit. While CLT predicts that abstract assessments of the future likewise obscure how specific cases depart from general theories, CCS 551 and Talisman were instead the products of planners who, lacking authority or effective policy guidance from top civilian policymakers, relied on the organizational knowledge they had available.

Ironically, but consistent with the predictions of CLT, those focused on immediate operations and events—individuals in the War Department, the FEA, and commanders at the front—were most sensitive to the feasibility of postwar plans meant to secure transformative objectives, rather than "far-sighted" officials with valued long-term aims. One might infer that this is simply because officials focused on the present also had better knowledge of conditions on the ground. However, this explanation cannot account for why Roosevelt remained fixated on dismantling Germany's economic capacity when the bulk of intelligence available to him indicated that Allied bombing had already accomplished this task. Information asymmetries also cannot explain why the president resisted detailed considerations of occupation plans. Roosevelt's consistent refusal to become engaged in concrete analysis, behavior CLT would expect of someone with an abstract mind-set, is laid out further in the next section. Information asymmetries also cannot explain why members of the State Department were so slow to update their beliefs about Germany. Even in July 1944, after its assumptions had been challenged by the FEA, State planners still thought the bulk of industrial reparations could be taken from Germany's "current production," and were depending on existing German administrative infrastructure to run their economic program.[86]

Some of the more worrisome assessments made prior to the occupation were affirmed by General Clay once he arrived in Germany. Clay tried to persuade leaders in Washington that the lack of focus on the immediate conditions in the country was endangering the United States' long-term goals. It is unlikely any of his objections to occupation policy arose because he wanted to be "soft" on the German people. Clay had written that he was "unwilling to concede that Germany became what it was in spite of the Germans, and merely due to their readiness to follow the leader," and held that "some cold and hunger will be necessary to make the German people realize the consequences of the war they caused."[87] Instead, he thought the civilian leadership had the wrong priorities and had failed to anticipate future conditions on the ground, having been overly focused on their ultimate goals. Early in the occupation Clay wrote that:

> Conditions in Germany are getting progressively worse . . . we have a *long range problem in preventing the restoration of Germany's war potential. However, this is not the short-range problem* as several years will be required to develop

a sustaining economy. . . . I think too much of our planning at home envisaged a Germany in which an existing government has surrendered with a large part of the country intact. In point of fact, it looks as if every foot of ground will have to be occupied. Destruction will be widespread, and government as we know it will be non-existent. *In solving the short-range problem we should find the answer to the long-range problem.*[88]

Privately, Clay's subordinates voiced the same opinions. At one of the first staff meetings after the defeat of Germany, a member of the U.S. military government there commented that "in Washington there is a much better understanding of the nature of the German problem than previously, although there are still traces of the earlier assumption that a large enough part of the German political and economic fabric still exists to provide workable machinery for the operation of Allied controls." A few days prior, Ambassador Murphy had presented two acts of surrender that were "totally different" from those the EAC had been instructed to prepare because the earlier documents had not considered the possibility there would be an absence of German government authorities with which occupation forces could deal.[89]

ZONES OF OCCUPATION

Another prominent area where a lack of feasibility concerns was apparent was the long-running debate over which zones the British and Americans should occupy in Germany after the war. Normally, Roosevelt was of a like-mind with Hull on matters of territorial issues in that neither man was inclined to deal with what they perceived to be "these piddling little things." Consistent with CLT, Kimball contends that Roosevelt and Hull's reluctance to deal with "lesser, excruciatingly detailed issues of borders" reflected their "broad conception" of postwar goals, as well as political leaders' general tendency to resist political commitments.[90] However, Roosevelt's postwar goals led him to become quite involved with a particular territorial issue relevant to the occupation of Germany. He demanded the United States be granted the northwestern zone of occupation due to his concern that southern Europe, and France in particular, could be chaotic after the war's conclusion.[91] As Roosevelt wrote Stettinius in February 1944, his objective was "not to take part in the internal problems in Southern Europe" but to eliminate Germany as a threat to world peace. Similarly, he would tell Churchill that France was "his baby" and insist that the prime minister discipline his own "children" on the Continent.[92] Roosevelt also worried that a U.S. presence in the southwestern zone, adjacent to areas of political disorder, would result in American forces staying in Europe for much longer than he could countenance.[93]

While Roosevelt's postwar goals provided some motivation to push for the northwest zone of occupation, he did not devote careful attention to whether or not he could feasibly avoid the difficulties which might accompany such a position. U.S. forces were to the south of British forces after the Normandy landing, and to reverse the zones of occupation would require a complicated crossing of the armies' lines of communication. Marshall and the American JCS first told Roosevelt that such a crossover would be very difficult, but possible.[94] Eventually, however, prominent U.S. officials came over to the British point of view that the complexity of the maneuver would be prohibitive. Stettinius informed Roosevelt of the difficulties of his plan and argued that northwest Germany, not the southwest, would be harder to control and require a longer occupation. The president wrote back that British objections "are specious . . . it is physically easy for [Allied forces] to go anywhere—north, east, or south."[95] Roosevelt would continue with this insistence for the next seven months. When Stettinius warned him again in August that "the northern area [of Germany] may have a good many headaches and not a little shooting will have to be done," Roosevelt rebuffed him, stating it would not be problematic for British soldiers to "march hand in hand with the supply of our troops."[96] At the Quebec Conference in September 1944, Admiral William Leahy told the president that, in line with General Eisenhower's thinking, a crossover of zones would be impractical. The president again rejected this assertion, telling him the objection was "nonsense. It could be done."[97]

Despite his protestation to Leahy at Quebec, Roosevelt reversed himself the next day, suddenly declaring his preference for the southwest zone. This reversal has puzzled historians, though Robert Dallek has advanced two possible explanations for the change in Roosevelt's position. First, the president might have come to accept the need for a prolonged presence of American forces in Europe. This seems unlikely, as after the conference the president continued to assert U.S. forces would leave quickly after Germany's surrender, telling Winant, "it is my intention to return from Europe to the United States as many of our troops as possible and at the earliest practicable date."[98] Dallek's second explanation for Roosevelt's reversal rests on Churchill's acceptance of Morgenthau's proposal for postwar Germany. Since the bulk of German industry that would have to be dismantled and monitored lay in the northwest, Roosevelt may have chosen to leave his position unsettled until Churchill's acceptance or rejection of the Treasury plan made it apparent which zone would carry the fewest demands for occupation forces.[99] This explanation also seems unlikely. The president's desire for the northwest zone had been unwavering for many months, prior to the formulation of Morgenthau's plan. For Roosevelt to complicate his relationship with his British ally would have been atypical unless he firmly believed his long-term interests were being threatened. Given his long-standing desire for Germany's deindustrialization, it would also be dubious to argue that Roosevelt could not have been expected to be aware of the geographic disposition of the German economy. The productive capacity of the country's different regions was not secret; the State Department had pointed out in 1942 that dividing Germany into separate units would give the northwest "highly disproportionate industrial strength."[100]

Unlike the preceding arguments, CLT's predictions on communication fluency can explain Roosevelt's new position on occupation zones at Quebec. He was determined to lay Germany low but had not thought much about what the blunting of German economic power would actually entail. In short, the president's insistence on the northwestern zone of occupation can be explained by his fixation on his goals—avoiding problems in southwestern Europe, quickly withdrawing U.S. forces, and deindustrializing Germany—combined with his resistance to information explaining the costs that his goals would entail. As shown above, Roosevelt was not at all receptive to information challenging the feasibility of his plan to occupy Germany's northwest. Furthermore, he was not interested in the complexities deindustrialization would present. He consistently refused to make decisions about postwar Germany when the subject came up, and was prone to avoid concrete information about postwar plans. Roosevelt was fixated on ends, not means, and his corresponding communication fluency meant he was inattentive to information highlighting the obstacles that would impede the attainment of his goals. The president wrote to Churchill that he had "been worrying a good deal of late on account of the tendency of all of us to prepare for future event is such detail that we may be letting ourselves in for trouble when the time arrives," adding that the thought of all the committees working on Germany's occupation caused him to "shudder." He regarded the "pages and pages with detailed instructions and appendices" he had been shown "as prophecies by prophets who cannot be infallible," further arguing such specificity was a constraint on his future freedom of action.[101] As late as October 1944 Roosevelt wrote Hull that "it is all very well for us to make all kinds of preparations for Germany but there are some matters in regard to such treatment that lead me to believe speed in such matters is not an essential. . . . I dislike making plans for a country which we do not yet occupy." In November he told Stettinius he particularly liked plans which "did not dot all the i's and cross all the t's," and thus, in deference to the president, State planners were instructed to avoid detailed suggestions of how to achieve ultimate objectives for Germany.[102]

Given the uncertainty Roosevelt faced, his fixation on broader goals and his qualms about plans being overly specific are understandable. However, all of Roosevelt's fears and objections to detailed plans for Germany's future were absent when he was presented with Morgenthau's proposal. The president's professed desire for flexibility was belied by his embrace of the harsh Treasury plan, and the lack of precautions Roosevelt took to keep the plan under wraps certainly resulted in constraints on his freedom to maneuver politically. Roosevelt's reluctance to deal with detailed schemes for Germany's future melted away because he attended to the objectives of Morgenthau's proposal rather than the means by which those objectives would be achieved. Had he considered in advance how deindustrialization would have to be carried out it is doubtful he would have continued to lobby for northwest zone of occupation, which contains the Ruhr and much of the Saar, until near the end of the Quebec Conference.

POSTWAR U.S.–SOVIET RELATIONS

One of Roosevelt's primary postwar goals was to enforce international security via the four regional "policemen," and he thus placed a premium on U.S. relations with the Soviets. The president was not entirely optimistic about Soviet postwar foreign policy. Besides recognizing the need to reach Berlin at the same time as the Red Army, Roosevelt's desire to make China a great power stemmed partially from his desire to check the USSR if necessary. Despite his refusal to allow territorial concessions in Eastern Europe to the Soviets in the early stages of the war, Roosevelt, Welles, and the JCS recognized that there might be little the United States could do to block some Soviet expansion once Germany was defeated. Roosevelt was more worried about losing the Soviets' trust and thus upsetting his plans for a prolonged postwar peace.[103]

Ironically, given the weight he attached to this postwar objective, Roosevelt never grasped how the United States and USSR could come to confront each other over a devastated Germany, and how his own reluctance to discuss concrete details of the occupation could encourage mistrust between the two states. This reluctance appears incongruous with Roosevelt's position before the United States' entry in the war that, while governments might agree on ultimate objectives, they would have greater difficulties reaching consensus on the machinery to attain their ends. But as John Gaddis surmises, once America joined the fighting Roosevelt became preoccupied with his ends, not the means by which they would be achieved.[104] CLT again explains why the president could remain focused on the desirability of his goal of postwar cooperation with the Soviet Union, but neglect and even resist collaboration on the details of occupation that would facilitate this goal.

As discussed, the British–American debate over zones of occupation lasted months. Meanwhile, the finer details of occupation policy were left unattended, causing increasing distress in some corners of Washington. In November 1943 the JCS told the president that the rapid progression of the war required an Allied agreement on Germany, asserting that the United States "must be prepared to occupy German-held Europe, or any areas from which she withdraws forces, on short notice" and thus asking the president to provide "an expression of your desires in these matters."[105] In the summer of 1944 Winant told Britain's impatient foreign minister Anthony Eden that he was still awaiting instructions on postwar Germany to deliver to the EAC.[106] Stimson became troubled by the "complete lack" of coherent U.S. plans for occupation even though Germany's military defeat seemed imminent. Driving through Europe in the winter of 1944, SHAEF was forced to apply the directions of CCS 551—a "pre-surrender" document—to Eclipse.[107]

Such delays would have proved nettlesome for postwar operations in Germany regardless of Roosevelt's postwar aims. Delay was riskier still given the effect it could have on Soviet perceptions of American intentions. The State Department concluded in August 1944 that too many important matters had been sidelined due to the British–American dispute over zones of occupation, noting "the slowness in arriving at agreed policies on the treatment of Germany has resulted primarily from the unwillingness of the Russians to discuss the control machinery proposal until the zones of occupation are definitely decided." Hull and Stettinius reflected the concerns of their departmental subordinates. In August 1944 Hull told the president that his reluctance to discuss the details of occupation was complicating Allied relations, while Stettinius asserted that the lack of direction given to U.S. representatives in the EAC had created a "danger of developing a bad situation between ourselves and the British of which the Russians and other countries will be aware."[108] Roosevelt replied that he was "unable to understand that any further discussion with Soviet [*sic*] is necessary at this time." He reiterated the next month to Hull that at "the present stage" he did not think "any good purpose would be served by having the State Department or any other department sound out the British and Russian views on the treatment of German industry." He recognized the U.S. government had "no idea" what Soviet policy toward Germany really was, but insisted he could not be put in the position of registering protests.[109]

Roosevelt's advisers worried that the president's resistance to addressing the details of Germany's occupation would prove injurious to Washington's relations with Moscow. Were such fears valid? Averell Harriman reported that, when informed of Morgenthau's proposal for Germany, Stalin approved.[110] However, this contradicted the position of Soviet diplomat Arkady Sobolev, who just days after Harriman's communication insisted to U.S. officials he "was certain that Mr. Morgenthau's type of thinking was not acceptable to the Soviet Government," continuing that "the efficacy of [postwar] control will depend on whether or not the principal victors stay together." While open to "a selective destruction of a relatively small number of branches of industry" in Germany, the Soviets still held that "Germany should be encouraged to develop production and export of coal, chemicals, textiles, and other consumption goods." This was likely because Russia's own economic future, like that of Britain, would suffer without German production.[111]

Perhaps Roosevelt was aware that his short-term objective of maintain the Allies' cohesion conflicted with his long-term objectives regarding postwar alliances, but felt he had to privilege the former over the latter. The problem with this assertion, however, is that uncertainty about the postwar management of Germany appeared to be upsetting allied relations as the war was ongoing. What is more, the British and Soviets had already been engaged in high-level discussions about Germany's occupation without the Americans, a fact which Winant and the JCS had communicated to Roosevelt.[112] This did not stop the president from believing his own private preferences for the disposition of Germany could come to fruition. As CLT predicts, his ideas were guided by his long-term aims without consideration for how his preferences might be constrained. Roosevelt had initially sketched his concept of how the Allied zones of administrative responsibility in Germany would be laid out on the way to the first Cairo Conference in 1943. He still held to them in 1944 when Winant told the president that the occupation zones he had drawn up were highly impractical. They contradicted the disposition of zones agreed on by the British and Soviets. Roosevelt's proposal would cut the area occupied by the USSR in half, something to which Stalin would not agree and that would lead him to be "highly suspicious" of U.S. motives, according to Winant.[113] Not only might Roosevelt's plans have been expected to upset the Allies' cohesion during and after the war, they were made without reference to existing German administrative boundaries. Jacob D. Beam, secretary of the U.S. embassy in London and later U.S. ambassador to the Soviet Union, understatedly called the president's zones "ill-considered."[114]

Alternative Explanations for Occupation Preparations

Both an appreciation of shifting opportunity costs and recognition of organizational factors add to an understanding of how the assessment and implementation of Germany's occupation unfolded. Allied power grew steadily relative to the Axis throughout the war, and as predicted the postwar world and the "German question" began to feature more heavily in American officials' public and private statements. An interrelated development was the increasing importance credited to the Civil Affairs Division in the U.S. Army over the course of the war. Consistent with organizational theory, the decision to dedicate personnel to improve on knowledge culled from previous military experience allowed the Army to effectively complete many short-term tasks in Germany. And, as already discussed, the military's overconfident position in CCS 551 is best explained by political constraints that forced excessive reliance on existing civil affairs doctrine, though such optimism was encouraged by Roosevelt and the State Department.

Despite these contributions, changes in the perceived military balance, information available to leaders, and organizational explanations are not themselves sufficient to account for the strategy initially adopted by the United States in Germany. Washington's awareness of its growing military advantage can account for officials' lengthening time horizons, but cannot explain their expectations about the postwar environment, nor the relatively lackadaisical procedures Roosevelt employed to manage occupation planning versus those used to manage the war. While organizational theory can account for the success of short-term military operations, it cannot explain the approach senior leaders took toward broader economic and political issues in Germany. Lastly, Roosevelt's assessments of the postwar occupation do not appear consistent with his management of combat operations during the war, nor are they attributable to his enduring personality traits.

ROOSEVELT'S PERSONAL ATTRIBUTES

Rather than CLT, it could be argued that Roosevelt's idiosyncrasies and leadership style accounted for his assessment of the occupation and delayed serious consideration of associated plans. Political scientists have characterized Roosevelt as an active president who immersed himself in most aspects of his administration in order to maximize control over policy. The substantial self-confidence evidenced by this approach was arguably associated with a belief that he could defer most political problems and still solve them when it became necessary to do so.[115] Roosevelt's managerial style also engendered conflict among those beneath him.[116] The president's aims, if not unknown to his subordinates, could often appear self-contradictory. It is not hard to understand how such a state of affairs could lead to clashes between members of the administration and hinder firm decisions on policy. What is more, some hold that Roosevelt's standard practice when dealing with disputes was to procrastinate or promise everything to all parties, thus sowing greater dissension and confusion.[117]

Self-confidence combined with a need for control might have encouraged the president to marginalize or ignore others' work on Germany until the war was nearing its conclusion. However, unlike CLT, personality-based explanations cannot account for differences between Roosevelt's short- and long-term assessments during the war. His assessments and actions regarding plans for the occupation of Germany were not at all consistent with the way he dealt with incoming information regarding combat operations. Historians have judged Roosevelt's handling of military affairs to have been quite capable. Eric Larrabee argues the president's "numerous" military instructions, issued at key points in the war, "were in the main concise and final, contrary to when the ebb and flow of politics was the determining factor." Rather than relying solely on himself to manage military issues, Roosevelt structured the JCS to coordinate strategic assessment of war plans. Frequent interactions between Roosevelt and his military advisers led to a high degree of concurrence between them. Early in the war Ambassador William Bullitt asserted that Stimson was a "mere housekeeper of the War Department now that the president had taken over all relations with the military men."[118] Intimates of the president such as his son Elliott, Hull, Churchill, and Welles agreed that if anything Roosevelt was overly concerned with the details of military operations.[119] Roosevelt's responsiveness to his generals, and his general receptivity to military advice on combat operations, stand in contrast to his insensitivity to military advice and officers' requests for guidance when postwar noncombat operations were in question—a clear shift in the president's communication fluency dependent on the phase of the war under consideration.

As to Roosevelt's managerial style, Arthur Schlesinger described the president as someone who believed "situations had to be permitted to develop, crystallize, to clarify; competing forces had to vindicate themselves in the actual pull and tug of conflict . . . only then, at the long frazzled end, would the President's intuitions consolidate and precipitate as a result."[120] According to Schlesinger, Roosevelt adopted this practice of postponing decisions because it allowed him greater access to opinions and information, which would then allow him to choose a course of action when the moment called for it. For Roosevelt's decision making in the case of Germany to fit the profile Schlesinger depicted, one would expect both efforts to seek out and weigh information from competing sources and the precipitation of policy as developments in the war demanded. Neither of these components feature in the case in question, however. American soldiers' movement into Germany prior to any settlement of occupation policy attests to the absence of the second point. Before his departure for the Allied conferences at Cairo and Tehran in 1943, the president appears to have relied mainly on a single report by Harriman on the USSR to draw indirect conclusions about what should be done in Germany. After the Tehran conference Roosevelt acted as if the German question had largely been settled even though no specific agreements had been arrived at.[121] Stimson still believed that the president had given little serious thought to occupation operations a year after Tehran. The Cabinet Committee on Germany, arranged by Stimson rather than the president, was meant to stimulate debate and action on the matter. The president, however, readily adopted Morgenthau's controversial plan with minimal deliberation.

Along with his personal traits and managerial style, Roosevelt's health was failing in the latter stages of the war due to cardiovascular disease. Stimson and others have tentatively attributed Roosevelt's decision to approve Morgenthau's plan for Germany at the Quebec Conference in September 1944 to the effects of his illness, which left the president unable to engage with the proposals being put before him.[122] However, arguments which appeal to Roosevelt's illness as an explanation for his acceptance of Treasury policy at Quebec must contend with the fact that the Morgenthau plan aligned with his long-standing beliefs about the militaristic nature of Germany. Roosevelt had a general inclination toward a "tough peace" before the Tehran conference, an inclination reinforced by his belief that such a plan would please Stalin.[123] Even after the president distanced himself from Morgenthau, he would tell Stettinius that he worried the proposed U.S. Control Council for the occupation would have an "insufficient representation of a tough civilian point of view."[124] Illness-related arguments must also explain why the president endorsed Morgenthau's plan at a cabinet meeting on September 9, two days before the Quebec Conference, while acknowledging he was aware that many disagreed with him.[125] Lastly, they must deal with the fact the Roosevelt chose to bring Morgenthau, not Hull or Stimson, with him to Quebec. The president wanted the treasury secretary and Anthony Eden at the conference because he believed both men would advocate tough policies.[126] Such choices and statements would not appear to emanate from a man whose illness left him unsure of his position on the German problem.

OPPORTUNITY COSTS AND THE FOG OF WAR

The first opportunity costs hypothesis is that state leaders focus more on the future as their relative power advantages over their adversaries grow. This is consistent with the behavior of U.S. policymakers' in World War II. Officials were initially discouraged from thinking about the more distant future. They were fighting a war with multiple fronts against enemies with substantial military might. It was also necessary to maintain wartime cohesion among the Allied powers. These two factors delayed consideration of postwar issues until the tide of the war had shifted in the Allies' favor. However, there is a lack of support for the second opportunity costs hypothesis that greater military advantages translate into more investment in strategic assessment of noncombat operations. Roosevelt was reluctant to develop concrete occupation plans until prodded to do so in the fall of 1944, well after the Normandy landing. The president's reluctance is made all the more remarkable by the nature of intelligence reports to which leaders in Washington were privy. The first fog-of-war hypothesis, that strategic assessments depend on the accuracy and consistency of information provided by intelligence estimates, is inconsistent with how Roosevelt insulated himself from pertinent information while formulating occupation policy. The greater accuracy and reliability of intelligence reports on combat versus noncombat operations is also called into question, given that Allied intelligence ministries thought that the war in Europe might be over as early as 1943. Though he was provided with this information, neither it nor the value Roosevelt placed on the future of Germany and Europe encouraged more rigorous assessment of occupation plans. As already shown, the president and many other top officials were considerably overconfident about the costs of occupying Germany, contra the hypothesis that leaders will be ambivalent or pessimistic when evaluating noncombat operations.

Though U.S. forces were not near parity with the Axis belligerents at the start of the war, the country's latent power was mobilized such that the Allies came to greatly outpace their enemies in production. In 2005 U.S. dollars, the United States' total military expenditures in 1939 were a little less than $1 billion; in 1945, the United States spent ninety times that amount.

The U.S. economy alone outpaced Germany and Japan by better than a three-to-two margin for half of the war's duration.[127] America's growing military strength coincided with reports that the enemy was weakening significantly. Though consistent, these reports did not paint an accurate picture of Nazi power. In January 1943, the American Board of Economic Warfare surmised that the German economy had peaked two years earlier and had since "passed the point of maximum exploitation of the resources of men and materials at its command."[128] While the board stressed that more bombing of German-held territory would be necessary before there was a steep drop-off in the country's capacity to wage war, other estimates indicated the Allied bombing campaign was having marked effects. Intelligence reports being consumed by top officials suggested the approach of a German collapse in 1943. Manpower was held to be the key factor which kept Germany's war machine running, and in that regard the Nazi regime was sorely lacking. A memorandum sent to Roosevelt in January reported that Germany no longer had enough men to satisfactorily equip its armed forces while meeting its industrial and agricultural needs. The manpower shortage would present Germany "with considerable economic risks." Comparing the country's situation with that faced by Wilhemine Germany in 1918, the report foresaw that the possibility of an economic collapse in 1943 could not be excluded, "and, if it came, it might come with startling rapidity."[129] Even reports which doubted a collapse was imminent wrongly asserted that Germany had been fully mobilized for war in 1939 and thus its economy was under great strain from manpower and other deficiencies.[130]

The United States' growing material advantage, coupled with an inflated sense of German weakness, led the Roosevelt administration to increasingly focus on its postwar objectives in 1943. In his annual budget message delivered in January, Roosevelt spoke for the first time of the importance of economic stabilization programs for domestic postwar prosperity and international reconstruction. He further highlighted his economic policies for postwar America in the State of the Union address that month, as well as noting that the balance of power had tipped decisively in the Allies' favor.[131] On his way to the Tehran conference in November Roosevelt predicted that the country's invasion would involve little or no fighting.[132] By January 1944, the president's annual budget message contained substantial sections on relief and rehabilitation in liberated Europe and "Wartime Readjustments and Preparation for Peace."[133]

While wartime information about Axis production capacity and the military balance of power encouraged U.S. leaders to place more emphasis on future policy toward Germany relative to ongoing combat operations, this shift manifested itself in a focus on high-level goals rather than increasing attention to how occupation policy would be executed. As already discussed, there would be no cabinet-level debates on this matter until September of 1944, by which time estimates on German economic capacity were being revised. Prior to this date Washington's awareness of its growing production advantages, coupled with an inflated estimate of Germany's economic struggles, should have provided the Roosevelt administration with an incentive—even a sense of urgency—to consider the details of an occupation in greater depth.

One might explain Washington's delay by referencing Roosevelt's concern for solidarity among the Allies. Though postwar policy was discussed among the three allied leaders at Tehran in 1943, the president was still adamant that nothing hinder the collective war effort, including disagreements over postwar plans.[134] At the same time, one must consider how a lack of discussion among the Allies could jeopardize U.S.–Soviet relations. While high-level talks could raise tensions between the wartime allies, they were necessary if the occupying powers were to trust one another not to use Germany for their own self-interested purposes. The opportunity costs framework predicts that, as the Allies' relative power advantage over the Axis grew, Roosevelt would begin to prize the postwar cohesion of the alliance an increasing amount given its importance to his plans for international security. During the war the Allies could rely on a common enemy to help maintain unity of effort, but after the war transparency would be necessary if confidence in one another's intentions was to be had. More intensive involvement in negotiations could have also provided information about Moscow's vision of the postwar world. By postponing the coordination of policy even as victory became more assured, Roosevelt was unwittingly harming his own long-term interests.

ORGANIZATIONAL EXPLANATIONS

The first organizational hypothesis, that the military invests fewer resources and makes poorer assessments of noncombat versus combat operations, is not well supported in the Germany case. Given the magnitude of the fighting in World War II, it would be nigh impossible to expect the U.S. Army to invest the same amount of time and effort into postwar plans as battlefield engagements. Yet even before hostilities in Europe had begun anew in 1939, a small but significant group of American officers pressed to develop lessons derived from the occupation of the Rhineland in World War I. The civil affairs sections of the Army would start out near the bottom of the chain of command, but came to be seen as more important as the war went on. By 1944, thousands of civil affairs officers were preparing to apply their knowledge in the field. U.S. troops in Germany were able to accomplish many crucial short-term occupation tasks once Berlin had been taken. However, the perspective of military planners would have little impact on high-level long-term strategy regarding the treatment of Germany. The hypothesis that organizational factors' importance hinges on the military's power and autonomy relative to civilian leadership is well supported by historical evidence from World War II. Roosevelt, when aware of specific military preparations for the occupation, exerted a strong influence over the substance of such plans.

The primary goal of the Army was to manage the occupation so that it furthered combat operations elsewhere while maintaining security in the European theater. This meant keeping the costs of occupation down, which in turn meant insuring that occupied populations became self-reliant. Such measures were intended to blunt the cost to the occupying power and maintain the security of military personnel. The School of Military Government, meant to prepare civil affairs officers to handle this task, opened its doors in May of 1942 with authorization from General Marshall. The president had expressed a strong preference for civilians to be in charge of occupied territories, and doubted the Army would turn out "first class" individuals in this regard.[135] However, the Army's trying experience with the management of civil affairs in North Africa after Operation Torch revealed that the U.S. government had underestimated the need for competent military administrators in the field. What is more, civilian agencies simply could not match the Army's resources and manpower, which would be necessary to effectively control territories and populations overseas.[136]

By the summer of 1943, Roosevelt had become grudgingly acceptant of the need for military government. However, norms and practical incentives dictating the separation of the political and military spheres made Army planners hesitant to consider broad issues of grand strategy without a mandate from Washington. The tenets of military necessity contradicted Roosevelt's fundamental aim that Germany should be stripped of the economic capacity to wage war, and the relative autonomy field commanders enjoyed when making combat decisions did not extend as far into civil affairs. Merle Fainsod, a member of the Roosevelt administration and associate director of Harvard's Civil Affairs Training School and School for Overseas Administration, argued that the Army's emphasis on flexibility in its doctrine of military government recognized the necessity of demurring to the judgment of the president and civilian officials on occupation policy.[137] As a result, officers actively assessed and prepared for contingencies which they felt fell within their authority but were silent when it came to advising civilian leadership about long-term goals. This inclination was one reason why Washington's occupation policy would not be effectively critiqued until operatives in Germany experienced firsthand how it hindered military efficiency.

Though officers were disinclined to stretch the limits of their authority in civil affairs matters, the need to develop occupation plans became more pressing as the war progressed.[138] There would be consequences when political leaders misinterpreted Army doctrine premised on military necessity as being driven by an inclination toward a "soft peace." Nearing German soil, SHAEF's German Country Unit published the *Handbook for Military Government in Germany* in August 1944. The book described potential conditions in Germany, the possible forms military government would take, and the primary roles of the civil affairs officer. When Morgenthau came into possession of the *Handbook* in August, he was disturbed that the Army appeared ready to treat Germany much as it was treating the countries it had liberated from Nazi occupation, and thought the Army's plan to make the population self-sufficient was inadequately harsh and even conducive to a third world war. When he brought the matter to the president in the late summer of 1944, Roosevelt concurred. The president told Stimson that the "so-called handbook is pretty bad" and ordered all copies to be withdrawn and revised.[139] SHAEF complied, informing the War Department that "it has been repeatedly stressed that the application of provisions relating to general economics and rehabilitation would be governed by military necessity. . . . However, if you so direct, we shall put out the directive and handbook with a covering note instructing commanders categorically not to apply the provisions relating to general economics and rehabilitation."[140]

This episode sheds light on the behavior of military officers who were involved in postwar policy formation in Washington. Consistent with organizational theory, officers on the Working Security Committee (WSC) responsible for advising Winant at the EAC were reluctant to allow nonmilitary entities much freedom to issue policy guidelines and thus could be accused of interfering with strategic assessment by impeding the formulation of plans by low-level civilians from other government agencies.[141] However, any organizational preferences were secondary to the fact that policy recommendations of the WSC were doomed to irrelevance by executive fiat. Aside from Roosevelt's unwillingness to give much autonomy to the EAC, the *Handbook* controversy illustrated that military officers were right to anticipate negative repercussions for allowing even modest policy recommendations through without the approval of top leadership. H. Freeman Matthews, head of State's Office of European Affairs, surmised that "ever since the President's letter on the Military *Handbook* which Mr. Morgenthau brought back and the subsequent setting up of the Cabinet Committee on Germany, our military authorities have felt that they were in no position to approve and, for a long time, even to discuss in the Working Security Committee, any documents affecting the treatment of Germany." The obstructionist actions of the military would not have been possible without the actions and approval of those in the White House.[142]

In its first three months in defeated Germany the Army disarmed and demobilized the Wehrmacht, took responsibility for millions of refugees, restored important civil services, and maintained order and a working system of justice.[143] This success was achieved despite a lack of direction from civilians. The military's doctrine, training, prior experience with occupation, and most importantly attitude toward postconflict operations explain the initiative shown despite the lack of pressure being applied by the Roosevelt administration. Had the Army wanted more control over matters perceived as overtly political, it is possible they could have had more influence on how

Roosevelt and others approached occupation policy. Still, given the president's negative reaction to military suggestions, and the authority he wielded over the policymaking process, such a scenario was unlikely. In sum, given the absence of collaboration with military advisers and civilian dominance over postwar policy, an organizational explanation is not adequate to account for senior officials' strategic assessment of the occupation. Though organizational theory can help account for many of the actions of the military's Civil Affairs Division, these actions ran contrary to the conventional wisdom that the U.S. armed forces systematically neglect noncombat operations.

Conclusion

The outcome of the U.S. occupation of Germany can be counted a success in that the United States oversaw its former enemy's democratization and eventual membership in NATO, the partition of the country notwithstanding. This success did not stem from accurate strategic assessments made during the planning for occupation, however, but from structural factors and a gradual shift in American strategy after the war had concluded. Overly abstract thinking and optimistic assumptions led to an often muddled decision-making process. Roosevelt and State officials were excessively confident in the ability of military forces to execute prohibitively difficult tasks and planned to rely on preexisting institutions and armed forces in Germany despite a war plan designed to cause their destruction. What is more, the president believed that the duration of the occupation could be kept short despite allies' security concerns, concerns that he largely dismissed. Finally, Roosevelt's reluctance to deliberate over detailed plans for Germany's occupation risked damaging America's long-term relations with the Soviets despite the importance he placed on such a postwar alliance.

As Elmer Plischke observes, in 1944 "documentation suggests that the distinction between *defining objectives*," which CLT would characterize as high-level cognition related to desirability, "and *detailed programs*," or concrete, context-dependent assessments at lower levels of construal, "was not clearly expressed or understood in Washington." Roosevelt and others were much more comfortable with the former than the latter. Due to this confusion, Plischke states, occupation guidance came about in a "piecemeal" fashion, leading to uneven implementation by units in the field.[144] Similarly, Fainsod opined that Roosevelt and other postwar planners had trouble understanding that political reconstruction entails more than simply the removal of the old regime.[145] CLT explains why Roosevelt and other "far-sighted" officials were unable to distinguish between America's abstract goals and the concrete means by which these objectives would be achieved. More "short-sighted" individuals such as Secretary Stimson and his colleagues at the War Department did not exhibit similar patterns of thought about what the U.S.

experience in postwar Europe would be like, even though they possessed policy preferences not unlike postwar planners at State.

The opportunity costs of focusing on postwar policy and noncombat operations while fighting is ongoing can successfully explain why and when Roosevelt became more inclined to think about ultimate objectives. Opportunity costs cannot, however, account for his resistance to his top advisers' efforts to press on him the need for detailed planning and greater inter-Allied deliberation on the occupation late in the war. Conversely, CLT predicts that those with an abstract mind-set will resist processing concrete information but will uncritically adopt plans which purport to advance their desired objectives, as was the case with Morgenthau's proposals.

Organizational theory can make sense of the overconfident predictions of CCS 551 and associated directives. Though contrary to the military's alleged resistance to noncombat operations, organizational theory also predicts the short-term tactical success of the U.S. Army in Germany given the developments in doctrine and training during the interwar years and early 1940s. The Army's preparations were not sufficient to overcome the lack of initiative on occupation policy in Washington, however, and organizational theory cannot explain why the initial strategy governing Germany's occupation took the form it did. U.S. soldiers did ably execute the short-term duties laid out for them in Eclipse but disarming surrendering German units is not equivalent to preparing a workable scheme for Germany's long-term reconstruction and political development.

Any analysis of the United States' preparations for occupation must not confuse the total personnel hours put into planning with the substance of those plans or state leaders' willingness to engage with the assessments of their subordinates. Nor should one conflate a multiplicity of working bodies concerned with the late stages of an intervention with interagency cooperation or coherent policymaking. Unless such processes are guided and critically assessed by top officials in government, operatives in the field will lack the confidence to perform needed tasks for fear that they are going against some unknown political aim of their superiors. Without leadership that balances abstract desires with a concern for the means, even well-resourced planning endeavors will generate more heat than light.

"Phase IV" and the Invasion of Iraq

The U.S.-led invasion of Iraq, named Operation Iraqi Freedom (OIF), began in March of 2003. The meager preparations for noncombat operations, anticipated to occur in "Phase IV" of the campaign, stood in stark contrast to the sixteen months of preparations for Phase III, or "major combat," operations. Whereas initial combat operations rapidly brought down Saddam Hussein and his Ba'ath regime, Phase IV operations could not prevent years of insurgent attacks on U.S. personnel and the Iraqi populace at large, nor high levels of ethnic and sectarian violence. Fewer than 200 U.S. troops had been killed in the war prior to May 1, 2003, when President George W. Bush declared the end of major combat operations. By December 2011, the official end of OIF, almost 4,300 additional American troops had been killed, along with an estimated 116,000 Iraqi civilians.[1]

Many features which might lead an occupied population to accept the presence of a foreign power were absent in Iraq. Unlike the occupation of Germany, the United States and Iraq did not share an external enemy like the Soviet Union, nor was there preexisting political cohesion within the occupied country. Clearly, such features were beyond the control of policymakers in Washington. Other important factors, including the Iraqi population's perception of whether they needed services such as security and public utilities that might be provided by their occupier, were more amenable to the Bush administration's control.[2] The consensus that emerged after the invasion, however, was that the U.S. government had not effectively prepared to shape conditions in Phase IV to its own benefit. According to the Special Inspector General for Iraq Reconstruction (SIGIR), "when Iraq's withering postinvasion reality superseded [officials'] expectations, there was no well-defined 'Plan B' as a fallback and no existing government structures or resources to support a quick response."[3] Leaders failed to foresee the rise of sectarian violence and ignored officials working on potential postwar problems or left them underresourced, without the necessary time or guidance necessary to effectively plan.[4]

The primary evidence that the administration had a good grasp of the difficulties they would face in Iraq was Secretary of Defense Donald Rumsfeld's "Parade of Horribles" memorandum drafted in October 2002. The memo listed many possible dire consequences of an invasion, including a U.S. occupation lasting eight to ten years.[5] However, this document creates more puzzles than it solves. Former national security adviser Condoleezza Rice contends Rumsfeld's department made no concrete plans to guard against the calamities outlined in the memo, an assertion that is consistent with other accounts and the aftermath of the war itself.[6] If Rumsfeld took his own warnings seriously, it is odd that they did not affect a postwar plan over which his department had substantial influence. Undersecretary of Defense for Policy Douglas Feith, whose job it was to oversee policy planning for postwar Iraq, gave briefings to the principals on the National Security Council (NSC) devoid of alarming predictions. After reviewing notes taken during Feith's March 4, 2003, briefing on postwar Iraq, Bob Woodward concluded that he had presented a "rosy, pie-in-the-sky" scenario lacking in particulars.[7] As detailed below, top administration officials believed postwar problems would amount to short-term humanitarian suffering due to the destruction wrought during the initial invasion. The president seemed confident that U.S. efforts to manage the effects of the war would be successful, saying that while there were "a lot of things that could go wrong," it would not be "for want of planning."[8] But a lack of planning, along with mistaken prior beliefs by senior policymakers, did in fact leave the administration and U.S. forces in Iraq unprepared to mitigate the gravest consequences of the invasion.

Planning for Phase IV

It would be inaccurate to say that the Bush administration did no planning for noncombat operations in Iraq. However, the planning that was done was disjointed and compartmentalized. Government departments did not communicate with one another, particularly Defense and State. Senior members of the administration transferred responsibility for postwar planning from one group to another unexpectedly. This served to create what British foreign secretary Jack Straw, representing the United States' primary ally in the Iraq War, understatedly called an "inter-agency row" in Washington. Major General Tim Cross, a British officer who served with American civilians in the early days of Phase IV, went further, saying "it was clear . . . that many in the State Department deeply resented the DOD and Rumsfeld, almost to the point of wishing strategic failure."[9] This conflict would continue even after OIF was launched in March.

The Pentagon's Joint Staff assigned postwar planning to General Tommy Franks and Central Command (CENTCOM) in the summer of 2002. The

CENTCOM staff, which had planned the invasion of Afghanistan in a very short period of time in the fall of 2001 and was working on combat plans for the invasion of Iraq, were surprised the job fell to them. Two mid-level officers were put in charge of Phase IV efforts.[10] The last war plan for Iraq prior to Bush assuming the presidency called for a deployment of 380,000 military personnel to the theater of operations. General Anthony Zinni, the since-retired commander of CENTCOM, believed at least that many troops would be necessary to secure Iraq's borders and prevent disorder if the Ba'ath regime fell.[11] Under Rumsfeld's direction, the new war plans for Iraq called for different, smaller invasion forces, which meant any postwar assumptions built into the plans of the 1990s would have to be significantly reworked.

As the start date for the invasion approached, General George Casey of the Joint Staff became concerned that CENTCOM was paying insufficient attention to Phase IV operations. As a result of Casey's concerns, a new group called Joint Task Force IV (JTF-IV) was created in late December 2002 to assist with postwar planning.[12] JTF-IV was led by Brigadier General Steven Hawkins, an officer with an engineering background and a great deal of experience with reconstruction operations. However, the creation of JTF-IV would not do much to augment the capacity of CENTCOM to plan for Phase IV. CENTCOM had not requested assistance from Hawkins or anyone else in regard to postconflict operations. In the assessment of one official government historian, the implication was that Franks and his officers "were not thinking ahead," and "had dropped the ball on Phase IV planning." This understandably created resentment within CENTCOM, and Hawkins did little to ingratiate himself there. His evaluation was that Franks's outfit had done "cursory planning" for Phase IV and "convinced themselves it was more detailed than it really was," and further implied they lacked the expertise for either reconstruction or civil administration tasks in Iraq.[13] What was more, CENTCOM headquarters in Tampa did not have the assets to set up the JTF headquarters. Hawkins's unit was given no budget of its own. By January 2003, according to CENTCOM colonel John Agoglia, his superiors realized the task force was "broken."[14]

Lieutenant General David McKiernan, commander of Combined Forces Land Component Command (CFLCC), worried he could find himself in charge of postwar Iraq with little direction from his superiors. He placed Albert Whitley, his senior British military officer, in charge of CFLCC's Phase IV planning. Whitley named his plan Eclipse II in an apparent reference to the occupation of Germany, though Eclipse II differed from its predecessor in significant respects. It relied on a large number of Iraqis to contribute to security efforts, and further assumed that a significant amount of assistance would be provided by the international community and nongovernmental organizations.[15] Coalition forces retained significant responsibilities under Eclipse II, but given the relatively small number of U.S. and British troops, the plan necessitated a functional Iraqi military and police force, as well as the somewhat immediate generation of Iraqi provincial governments, if order was to be maintained. According to Lieutenant General William Wallace, commander of the Army's 5th Corps, "the things that we assumed would be in place on the ground that make [Phase IV] operations extraordinarily easy if they are there or extraordinarily hard if they are not most had to do with Iraqi institutions and infrastructure."[16]

Multiple other bodies became involved in the planning for a post-Hussein Iraq. In the winter of 2001–2002 the State Department initiated a Future of Iraq project overseen by Tom Warrick. Along with input from American and international officials, the project incorporated a great deal of input from Iraqi exiles, who participated in working groups addressing diverse issues such as democracy and the rule of law, public finance, and oil. However, the Department of Defense, which ultimately became responsible for planning and executing Phase IV operations, did not participate nor draw on the work done by State. In fact, Rumsfeld and others in the administration actively worked to prevent Warrick from participating on postwar efforts in Iraq.[17] Furthermore, it did not appear that the Future of Iraq project made much of an impression on senior State Department officials, including Secretary of State Colin Powell. Though the project contained fourteen working groups producing tentative policies on postwar issues, it was largely conceptual in nature. It was not a plan to be implemented by the coalition but rather an exercise with the primary goal of getting Iraqi exile groups comfortable working with one another and thus facilitate the creation of an interim government.[18] This was not merely the opinion of interagency rivals in the United States. Carolyn Miller, a director at the UK Department for International Development focused on the Middle East, testified that the Future of Iraq project focused primarily on general principles rather than actionable plans. Likewise, Kevin Tebbit, the British under secretary at the Ministry of Defence, perceived State's work as "conceptual planning, academic work really" that never "amounted to anything real."[19]

The first effort at postwar planning directed by the White House began in the spring of 2002. The NSC deputies committee—second-level officials from State, Defense, and other departments—began meeting twice a week to discuss how Iraq would be administered once Hussein's regime was gone. According to SIGIR, however, the NSC machinery for dealing with Phase IV was largely "idle" by the middle of the year.[20] The NSC would eventually establish a Humanitarian Working Group headed by senior staffer Eliot Abrams and Associate Director of the Office of Management and Budget Robin Cleveland. Aside from humanitarian issues that might arise, with worst-case scenarios featuring Hussein launching chemical and biological weapons against his population, the group also looked at reconstruction tasks. However, the work done at the NSC was just as, if not more, underdeveloped as that by the Future of Iraq project. Though the Humanitarian Group accurately surmised that sanctions and other factors had hindered the recovery of Iraq's infrastructure since the Gulf War, it operated via guess-work on most matters. One Defense official noted they "had some financial estimate papers, but it was a lot of back-of-the-envelope, 'what will it take to fix the Ministry of fill-in-the-blank.' It was all guesstimates made on top of suppositions."[21]

The faults of the NSC working group would prove to be moot. With little prior warning, Bush signed National Security Presidential Directive 24 (NSPD-24) in January 2003. Feith's office drafted the directive, which gave control of Phase IV to the Department of Defense and the Office of Recon-struction and Humanitarian Assistance (ORHA), the first lead civilian body in postwar Iraq. Rumsfeld selected retired general Jay Garner as head of ORHA. Garner had been a commander in Operation Provide Comfort, a suc-cessfully executed humanitarian mission aiding Kurds in Iraq after the Gulf War. Other government agencies were to assist Defense and ORHA, but there was no specific guidance as to how. NSPD-24 authorized ORHA to deliver food and emergency supplies, aid refugees, reestablish electricity and other utilities, safeguard Iraqi infrastructure, and aid in the dismantling of weap-ons of mass destruction (WMD). While the administration was anticipating potentially dire short-term problems, the only ORHA objective with a some-what long-term focus was the restructuring of the Iraqi military, a task not fleshed out in any great detail.[22]

Feith's office formally oversaw Defense policy on Phase IV within its Of-fice of Special Plans, created in September of 2002. Feith himself had pre-saged ORHA's creation in October 2002 when he proposed Rumsfeld be in charge of all postwar operations. However, Garner was not approached by Rumsfeld to head the postwar effort until January 2003, and thus could not organize a major interagency meeting on postwar Iraq until a month prior to the invasion. He described his own organization as "glued together over about four or five weeks' time. [We] really didn't have enough time to plan."[23] This may appear to be a self-interested excuse, but Garner's assessment has become increasingly common since 2003. General Richard Dannatt, who had commanded ground forces in Iraq prior to becoming chief of Britain's Gen-eral Staff, characterized ORHA as a "very thin but well-meaning organiza-tion," and stated that while Garner was "excellent" in his own right, his "team was so thin they had no chance of being able to resurrect the situation."[24]

The administration's estimates of Phase IV costs were wildly off the mark. While prewar predictions of post-Hussein costs ranged from virtually noth-ing, an estimate made by Undersecretary of Defense Paul Wolfowitz, to $1.9 trillion, the Bush administration consistently embraced estimates at the low-est end of this spectrum.[25] Low estimates of costs were not merely attempts to persuade the American public to support the war. They were also consis-tent with private assumptions that U.S. forces could be extracted quickly once Hussein was deposed. Six months into war planning, Franks and CENTCOM projected that troop levels would decline from 265,000 to 50,000 over an

18-month period during Phase IV. Under pressure from Bush and Rumsfeld, CENTCOM changed the estimated pace of withdrawal to a drawdown from 140,000 troops at the end of combat operations to only 30,000 soldiers by September 2003, a period of four months. American commanders were given no orders regarding protocol for enforcing order after Hussein's regime fell.[26] According to Garner, the Office of the Secretary of Defense expected Iraqi ministries would be stood up, an interim government convened, and elections for a new Iraqi government would be held only five months after the invasion began.[27]

With the Iraqi government toppled and American personnel unable to fill the power vacuum, weeks of looting and destruction by civilians and Ba'athist elements took hold in Baghdad. Government buildings coalition forces had planned to use to administer the capital were raided and burned, as were banks, hospitals, universities, and museums. Though the oil ministry was preserved under guard of U.S. Marines, looting was responsible for almost $1 billion in damage to Iraq's oil infrastructure. The chaos greatly added to the costs of reconstruction. Most consequently, thousands of tons of munitions were stolen from weapons dumps around the country, literally providing ammunition for the insurgency that was to come.[28]

Garner had always known that he and his organization would be replaced by an American envoy to Iraq, but the speed with which ORHA was overtaken by L. Paul Bremer and the Coalition Provisional Authority (CPA) shocked the former general. Bremer arrived in Iraq a mere three weeks after Garner did.[29] Two of Bremer's first acts as head of the CPA were to disband the Iraqi Army and ban former members of the Ba'ath Party from jobs in the public sector. Garner had never contemplated taking these steps, which also appeared to take senior administration officials like Powell and Rice off guard. In the words of the president's Iraq coordinator on the NSC, the CPA orders put "300,000 men with guns in their hands on the street."[30] By June U.S. forces were being subjected to hit-and-run attacks in Baghdad, leading to new combat operations aimed at Hussein loyalists. In July General John Abizaid, the new head of CENTCOM, stated that coalition forces were facing "a classical guerrilla-type campaign."[31]

A Construal Level Theory (CLT) Explanation of Phase IV Preparations for Iraq

The parallels between the occupations of Germany and Iraq are striking. In both cases, policymakers exhibited overly optimistic assessments of the cost of noncombat operations following invasion. Like Franklin Roosevelt and many of his advisers, much of the Bush administration believed they could rely on the institutions and infrastructure of Iraq to manage the country immediately following regime change. At the same time, they adopted a draconian approach toward purging party members associated with the former regime that would make administering the country via its indigenous institutions difficult. Both administrations presumed their invasion forces could be withdrawn much earlier than would prove possible.

These similarities are not coincidental. Though Roosevelt looked on Germany as a defeated and occupied country while the Bush White House saw Iraq as a liberated one, both administrations believed that the political transformation of their targets would secure their own far-reaching policy objectives. In neither case did U.S. leaders seek to preserve the status quo; their goals led them to adopt a more distal temporal focus. The same mechanisms which impacted the strategic assessments of Roosevelt administration policymakers with long time horizons were present among officials with long time horizons in 2002 and 2003. As predicted by CLT, the degree to which they exhibited overconfidence depended on what phase of the war they were evaluating. Overconfidence regarding Phase IV arose because Bush and others emphasized the desirability of their ends over the feasibility of proposed means; relied on simple, preexisting theories about politics rather than context-specific information about Iraq; and were unreceptive to messages containing more concrete information about noncombat, postconflict operations. The analysis of alternative explanations for strategic assessment of Phase IV further increases confidence in the causal analysis which follows.

TIME HORIZONS

One prominent difference between the cases of Germany and Iraq is that, in the former, policymakers were in the midst of fighting a war while preparations for postwar noncombat operations were ongoing. Conversely, the United States was readying for war, rather than being engaged in combat, while the Bush administration was preparing for Phase IV. The first hypothesis derived from CLT is that, compared to combat operations, operations projected to occur postconflict will be assessed abstractly, promoting overconfidence. This is in part because postconflict operations are by definition more temporally distant than operations during the conflict itself. However, why would CLT predict that assessment of noncombat operations will be abstract and overconfident relative to those of preceding combat operations if combat also lies many months in the future, as in the Iraq case? Per the discussion in Chapter 1, it must be remembered that CLT holds that *sequence* should impact assessments as well as temporal distance. It is cognitively more difficult to ascertain contextual information about operations that are dependent on a preceding campaign, and the act of framing a set of activities as being distinct from earlier operations and coming late or last in a sequence should lead individuals to construe them more abstractly.

Previous accounts of the 2003 Iraq War have held that U.S. time horizons were relatively short due to a heightened sense of threat to the American homeland after September 11, 2001.[32] Bush and other officials did make public statements to this effect in the months before the invasion; the president argued that if the country waited "for threats to fully materialize, we will have waited too long," and that "time is not on our side. I will not wait on events, as dangers gather."[33] This is consistent with the opportunity costs framework that holds that time horizons are predominantly a function of subjective threat and security. However, as covered in Chapter 1, this is an overly narrow conceptualization of time horizons, which are established not only by the perceived temporal proximity of actions and events, but also by the type and magnitude of goals the leaders of military campaigns adopt. The two sections that follow demonstrate that Bush and other top officials placed substantial weight on their transformative, long-term goals for the invasion; that officials often adopted a distal temporal focus when considering how their military plans would affect Iraq and the Middle East; and that the Bush administration perceived the invasion and postwar campaigns as sequentially distinct phases.

War Conceived as Discrete Phases. One of the primary explanations for the lack of interagency coordination and detailed Phase IV plans offered by the administration's defenders is that postwar planning would have signaled other states that a U.S. invasion of Iraq was practically unavoidable.[34] Bush reportedly reversed Rumsfeld's decision to establish a civilian office for postwar plans in October 2002 because the president believed it would have damaged the diplomatic track of U.S. efforts against Hussein.[35] However, the United States had already devoted significant energy producing a plan to invade Iraq, planning which was public knowledge. It is hard to argue that the devotion of relatively insubstantial resources toward preparations for postwar Iraq would have put the United States past a metaphorical "point of no return" given that the same argument was not made about the much greater investment of resources in combat preparations. If postwar planning really was a costly signal of U.S. intentions, one could argue that acknowledging the existence of such plans would have further bolstered the credibility of the U.S. military threat and provided international negotiators and Hussein with additional incentives to reach a compromise.[36]

Although it is unclear how postwar planning would have short-circuited diplomacy, the preceding does provide insight into how distinct senior officials thought Phase IV planning was from combat plans. Bush apparently saw postconflict planning as a new, significant step on the path toward war, even though the United States had already devoted significant energy to producing a plan for Iraq's invasion. As one commentator has noted, the Bush administration's approach to Iraq artificially categorized certain issues as "'postwar' problems," and officials were "reluctant to recognize the establishment of economic and political order as part of war itself, not something which comes after."[37] Feith acknowledges he and others committed a "major error" in that "across the board, administration officials thought that postwar reconstruction would take place post—that is, after—the war."[38] This was also apparent in the sequential manner in which Bush and his advisers deliberated over war plans: senior officials spent roughly three months sporadically reviewing preparations for Phase IV, in isolation from the preceding discussions of major combat operations. The first major postconflict briefing at which Bush was present was given in January 2003, only three months prior to the invasion.[39]

One U.S. officer who has written on the Iraq War has noted the apparent strategic disconnect in leaders' thinking about postwar Iraq, arguing that if the initial conception of war had integrated the combat phase of battle with tasks to secure the peace, policymakers would have been encouraged to adopt a "radically different" campaign plan.[40] Reflecting this claim, CENTCOM's Lieutenant Colonel Steven Peterson tried to alert superiors to the fact that offensive operations of the campaign, designed to disrupt and disable Ba'athist ministries and control mechanisms, undermined Phase IV operations planning to utilize these very same institutions.[41] Simon Webb, the British policy director in the Ministry of Defence, said that ORHA's creation indicated that the Bush administration eventually "bought" the idea that there needed to be a more "integrated campaign, more closely integrated with the civil development, with the security and the follow-up military operation to follow."[42]

However, Garner's organization was never really integrated with military commands in Iraq. Major General Cross believed that the campaign aimed at regime removal should have been integrated with the one for regime replacement. Instead, in his view, the two were separated in time along with the transfer of authority from CENTCOM to ORHA. The experience of Colonel Kevin Benson, one of the few CFLCC planners who had contact with ORHA, supports this interpretation. He recalled his commander, General McKiernan, as disengaged from Phase IV. McKiernan replied to Benson's concerns about postwar plans by saying he did not have the energy to think about it and that his focus had to be on combat operations, as soldiers would be killed in Phase III. Benson protested that soldiers would also be killed in Phase IV, but said McKiernan was unresponsive. Despite the commander's orders to Whitely, Cross indicated that McKiernan saw CFLCC as separate from personnel dealing with postconflict operations. He testified that McKiernan's view was "we will fight the land campaign and essentially I will tell you [ORHA] when the time is right for you to come, when it's safe for you to come."[43] CENTCOM commander Franks also had the mind-set that combat and postconflict operations represented distinct sequential phases. Franks recalls his attitude was that civilian agencies should attend to the "day after" combat ceased, while he would "pay attention to the day of." USAID officials involved in postconflict planning also picked up on this attitude, and thought the military had a concept of the war that left Phase IV figuratively sealed off from earlier operations.[44]

Political Objectives. Private memos, correspondence within the Bush administration, interactions between Washington and London, and evidence in available secondary sources show that President Bush and his top advisers placed substantial weight on long-term goals to be achieved via the Iraq War.[45] Democracy promotion was a prevalent part of the Bush administration's strategy to achieve its long-term security objectives in the Middle East. It was especially embraced by the president when considering the benefits of intervention in Iraq. Many senior policymakers in the administration believed the country's democratic transformation would be a catalyst for similar events elsewhere in the region over time, and the idea of inspiring people to upend their ruling regimes appealed to the president. Rumsfeld, however, did not place much weight on this objective. Webb observed that the secretary's "strong view was that you couldn't give anybody democracy."[46] Rumsfeld had another set of transformative aims: strengthening the U.S. capacity to deter future attacks by demonstrating the country's ability to rapidly overthrow regimes via military force.

Regime change in Baghdad had been the official policy of the U.S. government since President Bill Clinton had signed into law the Iraq Liberation Act of 1998. This legislation had been preceded by a letter to Clinton from the Project for the New American Century urging him to remove Hussein from power; the letter was signed by many future members of the Bush administration, including Rumsfeld, Wolfowitz, and Powell's deputy secretary Richard L. Armitage.[47] However, Iraq was not the primary focus of Bush's foreign policy prior to the terrorist attacks in the United States on September 11, 2001. Though Rice, perhaps Bush's most trusted foreign policy adviser at the beginning of his presidency, had endorsed regime change in Iraq in the pages of *Foreign Affairs* in 2000, her article also accurately reflected what would be the main concerns of the new administration: Russia, the future power of China, and ballistic missile defense.[48]

Bush did not settle on a military invasion to overthrow Hussein in the weeks immediately following September 11, but he clearly had Iraq on his mind. Jonathan Powell, the chief of staff for British prime minister Tony Blair, testified that Bush brought up Iraq policy during his phone conversation with Blair on September 12, and again when the prime minister made his first visit following the attacks. This accords with the account of Richard Clarke, a senior White House adviser on terrorism, who claims the president was soon searching for links between Hussein and the September 11 terrorist attacks under the advice of Wolfowitz and Rumsfeld.[49] For Bush, merely disarming Hussein of his presumed stockpiles of WMD was an insufficient policy objective. David Manning, Blair's principal foreign policy adviser, recounted that his own government's policy on Iraq focused on disarmament, acknowledging that regime change might be a consequence. "For the Americans," Manning continued, "it was almost the opposite. It was, 'We want regime change in order to disarm Saddam Hussein.'" Toppling Hussein was meant to affect change beyond eliminating WMD, reflected by Wolfowitz's comments shortly after the invasion of Iraq that disarmament acted as a lowest common denominator that "everyone could agree on."[50]

Bush embraced what might be called "democratic domino theory," or in the words of one of the British government's Middle East experts, Edward Chaplin, the notion that "if democracy would break out in Iraq . . . then, lo and behold, democracy would break out in Palestine and this would be a terrifically good thing." Bush's aspirations extended beyond eventual democracy in Palestine, however. He told Prince Bandar of Saudi Arabia that a democratic Iraq would not only bring peace between Israelis and Palestinians, but would change the political order of the Middle East. Similar talks with Dick Cheney reportedly convinced the vice president of Bush's sincerity.[51] Manning, who was present at several private meetings between the president and Blair, believed Bush and his administration saw Iraq as part of a historic campaign, a "1945 or a 1991 moment when they were going to change the world for the better on their watch." He reiterated that "Americans had this vision and Bush had this vision of a new Middle East" that could be had by changing Iraq. Webb likewise recalled a "strong initiative from the White House . . . that we should be promoting democracy in the Middle East and we should be starting in Iraq."[52] Rice, conversely, argued that the administration "did not go to Iraq to bring democracy any more than Roosevelt went to war against Hitler to democratize Germany."[53] However, the president states in his memoir that

> If we had to remove Saddam from power, Tony [Blair] and I would have an obligation to help Iraqi people replace Saddam's tyranny with a democracy. The transformation would *have an impact beyond Iraq's borders*. The Middle East was the center of a global ideological struggle. On one side were decent people who wanted to live in dignity and peace. On the other were extremists who sought to impose their radical views through violence and intimidation. The best way to protect our countries *in the long run* was to counter dark vision with a more compelling alternative.[54]

Bush's recollection, like those of the officials around him, is consistent with high-level policy documents drafted under the supervision of Bush's national security adviser Rice. The "Liberation Strategy" for Iraq written in the summer of 2002 emphasized how regime change would help Iraqis and the Middle East as a whole. It was envisioned that toppling Hussein would lead to a democratic government in Iraq that could serve as an example to the region. An August meeting of the NSC principals chaired by Rice refined her initial document into a NSPD.[55] British ambassador to the United States Christopher Meyer expressed skepticism toward goals of democracy promotion that projected that if one were to "remove Saddam Hussein and the Ba'ath Party . . . a thousand [Edmund] Burkes, as it were, emerge." In his recollection, Rice responded by saying "that the trouble with the Europeans, that we were too sniffy, too . . . condescending about the Iraqi people, who were perfectly capable of running a democratic system and we should allow them to do so."[56]

Though he argued the president's emphasis on transforming Iraq was a mistake after the war, Feith—the lead Defense official on postwar policy—had long accepted the argument that democratizing the Middle East would bring the United States long-term security benefits. He had been one of the participants in a study group that advocated a "clean break" in which Israel would depose Hussein to benefit itself as well as the United States and its allies in the Middle East.[57] Just before leaving office, Feith reflected on his statement that "a humane representative government" in Iraq would "have beneficial spillover effects on the politics of the whole region" by stating "I must say, I'm damn proud of that sentence. That was right on the nose."[58] ORHA member Mike Ayoub recounted his plane ride from the United States to the Middle East seated next to Harold Rhode, who had been tasked by Feith to serve as liaison to Iraqi opposition parties. Ayoub remembered Rhode saying "the real objective was not Baghdad, it is Tehran, and after that As-sadville [Syria]."[59] Wolfowitz, Feith's superior in the Pentagon, shared these views. Ambassador Meyer recalled that Wolfowitz had broached the idea of invading southern Iraq and toppling Hussein with him roughly five years before the war began. In his memoirs Meyer writes that Wolfowitz "saw Iraq as the anvil on which a realignment of forces in the Middle East favorable to the United States and Israel would be struck." A stable democracy there would politically remake the region, provide territory for new U.S. military bases, and reduce dependence on Saudi oil.[60] Wolfowitz told reporters a few weeks before the war began that "if, when Iraq is liberated, it can come up with a representative government that treats its people decently, I think it can have significant effects throughout the Middle East."[61]

Though he had urged Clinton to make Hussein's overthrow U.S. policy in 1998, Rumsfeld was not like others in the administration who placed considerable weight on democracy promotion in the Middle East.[62] However, he was the primary proponent of another key long-term goal of the Bush administration regarding Iraq, namely the use of the invasion to strengthen U.S. deterrence. This desire was especially evident in Rumsfeld's internal government correspondence. Prior to September 11, 2001, the secretary had serious concerns that American operations in Iraq had become a series of "tit-for-tat" actions "without clear objectives or a discernable end state." Accordingly, in May of that year Rumsfeld composed a list for himself that placed Iraq as his top priority out of twelve areas of importance.[63] This focus overlapped with Rumsfeld's concerns about what he saw as a weakening U.S. deterrent against attacks from regimes like Hussein's. In "a world where more and more nations and non-state entities are going to have weapons of mass destruction," Rumsfeld wrote, the United States must "resolve to invest what is necessary to assure that we deter and dissuade and, if necessary, defend and prevail." Reviewing U.S. responses to a series of events beginning with the bombing of the World Trade Center in 1993 up to the attack on the USS *Cole* in 2000, Rumsfeld concluded that "for some eight years, the U.S. deterrent was weakened as a result of a series of actions that persuaded the world that the U.S. was 'leaning back,' not 'leaning forward,'" ending his review, in all capital letters, with the declaration "hardly a credible deterrent."[64]

This belief was only reinforced by the events of September 11. Rumsfeld told the *New York Times* that the terrorist attacks created "the kind of opportunities that World War II offered, to refashion the world."[65] Privately, he had informed America's combatant commanders that one of his key objectives in the war on terrorism was to demonstrate to terrorist-harboring states that they would incur great costs if the continued to target the United States. Bold military action, Rumsfeld concluded, could have this long-lasting deterrent effect.[66] He wrote that "If the war [on terror] does not significantly change the world's political map, the U.S. will not achieve its aim. . . . The [U.S. government] should envision a goal along these lines: New regimes in Afghanistan and [other states] that support terrorism (to strengthen political and military efforts to change policies elsewhere); Syria out of Lebanon; dismantlement or destruction of WMD in [key states]; end of many other countries support or tolerance of terrorism."[67] Rumsfeld and Wolfowitz doubted that U.S. operations in Afghanistan could achieve the "impressive results" necessary to have a deterrent effect, but thought an attack on Iraq would produce the desired outcome. Bush agreed with Rumsfeld that a backward-looking "retaliatory" approach should be rejected in favor of a forward-thinking strategy.[68] This was augmented by what Admiral Michael Boyce, chief of the British Defence Staff, called Rumsfeld's "obsession" with proving that doctrinal and technological innovation could minimize the number of troops and therefore time one needed to achieve military objectives, such as toppling dictators.[69]

The long time horizons of Bush, Rumsfeld, and top civilians in Defense were not shared by Secretary of State Powell. Powell was concerned about Iraq and the possibility that it might possess chemical, biological, and even nuclear weapons. He entered his job as secretary worried that sanctions could not forever contain the threat Hussein posed, a topic which he focused on in collaboration with his counterparts in the British government. Meyer testified that Powell treated the prospect of Hussein breaking containment "extremely seriously and he devoted a vast amount of energy to it."[70] However, he did not entertain transformative long-term goals for Iraq, favoring containment instead. He and Robin Cook, the UK's foreign secretary in 2000–2001, advocated improving containment via incremental changes in policy, including "smart" sanctions to contain threats from Hussein's regime.[71] Likewise, after September 11, Powell was focused narrowly on al-Qaida in Afghanistan rather than the "global" network of terrorist-supporting regimes hypothesized by Rumsfeld, Wolfowitz, and Feith, and did not seek the same transformation in the Middle East that other Washington officials did.[72] Generally speaking, Blair's chief of staff described Powell as "not at all happy with the way the wind was blowing" concerning the administration's policy on Iraq in 2002.[73]

Rice and, to an even greater degree, Cheney are the most difficult influential members of Bush's administration to categorize in terms of the value they placed on transformative goals vis-à-vis Iraq. In light of her 2000 *Foreign Affairs* article, Rice has been described as entering her job as national security adviser holding a "containment-plus" position similar to that of Powell. She wrote that, if a regime like Hussein's was to acquire WMD, the United States' first response should be that of "classical deterrence" because the weapons would be "unusable" unless the regime accepted "national obliteration."[74] However, Rice appeared to move from this more limited, conservative position to one closer to Bush's over time. Along with being responsible for drafting the administration's strategy laying out transformative objectives for Iraq, she opined that regime change would "open new opportunities for peace in the Middle East and new opportunities for Arab countries to give greater liberty and greater awareness to their own people."[75] Despite the fact that Rice distanced herself from such sentiments in her memoir, in 2008 she prominently asserted that the United States must "recognize that democratic state building is now an urgent component of our national interest. And in the broader Middle East, we recognize that freedom and democracy are the only ideas that can, over time, lead to just and lasting stability, especially in Afghanistan and Iraq."[76] Her private interactions with British officials such as Meyer indicate that she sincerely embraced such views in the run-up to war. Given her political stance in 2002–2003 as war plans were being crafted, Rice is cautiously categorized here as having long-term transformative aims regarding Iraq and the Middle East despite her earlier position.

Most accounts of Vice President Cheney portray him as placing much less weight on democracy promotion in the Middle East compared to Bush.[77] Instead, according to Feith, Cheney shared Rumsfeld's view that toppling Hussein would have widespread effects beyond Iraq, enhancing U.S. security by disrupting the presumed "nexus" between terrorist groups and their state sponsors. According to Aaron Friedberg, who became the director of planning on Cheney's foreign policy staff in the summer of 2003, Cheney believed overthrowing Hussein would produce a "demonstration effect" that would send a strong message to state sponsors of terrorism and reestablish America's capability to deter attacks. "I think the reason he wanted someone to do what he asked me to do was the hope, the assumption, of broadening out," Friedberg said, in reference to his own role as a long-term planner in the wake of the invasion. This corresponds with the observations of General Zinni who, serving as Bush's special envoy to Israel and the Palestinian Authority in 2002, reported hearing talk of "constructive destabilization" from people in Cheney's office, which he thought reflected the idea that "you could light this spark, cause a dramatic shift" in reference to the Middle East.[78]

Though the foregoing observations make it appear that Cheney's time horizons were similar to those of Rumsfeld, there are reasons to be cautious with such a conclusion. First, compared to other senior officials in the Bush administration, there are fewer available sources with which to corroborate the characterizations of Cheney just cited, which are drawn from a single (well-researched) biography. It might be argued the problem of limited information applies just as much to Rice. However, unlike Rice's actions as national security adviser in terms of forming a liberation concept and political objectives for Iraq, Cheney's contributions to postwar policy on Iraq prior to the war are much harder to discern. Biographies of Cheney, as well as his own memoirs, do not reveal much information on the matter. Unlike other members of the administration, his assessments of combat operations cannot be effectively compared with those of noncombat activities in the prospective postconflict stage. Despite Friedberg's and Feith's recollections, some of Cheney's most prominent public statements suggest he had short time horizons. Addressing the alleged threat from Iraq in August 2002, Cheney portrayed an attack as imminent, and drew analogies to the United States being caught off guard by the 1941 attack at Pearl Harbor. He cited Bush's comments in his second State of the Union address that "time is not on our side" vis-à-vis Iraq.[79]

While unwelcome, this gap in knowledge is not an insurmountable impediment to understanding how U.S. policy on postwar Iraq was formed. Though Cheney undoubtedly had great influence in the administration, available evidence indicates he was considerably less involved in plans for the aftermath of the invasion than policy leading to the invasion itself. Furthermore, while the apparent similarities between the vice president and Rumsfeld are not sufficient to conclude Cheney would have managed planning for Phase IV the same as the secretary of defense did, these similarities make any counterfactual claim that Cheney would have acted significantly differently appear dubious.

ATTENTION TO FEASIBILITY: COMBAT AND HUMANITARIAN AID VERSUS RECONSTRUCTION AND GOVERNANCE

Administration officials' tendency toward abstract thinking varied depending on the phase of the war plan considered. Bush was able to articulate his postwar goals—the desirability of his ends. For example, Rice's policy paper reflecting the president's views on Iraq enumerated thirteen high-level goals and objectives.[80] CPA head Bremer reflected that Bush was "quite clear" about his primary objectives, especially the establishment of democratic governance in a reconstructed Iraq.[81] However, the president, Rumsfeld, and top officials with long time horizons did not seriously attempt to assess the feasibility of postconflict operations to achieve their objectives. As a result, positive considerations of the war's potential payoffs overwhelmed considerations of potential costs, evidenced by overly optimistic estimates about the costs Phase IV would entail for coalition forces. The variation in the attention officials gave to feasibility concerns is especially striking when their assessments of combat plans are juxtaposed with assessments of noncombat operations.

Franks and others have characterized participation by Bush and his immediate subordinates as active and engaged during the war-planning process.[82] Rumsfeld was especially detail-oriented, becoming heavily involved in the process of targeting installations inside Iraq and the scheduled deployment of forces into the Iraqi theater. He was so engaged with the military's operational assumptions that CENTCOM characterized his conduct as bordering on harassment.[83] A concerned Powell informed former national security adviser Brent Scowcroft that the White House was focusing on the details of military planning at the expense of other considerations.[84] Because Bush, Rumsfeld, and others were attentive to details of how combat operations would be carried out, they were also aware of unwanted events that could happen as a result of the initial hostilities. Bush was particularly worried that Iraqi forces would entrench themselves in urban areas in an attempt to make the fighting as protracted as possible. Franks received a planning order in May 2002 to focus on countering urban warfare strategies that might be employed by the Iraqi military, and civilians returned to the topic of urban warfare repeatedly during briefings.[85] Administration principals were also troubled that Iraqi forces might launch missiles against Israel or other states, and that the initiation of hostilities would disrupt the international oil market. Bush, Cheney, and Rice all highlight these concerns in their memoirs.[86]

One of the foremost concerns of civilians in the United States and United Kingdom was that combat would create a humanitarian crisis in Iraq.[87] While being briefed by Franks in the summer prior to the invasion, Bush remarked that there had to be humanitarian assistance on the ground from the very start of OIF.[88] Five months later, Elliot Abrams briefed Bush on what the NSC saw as potential dangers following combat. Following the president's preferences, the focus was on displaced persons and potential food shortages. Bush regarded U.S. aid during the war as a mechanism to bolster the United States' image in the Middle East and at the same time expressed confidence in U.S. preparations in this regard. At a meeting on March 16, 2003, in the Azores, Bush told leaders of other countries in the OIF coalition that "we have to keep planning for a future postwar Iraq," emphasizing the possibility of a humanitarian crisis.[89]

These fears were not misplaced. The Ba'ath regime's past attacks on its civilian population and its torching of oil wells in the Gulf War showed it was willing to create human and environmental disasters when threatened. These same fears were circulated early among high-ranking members of the British government.[90] Furthermore, the administration integrated its thinking about humanitarian aid with its war plans. The conventional war-fighting phase of OIF was designed to proceed as quickly as possible in part to reduce the probability of a humanitarian disaster occurring.[91] However, the administration's focus was overly tilted toward humanitarian issues rather than the long-term governance and political solvency of Iraq. SIGIR noted this "striking asymmetry" in the planning process: "the U.S. government planned for the worst-case humanitarian scenario while it simultaneously planned for the best-case reconstruction one."[92] Likewise, the British secretary of state for international development wrote Prime Minister Blair that American plans for humanitarian assistance during and immediately after major combat operations were "quite comprehensive, but rely on the naïve assumptions that there will be no major problems and the conflict will be swift."[93] Cross, the United Kingdom's military liaison to ORHA, testified in 2009 that Garner was tasked with "immediate humanitarian issues" but that "the longer term view was this will all be okay."[94] Bush, Rumsfeld, and others with long time horizons were attentive to the context in which the invasion would be carried out, but not to the possible context of Phase IV, which in their minds was a distinct and temporally distant environment compared to the former. This mind-set led officials to think of a potential humanitarian crisis as occurring during the initial invasion, not a result of long-term difficulties of building a democratic Iraq or reconstructing the country's infrastructure. Ironically, this is best illustrated by a Defense memorandum which Feith claims contradicts the assertion that the administration underestimated the potential for long-term suffering and chaos in Iraq. The memo describes the task of providing humanitarian assistance and maintaining public order as an issue "during Combat Operations," not after.[95]

SIGIR found that the NSC working group on postwar Iraq, following the expectations of Rumsfeld, "assumed that long-term repairs could be undertaken and funded by the Iraqis," who would draw on oil revenues to do so. In testimony before the Senate, Feith appeared confident that Iraq's oil revenue would be able to cover the bulk of reconstruction costs, though he acknowledged that no plans for an organizational control mechanism to handle oil or other aspects of Iraq's resources and infrastructure had been laid out yet.[96] Gordon Brown, then chancellor of the British Exchequer, also thought that Iraqi oil revenues would pay for long-term repairs to the country.[97] At the same time, Rumsfeld and other senior officials did not account for how any noncombat expenses in the earliest days of Phase IV would be paid for. In contrast to the prevailing assumptions about Iraq's long-term requirements, members of the NSC's working group doubted that revenues from Iraq's oil would be available in time for urgent postwar needs. Garner also recounts being told by Rumsfeld's office that oil would pay for Iraq's reconstruction, and noting to himself that those funds would not be available for some time.[98] Given that one of the administration's predominant fears was that Hussein's regime might set the country's oil fields aflame during the invasion, and the extensive damage done to Iraq's oil infrastructure after Baghdad had been captured, this thinking highlights the severe disconnect between assessments of combat operations and the postconflict environment.

The optimism about oil revenues regarding Phase IV, in contradiction to wariness of the security of Iraq's oil during the invasion, was coupled with many other signs of overconfidence about the postconflict stage. American political leaders' waning focus on feasibility was demonstrated by an inattention to the mechanisms by which their political objectives would be accomplished. Debates between Rumsfeld and Franks about how many troops would be necessary for the invasion, for example, excluded Phase IV. Political conditions on the ground in Iraq were projected to help rather than impede U.S. objectives, and it was presumed U.S. forces could quickly redeploy once major combat operations ended.[99] Rice said the prevailing concept "was that we would defeat the [Iraqi] army, but the institutions would hold, everything from ministries to police forces," while General Carl Strock, a member of ORHA, concluded "we sort of made the assumption that the country was functioning beforehand."[100] It was presumed the Iraqi army would be available and willing to help the coalition maintain order, and Rumsfeld was confident that Iraqi exiles could quickly establish authority within the country. He testified in the Senate that "presumably Iraqis from inside the country and from outside the country would have some sort of a mechanism whereby they would decide what kind of a government or template would make sense" in the aftermath of regime change in Iraq. SIGIR noted a general presumption that the United States would magically "pull a 'Karzai' out of the hat," referring to Afghanistan's postinvasion president, and then Iraqis would take care of the rest.[101]

In light of the preceding, it is not surprising that the Defense Department's work on governance prior to the invasion reflected both an inattention to feasibility and communication fluency biased toward considerations of desirability. The documents from Feith's policy office that had emerged prior to the invasion focused on politics at the national level, suggesting that the Iraqi government be reformed from the top-down with provincial and municipal governments to follow. Feith asserts that his plan for an Iraqi Interim Authority (IIA), which would have quickly transferred a share of power to a provisional Iraqi council, would have prevented the United States from being viewed as an occupying power.[102] Feith and Wolfowitz had been quite receptive to advocacy on this point provided by Ahmed Chalabi, an influential Iraqi exile who promised precisely what they wanted to hear: the costs of deposing Hussein would be relatively low, and a liberal, democratic Iraq would promote similar transformations in Iran, Syria, and elsewhere in the region. They castigated and sidelined those who disagreed with such views.[103]

However, Feith himself says his IIA idea was a "concept" and not a concrete plan in March 2003. Ali Allawi, a member of the Iraqi exile community in Great Britain who held several senior posts in the Iraqi government from 2003 through 2006, surmised that Feith thought the transfer of power from the Ba'ath Party to a new governing entity would be unproblematic.[104]

Given this optimism, Washington stopped troop deployments and undermined a military command whose postwar structure and responsibilities were already unclear. With major combat operations still ongoing, Bush and Rumsfeld instructed their generals to "be prepared to take as much risk departing as they had in their push to Baghdad."[105] The official U.S. Army history of the Iraq intervention concluded that "it is questionable whether leaders at DOD, CENTCOM, and CFLCC conducted a thorough, coordinated, and realistic evaluation of the probable force levels required for Phase IV based on the realities of the new Iraq that were emerging in front of them."[106]

Powell, who did not place the same weight on long-term transformative goals for Iraq and the Middle East as Bush and Rumsfeld, was not disposed to give disproportionate attention to the "why" rather than "how" of future actions. The secretary privately told Bush that the United States would effectively become the government once the Ba'athists were deposed, an endeavor fraught with complications.[107] Consistent with CLT, Bush recalled his reaction to Powell's warning was to focus more on the potential benefits of transforming Iraq than chances of success, explaining that his job was to focus on higher level strategy rather than means of implementation.[108] Of course, this was not the president's attitude when considering damages that might occur during initial combat operations. CLT explains this discrepancy and Bush's puzzling admission that he did not categorize Powell's warning as a matter of high-level strategic concern—it was not central to the ends the president sought. Bush's admission is an example of the second intervening variable between abstraction and optimism regarding postconflict operations, that of communication fluency. In general, the State Department failed to frame its arguments in a way that would resonate with an abstract thinker. According to one senior State official, the department collectively "convinced ourselves that you could make these tactical arguments. . . . But we were guilty of ducking the big issue" of questioning the war's objectives.[109]

Powell was not the only one to try to persuade Bush to adjust his thinking regarding Phase IV. Dominick Chilcott, the head of the Iraq Planning Unit in Britain's Foreign and Commonwealth Office, noted the same lack of receptivity to details about postconflict operations. He reported that his team and others in his government had been attempting to "influence U.S. thinking for the better" since November of 2002. The British had "handed over a number of day-after papers to the Americans (but got very little back in return)."[110] Jonathan Powell testified that his government made repeated warnings to President Bush about the potential unintended consequences of the war that could arise in Phase IV, apparently to no avail.[111] Similarly, Iraqi exile Hatem Mukhlis said of his private meeting with Bush before the invasion that the president struck him as "unfocused on the key policy questions of the future of the Iraqi army, de-Ba'athification, and an interim government."[112] The one official Jonathan Powell noted who was receptive to such concerns, if not in need of much convincing, was Colin Powell, who was "particularly worried, I noticed, in July [2002], about the day after, what the preparations would be. . . . That was his focus at that stage."[113] Ironically, but in line with CLT, Powell was also the exception among senior administration officials in that he did not have valued long-term goals in regard to Iraq.

CLT also helps explain a puzzle regarding the differing assessments of Powell and Rice. In 2000 Rice wrote that the U.S. military "most certainly is not designed to build a civilian society," a prescient warning in light of the aftermath of the Iraq War. One analyst has noted that Rice's position at the time was largely in accordance with the "Powell Doctrine" regarding the use of military force.[114] One might then reasonably expect that Rice, like Powell, would be mindful of the likely costs facing the United States in Phase IV. Instead, Rice did not voice concerns to Bush as Powell did despite her access to the president. She apparently shared the assumption that the noncombat tasks in Iraq would be achieved relatively easily, and reportedly chastised British officials for thinking otherwise. This about-face in a period of two years is inexplicable unless the crucial differentiating factor between Powell and Rice, the disparate values they attached to long-term objectives of the Iraq War, is taken into account. When temporally distant noncombat operations were considered, the desirability of Rice's valued long-term objectives overshadowed considerations of feasibility. Powell, who lacked such objectives, did not face the same psychological barrier.

In contrast to the lack of communication fluency between top officials in regards to Phase IV, Bush, Rumsfeld, and others were receptive and willing to deliberate over concrete concerns relating to the feasibility of the combat phase of the intervention. In contrast to considerations of Phase IV, military historians describe the "numerous discussions" that Bush and members of the NSC had on the developing plan for Iraq as an "open, iterative process." One highly critical historian nevertheless characterizes Rumsfeld's participation with military planners updating war plans for Iraq as "not directive; it was more a dialogue to explore options."[115] Furthermore, collaboration between Rumsfeld and military officers regarding the invasion plan led to significant changes which departed from the secretary's initial preferences. Rumsfeld came to his position with the goal of transforming the way military forces deployed and fought in a theater of combat, emphasizing more agile forces that could rapidly defeat enemies. In June of 2002 he assigned the JCS and combatant commanders the task of developing strategic concepts for "'swiftly defeat' plans" to use in the administration's war on terror.[116] However, deliberations with his commanders led Rumsfeld to abandon his favored "hybrid" invasion plan in December 2002. The final invasion plan in large part resembled Franks's initial scheme, the "generated start," which Rumsfeld had at first rejected due to its large force size and lengthy deployment period prior to invasion.[117]

Unless it seem that Bush, Rumsfeld, and other top civilians were simply receptive to critiques from the military rather than State or British officials, it must be noted that senior policymakers were not receptive to the military's concerns or criticism regarding Phase IV. General John Jumper, chief of staff for the U.S. Air Force prior to the invasion, recalls that the JCS was at times asked by top Defense civilians whether they were comfortable with the war plan, but never about postwar operations.[118] Garner, a retired general hand-picked by Rumsfeld, was able to give one high-level briefing on Phase IV nine days before the start of hostilities. There was a general lack of inquisitiveness at Garner's briefing, at which the president and members of the NSC asked no questions and struck the head of ORHA as uninterested in his mission.[119] Cross testified that, during talks about Phase IV at which Rumsfeld was present, "it was quite clear . . . that he and the system had made up their mind how they were going to fight this campaign, so anybody speaking outside that paradigm was not particularly well received." Boyce remembered that the challenges he put to the Pentagon's assumptions about postwar Iraq were "absolutely not accepted." A retired U.S. Army colonel working in ORHA echoed the British officers' conclusions, saying that Rumsfeld and Wolfowitz "demonstrated repeatedly that they wanted information/advice that fit their preconceived ideas."[120] Perhaps the clearest signal military planners received from the civilian leadership was the very public rebuke of Army Chief of Staff Eric Shinseki by Wolfowitz and Rumsfeld after he suggested more soldiers would be necessary for Phase IV than the invasion. This was a forceful indicator that suggestions about postconflict operations that did not accord with administration views were unwelcome.

It has been argued that Rumsfeld and other civilians in the Defense Department resisted questions about postwar plans for Iraq because preparations for extensive stabilization and reconstruction activities would alarm the public and allow political opponents to prevent the invasion from taking place.[121] Much like the argument that postwar planning could have derailed the diplomatic process, these contentions are not convincing. First, it must be remembered that the private expectations of Rumsfeld and others in Defense matched their public pronouncements. Senior leaders at Defense believed only 30,000 U.S. soldiers would remain in Iraq by September 2003 and anticipated elections for a new Iraqi government would be held shortly after Hussein was deposed. Second, Defense officials were quite adept at denying information to others in Washington, as demonstrated by how the creation of ORHA surprised NSC and State officials. Even if senior Defense officials expected the costs of Phase IV to be high, assertions that political opponents could have acquired enough information from Defense about postwar operations to stop the war from happening are suspect. Third, top administration policymakers had repeatedly discussed possible calamitous events that could occur during the invasion itself: the use of WMD against Iraqi civilians and/or Israel; protracted urban fighting in Baghdad; and a surge in the cost of oil, to name a few. U.S. public opinion was surely sensitive to the costs of invasion before the war. Support for military action in Iraq reliably dropped when pollsters asked about the potential for U.S. casualties or the use of ground troops.[122] Why would there be a thorough discussion of these costs but not potential costs of Phase IV—even private deliberations among Rumsfeld and military planners in CENTCOM? Fourth, revelations that there had been a lack of planning for reconstruction, stabilization, and governance in Iraq were perhaps an even better tool for political opponents to use to slow the march to war. When polled, a majority of the U.S. public consistently demonstrated they were wary of military action against Iraq that lacked some international support.[123] The British government, the only member of the U.S.-led coalition in Iraq contributing substantial forces, was certainly alarmed by the lack of concrete plans for the war's aftermath. Boyce testified that "we kept on saying to the Americans all the way through that there were provisos about our commitment," including the need for parliamentary approval. The admiral continued that U.S. officials "understood absolutely that if Parliament had said no, we would not be going, and what contingency planning they were doing, if that were to happen, I have absolutely no idea."[124]

Rumsfeld was not indifferent or oblivious to potential costs of Phase IV. He recognized that if the United States and Iraqis could not effectively secure the peace following conventional combat operations, America could be stuck in Iraq regardless of his wishes, thus undermining his prized policy of military transformation. Speaking in September 2002, Rumsfeld stated the United States could not afford to be in a position where the failure to prepare for the political and physical reconstruction of Iraq "ties our forces down indefinitely."[125] Nevertheless, he did not attend to ways that worst-case scenarios could be prevented. The difference between Rumsfeld's detail-oriented approach to war plans and his hands-off approach to postconflict activities was a function of abstract thought, which led him to apply his own general preexisting beliefs rather than contextual information about Iraq when Phase IV was evaluated.

Rather than being worried about the political effects that a discussion of the costs of Phase IV could have, Rumsfeld's reliance on preexisting beliefs made him confident in the likelihood of a stable Iraqi state emerging from the war. One of Rumsfeld's important beliefs prior to the Iraq War was the undesirability of "nation building" by U.S. forces.[126] The secretary cited U.S. involvement in the Balkans as a model of how postwar policy could go wrong, specifically by breeding dependency on the United States and creating opportunities for moral hazard.[127] Rumsfeld drew on one of his assistant secretary's analysis of American policy toward France immediately after World

War II to persuade senior officials that U.S. military government in Iraq would have adverse consequences, and thus power should be quickly transferred to Iraqis.[128]

Correspondingly, Rumsfeld discounted information that did not fit with this set of beliefs. Manning noted the disconnect in strategic thinking, observing that "Americans had this vision and Bush had this vision of a new Middle East," but at the same time "they won't do nation building. They think this is a principle. So if you go into Iraq, how are you going to achieve this new Iraq?" He later explained the disconnect by stating there was "wishful thinking among some, that what would happen in Iraq would reflect something of what had happened after the Second World War in Japan or Germany."[129] Boyce concurred with Manning's assessment, saying Rumsfeld's notion that the United States should not do nation building was something he "passionately, passionately believed."[130] These beliefs did not appear to be based on any information about actual conditions in Iraq. Similarly, Wolfowitz and Feith relied on the examples of Poland, Hungary, the Czech Republic, and other former communist states to argue that countries could democratize after decades of authoritarian rule, and thus Iraq could do the same. Conversely, they seemed to discount the bloody postcommunist aftermath in the former Yugoslavia, even though that country was arguably a better analogy to use when thinking about Iraq.[131]

In sum, Rumsfeld had good reason to care about the success of Phase IV, but his assumptions of what success would require proved incorrect. His prior belief that nation building led the occupied population to become dependent on interveners was complemented by the desires and long-held beliefs of Feith, Wolfowitz, and others in his department that democracy would easily take hold in Iraq. According to Secretary of the Army Thomas E. White, the Defense mind-set was that Phase IV would be "straight forward" and "manageable . . . because this would be a war of liberation and therefore reconstruction would be short lived."[132] If Rumsfeld believed otherwise, it is hard to understand why he secured his department's authority over postwar policy. Rumsfeld did so to ensure that what he believed would be the best approach—a rapid transfer of power to an Iraqi authority and minimal U.S. engagement in Phase IV—would be implemented.[133]

The striking difference between Rumsfeld's engagement with combat and noncombat plans prior to the invasion was accompanied by a remarkable reorientation after the war had commenced. By March 2003 postconflict activities in Iraq were no longer last in a sequence of operations that had to be prepared for: they were the only activities remaining for which preparations were necessary. At that point, Rumsfeld's mind-set regarding postconflict operations shifted to a concrete mode of assessment that resembled how he had dealt with preparations for major combat. In the period from March 17 to April 23 the defense secretary began sending memorandums to Bush, Powell, Wolfowitz, Feith, and others about managing Iraq's currency; the political intricacies of the IIA; coordinating humanitarian relief efforts by ORHA and USAID; the possibility of Syria and Iran interfering in Iraqi political affairs; the recruitment of Arabic speakers; and the need for a comptroller managing American monetary expenditures in postwar Iraq.[134] Up until that time, there had been a conspicuous absence of attention to the details of postconflict activities in Rumsfeld's internal documents. At the time he was composing the newly oriented memorandums Rumsfeld had received no substantial new information from advisers or events on the ground in Iraq with which to update his beliefs. U.S. forces did not begin to report on looting in Baghdad until April 7.[135] This was after the secretary had already begun focusing on postwar challenges, and urban looting was not the subject of any of his correspondence about postconflict tasks during March and April. Rather, concrete assessment of the means by which the peace in Iraq would be secured corresponded with a shift in the sequential proximity of Phase IV.

In his memoirs, Rumsfeld remembers taking issue with Bush's pronouncement after Hussein had fallen that the United States would remain in Iraq for an indeterminate amount of time. The former secretary states bluntly "that was not the way I understood our plan."[136] Indeed, such a strategy was entirely contrary with Rumsfeld's views before the war. However, Rumsfeld's recollection of his postwar reaction is contradicted by the work he was doing at the time of Bush's announcement. In mid-May he composed a more detailed, updated version of Rice's document on U.S. political objectives in Iraq which added concrete recommendations for achieving those goals.[137] Most remarkable in comparison to Rumsfeld's earlier resistance to challenges to his thinking about postwar operations was a memorandum he dictated after a discussion with Federal Reserve Chairman Alan Greenspan. In light of his conversation, Rumsfeld wrote "The way to get a non-theocratic system is to go slowly. People have to begin to see what is in it for them. That suggests we should not rush to have elections. We can have votes on things like city councils with a limited mandate to help get garbage picked up, help get policemen out. Otherwise the fundamentalists will very likely sweep, in a way that is disadvantageous to the people in terms of their long-term future and benefit."[138] This opinion totally contradicted the secretary's prewar position and that of his department. It also stood in contrast to Rice's policy paper on goals and strategy for Iraq, which had set out that an interim administration be established to prepare for a "transition to an elected Iraqi government as quickly as practicable."[139] Greenspan's advice was just the sort of information that Rumsfeld had ignored or expressed hostility toward in the many months leading to war but now he appeared sensitive and receptive to such concerns.

Garner recalled that Rumsfeld had been much less invested in Chalabi and the IIA than Wolfowitz or Feith.[140] Clearly, however, Rumsfeld must have accepted or acquiesced to Feith's position on a rapid transfer of power before the war. By June 2003, however, Rumsfeld recognized that "without some additional element of Iraqi participation in the selection" of an interim administration, "there is risk that selectees will be tainted as creatures of the U.S."[141] Three days later he told Bremer that, in regard to peacekeeping in security environments such as that prevailing in Iraq, forces had to "plan on a decade, not months or years."[142] In contrast to the IIA plan, ORHA and CENTCOM had made the assumption a bottom-up approach would be necessary—it would be best to go from local elections to a constitutional convention and then to national elections.[143] Not only was Rumsfeld now receptive to such arguments, he was endorsing them. Again, the bulk of Rumsfeld's observations and directions on governance in Iraq came before any clear signs of an insurgency or Islamic fundamentalist influence in Iraqi politics had emerged, a sign that shifting temporal construal, rather than new information, was driving his assessments.

There are signs that others besides Rumsfeld became aware of the shortcomings in the IIA framework the Defense policy office had created. Though Feith says the IIA plan was embraced by President Bush on March 10, 2003, his book makes it clear that Bremer, the head of the CPA, was receiving garbled signals from the president and others on the administration's intentions for Iraq's new political order. Bremer contends that the president never instructed him to rapidly set up a power-sharing arrangement with Iraqis, and that his view was shared by Cheney and Powell. He also sensed that, after the war had commenced, there had been "considerable debate in the administration about what kind of an occupation it was going to be."[144] As CLT predicts, the question of how an occupation would be executed was not salient until Phase IV was impending.

ADDITIONAL CONTRADICTIONS IN ADMINISTRATION ASSESSMENTS

As the preceding shows, there was a jarring incongruity between the nature of the Bush administration's assessments of combat operations versus postconflict tasks. The shifting character and substance of Rumsfeld's thoughts about Phase IV shortly after the war commenced was almost as sharp. There are several other areas in which policymakers displayed an inattention to the mechanisms by which their goals would be accomplished, as well as a lack of receptivity to messages which contradicted established general beliefs. Prominent among such issues were the relationship of ORHA to Washington and CENTCOM; the role of the United Nations (UN) in Iraq; and the question of "de-Ba'athification."

ORHA and the Chain of Command. Because senior members of the Bush administration were not attentive to the means by which postconflict goals would be achieved, they also failed to clearly delineate the organizational relationships necessary for the successful execution of policy. Though sectors of the government such as the NSC and USAID had been making postwar preparations, the president's order establishing ORHA upended these efforts and showed little appreciation for what groundwork had been laid. NSPD-24 was seen by the NSC working group as ignoring the work they had done and usurping their authority, thus discouraging any collaboration with ORHA.[145] This foreshadowed ORHA being quickly and, from Garner's perspective, unexpectedly replaced by Bremer and the CPA.

ORHA itself was not structured with any particular attention to detail; Feith's Office of Special Plans delivered an initial layout of the organization that seemed lacking in preparation and thus in need of significant revision.[146] Strangely, even though Feith's office had been involved in creating ORHA, it did not share any of its work on Phase IV with Garner.[147] Furthermore, the Defense Department did not do much to assist Garner's attempts to acquire resources for his organization. Even after Bush had privately concluded war was virtually inevitable in January 2003, ORHA could not secure resources from other U.S. agencies when Garner made requests because the decision to invade had not been made public. When Garner met with Bush late in February, he reported there was no discussion of the problems with personnel or funding his organization was having. Of the twenty-three Iraqi ministries ORHA was to oversee, Garner deployed with senior advisers for only seven.[148]

While there was a clear chain of command for major combat operations, multiple sources have noted that military personnel were unsure of what relationship they had with ORHA during Phase IV, and coordination between the two was minimal as a result.[149] Of even greater concern is that Franks and his top commanders had the impression that responsibility for postwar operations lay with other parts of the government, whereas many civilians at the Pentagon were sure that CENTCOM knew it was in charge of Phase IV.[150] Powell informed Bush and Rice that the administration did not have unified command in Iraq because both Franks and Garner were placed directly under Rumsfeld, with neither answering to the other. Though incredulous when first told, both the president and national security adviser were surprised to find that dual chains of command did in fact exist. Once again, Powell was more cognizant of the details of Phase IV even though he had been largely excluded from postwar policymaking. ORHA would finally be brought under the CFLCC command in April, after the invasion.[151]

Like the difference between assessments of combat and noncombat operations, the absence of coherent command structures is peculiar to Phase IV. The existence of imprecise lines of authority was not characteristic of the Bush administration generally or Rumsfeld's department in particular. Both the Bush administration's transition into the White House in 2001 and its day-to-day operations were marked by discipline, efficiency, and clear lines of authority.[152] Others have observed that the authorization process at the

Pentagon while combat operations were being planned remained robust despite tension between civilians and uniformed officers.[153]

The Role of the UN. One of the major challenges facing explanations that hold the Bush administration had short time horizons before the Iraq War is the role the UN played in the intervention. These arguments expect Washington to have resisted engagement with multilateral institutions due to their immediate efficiency costs.[154] Yet Bush and others' approach to the UN varied noticeably according to the phase of the intervention under consideration. One of the most important provisos for Britain, the United States' primary ally in the war, was for the UN Security Council to sanction the invasion of Iraq. Key members of the Bush administration were quite resistant to this approach. However, just as civilian leaders were willing to compromise valued positions on invasion plans when challenged by the military, Bush and others were ultimately receptive to the British government's concerns about obtaining international support for the invasion.[155] American policymakers were willing to incur the delays that came with the UN process, contradicting claims they had short time horizons. However, the U.S. administration did not show similar receptivity to UK entreaties for UN involvement in Phase IV until after the war had begun. Alternative perspectives agree that this was because Bush and others grossly underestimated the operational commitment Phase IV would require.[156] They do not explain why officials did not make similarly optimistic assumptions about the initial invasion, or why they relied on information detached from the relevant context as well as flawed intelligence to arrive at their overconfident conclusions. CLT, however, does explain the variation in attitudes toward multilateralism as well as the overconfident assessments of Phase IV. American leaders' shifting levels of communication fluency in regard to UN diplomacy mirrored that regarding military plans.

Numerous UK officials stressed the vigorous debate within the Bush administration about attempting to secure a Security Council resolution prior to attacking Iraq, as well as their own roles in persuading their U.S. counterparts toward this track. According to Blair, it was a "perpetual focus" of his during discussions with Bush. Tebbit, British under secretary at the Ministry of Defence, likewise recalled that Blair's secretary of state for defence Geoff Hoon "continually emphasized to Rumsfeld the importance of pursuing the UN route" prior to the invasion of Iraq.[157] However, the British initially faced stiff resistance to this idea. Blair summarized the position of a sizable portion of the administration as thinking the British suggestion was "crazy." U.S. officials, he continued, thought the UN bureaucracy would go back to "playing around" with Hussein, and "in the meantime you have this guy doing what he is doing, sitting there and nothing is happening."[158] There were exceptions: Meyer stated that Powell's State Department was in favor of pursuing a UN resolution, but "you sure as hell had to argue it with the vice president and with Rumsfeld, and, up to a point, with Condoleezza Rice." More importantly, Meyer thought Bush "in his heart . . . just wanted to get over there and kick Saddam out."[159]

Even though the president and the majority of key actors near the White House did not prefer to pursue diplomacy through the UN, Bush was willing to entertain vigorous debate on the subject. Participants in the deliberations have cited August and September 2002 as the critical months in the president's decision making. In the first week of August Bush met privately with Secretary Powell and Rice, who presented the case for pursuing a new resolution. August was not the last time the president would seriously discuss the policy. In September, when Blair and Manning went to visit Bush at his ranch in Crawford, they were surprised to find the president had invited Cheney to participate in the discussions. Manning recounted how, over a period of hours, the prime minister laid out the case for pursuing more resolutions. Manning's belief was that Bush wanted to expose Cheney to the arguments the British were making. He also thought that Blair's reasoning had made a substantial impact on Bush's own beliefs. He recalled the president saying during the meeting that if Hussein were to accept and implement the terms of a UN resolution, the United States and United Kingdom would have largely succeeded. Manning testified that Bush used a "colorful phrase, which has stayed with me, he said: 'We would have cratered the guy [Hussein].'" There continued to be significant debate in the administration the second week of September before Bush decided to pursue further diplomacy in the UN.[160] Tebbit believed Rice's assertion "that U.S. policy had been transformed by being persuaded to go down the UN route." Boyce agreed with this assertion, speculating that the Bush administration was swayed in part because they wanted the United Kingdom "on board." At the same time, he also noted the United States was easily capable of invading Iraq without British assistance until very late in its preparations for war. Even as late as March 11, 2003, Rumsfeld publicly commented that British forces would be "helpful" but not essential for the invasion.[161]

Though Bush was willing to be exposed to vigorous debate about the UN resolutions related to the possible invasion of Iraq, he was not similarly disposed to engage with arguments about the potential role of a UN mandate and role in Phase IV of the upcoming war. Though Rice's policy paper on Iraq had listed contributions and participation from the "International Community" as part of U.S. strategy for postwar Iraq, it did not specifically lay out a role for the UN.[162] Peter Ricketts, of the Foreign and Commonwealth Office, testified that, just as his government argued for pursuing new Security Council resolutions on disarmament and the use of force, British officials "were clear that the preferred course, if it should come to a war and then a postconflict period, should be a UN-led administration."[163] In contrast to British input on the UN regarding resolutions pertinent to a potential invasion, however, proposals about UN involvement in Phase IV were not seriously considered. Aside from the State Department, which needed little persuasion, Ricketts believed "our arguments, certainly at my level, didn't have much impact." Like others, he attributed this lack of engagement to a "touching faith" among many in Washington that "Iraqis would some- how magically take over and restore their state to the democratic state that it should be in." When Phase IV was concerned, Ricketts concluded, admin- istration officials were most receptive to Iraqi opposition groups which pro- vided Bush and his advisers with forecasts that fit their preconceived beliefs— exactly as CLT predicts would be the case.[164]

Other UK officials had the same experience as Ricketts. Chaplin testified that he and his colleagues had "quite detailed discussions" with policymak- ers in Washington in November and January that touched on UN involve- ment in postwar Iraq. However, American political leaders did not deliber- ate over this possibility as they had when resolutions on the use of force were under consideration. Stephen Pattison, the head of Britain's UN Department in the Foreign and Commonwealth Office, stated that U.S. officials were still "implacably hostile" toward the possibility of a large UN role in February.[165] UK cabinet secretary Andrew Turnbull was equally blunt, saying "when Bush said the UN will have a vital role, he was fobbing us off, and he meant the UN agencies would have a vital role, but he was absolutely resistant."[166]

As opposed to their considerations of the merits of UN involvement in the coercive phase of diplomacy, there is no evidence to suggest that Bush and others with long time horizons seriously considered the benefits of sharing the burden of rebuilding Iraq with international organizations in Phase IV.[167] But just as Rumsfeld's lack of receptivity to detailed discussion of Phase IV lifted once the Iraq War commenced, Washington's implacability to consid- erations of a postwar role for the UN also came undone soon after the inva- sion. With the drive to Baghdad ongoing in early April, Bush and Blair reached an agreement at a summit in Belfast that the UN should have involvement in Iraq after Hussein was gone. Once again, this came prior to events in Iraq pointing to the need for international burden sharing during Phase IV. In Tebbit's view, British officials "thought we made a lot of progress over in- volving the UN" in the early days of the war. Chilcott also noted that by March and April it was clear British advice on governance in Iraq was be- coming more influential with Bush.[168] Once again, communication fluency and the administration's willingness to have its prior beliefs challenged in- creased as Phase IV became preeminent in the series of anticipated events.

De-Ba'athification. Along with the decision to disband the Iraqi army, the United States' de-Ba'athification policy in Iraq has been criticized as one of the main factors leading to an insurgency. De-Ba'athification should have ar- guably been central to the administration's thinking, as regime change was one of the primary objectives of OIF. However, it appears the administra- tion had no grasp of the Ba'ath Party's structure, and paid little attention to the feasibility of removing Ba'athists from government. This is not to suggest that there was a clearly "correct" policy for the United States to pursue in this regard but, as predicted by CLT, the majority of the Bush administration (with one important possible exception) neglected the details of implementing reform in Iraqi ministries and were blind to the costs of different policy options. Ultimately, the high-level goal of purging Ba'athists and transforming Iraq's government overshadowed considerations of feasibility.

Rice set the administration's initial tone on de-Ba'athification, and did so in a manner which does not fit comfortably with CLT. Rice's October 2002 policy paper on Iraq held that the United States would adopt a strategy that "substantially preserves but reforms the current Iraqi bureaucracy." Manning testified that his understanding in conversations with Rice was that "she was well aware of the desirability of trying to co-opt the army, trying to limit the degree of purge [sic] of the Ba'ath Party."[169] This appears inconsistent with the predictions of CLT: unlike Rice's presumptions about the ease with which Iraq could establish democracy and her notion that the United States would find Iraq's civil institutions largely intact, she appears to have considered the feasibility of allowing former Ba'ath Party members a role in government. One might tentatively attribute this to a mechanism consistent with CLT, namely a reliance on general beliefs about the political world. Before entering government, Rice's area of expertise was Soviet and Eastern European politics. Manning remembered telling Rice that "at the time of the collapse of the Soviet Union, we would never have said at this point that anybody who had belonged to one of the Communist parties in these countries could never take part in government again, and she absolutely accepted that."[170] However, it is not clear why some of Rice's general preexisting beliefs, such as those about transitioning autocracies, would influence her assessments of Iraq, while others—her belief in containment and skepticism toward nation building, for example—did not.

Regardless of the source of Rice's thinking, Tebbit believed his government "had an undertaking from the American administration that they were just going to do very light de-Ba'athification." Likewise, Garner presumed that the worst elements of the Ba'ath regime, those who would be subject to trial for crimes while in office, would be dead or in hiding by the time Hussein was overthrown, and urged members of ORHA not to expend much energy thinking about de-Ba'athification.[171] Garner himself presumed his organization would work with less notorious former party members, the bulk of Ba'ath members, in order to stabilize Iraq during Phase IV. Manning asserted that Garner "was absolutely clear that you should not disband the military, and he wasn't going in for great massive de-Ba'athification programs." He continued that, like the UK government, Garner preferred to work with Iraqi bureaucrats to "ensure the smooth administration of Iraq" and prepare the country for a new government.[172] This was consistent with assumptions made by CENTCOM and in Whitley's Eclipse II plan.

Despite the expressed position of the Bush administration as represented by Rice's paper in October, as well as the impressions of Garner and UK officials, most senior U.S. policymakers had plainly not given much thought to the matter of the Ba'ath Party in the lead-up to war. Graham Rudd, an embedded historian in ORHA, has done the most extensive work clarifying how Bremer's de-Ba'athification order came to be. Rumsfeld informed Garner on March 14 that the Defense Department, which had been officially in charge of Phase IV since January, had no formulated de-Ba'athification policy. As noted, Garner had not made it a matter of priority. He had initially assigned the task to someone in ORHA's civil administration staff, but Feith had objected that his office would be handling civil administration planning.[173]

The plan that Feith created, however, differed dramatically from what Garner and British officials had presumed postwar policy would be. The day before Bremer left for Iraq, Feith gave him a document on de-Ba'athification drafted in his office. Ambassador and ORHA member Robin Raphel said the document was "poorly written . . . almost incoherent" and proposed a severe approach to the removal of former Ba'athists.[174] Because the Ba'ath Party had been in power for decades, virtually all upper-middle and top members of Iraq's ministries had to be members regardless of their ideological dispositions, a point the policy did not appear to grasp. Garner objected to the plan, saying it would drive tens of thousands of Ba'athists underground if it were issued. Nevertheless, Bremer was determined to execute the orders he had been given. Both Rice and Powell appeared shocked by Bremer's de-Ba'athification order, and General Peter Pace, vice chairman of the JCS, said he was never consulted on the matter. Feith later said, "it appears I did not bring the matter to the Deputies Committee" of the NSC; neither could he confirm he received Rumsfeld's approval for the order.[175]

As Jonathan Powell observed, Bush administration policy toward the Ba'ath Party in postwar Iraq was "a similar mistake the Americans made after the Second World War with de-Nazification."[176] Like Roosevelt's relationship with Henry Morgenthau, Feith's decision reflected the mind-set of someone fixated on transforming a country to the exclusion of other considerations, and surrounded by individuals willing to provide information to reinforce this predisposition. Chalabi called for an extreme, top-down process of de-Ba'athification, the same form which appeared in the order drafted by the Defense policy office. The viewpoints were so similar that Zinni actually believed the CPA order came directly from pressure Chalabi applied on Bremer.[177] Rumsfeld came to be as critical of such estimates as he had been about military assumptions for the invasion plan, but not until momentous policy decisions had already been made in Baghdad.

It cannot be said with certainty how Phase IV might have developed in the absence of the CPA's de-Ba'athification order. On the one hand, it angered and drove away individuals with knowledge and experience of how Iraq could be governed. On the other hand, the majority of Iraqis may never have trusted even a temporary administration with a large number of former Ba'athists to help govern the country. What is evident is that the decision-making process leading to the de-Ba'athification order was far from rigorous, in both the absence of deliberation among policymakers and the method by which it was authorized. While an effective decision-making process may have ultimately led to the conclusion that wide-reaching de-Ba'athifcation was necessary, Feith's policy prematurely cut off discussion, not to mention access and influence over Iraqis that could be valuable assets or hostile opponents of U.S. forces. A well-considered policy of ambiguity toward former party members might have been preferable given the cross-cutting pressures facing foreign occupiers in Iraq. Instead, in the evaluation of Andy Bearpark, the CPA's director of operations and infrastructure for Iraq, "the fact is that Iraq had a perfectly good human capacity before we went and smashed it."[178]

JUXTAPOSING THE AMERICAN AND BRITISH GOVERNMENTS

Though it is beyond the scope of this study to closely trace how British officials came to their assessments of Phase IV, the contrast between the UK and U.S. governments is consistent with the predictions of CLT. The British adopted projections of postwar Iraq that were significantly less optimistic than those holding sway in the Bush administration. Furthermore, a conventional analysis would suggest the United Kingdom had every reason to be less mindful of the aftermath of the war than those in the United States. However, it is exactly because several factors influenced British officials to place significantly *less* weight on long-term goals, and spend more time focused on initial operations, that the contrast between the two countries fits well within the CLT framework.

British officials acknowledged several overly optimistic assessments they made prior to the invasion, especially in regard to the ease with which existing Iraqi institutions could be used to help administer the country after Hussein was deposed.[179] Despite this, they were not nearly as blind to potential challenges in Phase IV as their American counterparts. A year before the invasion, Hoon informed Blair that despite searching there was no "credible successor to Saddam," adding that "if a coalition takes control of Baghdad (especially without catching Saddam), it will probably have to stay there for many years."[180] Soon thereafter, Webb reported that "U.S. thinking has not identified either a successor or a constitutional restructuring to provide a more representative regime." Though he may not have discerned political destabilization in the Middle East was a goal of the administration, Webb aptly noted that governments in the region could not be presumed to support efforts to democratize Iraq "lest it prompted questions about their own structures." He warned that ethnic divisions in Iraq might produce a "fractured Iraq" and compel surrounding countries to intervene. Webb's conclusion was that the prospects of finding a short-term political solution to the question of governance in Iraq were poor, and thus any occupying force could expect to remain for quite some time. Straw and Jonathan Powell sent similar messages to Blair voicing concerns about U.S. preparations for Phase IV in July.[181]

In October Hoon again warned Blair that "there is likely to be a substantial and continuing post-conflict stabilization task in Iraq" that the United Kingdom might be asked to provide a large force to address. Several months later, Blair's private secretary for foreign affairs noted the prime minister wanted "much greater clarity about U.S. intentions" regarding the "aftermath" in Iraq.[182] At this point, in January 2003, Blair thought Phase IV was the primary issue regarding war plans, and was recorded saying the "Coalition must prevent anarchy and inter-Nicene fighting breaking out." Given that Iraqi Shiites had been brutally suppressed by Hussein and Sunnis loyal to him after the Gulf War, no access to secret information was necessary to see this was a possibility. Though British officials acknowledged post-Hussein operations might be short, they were "more likely to endure for years."[183]

The environment in which UK officials were making assessments should have influenced them to focus on near-term costs of war, not necessarily those they would face in the postconflict stage of the invasion. First, as the United States' junior partner, Britain was usually in a reactive position when it came to military policy on Iraq. UK officials were initially reluctant to appoint members to ORHA because they feared they would be put in a position in which they would be held responsible for decisions made by American officials in Iraq without having commensurate decision-making power.[184] Blair testified that one of the key lessons learned was that when Washington was "providing well over 90 percent of the assets . . . you are not going to be in a position where you are the driving party, for example, of what was happening in Baghdad."[185] Manning contended his government "had to be reactive" given the policy changes in America after the September 11 attacks. Tom McKane, deputy head in the Defence and Overseas Secretariat, likewise stressed critics should "keep very much at the front of your minds that the main player in all of this was the United States Government. They were going to be in the lead in whatever planning was being done, whether it was for the military operation itself or the arrangements that would come after."[186] While these statements may seem self-serving in that they deflect British responsibility for the aftermath of the invasion, it is hard to argue that they are not also true.

Related to its status as junior partner, Britain's military plans were in flux until late January. Such uncertainty had a much greater bearing on the United Kingdom's postwar preparations compared to the United States'. Washington was certain it would initially administer Baghdad and most of the rest of Iraq, whereas British officials could not know whether they would be in the north or south of the country until the military strategy stabilized. This was due to uncertainty as to whether or not coalition forces would be able to invade through Turkey. The Turkish option, which would have resulted in a British occupation of northern Iraq, remained on the table until January. Boyce testified that, though the British military had been making contingency plans, some British ships set sail for the Middle East "not knowing whether they'd turn left or turn right when they got into the Mediterranean."[187] When McKane was questioned about whether UK defense planners were thinking about a long-term occupation in Iraq, he pointed out that London was not even sure what the size or form of its military contribution would be in the spring of 2002, and "until one had addressed those points . . . the question of precisely what the aftermath was going to be was not something that could be settled."[188]

A third problem facing the United Kingdom was the government's concern that, without a UN mandate, it would be illegal to undertake noncombat tasks beyond humanitarian assistance in Iraq. Britain's Department for International Development took the position that it needed to acquire UN Security Council authorization for civil administration and reconstruction in Iraq, adding that "the absence of agreement with the U.S. is holding up international planning and the prospects of burden sharing."[189] Ricketts, of the Foreign and Commonwealth Office, summarized that "absent a UN Security Council resolution . . . our occupation was governed by the fourth Geneva Convention and the 1907 Hague powers, which are fairly restrictive in what they allow occupying forces to do."[190] Legal uncertainties would stymie efforts in some sectors of the government to progress in postwar planning.

Fourth, unlike officials in the United States, Iraq policy was not the most salient issue for many British officials for much of 2002. Manning held that the UK foreign policy agenda was "complicated and wide-ranging" in the first half of the year. While Iraq was "a constant theme" it was not consistently a "top priority . . . we were at least as pre-occupied in London with the crisis between India and Pakistan and the very serious situation in the confrontation between Israel and Palestine." Chaplin echoed these points, adding that in his view Blair had been "extremely seized" by the Second Intifada. Ricketts agreed, noting that "we now look at [Blair's April meeting with Bush at] Crawford as a key event in the Iraq saga, but for those of us preparing at the time for the Prime Minister's visit, the Arab/Israel issue was at least as major a concern."[191] Blair agreed, testifying that the Crawford discussion "was less to do with specifics about what we were going to do on Iraq or, indeed, the Middle East, because the Israel issue was a big, big issue at the time."[192] The competition for policymakers' attention that diluted their focus on Iraq was compounded by a lack of certainty of U.S. intentions toward military action. Boyce recounted it was not until June or July that British officials began to get access to military plans being developed in the United States.[193]

Fifth, the path to war was a much larger threat to Blair's political standing in the United Kingdom than it was to Bush's in the United States.[194] A year before the war began Blair wrote Jonathan Powell that "the persuasion job on this [the use of force in Iraq] seems very tough. My own side are [*sic*] worried. Public opinion is fragile. International opinion—as I found at the EU—is pretty skeptical." Blair's center-left Labour Party "was about to go into an alliance with a right-wing conservative Republican President," which troubled his fellow party members. In his words, "I was obviously going to get a huge political problem out of it." This meant that much of his focus had to be on managing immediate political challenges domestically, and was one reason why Blair pushed the United States so hard for a UN resolution legitimating military action. When asked if concentration on obtaining UN approval distracted from constructing a strategy for Phase IV, Blair answered in the negative but admitted "I was absorbed enormously by the politics and I accept that."[195] Deputy Prime Minister John Prescott said American officials never fully grasped the degree to which the Labour government was immersed in the immediate domestic implications of policy toward Iraq. Whereas Bush had considerable leeway moving ahead, Blair had to remind Washington "in a parliamentary system that is not the case. They can, in fact, remove us. They don't have to wait for November." Blair's chief of staff Powell recalled how "Andrew Turnbull used to regularly pop into my office in that period and ask me for the Labour Party rules on a change of Prime Minister, which wasn't altogether encouraging."[196]

Lastly, and most central to the theory presented in Chapter 1, Britain's primary aim in Iraq was disarmament, not regime change or a transformation of the Middle East. Though the means toward disarmament under discussion had changed, the policy was virtually the same as it had been in London since the end of the Gulf War. The UK government was not unaware of the potential long-term benefits of removing Hussein from power. The British Secret Intelligence Service wrote in 2001 that toppling Hussein "could give new security to oil supplies; engage a powerful and secular state in the fight against Sunni extremist terror; open political horizons in the [Gulf Cooperation Council]; remove a threat to Jordan/Israel; undermine the regional logic on WMD."[197] However, London never embraced the preceding logic like Washington did. Straw argued after the Iraq War that a major difference between Britain and the United States was that "however desirable the removal of Saddam Hussein might be, regime change could not be an objective of UK foreign policy, not least because military action for this purpose would palpably have been unlawful. Our objective was more constrained."[198] Several officials echoed Manning's comment cited above that, if anything, the UK government saw regime change as a potential side effect of disarmament, not an end in itself.[199] Because British officials did not place the same value on long-term objectives as their American counterparts did, desirability considerations were not going to overshadow feasibility concerns when they considered the more distant future. The one exception to this argument might have been Prime Minister Blair, who had long been driven to counter threats posed by Hussein and similar regime leaders.[200] Unlike Bush, however, Blair did not have a coterie of like-minded advisers, and—as demonstrated in this section—his government faced numerous factors shortening its time horizons. In sum, on the surface it might appear as though Blair and British officials should have been less mindful of Phase IV costs, and invested little time and energy in trying to turn transatlantic deliberations toward thinking about the postwar environment. That they behaved in contradiction to such expectations is consistent with CLT.

Alternative Explanations for Phase IV Preparations

The following explanations for U.S. preparations for postwar Iraq have been offered by participants in the planning process or scholars who have analyzed the case. While these explanations are plausible on their face, closer examination shows they are either inconsistent with case evidence, or fail to explain behavior accounted for by CLT. Those explanations derived from organizational theory and the scholarly literature on civil–military relations do account for key parts of the puzzle, but are inadequate by themselves to understand either military plans or the nature of political leaders' assessments of Phase IV.

OPPORTUNITY COSTS

The preceding has shown that, despite the Bush administration's threat perception following the September 11 attacks, the nature of its goals regarding Iraq along with the handling of the UN place arguments relying on short time horizons being dominant in Washington in serious doubt. However, perhaps it could still be that administration officials did not attend to the structure and relationships between bodies responsible for Phase IV because they did not feel they could afford to, rather than because abstract construal discouraged considerations of the means by which goals would be achieved. Colonel Peterson, the same CENTCOM officer who had tried to alert superiors to the strategic disconnect between plans for combat operations and noncombat operations in Phase IV, nevertheless defended preparations for the Iraq War by arguing that "only a fool would propose hurting the war fighting effort to address postwar conditions that might or might not occur." One British official, reflecting in 2004 on the lack of preparation for postwar operations, wrote in a memorandum that "it is inevitable that people dealing both with planning for a war and planning for the post-war will give priority to the former."[201] However, there were high stakes associated with the postwar stage of the Iraq intervention, and it seemed clear prior to the

117

invasion that U.S. forces would overpower the Iraqi military. The American power advantage certainly correlated with long time horizons, but not with an investment of resources into postconflict tasks commensurate with the challenges that lay ahead.

The possibility of urban warfare in Baghdad weighed on the minds of Bush and his advisers, and the administration also believed that Iraq might use chemical and biological weapons against civilians and coalition forces. Nevertheless, the military imbalance between coalition and Iraqi forces goes against the argument that opportunity costs explain why Phase IV operations received short shrift. When U.S. forces drove Hussein's troops from Kuwait in 1991, America's share of world military power was about eleven times greater than that of Iraq. By 2001, this disparity had doubled.[202] What is more, Iraqi commanders were unable to coordinate or effectively maneuver their units during the Gulf War, nor could they prepare proper defensive positions or implement modern combined-arms techniques.[203] While a WMD attack could be devastating to civilians, concerns in the Department of Defense focused less on how WMD would affect the performance of U.S. combatants and more about the proper response for the United States to take if unconventional weapons were used.[204]

Once again, civilian and military officials correctly believed that the first major offensive would conclude quickly and casualties would be light. Franks said Iraqi troops might "aggregate but probably not fight."[205] British officials made similar evaluations of their invasion in the south of the country. The UK Joint Intelligence Committee calculated that forces near Basra were "a relatively weak first line of conventional defense. They face rapid defeat. There is little evidence so far that the Iraqis are preparing for a hard-fought defense of Basra and other urban centers." General Dannatt observed that the United States "had significantly written down and destroyed the Iraqi capability in the first Gulf War so rolling it over a second time was probably not going to be that difficult."[206] Even though such beliefs were prevalent in early in the war planning, top U.S. officials continued to devote virtually all resources to refining the invasion plan. In light of the technological, numerical, and qualitative imbalances between U.S. and Iraqi forces, along with expressed confidence by the principal military and civilian actors, an opportunity costs framework cannot adequately explain the gross disparity in attention given to the different stages of the intervention. What is more, an opportunity costs framework cannot explain the disparate assessments of Phase IV made by the U.S. and UK governments given that both countries made the same basic evaluation of their strength relative to Iraq.

THE FOG OF WAR AND PHASE IV

As this and other studies have shown, little caution was apparent among top officials in the Bush administration when they considered postwar Iraq.

Perhaps this was because no source foresaw the possibility of an insurgency, as Feith claims, and thus there was no significant counterpoint to the information being provided by Iraqi exiles such as Chalabi.[207] American officials were not alone in claiming available intelligence did not prepare them for what awaited after Hussein fell. Pattison echoed the testimony of many UK officials when he said his government believed Iraq had "a reasonably well functioning state bureaucracy," and did not think anyone grasped the degree to which there would be a breakdown of law and order in Baghdad soon after the invasion.[208] Even if many of the difficulties in Iraq were foreseen by various people and organizations, high-ranking government officials might have been unaware of such opinions or distrusted them.[209] To the contrary, however, it appears officials ignored or rejected the sizable amount of trustworthy information indicating that Phase IV would be as challenging, if not more so, than the initial invasion.

There were numerous warnings from credible organizations that reconstruction and stability operations in Iraq would be difficult and costly. The Central Intelligence Agency and Defense Intelligence Agency began producing such assessments in the spring and summer of 2002. The National Defense University, Army War College, RAND Corporation, National Intelligence Council, and United States Institute of Peace all produced reports asserting that the United States would face many challenges in Iraq and need to maintain a large number of troops there for an extended period of time if it wished to maintain order.[210] These reports noted the potential for ethnic and sectarian strife in Iraq, and that the Iraqi economy might be severely battered after years of sanctions, mismanagement, and war. Contrary to assertions that an insurgency was unforeseen, one of two Intelligence Community Assessments issued in January 2003 stated that deposed Ba'athists "could forge an alliance with existing terrorist organizations or act independently to wage guerilla warfare against [Iraq's] new government or coalition forces."[211] The reports, which were disseminated to senior officials in the Bush administration, also predicted there was a "significant chance" of violent conflict between Iraqi ethnic and sectarian groups, and that Iran and Syria would hamper U.S. efforts to maintain security.[212] It appears, then, that intelligence on combat operations was only somewhat better than that on noncombat tasks postconflict. While combat estimates accurately reflected U.S. military dominance relative to Iraq, the "Fortress Baghdad" scenario, use of WMD against civilians, and other short-term predictions for the invasion did not come to pass.

Foreign policy principals may have believed these sources were opposed to war and thus prone to inflate estimates of intervention costs. However, outside backers of the invasion also opined that postwar operations could be long and costly. The warnings of the British government have already been covered in some detail. Jalal Talabani, leader of the Patriotic Union of Kurdistan, informed Rumsfeld and Cheney that they should expect looting and other civil disturbances in Baghdad once Hussein fell, while Mukhlis told them the city might become "Mogadishu" if the United States botched Phase IV.[213] Saudi crown prince Abdullah wrote to Bush that, while he supported efforts to remove Hussein, a politically destabilized Iraq could harm American and Saudi interests.[214] Brookings fellow Michael O'Hanlon, a proponent of military action targeting Iraq, warned it could take more than five years and a large portion of the U.S. military to stabilize the country. He was aghast at Rumsfeld's seeming indifference and outright hostility toward possible assistance from other countries in Phase IV; in response to the secretary's remarks discounting the importance of countries in "old Europe," O'Hanlon stated "if Rumsfeld had thought through how much we will need these allies for the occupation of Iraq, I presume he would not have made such a stupid comment."[215] Nevertheless, postwar security and stabilization continued to receive scant attention within the uppermost levels of the administration.

ORGANIZATIONAL THEORY AND THE CIVIL–MILITARY RIFT

If the doctrine, training, and incentive structure within military organizations lead them to neglect, misunderstand, or denigrate activities typical during postconflict operations, officers will not be able or willing to effectively advise civilian leaders on likely postwar costs, nor will they devote resources to planning for postconflict operations. The U.S. Army was not without doctrine or experience regarding stability and reconstruction operations prior to Iraq. Clinton-era interventions in Somalia, Bosnia, and Kosovo created a base of knowledge from which officers could draw, though the impact of such operations on doctrine is debatable.[216] In August 2003, Rumsfeld was briefed that the military's ability to adapt and demonstrate initiative during "post major combat operations" in Iraq exceeded expectations, while civil affairs activities, training, experience, and doctrine "demonstrated considerable effectiveness."[217]

The claim that the U.S. military resisted focusing on postconflict operations due to lack of interest, rather than lack of ability, is more consistent with the evidence. Retired general Ron Adams, Garner's deputy, said he was impressed with Eclipse II when compared to civilian concepts for Phase IV he had seen, but his briefing from a CENTCOM officer also made it clear that the military was not investing the necessary resources to implement the plans in place.[218] According to Cross, CENTCOM officers considered themselves "a war fighting team and as far as they were concerned, [Phase IV] was not their major business," comments echoed by Boyce. Likewise, General Mike Jackson, who immediately followed Boyce as British chief of the general staff, testified "anybody who knows the American Army will know that what they set out to do in Iraq was absolutely playing to their strengths and their doctrine of that time: mass maneuver," and that they were less concerned with the war's aftermath than their British counterparts.[219] Official military historians noted that "nowhere in CENTCOM or [land forces command] had there been a plan for Phase IV that was like the plan for Phase III, let alone all the preparations that accompanied it," while officers reported that their impression was one of "broad acquiescence by high ranking officers" to the lack of postconflict planning.[220]

Organizational preferences might account for poor assessment of postinvasion Iraq in conjunction with other factors. For example, if officials in Washington deferred to the military, officers would have been free to follow their own preferences. This was not the case, however, as civilians were politically dominant and freely interjected their views into military planning.[221] Though the military's inclination was to avoid nation-building duties, it appears they would have adopted the mission more readily if there had been a clear signal from civilians that Phase IV was a priority and responsibility for planning would fall into soldiers' hands. Planners at CENTCOM only disregarded Phase IV preparations as long as they thought the bulk of the responsibility lay with other agencies in the U.S. government; there was considerable confusion over what agencies would be responsible for postwar Iraq. By late August 2002, however, the Joint Staff began urging CENTCOM to focus more on postwar operations. Having already been charged with designing war plans for Afghanistan and Iraq in a very short time frame, it is understandable that strained officers would neglect postwar scenarios as long as it seemed they were also being considered elsewhere. By January 2003 certain elements of the armed forces and U.S. government were cognizant of the challenges Phase IV would pose, but they lacked the time necessary for rigorous planning and interagency collaboration.[222] Shinseki's treatment further removed officers' incentive to consider postconflict operations until ordered to do so.[223]

Rumsfeld's rebuke of Shinseki is consistent with an argument put forth by Risa Brooks, who holds that poor civil–military relations contributed to inadequate planning for Phase IV operations. Brooks posits that animosities between Rumsfeld and the uniformed military led to meager "strategic coordination," synonymous with the production and evaluation of contingency plans dealing with multiple potential scenarios.[224] There is merit to this argument. There had been significant tension between the defense secretary and generals on the JCS over plans to transform the military. Such tension could explain why senior officials ignored criticism of their assumptions. However, unlike the civil–military explanation, CLT can also account for why there *was* significant strategic coordination between Rumsfeld and the military regarding the combat phase of the war plan, as well as a sudden receptivity to constructive criticism of Phase IV plans once the war commenced. As Brooks notes, the civilian leadership's lack of engagement with the details of postwar plans when compared with major combat operations gave the military little incentive to prioritize Phase IV.[225] Still, the origins of this indifference are exogenous to Brooks's theory. By highlighting tendencies to privilege desirability over feasibility considerations, as well as discount information inconsistent with prior beliefs, CLT helps to explain the lack of civilian interest she cites.

Conclusion

Those ultimately responsible for the invasion of Iraq made many errors in judgment, errors which were reflected in the planning process for Phase IV. A focus on humanitarian issues, coupled with optimistic assumptions about political conditions in Iraq and the necessary length of military occupation, left soldiers in theater unable to perform key tasks once the initial combat phase was complete. Instead of maintaining the flow of forces into the theater of operations to enhance coalition and civilian security, principals in the United States stopped troop deployments and undermined a military command whose postwar structure and responsibilities were already unclear.

Existing theoretical frameworks cannot explain the inattention to detail or consequences exhibited by high-ranking officials in the Bush administration when they considered postwar Iraq. An opportunity costs perspective would not predict a state which vastly outmatched its opponent in military capabilities to focus on "easy" phases of an intervention—those requiring brute force—over the "hard" phase requiring the political transformation of an entire society, unless state leaders possessed a wealth of reliable information that the latter phase would not be difficult. Before the war, however, there was at least as much information coming from credible individuals and institutions to the contrary. Officials had an incentive to get in and out of Iraq as quickly as possible but not a reason to think that a quick exit would be probable.

Organizational theory is also an insufficient explanation for strategic assessment prior to the war. Though noncombat operations were hardly the primary focus of the U.S. military before the invasion of Iraq, the U.S. Army did possess doctrine for engaging in such operations, as well as senior personnel who had performed and commanded "unconventional" activities overseas. Though they were reluctant to take responsibility for postwar Iraq, planners in CENTCOM and CFLCC took the obligation to prepare for Phase IV seriously once it was clear the duty was going to fall to them. Rumsfeld and top civilians in the Defense Department were the dominant actors shaping Phase IV, and resisted or actively discouraged advice from the military as far as postwar operations were concerned.

The overconfidence of principal foreign policy actors that led to the mismanagement of postwar Iraq was produced by the mechanisms predicted by CLT. Individuals who sought transformative goals correspondingly had long time horizons, and displayed different attitudes than those focused on the short term. As these officials were in the majority at the top of the Bush administration, Washington became more concerned with the rewards of success than the probability of success in Iraq. General beliefs about nation building rather than specific, contextual information about Iraq informed officials' assessments. By January 2003 certain elements of the armed forces and U.S. government were cognizant of the challenges Phase IV would pose, but they lacked the time and resources necessary for rigorous planning and interagency collaboration.[226] Principals had not exhibited similar optimism nor inattention to detail in the fifteen to sixteen months of preparation for combat operations and the short-term humanitarian crises with which they believed could arise during the invasion.

An Occupation That Never Was

Korea, 1950–1951

When U.S. officials decided to send American ground forces to defend the Republic of Korea (ROK) against invading North Korean forces in June 1950, their objective was to preserve Syngman Rhee's regime in the southern half of the peninsula. More broadly, they saw the military intervention as necessary to counter what they perceived as a Soviet challenge to the containment of communism in Asia. By October, the Truman administration had changed its objective so that the unification of North and South Korea became its ultimate aim. The change in war aims also entailed planning for an occupation of territory held by the Democratic People's Republic of Korea (DPRK). American policymakers anticipated postwar operations would be conducted under United Nations (UN) auspices with a U.S. officer as theater commander, roughly the same command structure under which combat operations had taken place. However, neither the political unification of Korea nor the occupation of the North were to be. The U.S. decision to cross the 38th parallel line into DPRK territory was followed by a counterintervention by Chinese Communist Forces (CCF) that reversed much of the progress the UN coalition had made in 1950. The limited "police action" became a three-year conflict in which tens of thousands of armed combatants and millions of civilians were killed.[1] By the time major armed hostilities ended in 1953 the political border between the ROK and Kim Il Sung's DPRK lay approximately where it had been three years earlier.

Compared to policymakers' planning for occupations of Germany and Iraq, officials during the Korean War paid considerably less attention to their high-level political objectives and more to contextual information when assessing and planning for noncombat operations. In other words, they were in the main focused on the feasibility of occupying the North, and thus how the occupation would be carried out, more than the desirability of the ends to be accomplished by that mission. Furthermore, both the Roosevelt and

Bush administrations exhibited undue optimism about the risks and costs associated with noncombat operations they presumed would occur postconflict; this bias was not present in the Truman administration to nearly the same degree.

These findings may seem incongruous with the first hypothesis derived from construal level theory (CLT): that noncombat operations projected to occur postconflict will be assessed abstractly, promoting overconfidence about their costs and risks. However, the first hypothesis is contingent on leaders having long time horizons. The nature of President Harry S. Truman's political objectives, along with the context in which the war was fought, led the president and most of his key advisers to adopt much shorter time horizons than leaders considering occupations of Germany and Iraq. Officials in the United States and Seoul were surprised by North Korea's invasion, and compared to the previously studied cases had a considerably shorter period of time in which to prepare for combat and noncombat operations in the anticipated posthostilities period. Despite the shift in political objectives in the first months of the Korean War, most U.S. officials were focused on restoring the status quo ante rather than achieving a more transformative set of ends. The majority of American policymakers believed that crossing the 38th parallel was necessary to preserve the security of the allied South Korean regime, since it would deny communist forces a safe haven from which to reattack the ROK.

Given that most of the individuals in the Truman administration, including the president, had maintenance goals during the first year of the war, CLT predicts that the overall assessment of noncombat operations in the Korean War would fit closely with the pattern the Chapter 1 hypothesizes will characterize maintenance campaigns. This is borne out by the evidence: nearsighted policymakers carefully considered whether an occupation of the North was feasible given extant conditions on the peninsula in 1950. However, they were not motivated to think about whether an occupation would secure the ROK from a communist threat in the long run. Only George Kennan and John Foster Dulles seemed concerned that, even if U.S. and ROK forces could feasibly occupy North Korea in 1950, it would be difficult to maintain Korean security indefinitely with hundreds of thousands of CCF soldiers across the border. It was not until China's entrance into the war seemed imminent that others, such as Secretary of State Dean Acheson, came to this conclusion as well. Immediate means also became disconnected from ultimate ends. The subordinate goal of restoring and protecting Rhee's regime in Seoul became as salient as Truman's main priority, which was to check communist aggression in Asia while avoiding a wider war. The Truman administration was mindful of the details of how an occupation would be carried out and attentive to the possibility of China entering the war. However, officials never integrated their thinking on the two subjects; each possibility was considered separately from the other. This compartmentalization hindered the execution of noncombat operations in the months after China's entrance into the war.

A minority of important officials during the war saw the removal of the DPRK regime as a first step toward rolling back communism in Asia more generally, a decidedly more transformative and far-sighted interpretation of what the military mission entailed. For some, like State Department official John Allison, the mechanisms posited by CLT effectively account for the nature of strategic assessments of noncombat operations. Alternatively, the study of Korea shows that the dynamics predicted by CLT might be overwhelmed by individual characteristics. Most notably, commanding general Douglas MacArthur's assessments and behavior are more readily attributable to his personal characteristics than mechanisms posited by CLT.

Intervention and Evolving Objectives, June–December 1950

Korea, which had been occupied by Imperial Japan during World War II, was divided along the 38th parallel line in 1945. The United States proposed that the parallel demarcate the Soviet and American zones of occupation on the peninsula and did not intend for it to become a permanent political boundary. However, after the USSR refused to allow the UN into North Korea to supervise elections for a national government, the ROK became the UN-recognized government in the South while Kim's DPRK became the de facto authority in the North. Unlike Germany, where thousands of U.S. and Soviet military personnel remained for decades after the war, both superpowers quickly drew down from Korea. Only a few hundred American personnel constituting the Korean Military Advisory Group (KMAG) remained in the South by 1949.

With only a handful of soldiers on the peninsula, the United States was not in a position to fend off the large-scale invasion by the North Korean People's Army (KPA) that began on June 24 (local time), 1950. U.S. intelligence indicated a concentration of KPA forces that month, but it was not thought that the North would invade.[2] Secretary of Defense Louis Johnson admitted that his department had no plan for the contingency of a DPRK invasion.[3] The consensus in Washington was that the attack had been orchestrated by the Soviets to test U.S. containment. According to the U.S. embassy in Moscow, the invasion constituted a "clear-cut Soviet challenge" and a "direct threat [to] our leadership of [the] free world." The State Department's intelligence estimate of June 25 held that the invasion was meant to try U.S. resolve "on ground militarily most favorable to the Soviet Union."[4] On June 27 Acheson cabled the embassy in London that North Korea's action "makes amply clear centrally directed [i.e., Soviet] Communist imperialism" had substituted war for subversion in its efforts to conquer independent states.[5]

U.S. officials were quick to initiate UN resolutions condemning North Korean aggression, measures that were facilitated by the Soviet Union's absence from the Security Council. Security Council Resolution 82, passed on June 25, called for an immediate cessation of hostilities and for the KPA to be withdrawn back above the 38th parallel. With no cessation of the attack forthcoming, the council passed another resolution on the 27th recommending UN members provide assistance to the ROK in order to repel the invading forces.[6] Two days later, the Joint Chiefs of Staff (JCS) authorized MacArthur to carry out air strikes against targets north of the 38th parallel. The next day MacArthur requested that he be allowed to use U.S. troops to slow the KPA offensive, saying ROK forces could not handle the task alone. After discussing MacArthur's recommendation with the secretaries of defense and state, the various branches of the armed services, and the JCS, Truman authorized the deployment of American ground combat units from Japan. The U.S. objective would be to halt the North Korean offensive and force the invaders back, reestablishing the 38th parallel as the border between the DPRK and ROK.

Security Council Resolution 84, passed on July 7, created a unified UN command (UNC), to which Truman named MacArthur as commander. The command was under UN auspices, but not subject to the authority of the Security Council or General Assembly. Primary responsibility for the sixteen-member coalition fighting with the ROK was delegated to the United States, giving Washington substantial autonomy to plan and conduct wartime operations. This was true of noncombat operations as well. The next Security Council resolution, passed July 31, requested the UNC to determine "requirements for the relief and support of the civilian population of Korea, and for establishing in the field the procedures for providing such relief and support."[7]

The arrival of U.S. forces did little to hinder the KPA advance in the month of July. Nevertheless, on the 17th Truman ordered a review of whether or not UN forces should respect the 38th parallel.[8] After a four-day consultation with the British government near the end of the month, Ambassador-at-Large Philip C. Jessup and General Omar Bradley recommended the commencement of studies dealing with issues of unification and the long-term maintenance of UN forces in Korea. Subsequently, a draft memorandum by the Defense Department on July 31 recommended that Truman declare "at an appropriate time" that the UN should seek "a united, free, and independent Korea" and stated that this would require an occupation of both the North and South following the defeat of the KPA. It advised that a new multinational body under UN auspices be established to see to the "long-term reconstruction and security" of Korea and that U.S. military personnel would have to remain until an indigenous security force became operationally effective.[9] This proposed body would become the UN Commission for the Unification and Rehabilitation of Korea (UNCURK), created via a General Assembly resolution on October 7 and composed of representatives from Australia, Chile, Netherlands, Pakistan, Philippines, Thailand, and Turkey.[10]

The KPA offensive had begun to reach a point of exhaustion by the first week of September. American forces in the form of the 8th Army, allied with soldiers from the ROK and United Kingdom, formed a defensive perimeter around Pusan. Meanwhile, MacArthur and his staff had been planning an amphibious landing in Korea since early July. Operation Chromite called for units to land at the western port of Inchon, thus enveloping the overstretched KPA. The Navy and Marine Corps raised serious objections to the choice of Inchon as a landing site, pointing to the numerous natural obstacles which would have to be navigated to get ashore. MacArthur, confident that these very obstacles would provide his forces with the element of surprise, was able to convince the JCS to authorize the plan.[11] Chromite commenced September 15, and was a success. The landing at Inchon overlapped with the 8th Army's breakout from the Pusan perimeter. Thousands of KPA soldiers were either killed or captured as they retreated northward to avoid the closing pincers formed by MacArthur's forces. The allied armies under the UN were able to reinstall the ROK government in Seoul on September 29.

Concurrent with the Inchon landing, the Speaker of the Korean Assembly, the foreign minister, the ambassador to the United States, the acting prime minister, and President Rhee all issued statements calling for unification of Korea through military action north of 38th.[12] Further U.S. policy had emerged on this subject. National Security Council Document 81/1 (NSC 81/1), approved by Truman on September 7, stated that the United States and other UN forces could cross into DPRK territory if no overt military action by the Soviets or Chinese had been taken. Having ROK forces spearhead the UN offensive would help keep the Korean conflict localized. Due to concerns about America's widespread security commitments, the United States was not to allow itself to become engaged in a general war with China. In the end NSC 81/1 hedged by stating that a firm conclusion on crossing the 38th could not be drawn given uncertainty regarding Soviet and Chinese intentions. Still, it recommended that "UN forces should be developed and plans should be perfected with a view to the possible occupation of North Korea."[13]

Two days prior to the return of the South Korean government to Seoul, Truman and the JCS formally approved an alteration of U.S. objectives. The new U.S. policy was "the destruction of the North Korean armed forces" throughout the peninsula and MacArthur was authorized to conduct ground operations in North Korean territory. In line with evolving U.S. policy, the October 7 resolution establishing UNCURK also recommended that "all constituent acts be taken, including the holding of elections, under the auspices of the United Nations, for the establishment of a unified, independent, and democratic government in the sovereign State of Korea."[14] These new war aims were accompanied by directives that suggest that civilian leaders in Washington were paying less than careful attention to how their commander might implement the new policy. MacArthur was told that if the CCF intervened he was to "continue [military] action as long as action by your forces offers a reasonable chance of successful resistance."[15] This specific directive gave MacArthur considerable room to exercise his discretion. On September 29 George Marshall, who had replaced Johnson as secretary of defense, would reinforce the UNC's autonomy by cabling MacArthur that he should "feel unhampered tactically and strategically to proceed north of the 38th parallel." Marshall meant to communicate that Washington did not want to halt the progress of MacArthur's offensive nor put the UN General Assembly into a position in which it had to vote on whether or not to invade North Korea.[16] Nevertheless, it is not difficult to see how the general could have interpreted, or willfully misinterpreted, this message as adding to his authority.

UNC's communications to Washington were unperturbed on November 4, when it reported that a major intervention by China was unlikely.[17] However, two days later MacArthur ordered heavy air strikes to take out bridges over the Yalu River bordering Manchuria, reporting that "men and material in large force" were crossing the river's bridges. The JCS authorized bombing on the Korean side of the Yalu and stressed the importance of keeping the war localized.[18] In a personal letter Acheson wrote that in late October and early November "we in State were almost wild" because the Pentagon could not explain the rationale behind MacArthur's decisions. State's Policy Planning Staff (PPS) had grown so concerned it recommended that UN forces pull back to the 38th, declare an end to major military operations, and acknowledge that a portion of North Korea would remain under communist control.[19] On November 8, the JCS suggested MacArthur reexamine his mission's objectives and consolidate his gains rather than continue to pursue the KPA.[20] However, the U.S. 8th Army still proceeded northward without major contact with the CCF for the next two weeks.

New reports of heavy fighting began coming in from the front on November 27. A massive counteroffensive by hundreds of thousands of Chinese troops pushed the United States and its allies backward. The UN coalition was forced back below the 38th parallel, and communist forces recaptured Seoul in January 1951. Not only was this turn of events calamitous for UN forces from a combat perspective, it also threw noncombat plans for Korea into chaos. The October 7 General Assembly resolution had requested the Economic and Social Council (ECOSOC) to "develop plans for relief and rehabilitation on the termination of hostilities," and the United States had since been directing efforts to establish a UN Korean Reconstruction Agency (UNKRA) as "a special authority with broad powers to plan and supervise rehabilitation and relief" in coordination with UNCURK. The agency was necessary because Acheson and others in Washington envisioned UNCURK as primarily an advisory body, not an "operating organization." UNKRA had been established under the assumption that a final military victory would soon be forthcoming, but the body would now have to operate under an entirely different set of conditions than those intended by policymakers.[21] Though Seoul would be recaptured soon after China's entrance in the war and South Korea's independence preserved, the Truman administration's objective of unifying the peninsula was dropped. General MacArthur vigorously disagreed with this policy and his differences with Washington led to his dismissal in April.

CLT

As will be shown, unrealistic optimism about noncombat operations was not prevalent among Truman administration officials even though such actions were more temporally distant than large-scale combat operations. Why was this so? First, U.S. officials had no more than five months between the North Korean invasion and the entrance of the CCF into the conflict in which to consider the war's aftermath. High-level objectives also changed during the war, meaning the United States' more expansive aims were under consideration for less time than the five-month figure indicates. Second, in addition to the relatively short amount of time they had to prepare for the fighting's anticipated aftermath, many key officials' political objectives led them to have short time horizons. Individuals such as Truman, Acheson, Kennan, and members of the JCS consistently placed little value on Korea or its future prior to the war. Truman and Acheson viewed Europe as the primary front in the Cold War, and did not believe the United States was in a position to effect significant political change in Asia.[22] Ambassador to the ROK John Muccio reported after the war that he was sure the South Korean leadership was "astounded that we came in and that we came in time. . . . They must have known of our eagerness to get out of Korea that had been decided in [1947]."[23] Furthermore, such officials viewed the offensive in North Korea as a way of maintaining the U.S. position in Asia rather than enhancing it. In short, these individuals had not been in the mind-set to conceive of broad, long-term changes to be wrought in Korea or the region generally before the war's outset. This indicates Truman and like-minded individuals were primed to think in more concrete rather than abstract terms. Once people are primed to think abstractly or concretely, they tend to apply that level of construal to the events and actions they attend to.

TIME HORIZONS

Aside from President Truman, the main actors shaping U.S. postwar policy were located in the State and Defense Departments: Acheson; Acheson's special assistant, Dulles; officials in State's PPS and Northeast Asian Affairs; Secretary Marshall and the JCS; and General MacArthur. These officials are most frequently cited in the secondary literature as being responsible for influencing policy generally during the first year of the Korean War. Of these officials, only MacArthur and members of the Northeast Asian Affairs Office had long time horizons regarding the war's objectives.

Political Objectives. Though Truman sympathized with those pushing for Korean unification, he primarily viewed the war there in terms of his containment strategy, or maintenance of the status quo vis-à-vis the USSR. The president believed the United States could not afford to jeopardize the concept of collective security and embolden aggressors by doing nothing, an opinion shared by all the government figures discussed below. At the same time, he did not want to enter into another world war for which the United States was unprepared.[24] Due to his preoccupation with the threat posed by the USSR to Western Europe, the president placed relatively little value on the future of Korea itself. In an unsent letter, Truman reflected that he did not want to be "sucked into a bottomless pit" fighting on the peninsula.[25] Stressing this point in his memoirs, he further criticized the foreign policy of those he characterized as the "Asia-first advocates," referring to Republicans and members of the so-called China Lobby in which MacArthur fit.[26]

Truman readily accepted a reporter's characterization of U.S. involvement in Korea as a "police action" rather than a war. This framing served the president's dual goals of containing what was seen as a Soviet attempt to break containment, while limiting the conflict in such a way to keep it localized to the peninsula.[27] He initially saw an advance north of the 38th parallel as unnecessary to attain the former objective and potentially fatal to the latter. After committing ground forces, Truman asserted that nothing was to be done north of the parallel save what was necessary for the immediate security of civilians and coalition forces in the ROK.[28] Nevertheless, Truman and others in his administration began publicly adopting farther-reaching objectives for Korea early in the war. Before the success of Inchon, the president told the American people that "we believe the Koreans have a right to be free, independent, and united—as they want to be. Under the direction and guidance of the United Nations, we, with others, will do our part to help them enjoy that right."[29] However, there is reason to believe that the president continued to discount the future value of Korea relative to Europe and other areas of importance to U.S. strategy. For instance, General Robert B. Landry, Truman's Air Force aide during the Korean War, recalled that the president had been "very much worried" about the defense of Western Europe in mid-October during the Wake Island Conference with MacArthur and thus "was anxious to find out if he could pull some units out of Korea."[30] While the United States could contribute forces to the initial phase of the occupation, those in Washington would "gladly withdraw" their troops if other countries were able to pick up the slack and "would be delighted" if Asian countries were recruited while U.S. forces took positions south of the 38th.[31]

Administration member Richard Neustadt also argues that the president's thinking and actions in July and August of 1950 revealed that Korean unification was one of Truman's lesser objectives.[32] As discussed below, Truman's public declarations on the importance of Korean unification and political transformation were likely a by-product of concerns revolving around the continued threat North Korea could pose to the ROK from above the 38th parallel.

The Pentagon and JCS also placed little value on the future of Korea, as illustrated by internal Defense reports on the country. In 1947 the JCS concluded that the expense of occupying the South was providing "little, if any, lasting benefit to the security of the United States." They repeated this assertion in 1948, telling Truman it was important to avoid becoming "irrevocably involved" in the country's affairs.[33] The decision to remove U.S. occupation forces from Korea was backed by Truman, Acheson, and MacArthur. General Bradley also thought that it would be "unsound" to commit troops to the ROK's defense in the event of a communist attack.[34] Consistent with this line of thought, in July 1950 the JCS objected to maintaining a military presence in Korea in the event of intervention by Soviet combat units. They reasoned such a strategy to be unadvisable given Korea's "slight strategic importance."[35] Defense officials saw Formosa (Taiwan) as a crucial outpost in the Pacific in event of war with the Soviet Union, and Korea as a distraction.[36]

Acheson and his department did have a commitment to Korea before the war insofar as the policy of the United States since World War II had been the unification of the peninsula. State officials believed any precipitous withdrawal from the South would be potentially damaging to U.S. credibility.[37] Acheson's congressional testimony on Korea in 1949, however, was clearly directed at the maintenance of the status quo: "I believe we cannot possibly guarantee the southern Koreans their independence by American military power. However, we can, and should, we believe, give the Koreans economic help so that they can support themselves in their country and give them such military assistance as we are now giving and will have completed in the very near future so they can at least hold their own against the northern Koreans."[38] He also shared the president's preoccupation with Europe. After the Korean War Dean Rusk, assistant secretary of state for East Asian and Pacific affairs 1950–1951, pondered whether what he called Acheson's "strong orientation toward the North Atlantic" had led him to undervalue the importance of Korea. Early on in the conflict Deputy Under Secretary of State H. Freeman Matthews informed other State officials that Acheson thought too much attention was being given to Korea and not enough on the war's effects on international affairs generally.[39] The secretary of state told his embassy in Moscow that the U.S. intervention was necessary to deter the Kremlin from using "satellites or stooges" to commit future acts of aggression in areas of presumably greater import than Korea, a message he repeated in formal communications with Britain's foreign secretary Ernest Bevin in July.[40] Several historians hold that Acheson viewed the Korean War as a way to consolidate the alliance with Western Europe more than an avenue toward Asian security because the secretary was wedded to a Europe-first approach.[41]

The heads of the PPS discounted Korea's future to a greater extent than Acheson. Kennan, who remained a counselor in the PPS after being replaced by Paul Nitze as director in January 1950, viewed Korea as a "non-strategic" and unimportant area.[42] After Truman directed his advisers to determine a proper course of action once the 38th was reached, the PPS drafted a document stating that the "primary purpose" of the intervention was to force the KPA to withdraw beyond the parallel. This was differentiated from the "long-term effort to bring about [Korean] unity and independence." While acknowledging the latter policy, the document concluded that military operations in North Korea would "greatly" increase the chance of a conflict with the Soviet Union or China and recommended against such action.[43] Potential gains in the more distant future were not perceived to be worth the more immediate risks that would be necessary for their attainment.

The State Department was by no means composed entirely of individuals dedicated to preserving the status quo in Korea. John Allison of Northeast Asian Affairs and Rusk were both early proponents of rollback. Allison viewed an invasion of North Korea as necessary for securing the whole peninsula and desirable because of the long-term benefits it could yield in the global fight against communism. As early as July 1, 1950, before Truman had called for a review of U.S. policy on the 38th, he informed Rusk that the United States should "continue right on up to the Manchurian and Siberian border and . . . call for a UN-supervised election for all Korea."[44] Allison strongly objected to Nitze when the PPS recommended the military halt at the parallel. Though he recognized crossing the 38th could mean "war on a global scale," Allison asked, "when all legal and moral right is on our side why should we hesitate?"[45] For him, the near-term risks were justified by the long-term objectives he favored. Allison was somewhat placated once the PPS modified its earlier position by recommending that decisions on the 38th should be deferred, though the office's position still did not "go as far" as he would like.[46]

Lastly, the long time horizons of General MacArthur, who has been described as a "rabid Asia-firster," can be demonstrated clearly in regard to Asia and especially China.[47] Whereas Truman, Acheson, and others valued the maintenance of the status quo in Korea as a way to secure Europe, MacArthur saw the transformation of Korea as a stepping-stone to purging the communist regime in Beijing and spreading U.S. influence in Asia. Following a meeting with the general early in the conflict, W. Averell Harriman reported that MacArthur believed Korea could become a "strong influence in stabilizing the non-communist movement in the East."[48] Prior to the Inchon landing, MacArthur informed J. Lawton Collins and Admiral Forrest Sherman of the JCS that the operation would capture the hearts and minds across Asia, and told General Matthew Ridgway that a fight with the Chinese would provide the opportunity to turn back communism on that continent.[49] In his memoirs MacArthur wrote that Washington did not comprehend the "long-range" significance of the Korean War, and believed he could not only have defended Korea but inflicted such damage on China that Asia would not have known war "for generations to come."[50] After he was dismissed as commander of U.S. forces in Korea, he mistakenly testified to Congress that his "original mission . . . was to clear *all* Korea" of communist influence, a misperception which was telling in light of his long-term policy goals.[51] Scholars have argued that MacArthur deliberately sought to expand the war into China, an assessment which Kennan, Nitze, and Acheson adopted in light of the general's actions and personal policy goals.[52]

Commitment Problems. Despite Truman's political objectives, he also instructed U.S. officials to begin studying the question of whether the United States should cross the 38th parallel very soon after American troops were deployed. These instructions represent an obvious reason to doubt the validity of any assertion that Truman and other officials had short time horizons in the early months of the Korean War. Truman may have been motivated by concerns about how to maintain the ROK's independence well into the future, a long-term problem which perhaps drove early policy debates. Specifically, stopping at the 38th parallel could allow the KPA a safe haven to carry out future attacks.

Acheson, sorting through his own thoughts on the war in July, wrote "if we succeed in reoccupying the country, the question of garrisoning it and supporting it arises. This is expensive, requires troops needed elsewhere and presents a hard program to continue domestically. But I do not see how to avoid it."[53] The future costs of defending the ROK might be decreased, however, if UN forces occupied territory further north on the peninsula. Paul Nitze, head of the PPS, recalled after the war that "it was dangerous just to stop at the 38th parallel. . . . That would then mean that the North Koreans could regroup and that you'd be pinned down there in South Korea with this enormous percentage of your military forces, for a long period of time." Nitze claimed he and others contemplated how a settlement might satisfy communist demands while preserving the ROK.[54] However, in light of the deep mistrust which existed between Washington and communist governments, it seems doubtful either side would have seen the commitments of the other as credible. Likewise, Defense and State officials held that the only reason against moving across the 38th was a Soviet or Chinese countermove.[55] It has also been argued that there was a general consensus among American policymakers that the Soviet Union wished to avoid war with the United States, which encouraged officials to focus more on future commitment problems than contemporary signals about Moscow's intentions toward Korea.[56]

From these observations it could be inferred that policymakers were privileging long-term costs in their war plans.

However, there are more reasons to doubt American policymakers had adopted long time horizons in regards to Korea. For one thing, any long-term problems in officials' minds were overshadowed by worries about the more immediate costs a potential Soviet or Chinese counterintervention could inflict. The contents of NSC 81/1 clearly show that such concerns weighed heavily in Washington, heavily enough that MacArthur's incursion across the parallel was not authorized until late September. One point emerging from NSC deliberations the first week of September was that "final decisions cannot be made at this time concerning the future course of action in Korea, since the course of action which will best advance the national interest of the United States must be determined in the light of: the action of the Soviet Union and the Chinese Communists, consultation and agreement with friendly members of the United Nations, and appraisal of the risk of general war."[57]

Even if long-term security concerns mattered in the minds of policymakers, they were matched and likely outweighed by developments in September and October. The consensus in Washington was that a Soviet or Chinese entry into the war was more likely before U.S. forces had the chance to enter North Korea.[58] As a result, a possible counterintervention by one of these two powers was officials' foremost concern as MacArthur's offensive neared the 38th parallel. Top officials continued to be attentive to new information rather than being primarily interested in future commitment problems. On September 3, Indian ambassador K. M. Panikkar relayed information that China would be compelled to intervene if American soldiers crossed the 38th parallel. This possibility set off a flurry of correspondence between State Department officials in the United States and abroad.[59] Concerns about the U.S. offensive clearly weighed heavily on top policymakers in October: the day the 8th Army began moving across the parallel, the JCS sent MacArthur an "amplification" of his directive to obtain authorization from Washington before attacking objectives in China in the event of the entrance of the CCF.[60]

By October 12, the Central Intelligence Agency (CIA) asserted the Chinese were unlikely to become significantly involved in the fighting in part because "from a military standpoint the most favorable time for intervention in Korea has passed." This echoed NSC 81/1, which stated that in the "unlikely contingency" that outside communist powers did not attempt to occupy North Korea prior to UN forces reaching the 38th parallel, "it would seem probable that the Soviet Union had decided to follow a hands-off policy, even at the expense of the loss of control of Northern Korea."[61] However, on October 31 Acheson received a report from the consul general in Hong Kong that Moscow might be pushing for China to intervene. The report stated that Vyacheslav Molotov and other Soviet leaders had met in August and decided to support Chinese participation in the war. If the Inchon landing had not dispelled such notions, this would mean that China's military would have been preparing to attack the advancing UN coalition for two months.[62] The following day the director of the Office of Chinese Affairs at State informed Rusk that it was likely that China was considering a major intervention with Soviet approval.[63]

Aside from the salience of contemporaneous signals coming from the USSR and China, U.S. officials' considerations of the costs of holding North Korea were informed only by extant political and military conditions on the peninsula in the autumn of 1950, rather than by hypothetical future threats. Policymakers' views of the feasibility of upcoming noncombat operations were based on the immediate context in which they would take place. Having short time horizons, however, they were not motivated to think about hypothetical threats to Korea in the more distant future. Once they were so motivated they quickly concluded the costs of an occupation to unify the country were prohibitive. As has been made clear, administration intentions were to remove U.S. forces from Korea as soon as possible after victory given the unfavorable balance of power between the North Atlantic Treaty Organization (NATO) and the USSR in Europe. At the same time as the Wake Island Conference, the JCS was considering how to redeploy U.S. forces out of Korea and decided to cease the deployment of foreign troops to join the UN coalition.[64] When it appeared the large-scale involvement of the CCF might be imminent, the chiefs again showed how little value they placed on Korea by stressing that the United States could not leave its forces on the peninsula indefinitely.[65]

In hindsight, it is unclear why it would be any less costly to maintain a noncommunist regime throughout the whole of a peninsula bordering communist China than just preserving the ROK in Seoul. Deterring a future invasion by Chinese or Soviet forces meant U.S. troops would have to remain in Korea to act as a "trip wire" for a prolonged period of time, just as they would have to remain to defend the South if the 38th parallel line remained a de facto boundary. Kennan was unusual in that he was sensitive to the inconsistency between the administration's immediate plans and long-term priorities. He favored no more than the restoration of South Korea because, as he warned Acheson in August, it was beyond U.S. capabilities to keep the North out of the "Soviet orbit."[66]

The secretary of state belatedly came to agree with Kennan's views. Three days before the CCF launched it major offensive in November, Acheson asserted "our objective is not to defeat the Chinese Communists in Korea, since they will always be able to put in a little more than we can."[67] Like other policymakers, Acheson had tried to minimize the short-term probability of a Soviet or Chinese counterintervention. However, policymakers did not place much value on the future of Korea, and thus did not attend to the implications of a counterintervention for their occupation plans until China's full entrance into the war seemed a strong possibility. Immediate conditions were dictating assessments of the feasibility of an occupation, and it was not until late November that circumstances made such an operation appear unworkable. Even when an occupation of the North had appeared feasible, the endeavor was not weighed against the administration's ultimate goals. Avoidance of general war had been one of the Truman administration's primary objectives on entering the Korean conflict. However, high-level strategic objectives had become less salient relative to the immediate feasibility of offensive military operations in the early months of the Korean War. Many months after the entrance of the CCF, Acheson surmised the United States had a dilemma in which "the better we do in Korea the closer we get to World War III."[68] He recorded in his memoirs that the decision to unify Korea interfered with the primary objective of limiting the intensity and geographical scope of the war. He continued that it "was not thought through and masked . . . the difficulties and dangers against which Kennan had warned."[69]

There was variation in how U.S. policymakers justified crossing the 38th parallel, variation that reflects the different values officials attached to what the UN offensive could achieve in Asia in the long term. The vast majority of the Truman administration, including Acheson, the generals on the JCS, and the reluctant officials on the PPS, accepted crossing the 38th if it was necessary to preserve an independent ROK. For these individuals, restoring the recent status quo was key, and the unification of Korea a by-product of securing Rhee's regime in the South. An alternative perspective existed in the State Department's Northeast Asian Affairs Office. In light of their political objectives, officials there justified movement across the 38th as a way to roll back communism in Asia more generally—they sought to dramatically revise the former status quo.

Along with John Emmerson, Allison completed a proposal on August 21, a draft of which had been written earlier in the month, that articulated a rationale for crossing the parallel beyond maintaining extant U.S. interests. Instead, the Korean War was presented as an opportunity to roll back the Soviet sphere of influence in Asia. According to the memorandum, operations in Korea could "set the stage for the non-Communist penetration [sic] into an area under Soviet control," thus disturbing the USSR's political, economic, and military aims in East Asia. Korean unification, the memo continued, would carry with it "incalculable" benefits in Asia by shoring up the security of Japan and catalyzing a reorientation of China and unaligned countries toward the United States.[70] Allison and Emmerson's memo lifted much of the language from a draft issued by members of the Defense Department at the end of July, a paper that reflected the hard-line position of the soon-to-be dismissed Secretary Johnson and perhaps the importance Defense placed on Formosa.[71] Consistent with Allison's political objectives, his rationale for expanding the war into North Korea reflected a much more distal focus than other officials in the administration.

John Foster Dulles did not neatly align with any of the individuals or groups discussed so far. Unlike Truman and Acheson, he was critical of the idea that the United States should privilege the security of Europe over Asia, a position that was perhaps influenced by his intense involvement in UN negotiations over Korea in the 1940s. He was also an early proponent of roll-back or "liberation" rather than containment, a stance made plain in his 1950 book *War or Peace*.[72] Like Allison, another advocate of rollback, Dulles disagreed with the substance of the PPS's cautious recommendations about crossing the 38th parallel. Unlike Allison, however, Dulles saw a wider offensive as militarily necessary to maintain the administration's initial short-term goal of preserving peace and stability in Korea, maintaining Rhee's regime, and demonstrating American resolve to the Soviets. His internal communications with others in government did not focus on rollback or long-term benefits that could be garnered from defeating the communists in the North.[73] On the whole, then, his position was most representative of Truman and others who sought to restore the status quo ante in Korea. It will be shown that such differences within the administration further explain variation in officials' attention to concrete, contextual information when planning for the occupation of the DPRK.

ABSTRACT VS. CONCRETE THINKING: THE DEVELOPMENT OF OCCUPATION POLICY

Planning for the occupation of Korea departed from that done in Germany and Iraq in four key respects. First, officials did not presume they could rely on existing infrastructure and ministries in the North once the fighting had ceased. They thought that much of the economic and political assets of the country would have to be reestablished, and acknowledged that the United States and UN would have to shoulder much of the burden. As Gene M. Lyons surmises, the United States sponsored the formation of UNKRA with the assumption that "a unified Korea, striving for independence under the heavy burdens of military destruction, would require large sums of money in economic aid which the United States would be obliged to supply or risk losing Korea after winning the war."[74] Second, policymakers established a clear chain of command between Washington, MacArthur in the UNC, and the UN for the postwar phase. Officials made pains to address the finer details of how to involve other countries in the operations anticipated to come after the DPRK was defeated. Third, any government structures that did remain in the North would be allowed to operate similarly to how they had prior to the war. The United States would not systematically purge competent administrators that might remain as local governing structures were reestablished. Plans placed more weight on the feasibility of occupation governance than the desirability of ideological congruence with administrators in the North. Lastly, and in relation to point three, contemporary political dynamics in Korea rather than future political conditions policymakers wished to achieve drove American assessments and planning. In marked contrast to the Iraq case, U.S. officials did not presume that their Korean political allies during the war would be reliable partners once the fighting had ceased.

What factors might explain these differences between Korea and the other two cases examined? One might be the Truman administration's familiarity with the fragile political status of Korea in the years before the outbreak of the war. U.S. military advisers had been operating in the country since the end of World War II. In early 1947 Truman was told that the economic and political instability on the peninsula as a whole could lead to a civil war.[75] While this knowledge might explain officials' wariness of Rhee, it is difficult to argue that leaders in the U.S. government should have been expected to be less aware of political instability under the rule of Saddam Hussein, or in war-torn 1940s Germany. American policymakers' awareness of the difficulties of occupation may also have been heightened by their postwar difficulties regarding the occupation of Germany. Senator Henry Cabot Lodge Jr. stated in a meeting with policy planners that he did not want to see the United States again criticized for winning the war but losing the peace, indicating that perceptions of postwar Korea were not independent from recent experiences in Europe.[76] Nevertheless, policymakers did not refer to occupation experiences in Germany (or Japan) when considering plans for Korea, and the available evidence shows contextual circumstances on the peninsula informed assessments much more than lessons gleaned from prior endeavors.

Another explanation for how decision makers formulated occupation plans for Korea comes from CLT. It has been shown that the majority of officials had political objectives that reflected short time horizons: political goals focused attention on immediate U.S. security interests and existing conditions in Korea rather than some abstract future transformation. They also had less time to prepare for the war's aftermath than in the previously presented cases. Within the CLT framework, these antecedent conditions led to the prediction that Truman and the majority of his advisers, while seeking to create a new Korean state, would attach greater weight to the feasibility of their postwar actions than the desirability of their higher-level objectives. The historical record shows this to have been the case. Officials with short time horizons evaluated a future occupation of Korea in ways predicted by CLT. Rather than focusing on ends, deducing likely outcomes from abstractions, and succumbing to overconfidence, postwar planners were highly attentive to contextual information about political conditions in the South and North on which they based their plans. Furthermore, policymakers were more receptive to concrete contextual information about means than abstract information about ends.

Expected Costs of Occupation. In his speech upon returning from his Wake Island meeting with MacArthur, Truman briefly mentioned the postwar tasks he anticipated would face the United States and its UN allies in Korea. The president detailed how "thousands upon thousands" of Koreans had been left homeless and faced "serious danger of famine and disease in the coming winter months." Military personnel, he continued, were already in the process of reconstructing transportation infrastructure and public utilities. The U.S. Army and the Economic Cooperation Administration (ECA) would be the primary organizations by which the United States would "do its full part to help build a free, united, and self-supporting Korean Republic."[77]

Truman's words on Korean reconstruction composed a small portion of his long address that day. It would have been understandable if American policymakers had spent relatively little time thinking about noncombat operations in Korea compared to officials planning for Germany and Iraq, but this was not the case. Senior officials in Washington were privy to regular damage reports from the Korean theater, and their plans for postwar noncombat operations were made concurrently as updates arrived. This demonstrated a receptivity to—or communication fluency with—concrete, contextual information emerging from the front, something largely absent from the Roosevelt administration during World War II. Rather than varying widely as in the Iraq case, the estimates of necessary aid produced by senior Washington officials were congruent with those of the ECA and other institutions performing damage surveys in theater. The amounts proposed were consistent with the limited goals the Truman administration had set for its efforts in Korea.

Along with defeating communist forces in Korea militarily, NSC 81/1 asserted that "social and economic reforms will be necessary in order to reduce the Communist menace to manageable proportions."[78] This senior-level recommendation reflected the consensus of the CIA and American embassy in South Korea, which were providing regular reports on the socioeconomic status of the South. Given the damage within the ROK and the intelligence gathered as the UN offensive advanced, similarly dire conditions could be projected in North Korea. October 31, the same day MacArthur's finalized directive on occupation policy was issued, the CIA reported that "present conduct of civil affairs in [Pyongyang] and elsewhere in North Korea is not conducive to good government or the accomplishment of UN aims. All Communist government officials have left the city and there are no citizens with pre-Communist government experience."[79] Though a "substantial" portion of the industrial plant "could be made operable with minor repairs," UN forces also found industrial activity in the Pyongyang area to be nonexistent due to war damage or removal of machinery. Edgar Johnson, director of the ECA's Korean Program, claimed that industry in the North had been so heavily bombed that it would "contribute very little to national production for several years, and only then if a program of repair and reconstruction is systematically undertaken."[80] At the end of November, the ROK minister of social affairs estimated there were one million "destitute" North Koreans, to go along with the two million destitute in the South.[81]

Less than a week after the final day of UK–U.S. meetings Acheson and the State Department had prepared a resolution that requested specialized UN agencies be able to undertake such tasks without the need for further Security Council actions.[82] Prior to the war, the ECA had estimated aid to the ROK would total $115 million for fiscal year 1951.[83] The second week of October Acheson recommended to Truman the international agency responsible for fixing war damage in Korea would need an annual budget of $200 to $300 million for a period of three years. Acheson proposed the United States provide 70 percent of this total. This amount was less than what would have been necessary to furnish economic development in Korea beyond 1950 levels; consistent with the administration's goals for the country, Acheson did not intend for reconstruction activities to do anything more than restore the recent status quo in Korea. In December he wrote that developing countries had "incorrectly interpreted reconstruction aspects [of the Korean Relief and Reconstruction Program] to increase Korean economic resources and therefore for development. . . . Actually, reconstruction program designed only assist Korea's own efforts in restoring economy to level obtaining prior being made victim aggression."[84] Initial estimates by Acheson and State closely matched those coming from the Korean theater and the UN, showing that officials in Washington were attentive to information relevant to noncombat operations. Preliminary surveys of war damage in South Korea conducted by the UN Command, ECA, and ROK were completed the first week of November. They estimated the cost of imports necessary to restore production levels in the ROK to prewar output to be $203.8 million, not including transportation costs, local materials and labor, and "foreign technical assistance." ECOSOC arrived at similar estimates that week, recommending a UN program of relief and rehabilitation for Korea to provide $250 million from January 1, 1951, through early 1952.[85]

The only senior U.S. official who differed from the preceding assessments about damage in Korea and the costs of reconstruction was MacArthur. He portrayed the damage and assistance estimates emerging as exaggerated. His assessment makes for an interesting contrast with Dwight Eisenhower, whose observations of Europe as a general during World War II had led him to believe American estimates of war damage were significantly low. MacArthur, conversely, informed Truman and others present at the Wake Island Conference that the reconstruction of Korea would be unproblematic. When the president consulted him about the state of utilities, railroads, and other infrastructure in the country MacArthur reported that the KPA had not been in the South long enough to do anything but "ordinary looting" and that industry had not been seriously damaged, a claim significantly at odds with other reports from the theater. The CIA had reported that food and water were scarce in Seoul and "prohibitive in price," while the U.S. embassy recorded that damages in Seoul and the surrounding area were "terrible and beyond description" and that industry in the area was "largely destroyed or burned out."[86] MacArthur also doubted that the financial cost of rebuilding Korea would be as high as contemporary estimates, stating the country would require $150 million or less a year. Muccio characterized MacArthur's Wake Island estimate as something of a surprise, as in his recollection the general had very recently told him Korea would need $250 million—the consensus amount that had emerged elsewhere.[87]

On the other end of the spectrum, Edgar Johnson publicly criticized the UN in June 1951 for avoiding "realistic estimates of the probable cost of a comprehensive reconstruction program," saying the organization should have been "thinking in terms of two or three billions of dollars" for its programs.[88] It is unclear whether Johnson believed $250 million was unrealistic prior to China's entrance into the war; the ECA had concurred with the UN's estimate of $203.8 million in November. It is also hard to tell whether he thought the lower figure was insufficient on a per annum basis or as an overall package; the total property damage in the ROK at the end of the war was estimated to be roughly $3 billion.[89] Nevertheless, these uncertainties reveal another point: U.S. thinking about the costs of the occupation, stabilization, and reconstruction of North Korea never factored in the possibility of significant Chinese involvement in the fighting on the peninsula, even though this possibility was always on policymakers minds as the military offensive proceeded that fall.

Institutional Framework for Occupation. Like the Roosevelt and Bush administrations, Truman and his advisers had to manage a multitude of different actors who were to be involved in the occupation of North Korea. Aside from U.S. military personnel on the ground, several UN agencies and the ROK government also had a voice in postwar plans. As with the Nazi and Ba'ath Parties, officials in the Korean War also faced questions about how to deal with communists in Korea. The Truman administration was considerably better at managing the task of establishing coherent, structured relationships among these different groups and making policy in light of their competing interests. This supports the CLT-generated hypothesis that officials with short time horizons will be more mindful of institutional mechanisms for managing noncombat operations than their far-sighted counterparts seeking transformation.

Given the motivation to minimize the number of American personnel in the postwar period, UN involvement in Korea was to be a consistent theme in planning efforts. Early in September, NSC 81/1 advised the president that the obligation of solving "the tremendous economic, social and political problems certain to confront a unified and independent Korea" should rest mainly on other UN members, especially Asian countries that were presumably best suited geographically, politically, and culturally for those tasks. Though the United States would make its own forces available if needed to deter renewed aggression or internal strife, American troop numbers "should be reduced so far as possible" and "serve only in conjunction with other UN contingents, preferably including some Asiatic contingents."[90] Consistent with this advice, the final directive on occupation policy approved by Truman opened by stating that "the purpose of the occupation will be to establish peace and security so that the Koreans themselves may solve the Korean problem with the aid and assistance of the United Nations."[91] Emphasizing international cooperation also countered Soviet assertions that the Korean War was an example of American imperialism. This was true of the war's anticipated post-conflict stage as well. Upon his return from the Wake Island Conference in October, Truman spoke publicly that

> the job of the United Nations in Korea will not end when the fighting stops. There is a big task of rehabilitation to be done. As a result of the Communist aggression, Korea has suffered terrible destruction. . . . The United Nations is already extending relief to ease the suffering which the Communist invasion has brought about and it is preparing to help the Koreans rebuild their homes and restore their factories. . . . We will give our strong support to the United Nations program of relief and reconstruction that will soon be started. The United States will do its full part to help build a free, united, and self-supporting Korean Republic.[92]

The precise relationship between the United States and the UN regarding noncombat responsibilities became a focus of war planning at least a month and a half before the Inchon landing. Acheson relayed information regarding efforts "to clarify relations and procedures" between the UN and MacArthur's command in matters of "non-military assistance" to the American UN delegation the first week of August. Along with the State Department, the Army and ECA concurred that the U.S. government would be the primary channel for everything other than "local procurement."[93] On August 17 Philip Jessup recommended that the State Department begin to formulate more detailed plans for Korea's future, under which the country would be governed for a time by a UN authority. Later that month the State Department again stressed that UN support and involvement in the political and physical reconstruction of Korea "must be assured and solidified" and a UN body formed to assist with planning and administration.[94] The NSC incorporated the State–Defense consensus by inserting into NSC 81/1 recommendations that UN forces be developed for the contingency of an occupation of North Korea. By the end of September it had been decided that the UNC would continue to run relief and rehabilitation efforts after the war ended until another body was in a position to take over. In anticipation of this transition, Washington proposed that UNKRA be established to work

143

with the ROK, with an agent general appointed by Secretary-General Trygve Lie.[95]

Truman was involved in policy deliberations about the transition period between combat and noncombat. In the words of a study commissioned by the Department of the Army during the war, Truman achieved a "clear-cut designation of instruments" for managing civil affairs in Korea.[96] Writing to the ECA the first week of October, the president stated "it is my earnest desire that continuity be maintained in the flow of economic aid to the Republic of Korea," continuing that the ECA would oversee such efforts pending the final adoption of a United Nations program for relief and rehabilitation in Korea. Truman specified that the agency manage how aid and assistance was directed to agriculture, fisheries, and civilian industry; work on combating inflation while training personnel to operate Korean economic agencies and enterprises; begin plans for postwar rehabilitation of public utilities, mines, harbors, and other facilities important to ROK economy; conduct analyses of economic problems in the ROK to assist with future plans; and, on request of military commanders, assist with the proper distribution of supplies to prevent disease and unrest. Recognizing the depth and breadth of his directive, Truman relieved the ECA of responsibility for financing requirements in Korea for direct civilian relief assistance and "as a general rule, of responsibility for the provision of other categories of needed supplies which serve common military and civilian purposes." The Defense Department would become responsible for those matters "during the period of hostility."[97]

John Emmerson of Far Eastern Affairs had prepared a "Program for Bringing Korean Hostilities to an End" for discussion by the State and Defense Departments by September 22. It was mainly a recapitulation of NSC 81/1; ten of its thirteen points on occupation and "political actions in the post-hostilities period" were taken from the prior document.[98] Marshall wrote Acheson that the Defense Department had no objections to Emmerson's draft memorandum, since it was based almost entirely on existing policy. However, he added that Defense Department studies indicated that plans needed to allow for the possibility that "North Korean civil authorities may not be able or willing to maintain law and order north of the 38°" and thus UN forces would have to be prepared to assume complete authority over civil affairs.[99] This advice would prove prescient as MacArthur's offensive continued.

During Acheson's September 26 meeting with the U.S. delegation at the UN, it was agreed that there was "grave danger" in thinking about humanitarian relief separately from matters of political reconstruction—a stark contrast with the approach later taken by the United States in Iraq.[100] This did not appear to be empty rhetoric, for the shape of the proposed occupation became clearer as October progressed. On the second, Emmerson proposed a three-stage framework in which the arrival of the new UN authority would be accompanied by the demobilization and disarming of the North Korean forces, provision of humanitarian aid, and the reestablishment of public services. Consistent with NSC 81/1, this period would be followed by the planning of national elections under UN auspices. Finally, elections would be held and military occupation forces would be withdrawn.[101] The Department of the Army presented a draft paper on occupation the following day that also adopted a three-phase plan, but was nevertheless much more detailed. The primary differences were that the Army draft, in line with Marshall's warnings of disorder north of the 38th parallel, held that "conditions of security [would] be paramount" in the first phase, as would the "maintenance of law and order." Though Emmerson's draft included a provision for the "filling of minimum essential government positions" by Koreans serving in temporary roles, the Army explicitly called for the "establishment or re-activation of *de facto* local and provincial governments" in the North, which could relieve governance demands on occupation forces and act as temporary substitutes for centralized government. The second phase would revolve around preparations for national elections, and the third would involve the withdrawal of occupation forces while the new government assumed authority.[102]

The Army plan implied that available communist officials would be allowed to serve in civil affairs roles, at least temporarily. This aspect of the draft was consistent with the larger outlines of the Army's proposed occupation directive. Participation in North Korean affairs was to be "limited to the minimum necessary to assure law and order and tranquility," and any amendments to North Korean law limited to those necessary to maintain "military security."[103] It also echoed U.S. military government actions in Korea after World War II prior to the establishment of the ROK. Rather than embrace the popular leftist political organizations in the South, the United States had chosen to utilize and reconstitute the centralized bureaucracy Japan had used to govern the country. This was due not only to suspicions that Korean leftists were tied to international communism, but also the belief that they had no idea how to govern.[104] Conservative nationalists who were tainted by their collaboration with Japanese colonialism nevertheless had more recent governing experience and familiarity with established institutions. In the fall of 1950 the Army again prepared to utilize established institutions and Koreans with experience therein, only now it was willing to temporarily embrace individuals from the opposite side of the political spectrum.

In sum, almost all the U.S. effort was focused on how an occupation would be executed, rather than what it was to accomplish. The Army proposal that formed the template for overall policy reflected the tenets of military necessity over ideological purity, just as Army proposals for Germany's occupation during World War II had. Its emphasis was on minimizing the costs and risks to military forces conducting noncombat activities in Korea. In both Germany and Iraq top civilian officials resisted the adoption of military plans for noncombat operations. In line with the tenets of military necessity, these plans stressed feasibility concerns above the desirability of punishing and purging Nazis or Ba'athists, and had thus not appealed to civilian policy-makers with long time horizons. Conversely, Truman and his advisers lacked transformative goals and, demonstrating the communication fluency expected by CLT, adopted the military's perspective that feasibility be the foremost concern in postwar Korea. The Army plan was largely affirmed in an October 28 directive to MacArthur that was approved by Truman, the JCS, Acheson, and the Department of Defense.

Acheson and his advisers also paid close attention to the composition of UNCURK. This might reflect a lesson learned from the American preparations for occupation during World War II. Senator Lodge, who had warned the United States must avoid once again "losing the peace," was recorded as saying that "if we [consider] the choice of this commission in the abstract, we might get into trouble," a likely reference to postwar difficulties with the USSR in Germany.[105] Consistent with this view, Acheson believed that UNCURK would need to be composed of small states and not feature the United States or USSR if political progress was to be made. The experience of Germany's occupation was not sufficient to explain policy choices in Korea, however, given that the appropriate "lessons" to be derived were not shared by all policymakers. For example, Acheson's position was not obvious to Ambassador Warren Austin, who initially held that the United States should head the commission given its stake in Korea but was persuaded by Acheson's reasoning. Acheson himself thought that the commission might suffer from a lack of American leadership, and believed it would be highly desirable, but ultimately impractical, for the United States to have a position while excluding the Soviets.[106] In comparison to Germany, then, officials did not avoid debate over the parameters of the occupation's control machinery with other states, as they had when dealing with the USSR and Great Britain, and privileged feasibility over desirability considerations. It could be argued that the U.S. situation vis-à-vis the Soviet Union was more delicate near the end of World War II because of Franklin Roosevelt's desire for a long-term partnership with Moscow and the need to defeat Japan once Germany was knocked out of the fighting. However, the United States was seeking to set up a reliable network of states to contain the USSR in 1950, not just attempting to placate one ally, and thus the government's diplomatic position was not necessarily less precarious.

While Washington deferred to its theater commander in regard to combat operations, there was no such norm when it came to civil affairs. The Truman administration was assertive in restraining MacArthur, who had been given great freedom in governing Japan. Subject to the control of Washington and the UN, the UNC was to have greatest jurisdiction in the occupation's first phase. In the second phase the UNC retained its authority but would give "utmost consideration" to UNCURK as long as doing so did not interfere with military security. The directive stated that until the UN commission was ready to put forward its recommendations, the ROK government's authority would not be recognized north of the 38th parallel, though MacArthur was to consult with them to "facilitate eventual re-unification."[107] The directive on occupation policy gave the general the responsibility to "facilitate public order, economic rehabilitation, and the democratic mode of life." The key word was "facilitate"—MacArthur was told to refrain from making major economic or political decisions, which were to be left to the new Korean government.[108] He was to adopt the role of coordinator and implementer vis-à-vis the U.S. government and the UN. Washington would act as the UN's "executive agent" as it had during combat operations. The UNC would receive instructions through the JCS.[109] Though MacArthur was to work with UNCURK and follow their recommendations "as far as possible," he was not subject to the commission's jurisdiction and had the authority to dismiss UNCURK personnel. Despite the numerous agencies involved in noncombat operations in Korea, according to one historian of the war, a "great advantage enjoyed by the UN Command in this relief work was that the UN commander had the final say on all of these civil and military projects and shipments."[110] There were no accidental dual chains of command, as there would be in Iraq.

The main complicating factor in occupation plans was the ROK, which was recognized by the UN as the legitimate sovereign government of Korea. Analysts at the time cited the lack of a formal agreement with Seoul defining the scope of U.S. authority in civil matters as perhaps the Truman administration's greatest failure in respect to noncombat operations in 1950.[111] Technically MacArthur was to operate coequally with the ROK government, though Washington would take steps to try to limit the influence of Rhee's regime as the following section shows. One check on the ROK was the directive that MacArthur retain the native governmental apparatus of the North rather than establish a central government that would likely be laden with ROK operatives.

Rhee, Communism, and Postwar Plans. CLT predicts that the assessments of individuals with short time horizons will be largely based on contextual information flowing from immediate events in a specific case, rather than deduced from preexisting general beliefs about a broader class of phenomenon in which a specific case nominally fits. As Truman and his top advisers planned for a transitional government that would be the bridge between the conclusion of hostilities and a unified Korean state, they were very attentive to the political situation on the peninsula. Their conclusions were not governed by analogies drawn from other cases. Attuned to Rhee's political expectations as well as those of the international community, the administration ably balanced their desire to limit Rhee's authority with the need to secure a degree of cooperation from the South Korean government. Another delicate political question concerned the fate of communist officials in the DPRK. Despite being engaged in a global effort to contain communist expansion, an endeavor which could predispose policymakers to perceive communists in Korea as part of a monolithic international bloc, Truman and Acheson rejected such simplistic portrayals of North Korean officials. Instead of relying on general beliefs about communism, which CLT would expect from individuals with long time horizons, top U.S. officials distinguished between Soviet and local communism. Likewise, they privileged feasibility concerns by asserting that a large number of North Korean personnel could assist U.S. and UN efforts to stabilize and govern affairs north of the 38th parallel in the postconflict period.

Though the United States had backed conservative nationalists like Rhee over their leftist challengers in Korea, Rhee and his government pursued policies that from an American perspective were unilateral, opaque, and contrary to U.S. interests. Rhee had worked to sabotage negotiations between the United States and Soviet Union regarding a unified Korean government, and American officials observed his autocratic governing practices with displeasure.[112] When UN forces were able to retake territory in South Korea in the fall of 1950, Rhee's police shocked members of the coalition by brutally punishing and in many instances killing leftists who had assisted the DPRK occupiers.[113] Truman and others were often dissatisfied with Rhee's government, whose actions fostered skepticism about the prospects of a peaceful transition to democratic rule.[114] From the South Korean perspective, conversely, such policies were necessary to assert their sovereignty on the peninsula. Ambassador Muccio claimed that South Koreans were understandably suspicious of American intentions given their history of being occupied by foreign powers. "When we first arrived there," Muccio recounted, "the Korean attitude was that American 'overlords' had merely replaced Japanese overlords. There was practically no cooperation, no response from the Koreans."[115] Though it was helping Rhee raise a defense force, the U.S. government would not provide the ROK with equipment necessary to wage a sustained offensive campaign. This reluctance was a product of distrust between Washington and Seoul, and fed Rhee's resentment.[116]

The Truman administration's distrust of Rhee was evident in its disinclination to share postwar plans with the South Korean president. When queried, Muccio insisted that the U.S. government did not discuss the administration of a unified Korea with Rhee except in the most superficial ways.[117] Evidence from 1950 is consistent with this recollection. A Defense memo of July 31 held that "political reconstruction in Korea will present a complex challenge" in light of Rhee's political ambitions, and Acheson acknowledged in early October that political reunification would be made quite difficult if Rhee declared his authority over the whole of Korea prior to elections.[118] American worries were soon affirmed, as the State Department received word that ROK police were operating in the DPRK. Fearing this would damage international support for the UN mission, Acheson urged Muccio to stress that these police were under the authority of the UNC and acting in accordance with Security Council resolutions, though he was unsure of whether this was the case.[119] Things were to get worse for U.S. officials when Rhee told Truman that the UN was not allowing the ROK government enough control over the future administration of North Korea. Rhee asserted his government would take over the administration of areas in the North "whenever hostilities cease" by dispatching governors appointed by the ROK.[120] Acheson was distressed by this turn of events, which he thought would lead to pressure within the UN for a nationwide election, thus putting the international community and the ROK regime at loggerheads. He also feared early elections would leave Rhee in a position to dominate any new government.[121]

The CIA warned that Rhee should not be expected to act "completely in accord with decisions of the UN Interim Committee on Korea if the Republic of Korea as an interested party is not previously consulted in formation of Committee decisions."[122] Everett Drumright in the U.S. embassy likewise communicated that "any programs disregarding the ROK . . . would have disastrous effect here."[123] This advice, however, conflicted with the U.S. government's desire to sideline ROK leadership during postwar preparations. Washington thus walked a fine line between appeasing Rhee and not allowing him too much autonomy. Throughout October this careful balancing act wobbled between success and failure. Acheson instructed Muccio to tell Rhee that if the ROK president insisted on "outright defiance" of UN principles aimed at achieving Korean unification, the United States would find it "increasingly difficult if not impossible to continue its support and defense of Rhee administration in UN and elsewhere against pressure, in many quarters, for holding new elections throughout [Korea]."[124] Muccio responded the next day that, after speaking with Rhee, it appeared the ROK would not challenge the "supreme authority" of the UNC in North Korea during the occupation period. But just a few days later Rhee declared that he was to assume temporary civil control of all of Korea despite UN resolutions to the contrary.[125]

A related point of contention between the U.S. government and the ROK was the future of the Communist Party in North Korea. Though the containment of communism motivated American participation in the Korean War, the Truman administration's position toward Korean communists trended toward leniency as far as the transitional postconflict period was concerned. NSC 81/1 held that in the event of an occupation of North Korea "the United States should recognize that the Government of the ROK will have to take strong measures against Communist efforts to cause trouble in Korea and that it may require support in these measures from the United States."[126] However, logistical necessity made large-scale purges of communist personnel from public life unappealing. The administration's broader concerns about global containment meant it was essential to prevent U.S. manpower from being concentrated in Korea long after the war ended. Coupled with the backlash that might arise due to Korean nationalism, as well as the political sensitivities of Beijing, it appeared prudent to deploy as few U.S. and ROK troops in North Korea during an occupation as possible. Aside from turning to UN members for the personnel needed in the postwar period, reliance on North Koreans with governmental experience could also relieve the strain on U.S. forces while limiting Rhee's authority. There were indications that some North Koreans could be reliable in this role. While some KPA prisoners claimed that their North Korean countrymen believed their cause to be righteous, others asserted Northerners were skeptical of Communist claims and had "considerable faith in U.S. intentions and capabilities in Korea."[127] The JCS thus informed MacArthur at the end of September that "North Korean civil authorities should be held responsible for the maintenance of law and order north of the 38th parallel under the supervision of such UN Forces as are in the area." Aside from war criminals, amnesty would be declared for "all North Koreans, including political prisoners."[128]

The initial draft of the Truman administration's final directive on occupation policy likewise allowed former DPRK officials a role to play in the administration of occupied northern territory. MacArthur was to dissolve the DPRK and the Communist Party apparatus therein. At the same time, the draft directive stated that "it is desirable that, to the extent practicable, native government be retained or re-established at the local and provincial levels." MacArthur would be authorized to appoint and remove officials at all levels of government, with the qualification that "the mere fact that an individual is or was a member of the armed forces of the North Korean government, an official of that government or any local government, or a member of any political party will not subject him to prosecution or reprisal and will not, by that reason alone, bar him from office or employment." Furthermore, in line with existing U.S. and UN policy, MacArthur was not to recognize the ROK government as having authority north of 38th parallel, though he was to consult with the South Koreans on policy matters.[129] Acheson and the American delegation to the UN sought to placate Rhee by allowing current ROK representatives to retain their seats in any new government and hold new elections only for representatives from the North.[130] This tact would establish a government that would have a degree of legitimacy throughout the country and held out the best chance that neither Rhee loyalists nor communist representatives would represent an overwhelming bloc.

Rhee correctly surmised that Washington was inclined toward a lenient postwar policy regarding Korean communists. His October 16 telegram to Truman forcefully asserted that "to protect and revive communism in the North is unthinkable." This message also contained Rhee's first declaration of intent to take over civilian administration in North Korea since the war had begun.[131] ROK laws forbid communist political activities, and Drumright advised Acheson that the United States should consider extending these laws to the North when it was occupied. Drumright also recommended that the political history of any North Korean interested in working in government after the war be carefully investigated. Allowing individuals with ties to communism to serve in the public sector ignored that the party was a "monolithic organization" and "an agency of Russian Communist party."[132] He reiterated that if the United States could "assure [Rhee] Communists will not be utilized in North Korean Interim Administration and if a satisfactory arrangement can be made to utilize Korean[s] South of parallel, including North Korean refugees, in setting up Interim Administration in North, Embassy feels Rhee's principal points of opposition will have been surmounted."[133]

Superficially, Acheson appeared to yield to Drumright's concerns. The secretary telegrammed Muccio on the 25th to let the embassy know that the provision on retaining local and provincial North Korean governments was being removed from the directive.[134] However, this would have augmented Rhee's authority and control north of the 38th parallel, and thus his ability to work at cross-purposes with the UN, a scenario the Truman administration clearly wanted to avoid. In fact, it seems that Acheson and Truman tried to finesse this problem by making U.S. concessions appear greater to the embassy in Seoul than they really were. The president approved a draft directive on the 28th which stated that occupation forces were to "establish and maintain *supervision and controls* over North Korean *de facto* provincial and local governments."[135] It is fair to characterize this as a bit of deception directed toward Seoul via massaging of policy language. Rather than specifically retaining or establishing native governments in the North, as had been the case in the October 3 draft, the United States government would only establish controls over governments that existed independently of American actions. Clearly, the amendments in the directive Truman approved on the 28th were slight. U.S. policy still held that North Koreans' eligibility for public posts was to be independent of their prior status in the Communist Party or KPA. The altered language in the directive may have also reflected new intelligence about the status of government in North Korea. At the Wake Island Conference in the middle of the month, MacArthur had said that maintaining local government in the North would be moot, as most DPRK officials would have been killed or fled.[136] This prediction was upheld by the CIA's report of October 30.[137] Under such conditions, it would be easier to monitor what local DPRK institutions remained than to actively work toward establishing and maintaining local governments.

On the whole, then, Truman, Acheson, and other officials were highly attentive to the political signals emerging from Seoul as occupation plans were being formed in late September and October. They did not move toward either extreme of the policy spectrum. There were no plans to hold elections in South Korea as well as the North; even though that might weaken Rhee's grip on power in the long run, it would make cooperation between the United States and ROK much more difficult in the near term. At the same time, there was not going to be a broad purging of communists from public life in the

North despite Rhee's insistence on the matter. Truman and those in Washington likewise resisted similar entreaties from U.S. officials in the theater of operations. By allowing individuals—aside from war criminals—to aid occupation forces, policymakers privileged feasibility concerns to a greater extent than did U.S. officials planning the occupations of Germany and Iraq. Though the containment of global communism was one of the administration's high-level goals, antipathy toward communism did not dictate the means by which postconflict noncombat operations would be conducted. While the Soviet Union was (correctly) seen as supportive of the North Korean invasion of the ROK, simple arguments such as Drumright's characterization of all DPRK officials as part of a monolithic communist bloc were rejected.

Despite Truman and Acheson's clear attentiveness to the immediate political context in Korea, it is also plain that their short time horizons discouraged them from considering how a Chinese military intervention—even one limited in its scope—could upset their plans regarding the composition of temporary government in North Korea. On November 14, the ECA reported that any enthusiasm North Koreans had for the presence of UN forces had been dampened due to fears of communist reoccupation. When China invaded, there was an immense flow of refugees from the DPRK.[138] Even if UN forces had been able to slow the CCF advance to a greater extent than they did, it is still likely a flow of refugees would have left the UNC with little in the way of temporary indigenous civil affairs personnel. In an anticlimactic note, the 8th Army's civil assistance headquarters recorded the arrival of a letter in early December on the "Utilization of Qualified Koreans, North and South, in Accomplishment of Civil Assistance Missions." The report stated dryly that "owing, of course, to the situation, this directive was not fully implemented."[139]

VARIATIONS IN ASSESSMENT: ALLISON, MACARTHUR, AND DULLES

Actors with short time horizons behaved as CLT predicts they would. Having little time to prepare for postwar noncombat operations, and having placed little value in Korea relative to America's other global commitments prior to the war, their assessments were highly dependent on immediate contextual information rather than prior beliefs or long-term objectives. Their choices reflected a preference for plans that could be most feasibly executed. However, their short time horizons hindered the consideration of how threats from China might impact their plans for a unified Korea until late November. Though attentive to the possibility of China's entry into the war, officials did not evaluate how this would affect occupation plans. Still, individuals who saw crossing the 38th as an avenue toward rolling back communism in Asia were even less attuned to the challenges a Korean occupation could present. For the minority of actors who appeared to have relatively long time horizons, however, the task of developing a causal link between time horizons and the strategic assessment of noncombat operations is more difficult.

In evaluating the case of John Allison, a planner and vocal critic of long-term policy toward Korea, and his colleagues in Northeast Asian Affairs, there is a problem of endogeneity. Though it is true that Allison and others in his office saw long-term benefits to unifying Korea not emphasized by others in the administration, they articulated these views after the war had already begun. Thus, it is difficult to say whether the higher value they assigned to transformative future outcomes affected their strategic assessment or vice versa. In the studies of Iraq and the planning for the occupation of Germany, endogeneity problems could be rectified by demonstrating how actors' assessments varied as they focused on short versus long-term tasks. Allison and his office mates' focus remained generally on more distant events, however, so this means of clarification is unavailable. General MacArthur is also a difficult individual to analyze. The endogeneity problem present when examining Allison's actions is absent in the case of MacArthur. He had a long-standing view that reversing communist gains in Asia was the key to U.S. success in the Cold War.[140] Besides his time horizons, though, there is another likely factor which influenced MacArthur's assessments that cannot be dismissed, namely his general tendency toward overconfidence prior to the Korean War and during the intervention itself.

The striking difference between the strategic assessments of Allison and colleagues, on the one hand, and those of Dulles on the other, helps to resolve the analytical bind regarding members of Northeast Asian Affairs. Like Allison, Dulles was a critic of the status quo orientation of Truman's containment strategy, placed more weight on Asia than did the president or Acheson, and was an early proponent of crossing the 38th parallel. However, Dulles portrayed a move into North Korea as a necessary step to maintain the security of the ROK, a goal focused on restoring the status quo ante, whereas Allison and colleagues saw it as an avenue toward rolling back communism in Asia—a transformative goal with the future as the point of reference. Along with a different understanding of the purpose of crossing the parallel, these individuals differed in how they assessed a potential occupation. Like most of the Truman administration, Dulles was less focused on the desirability of unifying the country and gave greater weight to potential pitfalls that could await the United States. Allison and like-minded officials' assessments of postconflict operations were thus substantively different from those of administration officials who both did and did not share their more general policy preferences. This supports the conclusion that officials' views of the UN offensive as either serving maintenance or transformative goals are important for explaining the degree to which feasibility concerns featured in their assessments.

Though those in Northeast Asian Affairs saw the potential benefits of using Korea to roll back communism in Asia as "incalculable," it would be inaccurate to assert that Allison and like-minded officials were totally blind to the risks and costs an occupation of North Korea would entail. In their August 21 memorandum titled "U.S. Course of Action in Korea," they recognized the need to maintain enough reserve manpower to meet a Soviet challenge in Europe and that attempting to unify Korea by force increased the chances of a wider war. They also stated that America had to make sure it did not alienate its allies by insisting on reunification of Korea by force. Finally, they insisted the UN would have to play a major role in Korea's future given the "tremendous problem" that economic and political reconstruction in Korea would pose.[141] In short, recommendations coming from Northeast Asian Affairs acknowledged the global challenges facing the United States and some of the postwar costs America and the UN would face in Korea.

What most distinguished Allison and Emmerson's assessments from those of other U.S. officials was the formers' complacency regarding the specific political challenges facing the United States in Korea. They consistently ignored or discounted contextual information about how political friction between Washington and Seoul could complicate operations to unify the country. As already discussed, Emmerson's recommendations in September and October regarding the occupation of North Korea did not stress the importance of maintaining security and law and order the way the Army's concurrent memorandum did, nor were they open to the use of North Korean personnel to help administer occupied territory. This was not a singular example, but rather a continuation of an earlier line of reasoning. Allison's first August memo discussing "political factors" in Korea began with four paragraphs related to U.S. actions supporting unification. The memo held that after years of "colonialism and division, the people of Korea have an irrepressible urge for the unification of their country." While this may seem unremarkable, it illustrates that Allison's line of argumentation was first motivated by the higher-level transformative objective of uniting the country, rather immediate concerns of securing the ROK from future attacks. It did not address whether years of division along with the brutal period of internecine fighting in the years after World War II had left the Korean people in a position to agree on how to achieve unification. Instead, Allison stressed a UN report of June 26, 1950, which stated that political and economic conditions in the country were improving, leading him to dismiss critics who had called South Korea a "police state." Of course, any prognostications made in the UN report had been overtaken by the North Korean invasion, a point Allison neglected. Instead of being wary of Rhee's regime as others in the administration had been, his memo proclaimed, "the leaders of the Republic of Korea have stressed that the aggression from the North provides the opportunity to abolish the 38th parallel and unify all of

Korea under UN auspices."[142] Allison did not discuss means of restraining Rhee's political ambition, nor whether Rhee's regime would act in ways contrary to the interests of the United States and its coalition allies if allowed influence in the North, the primary concern of Acheson and others in the administration. All of Allison and Emmerson's observations about Korea's domestic political situation cited in August supported the conclusion that circumstances there would facilitate unification.

Although much of the disagreement between the U.S. government and the ROK regarding the administration of the North emerged in October 1950, Allison and colleagues should have been aware of such potential complicating factors in August and September. It must be remembered that Truman and others in his administration had become skeptical of, if not openly unsympathetic toward, Rhee's regime in the 1940s. Furthermore, a CIA report delivered to the NSC in the period between Allison's solo and coauthored memos in August painted a very different picture of politics in Korea as well as U.S.–ROK relations. The agency's analysis was that a nationwide election could still leave a large portion of the Korean government under communist control. If, however, Rhee's regime was restored as it had been prior to the conflict, his lack of popular support would lead to political instability. This, in turn, would require a long-term commitment by the United States to provide financial aid. Alternatively, attempts by the United States and UN to govern Korea via trusteeship would stir up nationalist resistance and serve to continue the country's status as "the catspaw of international politics."[143] Northeast Asian Affairs cited none of the CIA's concerns. Allison and Emmerson, who had been working on issues relating to Asia and Korea their entire careers in government, could reasonably be expected to be aware of the issues cited by the CIA prior to October 1950.

Dulles, who shared much of Allison's political outlook but nevertheless maintained a narrow, short-term view of the Korean problem, was significantly more mindful of the problems posed by an occupation. Dulles was clearly ambivalent about Rhee. While he regarded the ROK president as a "great patriot and anti-communist," his deliberations with Acheson in September had also led him to fear he might have given the impression he wanted "to ditch Syngman Rhee."[144] Though he did not endorse such a move, he must have voiced concerns to the secretary of state that prompted this clarifying note. In discussions with Acheson and the U.S. mission to the UN during the last two weeks of that month, Dulles echoed the CIA report by holding it was unrealistic to assume elections would be held throughout Korea, or that the United States could occupy all of the North. He was recorded cautioning those present against "committing ourselves to an impossible objective."[145] Dulles also foresaw friction between UNCURK and the UNC, noting that the General Assembly's October 7 resolution was vague and was likely to be interpreted by MacArthur so as to give himself as much authority as possible.[146]

It does not appear that Dulles had privileged access to information that would lead him to draw conclusions so disparate from those of Allison. What is more, Dulles was more perceptive about problems China and the USSR could pose to postwar plans than were Acheson or Truman. On September 22 Dulles wrote Acheson that, while the United States could not repudiate the idea of a united Korea, it also could not be sure whether the USSR or China would allow such an event to come to fruition.[147] Like Kennan, Dulles warned that an extension of U.S. influence near territories the large communist powers considered vital might not be feasible unless Washington was willing to commit forces to an extent which might endanger U.S. interests elsewhere. Even in the event that neither the USSR nor China occupied territory in the North, Dulles believed that free elections could result in a significant communist contingent being placed in the new government. Again echoing Kennan, the following week he argued that in all likelihood "a united whole Korea could never be obtained."[148]

MacArthur's evaluations of domestic politics in Korea were similar to Allison's in their optimism. He expressed confidence that, once the ROK was reestablished in Seoul and Kim's regime had been toppled, the Korean people would vote overwhelmingly for a new noncommunist government.[149] This was in addition to his estimates of the costs of reconstruction and stabilization in Korea, which were roughly a third lower than the consensus emerging between Washington and the UN. MacArthur's long time horizons and his relatively optimistic assessments of noncombat operations in the postwar phase align with the expectations of CLT. However, it appears unlikely that the substance of MacArthur's assessments can be attributed primarily to the effects of temporal construal. First, rather than being blind to the future risks that would face his forces, as officials with long time horizons in the Germany and Iraq cases were, MacArthur was risk-acceptant: he was aware of the dangers that rollback entailed. MacArthur told one of his political advisers that if his push to the Yalu failed he saw no alternative but to bomb "key points in Manchuria," a decision he believed would bring the Soviets into the fighting. Such an outcome was not necessarily unwelcome in MacArthur's eyes. In August MacArthur told General Ridgway, his future replacement as commander of UN forces in Korea, that he prayed "nightly" that China would enter the war.[150]

Second, MacArthur's confidence was temporally invariant. His assessments of combat and postconflict noncombat operations were marked by similar levels of optimism. This is clearest in regard to Operation Chromite. While other senior military officials, including the JCS, expressed doubts about the practicality of Inchon as a landing site, MacArthur's evaluations of the chances of success were characterized by "extreme optimism." He believed that, despite what he called "5,000 to 1" odds, the operation would crush the North Koreans. The commander of a Marine assault division at Inchon reported that MacArthur had an "almost mystical faith" that the operation could not fail.[151] This reflected a proclivity toward overconfidence that existed well before the Korean War. The autonomy of action to which MacArthur had grown accustomed may have bolstered the general's confidence, and his experience as occupation commander in Japan increased his already inflated sense of his own abilities.[152] Washington's communication of September of 1950 that MacArthur should "feel unhampered tactically and strategically" during the offensive and use his own judgment regarding the likelihood of an intervention by China would only have increased his self-assurance. In sum, while CLT appears to offer a plausible explanation for assessments of individuals in State's Northeast Asian Affairs Office, one cannot be as confident that temporal construal drove MacArthur's thinking.

Alternative Explanations for Occupation Plans

In contrast to the preceding account, some have argued that American postwar plans were driven by long-term aims and that these aims distracted Washington from the dangers of China entering the war as the military campaign progressed. It is beyond the scope of this book to provide comprehensive coverage of American evaluations of China's intentions in the summer and fall of 1950. Still, evidence shows that top officials had not become so focused on long-term objectives that signals about Chinese intentions went unnoticed. Instead, they based their assessments on the feasibility of ongoing operations and potential *immediate* negative consequences of allowing the UN offensive to proceed. The question of whether Korea could be secured into the more distant future, even if China did not enter the war in the near term, did not impinge on decision making. As CLT expects, officials had decomposed the ultimate aims of the Korean War into subordinate goals that were compartmentalized from one another. They were attuned to the feasibility of combat and noncombat operations but never considered how obstacles to the success of the former might impact the long-term success of the latter. This is similar to the strategic disconnect between combat and noncombat operations apparent in the minds of top U.S. policymakers in Germany and Iraq. However, in those two cases feasibility considerations were only dominant when initial combat operations were considered, whereas feasibility concerns were foremost in most officials' minds regardless of what phase of the Korean campaign they evaluated.

THE LOCAL AND GLOBAL BALANCE OF POWER

Contrary to an opportunity costs perspective, officials began formulating policy on crossing the 38th parallel, which implied an eventual occupation of North Korean territory, before it was remotely clear that the United States' defense of the South would be successful.[153] Since only MacArthur was confident that Chromite would succeed, there is no reason to think optimism among other decision makers prior to Inchon led to expanded war aims. Ultimately, neither perceptions of the local or global distribution of power adequately explain the timing of internal administration debates over war aims. Decision makers' concerns about the commitment problem perform much better in this regard, but the preceding examination of officials' thinking about this issue demonstrates that time horizons in Washington were relatively short even after the Inchon landing.

State and Defense considered it a distinct possibility that the USSR was using the attack in Korea to draw the United States into a quagmire in Asia, thus presenting an opportunity for Soviet expansion in other areas of strategic importance. This assessment was made in the context of severe manpower constraints; the number of personnel in the Army had declined from 6.1 million to 592,000 between August 1945 and June 1950.[154] The local balance of power on the peninsula was also initially unfavorable for Washington. A month prior to the war's beginning the Department of the Army had estimated the combat efficiency of the divisions under MacArthur to be anywhere from 65 percent to 85 percent.[155] From the war's outset the KPA made what were seen as stunning gains against U.S. forces. By the end of June almost half the ROK army was killed, missing in action, or had been captured. 70 percent of ROK supplies and equipment had been lost by the end of July. Acheson proclaimed that the United States had underestimated North Korea's "war footing and armament" given the advances that had been made against American resistance.[156]

Why did the debate over crossing the 38th parallel, which would culminate in an occupation directive for UN forces in North Korea, begin when there was still great danger that U.S. forces would be unable to save Rhee's regime? It may have been that many in Washington did not think the Soviets would enter the conflict. Soviet officials, including future foreign minister Andrei Gromyko, began communicating the possibility of an early peace settlement the first week of July. U.S. officials such as ambassador to the USSR Alan Kirk and future ambassador Charles E. Bohlen believed these offers to be genuine, and Acheson was inclined to take them seriously as well.[157] Still, the likelihood of a military defeat was by no means trivial even in late August. Near the end of that month the NSC was still considering the possibility that the KPA, with or without covert assistance from China and the USSR, might compel the withdrawal of UN forces from Korea.[158]

THE FOG OF WAR AND DOMESTIC POLITICS: PRELUDE TO THE CCF'S ENTRANCE

Scholars have asserted that key policymakers in the Truman administration became "insensitive to the marginal costs associated with [the military] offensive" and "simply did not reassess the feasibility" of taking North

Korea, or similarly, that they exhibited a "rigid adherence to previous decisions and an inability to receive and interpret new and countervailing evidence."[159] If correct, these assertions would contradict the CLT hypothesis that policymakers—especially those with short time horizons—are attentive to the concrete details of ongoing military operations, receptive to contextual information, and carefully assess the feasibility of existing plans. Contrary to what other accounts of the Korean War have argued, information about a potential counterintervention was given careful attention, but the intelligence on China being gathered by multiple sources was both contradictory and vague.[160] Furthermore, Truman and other officials clearly did not express more ambivalence or pessimism about the anticipated occupation of Korea compared to MacArthur's ongoing offensive. Nevertheless, they allowed his advance to continue due to the uncertainty surrounding China's intentions and domestic political considerations.

The entrance of large numbers of Chinese forces into the Korean War in November 1950 was the conflict's watershed moment. Rather than a victory, leaders in Washington once again found themselves facing the prospect of being forced from Korea. This problem was compounded by Truman and other officials' public pronouncements committing the United States to reuniting Korea. The constraining impact of this commitment was reinforced by the ambiguous nature of the intelligence available to senior officials and largely unknown to the public. It is not that domestic pressures forced the Truman administration to cross the 38th parallel, even though some later recalled this to be the case.[161] Instead, the evidence demonstrates that the overt commitment to the reunification of Korea made it costly to halt or reverse the course of the campaign after the 38th had been crossed. Administration fears revolved around potential near-term losses, rather than the perceived need to make up for "sunk costs."[162]

Evidence shows that Washington's public commitment to reuniting Korea made officials believe it would be politically costly to reverse the intervention's course during the fateful month of November.[163] This is especially the case given that the public perceived the war was progressing favorably, a perception which would have made any reversal appear dubious. Sixty-four percent of those polled immediately after Inchon favored taking the war into DPRK territory, and of these, 78 percent favored continuing "beyond the border line" even if it meant war with the USSR or China.[164] Harriman recalled that popular sentiment for a solution to the Korean crisis made it "psychologically . . . almost impossible not to go ahead and complete the job."[165] At an NSC meeting with the president on November 10, JCS chairman Bradley observed that, in the event of China's entry into the war, UN forces would be in a better defensive position the farther south they held the line in North Korea. Nevertheless, he followed this observation by noting that "such a retrograde movement would probably lose political support and might lose the South Koreans' will to fight." Even NSC vice chairman

Robert J. Smith, who advocated a U.S. withdrawal from Korea in mid-November, noted that such a move could "prove embarrassing at home and among our allies abroad."[166]

That the personage of Douglas MacArthur continued to strongly advocate his forces' continued advance complicated matters further. Besides the traditional deference given to the top commander in a theater of operations, MacArthur's status as the most senior Army general meant even his nominal superiors were reluctant to challenge his judgment. Before he became president, Eisenhower informed Ridgway that MacArthur was "an 'untouchable' whose actions you cannot predict and who will himself decide what information he wants Washington to have and what he will withhold." Kennan commented that MacArthur was "so distant and full of mistrust" toward the Truman administration that during his 1948 trip to Tokyo he felt like "an envoy charged with opening communications . . . with a hostile and suspicious foreign government."[167] MacArthur also had a history of publicly criticizing administration policies of which he did not approve. In August he had attacked Truman and Acheson's decision to keep Formosa out of the Korean conflict in a letter to the head of the Veterans of Foreign Wars. He saw the administration's attitude toward the Nationalists during the war as defeatist, calling the neutral policy a "threadbare argument" put forward by those who favored "appeasement."[168] In light of such considerations, it is not surprising that U. Alexis Johnson, who had been a deputy director at the State Department in 1950, later asserted that MacArthur's presence made the matter of approaching the Yalu "very, very much a domestic issue." In his opinion, "the Chiefs were *very, very* reluctant to try to 'beard,' if I can use that term, MacArthur on this."[169]

The clearest sign that domestic political considerations were blocking Truman's inclination to halt MacArthur's offensive emerged during the seventy-third meeting of the NSC in late November. The meeting followed a political campaign season in which Republican candidates for office had shown that attacking Truman's policies on communism could give them traction with voters.[170] During the meeting, the president was recorded as saying that "the present campaign of vilification and plain lies in this country was the greatest asset the Soviets had," creating "doubt" in the minds of the American public. He then asserted that the country was in the same situation as it had been in 1840.[171] While this comment is not explained further in the meeting notes, Truman was quite likely making a comparison between his own situation with MacArthur and the presidential election of 1840. That year President Martin Van Buren sought reelection against William Henry Harrison, a war hero like MacArthur who had achieved fame as a general in the War of 1812 and conflicts with American Indians. With the country in a depression and a famed war veteran as an opponent, Van Buren had been defeated.

As the UN offensive proceeded in November, the JCS and Marshall lapsed into ineffectiveness. Nitze's recollection of "the majority view" was that "U.S.

forces should stop at the narrow neck of land" south of the Yalu. Despite sharing this view, Marshall also believed that tradition dictated MacArthur be given as much freedom as possible as field commander.[172] Marshall and the JCS ultimately appealed to Acheson, asking him to advise Truman that MacArthur must halt and consolidate his advance. Unsurprisingly, Acheson replied he could not possibly provide military advice to the president if the generals and defense secretary themselves were unwilling to broach the matter. Aware of the costs that might be incurred if MacArthur continued his offensive, the JCS proceeded to advise but not order him to take up defensive positions south of the Yalu as a precautionary measure, advice he dismissed as politically and militarily unsound.[173] After the war, in Acheson's correspondence with the scholar Harold Stein, the former secretary wrote that November 1950 had been "a nightmare. . . . We had increasing meetings between State and Defense, Matt Ridgway at the map, Marshall, Lovett, and the JCS, together with Nitze, Matthews, Rusk and me around the table. The tradition from [Ulysses S.] Grant's day of the position of the theater commander, MacArthur's reputation, the vast distance separating us added to the trouble at this end."[174]

Despite the preceding evidence, Truman did not readily bend to domestic political considerations and popular opinion at other crucial points in the war.[175] Just as important for understanding why the UN offensive was allowed to continue in November is the nature of incoming intelligence in the fall of 1950. While it indeed suggested a greater risk of war with China, no firm conclusions about Beijing's intentions could be drawn even in late November. Lacking a clear picture of what the military consequences of continuing the Korean offensive would be, the idea of losing political influence domestically by halting MacArthur's advance would have been even less palatable to those in Washington.

While NSC 81/1 acknowledged the possibility of China's entrance into the Korean War, the document held that it was "unlikely" that foreign communist forces would be employed "in major units" in the South.[176] Though Indian ambassador K. M. Panikkar relayed information that China would be compelled to intervene if American soldiers crossed the 38th parallel, he was not seen as credible. Panikkar was perceived as sympathetic to communism, and had previously provided contradictory information.[177] Acheson also observed that China's threats had been made in private through intermediaries, and thus contended officials in Beijing were taking little to no risk as they could disavow such statements.[178] China's foreign minister Zhou Enlai made public comments forcefully condemning America's "imperialist" actions in Korea and had vowed to support the Korean people, warnings he repeated after the Wake Island Conference.[179] However, Zhou's threats came after Truman had authorized ground forces to enter North Korea, an act which led the UN to all but demand the DPRK's capitulation. Rather than deterring the United States, then, China's timing meant it would have to force the UN coalition to reverse course after being publicly threatened, a more difficult order of business. Any delay would have compromised the military advantage over the KPA and would have appeared to have been a result of diplomatic pressure.[180]

Even after UN forces made contact with heavy resistance as they drove north, the 8th Army was skeptical of reports that the CCF were present in "substantial" numbers. It was at first believed that there were only two regiments of Chinese soldiers operating near the 8th Army, and it was unclear whether the CCF were fighting independently of the KPA or not.[181] While it was possible China would send hundreds of thousands of soldiers into North Korea against the United States, it was also possible the intervention would be a limited, covert effort by the Chinese to "save face." Walter Bedell Smith, the new director of central intelligence, informed Truman on November 1 that the intention of the CCF appeared to be "to establish a limited 'cordon sanitaire' south of the Yalu River."[182] This prediction was reinforced by the absence of contact with the enemy from November 9 until the end of the month. The 8th Army and the Marines X Corps proposed that Chinese forces were likely assuming a defensive posture.[183] The CIA relayed the American embassy's conclusion that "unless the Chinese Communists intervene much more actively than they have during the past two weeks, it may be concluded that the Chinese are fighting a delaying action and are not committed to all-out intervention . . . available information favors the conclusion that Chinese intervention will in the end 'fall short of all-out war.' "[184] On the 24th, a new National Intelligence Estimate held that "available evidence is not conclusive as to whether or not the Chinese Communists are as yet committed to a full-scale offensive effort."[185]

In the face of inconclusive evidence, it was difficult for leaders to accept the political costs they would incur if UN forces halted or even retreated and no Chinese intervention took place. What is more, it was feared that hesitation might provoke the very counterintervention the United States sought to avoid. During discussions of whether or not to cross the 38th, Acheson had argued that American timidity was most likely to encourage Chinese involvement in the war.[186] Domestic critics could charge that perceived American weakness made the costs of entry appear lower to Beijing. Furthermore, MacArthur vigorously rejected any suggestion that he stop his advance north, informing a growingly cautious JCS that "it would be fatal" to slow down and that to surrender "any portion" of Korea to China "would be the greatest defeat of the free world in recent times." Failing to unite Korea would be "immoral," a defeat that would "bankrupt [U.S.] leadership and influence in Asia."[187]

In short, decision making in Washington was not driven by a blind commitment to postwar goals and inattention to associated risks. Policymakers remained attuned to incoming information about China's intentions. The commitment to uniting Korea, made before Zhou made any public warnings about crossing the 38th, significantly raised the political stakes for the Truman administration. MacArthur's autonomy as the theater commander, his strong reputation in the United States relative to the president and State Department, and his willingness to publicize his views made any challenge of his authority a costly endeavor. Even if another, less influential figure had been theater commander, the public commitment to reuniting Korea would have made altering policy in the face of severe uncertainty an unappealing choice. MacArthur's influence probably is necessary to explain why Truman allowed his forces to proceed as aggressively as they did during the "unprecedented" period of meetings in November among upper-level officials cited by Acheson. The JCS may have framed their advice to adopt a more defensive posture as an order, rather than a suggestion, had not the prestigious commander in chief, Far East (CINCFE), been heading the charge.

ORGANIZATIONAL POLITICS AND NONCOMBAT OPERATIONS

Observing Army operations in Korea in 1947, the former division commander of the Army's Civil Affairs Division in World War II wrote privately that "after six years we are in no better shape to handle military government than we were in 1941."[188] This assertion is consistent with the hypothesis that the military will not invest many resources into noncombat operations. Furthermore, MacArthur's autonomy and power relative to civilian leaders clearly made organizational factors a salient issue in 1950–1951, hindering effective strategy pertaining to combat operations. However, MacArthur's relations with civilian and uniformed officials did not appear as problematic when Washington was formulating plans for occupation. Signs of difficulties relating to interorganizational conflict only emerged after the Chinese counterintervention, and stemmed more from policymakers' short time horizons than anything else.

Johnson, head of the ECA, recorded the interorganizational problems that emerged in December 1950. In his account, the ECA had been trying to "liquidate" its Korean Program ever since December 1, when the UN passed a resolution giving its own bodies the responsibility for Korean relief and reconstruction in the posthostilities period. However, ECA had been stymied by what Johnson described as "very difficult inter-agency problems to resolve." There had arisen an unanticipated and "amazing series of disagreements between State, Defense, UN and CINCFE," with the ECA stuck assuming the role of mediator.[189] The State Department's position, as Johnson described it, was that the UN should take over the entirety of reconstruction and rehabilitation activities without the aid of the ECA. This would require the earliest possible activation of UNKRA, but "State became engaged in interminable wrangels [sic] of how, when, and to what extent the U.S.

should receive credit for its expenditures on behalf of Korea," Johnson recorded. In the meantime, "politics, jealousy, and indecision in the UN delayed the appointment of an Agent-General" for UNKRA. Further complicating matters was that U.S. military commanders showed no interest in replacing ECA with UNKRA. Their opinion was that "UNCURK . . . had come out 100 strong using up limited billeting space and accomplishing little if anything," and thus were not eager for more duties to be passed to another UN body.[190]

Because of the military's concerns, it was ultimately agreed that UNKRA would not take on operational duties "until peace and security had been restored in Korea or a designated part thereof." This was consistent with previous directives from Washington, but the Army soon proclaimed it had a mandate to take over the whole task of civil assistance in Korea "lock, stock and barrel," which led to "vigorous objections" by the State Department and ECA. Johnson concluded that "the intransigent attitude of Army has made it extremely difficult to reach agreement on the language of a Presidential letter that will relieve the [ECA] Administrator of responsibility for aid to Korea, especially since Army takes the position that MacArthur's staff must be consulted, even on questions where such consultation can have no fruitful result."[191]

Johnson's forceful criticism of interorganizational disputes and accompanying confusion regarding postconflict operations is supported by a contemporary account commissioned by the Department of the Army.[192] It also conforms to several aspects of the theoretical literature on bureaucratic politics. Army officials, whose officers in the field were actually responsible for executing noncombat operations with the war ongoing, jealously guarded the autonomy of their institution. The State Department, which had placed the UN at the center of its postwar plans in Korea as well as U.S. foreign policy generally, did not wish to harm relations with members of the American-led coalition. However, the interorganizational struggles Johnson described would not have emerged without China's entrance into the war, an event on which U.S. intelligence had not previously established a firm position. The tumult created by China's involvement upset existing timetables on the transition to postconflict operations, leading to the conflict and confusion over organizational responsibilities that existed in the winter of 1950–1951. It also clearly showed that the potential impact of a Chinese intervention had not been factored into noncombat plans, even though the possibility of such an intervention was being given close attention by those reviewing ongoing combat operations. The Department of the Army's commissioned study was thus highly critical of the lack of integrated policy that resulted from a multiplicity of U.S. and UN bodies trying to simultaneously exercise control over civil affairs in Korea by 1951, a problem that would have been avoided had the assumption of an early end to hostilities been met.[193]

It was not only the Army that exhibited confusion about its authority vis-à-vis noncombat operations in the aftermath of China's invasion. The main UN bodies could not even agree among themselves who was responsible for what domain. UNCURK reported that, pending termination of hostilities with China, reconstruction operations in Korea "would obviously be unfeasible," and any such activities would be carried out just as well by the military for the time being. Despite this report, Acheson still insisted that an agent general of UNKRA be appointed "promptly" since a "large and serious refugee problem" could develop. In his view, the availability of further relief assistance from UN members depended on the existence of an agent general who could solicit contributions.[194] After J. Donald Kingsley had been appointed agent general, he complained that MacArthur had indicated relief responsibilities would remain a military responsibility and that UN staff would fall under military command. Acheson had to explain that, consistent with plans prior to China's intervention, such responsibilities were to remain within the military's purview as long as hostilities were ongoing.[195] The secretary did not note that Kingsley's complaint was a *reversal* of UNCURK's position a few weeks prior, which indicated a preference that the UNC retain its lead role.

In any regard, the consequences of organizational disputes were muted by the fact that China's entrance into the war had pushed postconflict activities an indefinite length of time into the future. Prior to that point, the Army's actions had not hindered preparations for noncombat operations. In fact, the Army's recommendations for the postconflict period had been embraced by Truman and other senior officials as the template to guide occupation policy, and had been judged superior to efforts coming from the State Department's Northeast Asian Affairs Office. The military did not resist investing resources in planning noncombat operations. Furthermore, its assessments of noncombat operations were no worse than that of the fall offensive, as neither accurately predicted costs that would be incurred by the Chinese entrance into the war.

Conclusion

The strategic assessments made at the highest levels in the Truman administration during the Korean War were sound in that they made use of available information and attempted to enumerate the short-term costs and risks that could impact the success of the occupation of the peninsula. For the majority of officials, concerns about the feasibility of ongoing and near-future military operations trumped evaluations of the desirability of unifying Korea, since that goal was never given much weight prior to the war. Even after the U.S. government decided to expand its war aims, most framed the decision as a necessary response to defend the ROK and the status quo ante. The surprise of the attack, the fluid military situation in Korea, and the short period of time that policymakers perceived was available to prepare for the war's aftermath reinforced the short time horizons arising from the nature of their political objectives.

Given policymakers' short time horizons, CLT predicts that low-level issues would be given careful consideration, but officials would not necessarily attend to long-run risks and costs unless prompted to do so. Even then, CLT expects there to be a lack of communication fluency between short-sighted individuals thinking concretely and the more abstract viewpoints of their relatively far-sighted counterparts. This was reflected in the relative meager impact the evaluations of Allison, Emmerson, and like-minded officials had on overall postwar policy in Korea. If Truman and others in his administration had been more inclined to take the long view, they may also have been more cognizant of the warnings proffered by Kennan and Dulles concerning the long-range challenges of maintaining a unified Korea on China's borders.

Finally, the study of Korea highlights the importance of individual characteristics. MacArthur's assessments appear better explained by a general tendency toward overconfidence rather than his temporal construal. Kennan's assessments are also problematic from the perspective of CLT. Like Truman, Acheson, members of the JCS, and others, he attached little importance to Korea prior to the war. Why was Kennan more alert to the long-term difficulties an attempt to unify the peninsula might entail than those with similar political views? Though possible interactions between personality traits and situational factors emphasized by CLT are beyond the scope of this book, more research is needed on these dynamics.

State Building during Escalation in Vietnam

Though the United States' military involvement in South Vietnam (RVN) began much earlier than 1965, it was not until that year that the primary mission of American forces became the conduct of combat operations against the communist insurgency there. American programs meant to quell unrest in the Vietnamese countryside had been unsuccessful. As the communist insurgency in the South intensified with the formation of the National Liberation Front (or Vietcong) in 1960, U.S. efforts in the country became increasingly focused on combat. The number of U.S. military advisers increased from 680 to 16,000 by the end of 1963 and, in the assessment of one historian, "the twin aims of economic development and state building . . . fell into abeyance."[1] Noncombat activities were increasingly overshadowed by missions to kill insurgents and coerce the government of North Vietnam (DRV). Assuming the presidency following the assassination of John F. Kennedy, Lyndon Johnson initiated a prolonged bombing campaign in the spring of 1965 and, in July of that year, authorized the deployment of more than 100,000 ground troops to the RVN.

The predominant view in the political psychology literature on the Vietnam War is that Johnson and his advisers were rigidly focused on a military solution to the conflict, to the exclusion of political negotiations with the DRV or political reform in Saigon. Johnson's personal beliefs and interpretation of history allegedly led him to perceive external aggression as the primary problem facing the RVN, and place greater emphasis on combat operations as the solution.[2] Noncombat tasks "fell into abeyance," according to these arguments, in part because leaders' biases left them unable or reluctant to engage with a full range of policy options. Such explanations are complemented by works that draw from organizational theory to assert that the U.S. Army was not inclined to engage in state building or counterinsurgency campaigns. Instead officers advanced plans that would use firepower to overwhelm the enemy and achieve victory, as U.S. armed forces had done in previous wars.[3]

As opposed to the preceding arguments, the historical record for 1964 and 1965 shows that the president and key officials—civilian and uniformed—

acknowledged that the problem in the RVN was fundamentally related to politics in that country, rather than the threat emanating from the DRV. Johnson and others repeatedly stressed that the use of force was insufficient to secure a favorable outcome. This remained the case even as the security situation in the country deteriorated. Consistent with an opportunity costs perspective, combat operations became more prominent as the military advantage shifted in favor of communist forces. Contrary to the opportunity cost hypothesis, however, noncombat activities also remained at the forefront of deliberations, rather than receding into the background. Members of the administration were well aware of the delicate status of the RVN government (the GVN), and had no illusions that it could be made solvent without great cost.

Concerns about the military balance between the South Vietnamese army (ARVN) and communist forces, along with worries about the political fragility of the GVN, compelled officials overseeing Vietnam policy to adopt short time horizons. At many points Americans in Washington and Saigon did not take it for granted that the South could hold together for more than two or three months into the future. Furthermore, despite the attention given to the workings of the GVN, the administration's objective was to reform politics in the RVN so as to prevent a communist victory—to protect the status quo rather than secure future gains. To put it another way, Washington's means could be described as transformative, but its ends could not. Construal level theory (CLT) predicts actors focused on the near term will be biased toward concrete modes of thought, discouraging overconfident assessments while inclining policymakers to evaluate the feasibility of low-level operations over and above the desirability of high-level objectives those operations are meant to achieve. The decision-making process in the Johnson administration from 1964 through the summer of 1965 meets these expectations. Policy deliberations were marked by an intense focus on the means by which the GVN could be saved, both from communist insurgents and its own internal weaknesses. Both combat and noncombat actions were given careful consideration. The concrete steps that had to be taken to make the GVN durable in the long term were salient *because* of officials' short time horizons, not despite them.

Conversely, policymakers in the Johnson administration struggled to articulate their ultimate, high-level aims in Vietnam. In the German case, Franklin Roosevelt failed to make his objectives clear to his subordinates. In 1964 and 1965 political leaders in the Johnson administration could not make their objectives clear to themselves. Policies in Vietnam were advanced if they could be feasibly executed in the short term, not necessarily because they advanced high-level strategic ends. As one observer of the war stated, the utility of a given action was judged "not in terms of publicly avowed long-range aims, but in terms of the successive short-range aims and expectations that were actually . . . salient in the White House."[4] Beyond a general agreement that the consequences of a communist takeover of the RVN would be bad for the United States, there was little understanding among the president and his advisers concerning the country's purpose in Vietnam, what ultimate "success" would look like, and how much it was worth. As such, strategic assessments were skewed toward weighting the costs and feasibility of U.S. actions in Vietnam over the desirability of the (murky) objectives these actions were to achieve. What is more, this short-term focus made the possible immediate consequences of withdrawal much more salient than the possible long-term consequences of military escalation, even though officials harbored few illusions of what the latter might be.

Key Decisions and Events in Saigon and Washington, 1964–1965

Until 1965, U.S. forces had acted in an advisory and assistance role vis-à-vis the ARVN. Besides assisting with combat operations, U.S. personnel were taking part in a state-building effort on par with those immediately following World War II. Since the 1950s the United States had provided financial and technical assistance to train an RVN national police force, provide education in governmental administration, modernize elements of the country's infrastructure, and deliver food and other forms of humanitarian assistance in an attempt to provide the South Vietnamese with a higher standard of living. Johnson assumed the presidency with serious misgivings about the American presence in the RVN, but would still greatly increase U.S. involvement in the country. National Security Action Memorandum 273 (NSAM-273), Johnson's first as president, held "it remains the central object of the United States in South Vietnam to assist the people and Government of that country to win their contest against the externally directed and supported Communist conspiracy."[5] In February 1964 Johnson established a committee to manage U.S. policy and operations in the RVN, to be headed by the State Department's William Sullivan under the supervision of Secretary of State Dean Rusk.[6]

Upon his return from the RVN in March, Secretary of Defense Robert McNamara told Johnson that if the country did not remain independent "almost all of Southeast Asia will probably fall under Communist dominance."[7] This assessment intensified considerations of increased U.S. military involvement in the country. In May Assistant Secretary of Defense John McNaughton headed up an effort to assess the costs and risks of taking "graduated action" in the form of air strikes against the DRV. Johnson was given a Defense memo on the hypothesized effects of different air strike packages and the possible responses by the DRV and China on May 24.[8] In June McNamara went to Honolulu to meet with Henry Cabot Lodge and General William Westmoreland, head of the Military Assistance Command in Vietnam (MACV). The three agreed that the increased Vietcong activity in the

RVN in the preceding months called for additional actions on the part of the United States.[9] After taking over for Lodge as ambassador at the end of June, General Maxwell Taylor began formulating potential cross-border raids into Laos, air attacks against targets in the DRV, and plans for defending against retaliatory attacks by the North.

Officials received word the first week of August that North Vietnamese patrol boats had made two attacks on U.S. destroyers collecting signals intelligence on the DRV from the Tonkin Gulf. Though it is likely that the second attack never occurred, it appeared in Washington that the DRV was conducting a deliberate campaign against U.S. warships. On August 10 Congress passed what came to be called the Tonkin Gulf Resolution, which read that "the Congress approves and supports the determination of the President . . . to take all necessary measures to repel any armed attack against the forces of the United States and to prevent further aggression." The next month NSAM-314 specified that the United States should prepare for more attacks by the DRV and Vietcong, and approved continued naval patrols in the Tonkin Gulf as well as covert military operations against the North.[10]

Following a high-level meeting with the president on November 2, a new working group on Vietnam, also called the Executive Committee or "Excom," was formed. It was chaired by Assistant Secretary of State William Bundy, and included officials at the assistant-secretary level from the Joint Chiefs of Staff (JCS), Central Intelligence Agency (CIA), and Defense Department. The broad options in Vietnam, as the Excom saw them, were for U.S. forces to continue along present lines; begin to apply military pressure on the DRV via "a systematic program of attacks of increasing intensity" in which efforts at negotiations would be tabled; or utilize a more gradual bombing campaign against the DRV akin to a "slow, controlled squeeze" in order to bring about negotiations with Hanoi. Given the perceived costs and risks associated with the three options, McNamara and National Security Adviser McGeorge Bundy (William's brother) informed Johnson that planners were leaning toward the graduated bombing campaign.[11]

Johnson had also inquired in November as to whether U.S. ground forces would be necessary in the RVN to protect bases and personnel stationed there. Westmoreland informed Taylor the first week of January that 75,000 troops would be required to secure U.S. facilities in the RVN. Taylor was quite apprehensive, telling Johnson that he found the MACV recommendation "startling." He advised the JCS that, once the policy of keeping combat units out of the RVN was breached, "it will be very difficult to hold the line" against future commitments.[12] Meanwhile, support for bombing the DRV within the administration continued to grow. On February 8, 1965, Johnson informed his top advisers that he had chosen to move forward with greater military action against the DRV. The only question left, he said, was how fast and at what magnitude this force would be applied.[13] The bombing of the DRV, Operation Rolling Thunder, began in March, as a limited but sustained campaign (or "slow squeeze") meant to coerce the North to stop supporting the Vietcong in the South.

While preparations for large-scale combat operations were being made behind the scenes in Washington and Saigon, Johnson publicly emphasized the noncombat aspects of the U.S. presence in Vietnam. In a speech at Johns Hopkins University in April, the president proposed a $1-billion aid package that would develop the Mekong Delta much like the Tennessee Valley in the United States. Johnson had been exposed to ideas for such a project while he was still vice president and had expressed enthusiasm for them, remarking that "all my life I have been interested in rivers and their development." Some have drawn parallels between Johnson's Great Society programs for America and his views on development in Southeast Asia. As Lloyd Gardner observes, from Congress to the White House "Johnson's whole career *was* the politics of economic development."[14] The proposal for the Mekong Delta area could be seen as an outgrowth of ideas behind the Strategic Hamlet program that Kennedy had initiated. Aside from separating South Vietnamese villagers from insurgents, American officials had hoped strategic hamlets could be used to modernize rural economies and, even more ambitiously, establish a strong national identity among a people they thought lacked one.[15] Even as combat operations were ramped up in 1965, nonmilitary assistance to the RVN increased 36 percent to $216 million.[16]

NSAM-328, released the first week of April, formally approved an 18,000-to-20,000 increase in U.S. military support personnel, as well as two additional Marine battalions and a Marine air squadron to deploy to the RVN. Johnson also authorized a change in the Marines' mission which would "permit their more active use" than had been granted previously in their role defending U.S. airbases. The president directed that the tempo of Rolling Thunder and air operations in Laos be increased, and that the possible use of aerial mining or a blockade of North Vietnamese ports be subjected to further study.[17] By June 8, those in Washington were discussing whether or not to approve Westmoreland's request to raise total deployments to 34 battalions, or 175,000 men. There was broad opposition to this number of American personnel operating in the RVN among Johnson's top advisers. On June 18 the president approved a deployment of up to 115,000 troops, with the possibility that only 95,000 would be sent.[18]

By the end of June, McNamara and Under Secretary of State George Ball had prepared opposing papers stating their views of the U.S. intervention. Ball recommended withdrawal, arguing that the RVN lacked the political will to keep fighting and that there "could not be worse" terrain for the U.S. military to operate in. Observing that the French had tried to adapt their forces to guerilla fighting in Indochina and failed, Taylor also remarked, "I doubt that U.S. forces could do much better."[19] McNamara, however, thought an additional 34 battalions could make "a significant difference" in the war. As to whether such a large expansion of the U.S. presence in the RVN would hurt the GVN politically, McNamara acknowledged "we do not know."[20] Ultimately, after continuing deliberations throughout July, Johnson publicly announced on the 28th that the total number of U.S. forces in the RVN would be increased to 125,000, adding that "additional forces will be needed later, and they will be sent as requested."[21]

CLT

Historians of the Vietnam War have made an observation this section seeks to more fully develop, namely that the means by which U.S. policymakers believed they could preserve the RVN were much more salient than the actual ends these operations were to achieve. A pattern of thinking in which top officials largely considered questions of "how" rather than "why" defined decision making among Johnson and his advisers. This is because Johnson and his advisers had short time horizons. First, Johnson's domestic political agenda discouraged him from thinking ahead toward future Vietnam policy for much of 1964. After the 1964 election Johnson began giving Vietnam more attention, but events in the RVN compelled him and his advisers to focus overwhelmingly on the country's immediate political and military situation. Lastly, policymakers sought maintenance objectives rather than transformative goals. Johnson consistently stressed the importance of minimizing near-term losses, even if this strategy could lead to substantial problems later on. Given the administration's short time horizons, CLT predicts that officials would focus on their proposed actions' feasibility more than the desirability of the ends they were supposed to achieve.

The administration's focus on the means rather than ends of policy might be taken as a way of coping with cognitive dissonance: officials found themselves in a losing war whose ultimate objectives were unattainable and responded by focusing on immediate operations they could control. The problem with this interpretation, as shown in the following sections, is that officials were overwhelmingly pessimistic that ongoing operations were having even modest positive effects; they did not eschew information that caused them mental discomfort. Furthermore, individuals tend to alleviate dissonance by exaggerating the importance and desirability of the goals they seek, the exact opposite of behavior of those in the Johnson administration who were largely unable to articulate high-level objectives.[22] By and large, officials sought to craft policies that could be feasibly executed given the constraints they faced, feeling compelled to take action without a clear idea of what their actions would accomplish.

When it came to Vietnam policy, time horizons in the Johnson White House were short. An actor's time horizon is partially determined by the value he attaches to certain objectives across time, and Johnson's choices in 1964–1965 indicated that Vietnam's future carried less weight than other political concerns. The president placed greater priority on domestic policy even after his electoral victory in November. He thought he had a narrow window of time in which to move his Great Society programs forward, a belief which kept his attention focused on the immediate future. While he may have eventually escalated U.S. military involvement in Vietnam regardless, he was determined that nothing upset his ongoing efforts to push his legislative agenda. Vietnam policy was designed to protect Johnson's immediate goals, even though he was aware his choices could carry costly long-term consequences.

Most importantly, even when Johnson became more focused on Vietnam in late 1964, he and his advisers felt a considerable amount of time pressure to get things accomplished. Numerous indicators supported the conclusion that a South Vietnamese collapse could occur in the near future and thus policy initiatives had to be aimed at achieving immediate improvements. The goal was to preserve the United States' current position in Southeast Asia, and thus the status quo, not some unrealized future state of affairs, served as a focal point. Any long-term fears about Vietnam setting off communist takeovers in other states—"domino theory," an idea Johnson did not put great stock in—were offset by more pressing concerns about the short-term viability of the RVN.

Domestic Politics. Though he did not ignore developments in Vietnam, Johnson's primary concern in 1964 was winning election to the presidency in November and passing his Great Society legislation. According to aide Jack Valenti, when Johnson entered office Vietnam did not carry much weight with the president: it "was a cloud no bigger than a man's fist on the horizon."[23] Bundy's recollection was that the campaign dominated the collective attention of officials in the White House, making Vietnam policy seem minor by comparison. In a 1969 interview he recalled that Johnson paid attention to Vietnam "in the sense that he had it on his mind, but it was not his main account. His main account was the election of 1964, the nomination first, the securing of his political flanks against what he saw as the Kennedy threat, and the effective choice of the right vice president; all this is the period of sort of spring-summer. The immediate business was to govern the country. And while Vietnam was certainly the principal overseas problem, it wasn't one that he had to deal with right then."[24] Johnson's other advisers concurred with Bundy's judgment. Clark Clifford believed that "Vietnam was not particularly prominent [in 1964]; it was there . . . but I do not recall it as being a major issue at that time." Ball likewise reflected after the war that while Vietnam "had begun to fill up more and more of the kind of screen through which we view things, at that time it was just one of a lot of things that were ongoing."[25] This was apparent in Johnson's 1964 reelection bid. A State Department official sent a memorandum to Bundy listing Vietnam as one of the issues that "received little or no attention during the campaign."[26] While he clearly was not going to abandon the GVN, Johnson told aide Bill Moyers, "I want 'em to leave me alone, because I've got some bigger things to do right here at home."[27] At points in 1964 Johnson seemed to wish the Vietnam conflict would disappear. He complained to his national security adviser and Senator Richard Russell that, though he did not believe the United States could withdraw, he also could not help but think the RVN was not "worth fighting for."[28]

Given Johnson's sentiments in 1964, some have argued that domestic politics were the primary factor determining why the president chose to dramatically escalate U.S. military involvement the following year. Though Johnson placed little weight on Vietnam, according to this argument, he may have believed his treasured Great Society programs would be defeated if he allowed the RVN to fall.[29] What emerges most clearly in the historical record is that domestic considerations affected *how* Johnson chose to apply force against the DRV, if not why he chose to do so. The actions he took were designed to leave as small an impression on the American people as possible. He simultaneously sought to limit information available to the public so as to minimize potential negative reactions, even though the effects of his deceptions could eventually prove politically damaging at home and hurt the war effort. He did so in accordance with his short time horizons, which made the president considerably more sensitive to any immediate domestic upheaval that could damage him politically than long-term consequences of U.S. actions in Southeast Asia.

Johnson was quite wary of the public's possible reactions to greater military involvement in Vietnam. McNamara had told the president that the stakes in Vietnam were made greater by "domestic factors," and Johnson wondered on more than one occasion whether or not a communist victory in the RVN would lead to his impeachment.[30] In January 1964 Bundy reminded Johnson of the political losses suffered by President Harry Truman after the communists prevailed in China's civil war, saying that Americans thought the White House had not done all it could to back the Nationalist forces there. A year later Bundy argued that a larger military intervention would deter accusations that "we did not do all that we could have done," which would be important to U.S. citizens.[31] However, Johnson's countervailing apprehensions about the public's tolerance for U.S. involvement in Vietnam were also clearly evident in 1964. The JCS made a private assessment that Johnson did not want to "lose" the RVN before the presidential election in November, "nor did he want the country to go to war." In fact, Johnson had told advisers that he planned to "maintain the status quo" in

Vietnam until after the election, though he was open to new "social work" programs.[32] Johnson informed Bundy in March that "we haven't got any Congress that will go with us, and we haven't got any mothers that will go with us in war."[33] In May he asked McNamara, Bundy, and Ball how he could carry a "united country" with him to war "under conditions where the rest of the world would regard us as wrong-headed." That same month he told his friend Senator Russell that the casualties that came with escalation would undermine his public support and spawn Republican criticism.[34]

At a National Security Council (NSC) meeting in the spring of 1965, the president complained that he could not be certain of congressional support in the event of war, and that constituent mail was running 50-to-1 against administration policy during Rolling Thunder.[35] Johnson would have been right to be wary about the level of domestic support for military action. At the time, U.S. citizens' expressed preferences in response to an open-ended question about Vietnam policy clustered together; sticking with present policies, negotiating with Vietnamese communists, withdrawing U.S. forces, and sending U.S. troops to war were all significantly outweighed by the modal response "don't know."[36] Johnson feared the public's response to a greater U.S. role in the fighting in Vietnam almost as much as he feared its response to a communist victory. Given this dilemma, and his sensitivity to immediate losses that could upset his valued domestic agenda, Johnson chose to avoid extreme actions in the direction of either withdrawal or escalation. He was determined to keep Vietnam policy from national attention, as he thought he had a very limited period of time in which to make legislative progress on the Great Society. As a result, he pursued options he thought would give him the "maximum protection at the least cost."[37] Bundy thought the decision to keep information about the administration's policy from the American people was a mistake, but reflected after the war that the president was fixated on "a legislative program as long as your arm, and he made a conscious decision that he was not going to explain [Vietnam policy]."[38]

When he was presented with Westmoreland's plan to send in ground forces in 1965, the president deliberately rejected every part of the recommendation that would have raised the public profile of the new policy. Johnson instructed Rusk, McNamara and Director of Central Intelligence John McCone that "it was a matter of the highest importance" that decisions on Vietnam policy not become public. Bundy reassured the president that it was understood he did not want "a loud public signal of a major change in policy right now." Rusk reiterated Johnson's concerns to the embassy in Saigon, avowing that "if U.S. sources sternly refused details, few reporters will seek out accurate facts by themselves."[39] When he authorized the expansion of ground operations in April, he directed that the administration seek to "minimize any appearance of sudden changes in policy," and communicate that such actions "be understood as being gradual and wholly consistent with existing policy."[40]

By failing to invite public debate while neglecting to call up the reserves or declare a national emergency, Johnson protected his immediate interests but invited long-term costs. His chosen approach minimized the likelihood of a negative public reaction in the short term, but courted inflation and placed a greater portion of Vietnam's fate in the hands of draftees.[41] Similarly, employing a "slow squeeze" strategy when bombing the North was cost-averse from the immediate standpoint of domestic politics. The president's domestic assistants wrote as Rolling Thunder began that the president faced the danger that the bombing would appear on "front page of every newspaper" and damage the "consensus on which domestic progress depended."[42] Perhaps the clearest indicator that Johnson privileged short-term over long-term considerations is that he knowingly jeopardized his future political standing. He confided in McNamara that when he sought the Tonkin Gulf Resolution he "had no intention of committing this many ground troops. We're doing so now, and we know it's going to be bad. And the question is, do we just want to do it out on a limb by ourselves?"[43] Avoiding open discussion of Vietnam policy increased the likelihood that blame for a long and costly war would eventually fall on the White House, more so than Congress or others who would have been involved in a wider debate.[44] Nevertheless, Johnson did not seek a second congressional resolution and, against his advisers counsel, obscured the military path on which he had set the country. Bundy characterized Johnson's attitude as follows: "I don't want to louse up and lose a month of laws over a resolution [on Vietnam] that will preoccupy the Senate and make people angry, and upset half the people. They don't want it and I don't want it."[45]

Time Pressure. After Johnson secured the presidency in November the perceived importance of Vietnam began to rise. By then, however, a constant sense of time pressure permeated the Johnson administration, preventing officials from looking very far into the future. The overarching substance of much of the deliberations and intelligence gathering in 1964 and 1965 was that the noncommunist regime in Saigon had little time to live. It was frequently hypothesized that it was not a matter of years, but rather a few months or even weeks until the GVN collapsed or sought neutralization and an agreement with the communist opposition, two possibilities which were more or less equivalent in the mind of U.S. leaders.[46] This meant that policymakers had even less time to formulate and implement a plan of action to preserve the GVN.

Though Saigon had not fallen despite continuous negative reports from the field in 1964, McNamara thought that the situation could "disintegrate."[47] Despite his preoccupation with domestic affairs, Johnson was not deaf to these signals. In May he informed Lodge that, in his opinion, time was not on Washington's side in Southeast Asia, and requested that Bundy and the NSC staff provide him with an assessment of how big a window the United

States had to work with in Vietnam. Communicating to the president on behalf of Bundy, Michael Forrestal replied that any improvements that had been made were not enough "to indicate a trend for the better." He saw an increasing chance of a "political accident or upheaval" in the RVN and felt that the United States would need to take some action in the next four to six weeks that would communicate to Saigon that the Vietcong could be resisted.[48]

The political accident or upheaval of which Forrestal spoke reflected the instability of the GVN; Taylor's evaluation August 10 was that General Ngyuen Khanh's government, which had come in the months after Ngo Dinh Diem's overthrow, had a "50-50 chance of lasting out the year." He advised that the United States would have to prepare to militarily compel the DRV to stop supporting the insurgency. Taylor set January 1, 1965, a date less than five months away, as a target for escalation, though events might force the United States into action at "a considerably earlier date."[49] Shortly thereafter Rusk cabled Taylor that the "deterioration of governmental processes" in Saigon was "proceeding faster than we had anticipated." On August 27 the JCS advised McNamara it was their opinion that Taylor was right to say the GVN could fall considerably earlier than January 1 and advised "an accelerated program of actions with respect to the DRV is essential to prevent a complete collapse of the U.S. position in Southeast Asia." The feeling in Washington was that the South was slipping from its grasp at a quickening pace.[50]

As 1964 drew to a close, Bundy reported to Johnson that the North Vietnamese appeared "confident that time is on their side" and that the evidence supported the "general conclusion that the situation is going steadily but slowly against us there."[51] Messages indicating time was increasingly short for the regime in Saigon continued unabated into 1965. In the words of one historian, the RVN's collapse was seen as "imminent" by "nearly everyone" in the administration that year; Johnson later noted it became clear in early 1965 "gradually but unmistakably, that Hanoi was moving in for the kill."[52] While the Excom had in late 1964 assessed that the political situation in the RVN was "critical and extremely fragile," in January Bundy told Rusk that "the situation in Vietnam is now likely to come apart more rapidly than we had anticipated in November." At the same time, Taylor's message from Saigon was that the "seriously deteriorating situation" there meant "there is a comparatively short time fuse on this situation."[53]

In January Johnson faced heavy pressure from his top advisers as they began to contemplate an impending defeat. Bundy insisted to the president that without new military action "defeat appears inevitable—probably not in a matter of weeks or perhaps even months, but within the next year or so. There is still time to turn it around, but not much." He concluded that "to be an American in Saigon today is to have a gnawing feeling that time is against us."[54] Then, on January 27, Bundy and McNamara reported they were both convinced that the course the United States was on could "only lead to disastrous defeat." This message was echoed by General Harold Johnson, who on returning from the RVN on March 14 told the president that "time was running out swiftly" and that the prospect of a stable GVN was poor.[55] While Taylor asserted that the situation in Saigon showed signs of improvement in April, a change he attributed to the Rolling Thunder campaign, such hopes were quickly dashed. By May, concentrated Vietcong attacks were devastating the RVN's military, and Westmoreland reported that ARVN battalions were being destroyed faster than new ones could be raised.[56]

Maintenance Objectives. U.S. objectives in Vietnam shifted considerably in the decade following the 1954 Geneva Accords. The record shows that, whatever the intentions of earlier administrations may have been, Johnson and top foreign policy officials under him were focused on maintaining a noncommunist regime in the RVN to the exclusion of other goals. For example, the Eisenhower administration had been concerned not only with preserving the RVN but incorporating it into a collective security organization for the future defense of Southeast Asia.[57] By way of contrast, in 1964 McNamara told Johnson that while the United States sought "an independent non-Communist South Vietnam," it was not necessary "that it serve as a Western base or as a member of a Western Alliance." In December an administration position paper on Southeast Asia endorsed by Johnson held that U.S. objectives were first to "get Hanoi and North Vietnam (DRV) support and direction removed from South Vietnam," second to "re-establish an independent and secure South Vietnam with appropriate international safeguards," and third, to "maintain the security of other non-Communist nations in Southeast Asia," especially Laos.[58] Six months later, a similar paper stated that "we take US objectives in Vietnam to be the reduction of Viet Cong insurgency to manageable levels and, as part of this, forcing the DRV to cease promoting that insurgency." Any other goals were seen as "more specific and limited."[59]

Some of Johnson's top advisers had previously asserted broad transformative aims for Vietnam. Early in Kennedy's presidency Bundy had envisioned that a successful U.S. intervention in Vietnam could have "great effects all over the world" in combating communism, a statement akin to those who thought the unification of Korea would have long-term effects in rolling back communism in Asia.[60] However, under Johnson this type of transformative language was muted. McCone recorded that Johnson made it "abundantly clear" to his top advisers in November 1963 "that he did not think we had to reform every Asian into our own image" and that to do so in Vietnam would be a mistake. He desired an ambassador in Saigon with "enough judgment to realize he can't make Vietnam into an America *overnight*."[61] By July 1965 Rusk believed that the preservation of a noncommunist RVN was quite independent from the future course that country would take, writing "the 'war aim' of the United States is not concerned with what the South Vietnamese would do if they were left alone. . . . U.S. forces are present in South Viet-Nam only because of the aggression of Hanoi in sending men and arms into the South."[62]

Besides Johnson's possible influence on his advisers, the negative trends the Saigon embassy relayed to Washington likely made near-term events much more salient than any long-term fears or objectives. In late 1964, Bundy's reaction to Senator Mike Mansfield's inquiries into U.S. policy was a far cry from the aims he had articulated under Kennedy. He told Mansfield that the administration's goals were limited to stability in the RVN, saying "it is not clear to us that peaceful unification of all Vietnam is the best slogan for a government [the GVN] which has all it can do to deal with its own immediate problems."[63] Whatever value had been attached to the RVN's political development declined as the year wore on. While preparing to begin the ground war in July, McNamara wrote that an acceptable outcome would be one in which the GVN remained independent—hopefully siding with the United States in the Cold War, but perhaps genuinely neutral. He added that "a favorable outcome could include also arrangements regarding elections" and "relations between North and South Vietnam," but liberalizing the RVN and improving North–South relations were secondary considerations relative to simply maintaining the status quo.[64]

Though he attended to noncombat activities that could potentially preserve the GVN, Johnson did not view these operations as having wider implications for the South Vietnamese people or the region. For example, in his speech at Johns Hopkins University in April 1965, Johnson gave what could be interpreted as his most prominent articulation of a transformative vision for Vietnam prior to the commencement of the U.S.-led ground war. He laid out a picture of the Mekong Delta being developed much like the Tennessee Valley in the United States, an action which could be seen as having long-range consequences if realized. However, the historical consensus is that Johnson intended this statement mainly for public consumption to appease liberal critics of his increased troop deployments to Vietnam. Johnson hoped drawing attention to economic development projects in Southeast Asia would quiet the "sob sisters and peace societies domestically."[65] NSC staff member Chester Cooper wrote a memorandum on "Analysis of White House Mail on Vietnam" shortly thereafter which reported the speech "brought a sharp reversal in the heavy flow of critical mail," reaffirming the notion that its primary purpose had been to shape public attitudes.[66] Accordingly, NSAM-329 on the establishment of a task force on economic and social development in Southeast Asia charged those responsible for development tasks first and foremost with ensuring "public confidence in their effectiveness."[67] In short, the development of Vietnam was a means of stabilizing the GVN and a strategic tool for dealing with domestic political audiences, not one of the president's long-term goals.

Domino Theory. Washington officials sometimes asserted that the fall of the RVN would lead to Chinese expansion and more Southeast Asian states capitulating to communism—the so-called "domino theory" (DT). DT was inherently future-oriented, focusing on eventual costs U.S. leaders could expect to pay if their intervention in Vietnam was unsuccessful. It was thought Vietnam could be used as a base for communist aggression elsewhere in the region, and that U.S. prestige and resolve would appear weaker to allies and adversaries in future crises. However, aside from the immediate vulnerability of the GVN driving aside other concerns in 1965, DT became increasingly discredited in the first two years of Johnson's presidency. Intelligence indicated the fortunes of countries in Southeast Asia would be largely unaffected by whether the United States "lost" Vietnam or not.

Bundy had told Johnson in early 1964 that even the neutralization of the RVN would lead to neutrality in Thailand, the collapse anticommunism in Laos, heavy communist pressure on Malaya and Malaysia, and even a shift toward neutrality in Japan and the Philippines. The United States would need to increase its security commitments in South Korea and Taiwan as a result. McNamara spoke of even broader consequences, postulating that the communist threat to Australia and New Zealand would also increase.[68] In March Bundy wrote to himself that America's primary interest in Vietnam was to not be seen as a "paper tiger," and that it would be better to commit 100,000 troops and lose than lose without fighting.[69] The United States' reputation could be preserved if it played the "good doctor" who stuck by its dying South Vietnamese patient come what may.[70] When Johnson asked top advisers that September whether or not they doubted the RVN was worth continuing U.S. efforts, the vast majority of them strongly endorsed DT in response.[71] McNaughton believed that, whereas improving the lives of South Vietnamese barely registered as an objective, the administration's primary goals were to avoid a defeat that would damage U.S. credibility in the Cold War, and to keep Vietnam out of China's control.[72]

In line with CLT, however, individuals with short time horizons sought to examine the assumptions of DT rather than taking the theory at face value. When Johnson asked Senator Russell about the military significance of the RVN in May of 1964, Russell replied, "it isn't important a damn bit," though both men agreed that the country was still important from a "psychological standpoint."[73] Shortly thereafter Johnson asked the CIA to answer the question "would the rest of Southeast Asia necessarily fall?" if Saigon did. The agency provided a mixed assessment. It reported that such an event would be "damaging to U.S. prestige and seriously debase the credibility of US will and capability to contain the spread of Communism elsewhere in the area," but at the same time predicted that Cambodia was the only state likely to become communist if the RVN's regime fell.[74] The Excom dealt a less ambiguous blow to DT in the fall of 1964, calling it "over-simplified" and advancing the argument that events in Asia "would depend heavily on the circumstances in which South Vietnam was lost and whether the loss did in fact greatly weaken or lead to the early loss of other areas of Southeast Asia." William Bundy asserted that other Asian nations were unlikely to believe the United States could not come to their aid if the RVN became communist, describing DT as "much too pat."[75] In other words, contextual details drove the Excom's expectations, not an abstract theory.

McNamara, who had most strenuously pushed DT as a reason for increasing the U.S. military commitment to the RVN, clearly did not put much stock in that rationale by June and July 1965. If the consequences of a Vietnam unified under communist rule were as ominous as he and others had previously claimed, it is hard to understand why he might seriously consider accepting neutralization in July. He assured Johnson that he had "a very definite limitation on commitment in mind," continuing, "unless we're really willing to go to a full potential land war, we've got to slow down here and try to halt, at some point, the ground troop commitment." Such policy positions reveal the ever-decreasing weight officials placed on long-term consequences of a communist Vietnam, and lend credence to Gareth Porter's argument that DT was deployed in 1965 principally to influence Congress and the public to acquiesce to administration policies.[76]

It was clear to William Raborn, McCone's successor at the CIA, that the RVN was not the key to containing communism in Asia, and that the administration was overwhelmingly focused on the immediate rather than more distant future. As the United States prepared to undertake a major ground combat role in July 1965, he sent a long message to Johnson arguing that "achievement of our military objectives in Vietnam—a halting of DRV intervention and a reduction of the insurrection to manageable proportions—would leave unsolved a number of broader problems in Southeast Asia." Raborn continued that "even if we are successful in our short-term aims in South Vietnam, Southeast Asia will continue to be plagued by suspicions and fears, political and economic problems, and various forms of Communist subversion." He concluded that "we face a long-term strategic challenge is Southeast Asia," adding "I believe it is not too early to focus on these long-term problems."[77] The implication was that Johnson and his adviser's short-term worries about the RVN were crowding out concerns that were broader, more distant, and perhaps more important.

EFFORTS AT STABILIZING THE RVN

From the preceding, the United States may not have been expected to devote much time or effort assessing and implementing noncombat operations in the RVN. Johnson placed little weight on Vietnam policy for most of 1964, instead focusing on domestic concerns. By 1965, the RVN's security and political situation was seen to be in such a rapid state of deterioration that combat operations were increasingly seen as necessary to save the country. What is more, the administration lacked transformative goals for Vietnam. However, the evidence shows that neither the dire situation in the RVN nor Johnson's lack of interest in transforming the country led the administration to ignore the internal problems facing it. Noncombat operations designed to stabilize the government coexisted with efforts to address external threats from the DRV, and at many times surpassed conventional military concerns. Unlike assessment of noncombat operations in Germany and Iraq, the details and feasibility of stabilization efforts were prominent features of senior officials' assessments, even though noncombat activities were not linked to transformative ends in the Vietnam case. Johnson in particular was acutely aware of the South's political problems. CLT, which explains why policymakers with short time horizons would focus on the concrete details and feasibility of their actions, unravels behavior that would otherwise appear paradoxical.

Though they would call for the United States to take on a greater combat role in Vietnam in early 1965, Johnson's advisers also pushed for more expansive noncombat activities for most of the preceding year. In January 1964 Bundy told the president that the United States needed to pursue a "rapidly stepped-up political effort" to reverse negative trends in Saigon. Not long after he recommended the president read a memorandum by outgoing assistant secretary of state Roger Hilsman which emphasized, in Orwellian language, that the United States must not "over-militarize the war."[78] Bundy further stressed that Johnson needed the "strongest possible U.S. effort to move ahead *within* South Vietnam" and that action against the DRV was not called for: "the *first* task of this U.S. team is to strengthen the effectiveness of Khanh and his colleagues, at *every* level, and by *every* means."[79] McNamara presented Johnson with a detailed report endorsing an "oil-spot" strategy that would focus on providing security for the South Vietnamese population. In addition to a 50,000-man increase in the RVN's armed forces, McNamara told Johnson that a civil administrative corps of around 40,000 would be necessary to rehabilitate security and pacification efforts.[80] Bundy would later record that McNamara insisted the United States should have been "concentrating on intense police control from the individual villages on up" rather than "military results against guerillas in the field."[81] Even Rusk, who has been portrayed elsewhere as most insistent on the use of force against the DRV due to his experience in Korea, expressed his view that "experience in Greece, Malaya and Korea demonstrates the need for a sound structure of support before active advances can be made, and this would seem to mean genuine progress in South Viet Nam before action against the North."[82]

Johnson had not been inclined to focus on the workings of foreign governments in prior U.S. efforts to contain communism.[83] However, like his advisers he was quite cognizant of the problems of the GVN, though he lacked transformative objectives for the RVN. He saw a stable government as essential to the effective prosecution of the counterinsurgency by the ARVN, and was receptive to advice along these lines. Because Johnson shared his advisers' short time horizons and concrete mind-set, he was open to the information they provided him, or exhibited high communication fluency to use the language of CLT. Aside from responding to advisers' concerns, he was also willing to push advisers to intensify their efforts at improving the political situation in Saigon and the surrounding provinces. Above all, he was cautious when considering whether a proposed course of action might do more to destabilize the GVN then solidify it, and would change course when a policy seemed infeasible.

In May 1964 Johnson told Bundy that if the United States could "furnish the military government people that are trained in civil administration, the mayors, and the councilmen and folks of that type . . . I think that'll improve that situation a good deal."[84] By the end of May William Sullivan's committee had prepared a statement detailing a three-to-six month program that would "marry" American personnel to their Southern Vietnamese counterparts at every level in the civilian and military apparatus in the RVN. This process was driven by Johnson and officials in Washington; as Bundy reported to the president, "Lodge, and to a much less extent Westmoreland, are very wary of major U.S. 'encadrement' or 'interlarding' and are accepting this plan more because Washington urges it than because of deep belief in it." It was under Jonson's "spur" that his advisers had "begun an intensive study of new and additional steps that could be taken on the basic theory that Americans can and should do more."[85] Rusk cabled Ambassador Taylor in July that the president had concluded U.S. assistance should be directed toward a "dramatic social and economic effort" on a project to highlight the "opportunity for progress after pacification." Taylor agreed that there was a greater need to focus on political, social, and economic developments, arguing that the GVN was the biggest obstacle in fighting the insurgency.[86]

Even as Johnson began seriously considering a large, sustained U.S. combat role in Vietnam, he did not see military pressure against Hanoi as a substitute for political projects in the RVN. After the Gulf of Tonkin incident, the president reemphasized in NSAM-314 "the importance of economic and political actions having immediate impact in South Vietnam," such as government pay raises and "spot projects" throughout the country. The memo read that "the first order of business" was to "strengthen the fabric of the Government of South Vietnam."[87] Starting in September, at Johnson's request, Taylor sent weekly progress assessments of the pacification program to the president which detailed both military and political developments.[88] Having told Lodge in January that "political energy is at the center of the government's problem in South Vietnam," Johnson was reluctant to approve actions that might sap whatever energy the GVN had left.[89]

When pressured to assign an active combat role to U.S. forces in September, Johnson pointedly asked his top civilian and military advisers whether doing so might make the GVN weaker. At the same time the president resisted any negotiations with the communists due to the same fears.[90] In late 1964, Taylor informed Washington that the "hopelessness" which pervaded the RVN would necessitate a U.S. bombing campaign if the GVN was to be preserved. Johnson's reaction to this advice was quite inconsistent with the argument that his actions derived from preexisting beliefs about the "external" nature of communist threats or simplistic analogies drawn from the Korea War.[91] Instead, consistent with CLT, he cited the specific context at hand—the extant political situation in Saigon—to rebut Taylor's recommendations. At a December 1 meeting with Taylor and his other top advisers, the president argued that there was no point in striking targets in the DRV if the RVN was not solid enough to absorb a counterattack.[92] Further elaborating his position two days later, the president told Taylor he thought North Vietnamese actions were *"contributory, not central"* to instability in the GVN and that an expansion of hostilities was unwise until the government could "at a minimum" reflect the will of the South Vietnamese people; maintain order in major population centers; and be able to make plans for the conduct of counterinsurgency operations. The United States should help and encourage the GVN to "broaden and intensify the civic action program . . . to produce tangible evidence of the desire of the government to help the hamlets and villages." Responses to insurgent attacks on U.S. personnel had to be sensitive "first and foremost" to "the continuing political turmoil in Saigon," and thus Johnson recommended noncombat actions "mainly within South Vietnam, which can help to turn the tide."[93] Reflecting such assertions, Bundy responded to one of Senator Mansfield's December inquiries into the administration's thinking on Vietnam by noting that the president had "hammered" on establishing a more effective Saigon government in "every meeting in recent months."[94]

The administration had largely settled on an escalation of force in Vietnam in early 1965, though it was unclear what limits would be placed on combat missions. At the same time, echoing the point Johnson had emphasized in the previous months, Bundy noted that next to fighting the Vietcong, "the shape, and structure of the government is the most important element of the Saigon situation." He believed that "the most urgent order of business" was the "improvement and broadening of the pacification program, especially its non-military [i.e., noncombat] elements." American ambitions for the GVN were modest, however, reflecting the administration's maintenance objectives and the complexities of the political environment in the RVN. Bundy hoped for a GVN that could "maintain its political authority against all challenges over a longer time than the governments of the last year and a half," a fairly low hurdle to clear.[95] Johnson soon told Ball he endorsed strengthening "by all available means the program of pacification within SVN." Such efforts would be greatly hindered by political instability that month, though, as an attempted coup was suppressed and Khanh removed from his position as commander in chief. Rusk's memo to the president following the latest round of upheaval held that the "highest possible priority must be given by us and the South Vietnamese to the establishment of a government and leadership which not only is stable but looks stable." Without that all other efforts would "prove fruitless," including pacification and "nonmilitary measures required to organize the countryside."[96]

Once again, unlike his presidential counterparts in Germany or Iraq, Johnson was responsive to his advisers' concerns and delved into a new set of programs that were notable for the number of concrete actions outlined to stabilize the RVN. In a memorandum for discussion, Bundy wrote that efforts were proceeding apace on Rolling Thunder and ground deployments of U.S. troops. He then stated that "at the President's direction, State, AID, and USIA [the U.S. Information Agency], with the White House Staff, are framing a program designed to match and even out-match the military efforts outlined above." In a list Bundy described as "non-exhaustive," he outlined that the noncombat programs would be designed to achieve "close control of the population; new programs to encourage Viet Cong defection; land reform operations; new information and propaganda programs; new incentives to university students; new programs of guerilla action in Viet Cong-controlled areas; intensified housing and agricultural programs; progressive U.S. political announcements; increased contact at all levels with political and religious groups; greatly increased decentralization of all U.S. efforts in the light of weakness and instability of central government."[97] By the first week of April Johnson had approved a *41-point* "non-military" program for the RVN. As summarized in a message from the American embassy in Saigon, the "highest authority" believed that "in addition to actions against the North, something new must be added in the South to achieve victory." Along with the 41-point program, general officers in MACV including Westmoreland would be working on providing provincial government with Army civil affairs personnel, as well as trying an experimental food distribution program targeting Vietnamese paramilitaries and their families.[98]

Despite his long-standing commitments to political stabilization efforts in Vietnam, Johnson was still willing to be flexible in response to information regarding the feasibility of actions he favored. This was evident in his response to Taylor's objections to the noncombat programs Washington was proposing. Though he had initially approved of the new stabilization efforts in the RVN, Taylor soon grew wary of their potential effects. He pointed out to Bundy that the two-month-old government that had succeeded Khanh could hardly be expected to manage the execution of what Washington had been drawing up: a proposed 21-point military program, a 41-point nonmilitary program, a 16-point program put forth by the USIA, and a 12-point program drawn up by the CIA.[99] Bundy and Rusk conveyed Taylor's concerns to Johnson, who directed all actions to be suspended pending McNamara's upcoming meeting with Westmoreland.[100]

Taylor's objections were not the end of proposals regarding pacification and stabilization in the RVN that spring and summer; in the same memo in which he recommended U.S. and allied forces insert forty-four battalions into the RVN, McNamara argued for large new construction projects and improvements in the country's food distribution system.[101] However, it did appear that officials in Washington had grown as pessimistic as Taylor regarding what, if anything, noncombat operations could accomplish in the near future. From May through July, state-building activities were mainly discussed in connection with military logistics. Efforts to deepen ports and improve airfields and access roads for supply began apace. Preparedness for combat, rather than stabilization and economic development, took center stage.[102] Even then, Taylor reminded officials in Washington of the economic and political problems these new projects created, as sharp increases in military personnel and money for construction strained local resources and pushed inflation. Strong government action would be necessary to counteract these pressures.[103]

Given the impracticality of implementing the noncombat programs under consideration in Washington in the spring of 1965, one might wonder at the seriousness of the proposal. The shift in the administration's emphasis toward combat operations further contributes to this suspicion. Yet Johnson was aware that the distribution of resources between combat and noncombat activities was becoming unbalanced, and his efforts to address the issue kept pacification from falling off the policy agenda in 1965 and 1966.[104] In February of 1966 Johnson took the initiative to organize a "heads of state" conference in Honolulu between himself and top GVN officials, mainly to address how noncombat operations could aid the war effort. Like his speech at Johns Hopkins, the Honolulu conference was partially meant to drum up public support for continued U.S. involvement in Vietnam.[105] However, the conference also laid out a detailed agenda for addressing issues of governance, economics, rural construction, health, education, and agriculture.[106] The agenda reflected many of the concerns the 41-point program Johnson and senior Washington officials had proposed a year earlier, and would catalyze a reorganization of how U.S. noncombat operations were managed in the RVN. Throughout 1966 the Johnson administration would build on the groundwork laid in Honolulu to create a new program, Civil Operations and Revolutionary Development Support (CORDS). The CORDS program was implemented in 1967, and remained in charge of overseeing noncombat operations in Vietnam until 1973.

DEFINED MEANS, OBSCURE AIMS

Given the developing security situation in the RVN, it is striking that the Johnson administration remained as devoted and attentive to noncombat operations as it did. It was not rigid in its approach to stabilization and pacification tasks; the president and his advisers adjusted their plans as information from Saigon appeared to dictate. Conversely, policy adjustments in the face of criticism were largely absent in the cases of Germany and Iraq. Neither general beliefs related to DT nor decontextualized analogies to previous U.S. wars explain Johnson's approach to noncombat activities. But the behavior of Johnson and his top advisers described so far may be attributed to mechanisms other than CLT. For example, Johnson's reluctance to alert the American public to changes in U.S. policy toward Vietnam would necessarily make relatively low-visibility stabilization and reconstruction operations appear preferential to a course of intensified combat, perhaps even in the context of a deteriorating security situation. Additional evidence is necessary to show that temporal construal effects account for the administration's assessments of noncombat activities.

As it was in previous cases, CLT demonstrates its explanatory utility by accounting for additional decision-making dynamics that other plausible explanations cannot address. Johnson's domestic legislative agenda can partially explain the way in which he chose to escalate U.S. military involvement in Vietnam. Domestic factors, however, have difficulty accounting for an additional facet of the Vietnam case that has been noted in previous works: officials' had significant difficulties articulating and, relatedly, reaching consensus on the higher-level objectives military intervention in Vietnam was supposed to achieve. CLT demonstrates how this latter feature of officials' strategic assessment is not independent from their short time horizons, but rather a product of them. CLT predicts that, compared to actors concerned with the more distant future, those with short time horizons will focus more on how proposed actions will be carried out relative to the reasons why those actions should be taken. Present-minded individuals will also weight the feasibility of proposed actions highly relative to the desirability of anticipated ends. Consistent with evidence suggesting members of Johnson's administration had short time horizons, the historical record shows that officials' questions of "how," and attention to low-level operational details, trumped high-level considerations of "why" when considering what to do in Vietnam through 1964 and 1965. In line with CLT, Porter contends that propping up the RVN became "an end in itself" regardless of the effect it would have on high-level political objectives.[107]

The communication fluency Johnson had exhibited in relation to *how* noncombat operations were to be executed was missing in regard to *why* these and other military activities should take place. Ball pointed out in the spring of 1964 that many in the government were intent on constructing a "more decisive plan" for Vietnam, without explaining what the expected payoffs of an expansion of the U.S. intervention would be. He detected "an inarticulate wish to sweep the difficult issues under the bed," and agreed with Walter Lippmann that the government was "unwilling to ask questions about the nature of the conflict" in Vietnam.[108] Ball perceived that "the president and Secretary McNamara were primarily preoccupied with operational problems" and were less receptive to other issues.[109] Air Force officer Edward Lansdale, whose experience as a military adviser in Indochina began in the early 1950s, felt he had to remind senior officials that "the psychological, military, and socio-economic programs are [the war's] instruments, not ends in themselves."[110] Bundy also thought that despite McNamara's attention to the details of noncombat operations "in a curious way, he has rather mechanized the problem [of U.S. policy toward Vietnam] so that he misses some of its real political flavor."[111] These were conclusions McNamara would arrive at thirty years later, stating that he and other top officials "had not truly investigated what was essentially at stake and important to us," and as a result "were left harried, overburdened, and holding a map with only one road on it."[112] With the benefit of hindsight, McNamara connected the sense of time pressure and corresponding shortened time horizons with policymakers' difficulty contemplating the value of their ultimate goals.

Perhaps it is unsurprising that Ball, who was the chief internal critic of the administration's militarized Vietnam policy, argued that the president, McNamara, and others made poor assessments of the United States' interests in Southeast Asia. However, the observations of the members of the JCS, who also remarked on the lack of clear objectives in Vietnam, cannot be attributed to any reluctance to use greater force to achieve U.S. aims. The chiefs had told McNamara in 1964 that there was "a lack of definition, even a confusion in respect to objectives and [the] courses of action related to each objective." This was still the case once Rolling Thunder commenced in March the following year—the JCS was as perplexed as Johnson by McNamara's alternate depictions of the campaign as a tool to coerce the DRV versus one focused on attrition and interdiction.[113] According to William Bundy's notes, the Excom had had to weigh every possible reaction to the bombing campaign by the U.S. Congress, Saigon, Hanoi, and Beijing, while including a precise layout of time-phased deployments, bombing targets, the number of sorties per target, and so forth.[114] This left little time for consideration of broader strategic ends. This task would have thus seemed to have been the purview of more senior decision makers, out of necessity as much as senior officials' political authority. However, according to Leslie Gelb and Richard Betts, "administration leaders persistently failed to clarify U.S. objectives in concrete and specific terms." William Conrad Gibbons also surmises that the planning process regarding air strikes in November was "action-oriented. . . . There was almost no debate over U.S. diplomatic or strategic interests in Vietnam."[115]

The military's uncertainty of ultimate aims in Vietnam may have contributed to how it prosecuted the war there. Although still attentive to noncombat activities in the spring of 1965, Johnson also became focused on the weekly numbers of communist insurgents being killed by U.S. actions. This was a low-level detail CLT would predict to be salient to someone with short time horizons. Given that the JCS lacked a sense of Washington's ultimate aims, the president's pronouncement that the military concentrate on "killing more Viet Cong" became, in H.R. McMaster's words, "the basis for JCS plans and recommendations."[116] General Bruce Palmer Jr., deputy chief of staff for operations, observed that by February 1965 the generals had already been reduced to proposing courses of action just "to 'see' if they could work"—that is, discern whether they could be feasibly executed—while remaining unsure of the ends being sought. Likewise, Palmer said that Westmoreland "made successive requests for larger and larger force levels without the benefit of an overall concept and plan."[117] A senior intelligence officer complained that the "Johnson administration attempted to fight the Vietnam War without clear, tangible, or measurable objectives, both military and political."[118]

The largely "action-oriented" reasoning in Washington remained undisturbed through 1965. While there had been much speculation and general consensus about the military costs in Vietnam, there had been less so regarding the United States' purpose. Once again, the juxtaposition of the administration's means and its objectives was striking. Bundy's advice had been crucial in convincing Johnson to increase U.S. military involvement in Vietnam, and thus his contemporaneous observations cannot be discounted as easily as those of Ball's. Bundy believed that, though officials worked hard to preserve the GVN, they did not pay much attention to its "composition and direction," which was a "most difficult problem."[119] Lacking transformative aims for the RVN, these questions were not predominant in the minds of officials, and their focus on the immediate rather than more distant future further discouraged such assessments. What had been the simple task in Germany and Iraq—articulating ultimate objectives—was seen as the most difficult problem in Vietnam, and as Ball had indicated, policymakers felt more comfortable sweeping such issues under the bed.

In a private message to Johnson in April, Bundy wrote that he had "deliberately put the political problems up near the front because they are the harder ones." Consistent with the evidence in the previous section, he believed that concrete issues surrounding the "military and non-military action programs summarized in later parts of the memo do not seem as controversial or difficult today."[120] Just two weeks earlier, he had postulated that an eventual settlement might take several forms, but it was not clear which the administration was trying to achieve. Of maintaining a "wholly non-Communist South Vietnam," Bundy remarked with apparent uncertainty that "*if* this is our real target, it is doubtful we want an early settlement." Possible alternatives were a partitioned RVN or a national unity government with de facto Vietcong control of some territory, but to Bundy's mind it did not at the time "appear necessary today to decide among these three alternatives."[121] As Rolling Thunder was getting its start, the administration had still given little consideration to the form the GVN might take, or what type of political settlement it would prefer.

The evidence does not make it appear that the disparity between the focus on means and ends was undone in the months that followed. Gibbons notes that, when Johnson asked senior officials on June 10 what the objective was in the RVN, there were "divergent answers." Some proposed trying to achieve a "stalemate" between U.S. and communist forces, only to pull back when manpower constraints were identified. Others suggested negotiations with Hanoi, a prospect that was criticized and withdrawn.[122] It must be noted that the "objectives" being discussed were actually means to an unspoken end; negotiations or a stalemate could not be considered ultimate aims. In line with Daniel Ellsberg's critique, the administration had only short-range objectives—what CLT refers to as subordinate goals.[123] In the final weeks before Johnson announced a formal U.S. combat role in Vietnam, policymakers remained overwhelmingly focused on means rather than ends. Revealingly, when the last deliberations over the deployment of ground forces were being made in July, JCS chairman Earle Wheeler was caught off guard by Clark Clifford's question concerning what "success" in Vietnam would look like. Taking Johnson aside afterward, Clifford asked him to reflect on whether a military victory could be won and, just as importantly, "what do we have if we do win? Based on what we have heard, I do not know the answers to these questions."[124]

In an unsigned document that nevertheless appears several times in collections of Johnson's papers on Vietnam, an administration official listed as a possible item for discussion "what are our war aims? What is the answer to Walter Lippmann's question on this point?" The document was dated July 22, meaning the decision to deploy major ground forces to the RVN had already been settled.[125] John Burke and Fred Greenstein note that "the failure to specify the goals of the 1965 intervention [was] especially conspicuous because civilian leaders deliberately attempted to exercise control over the military."[126] This dynamic only appears incongruous if one assumes that attention to the feasibility of one's means and attention to the desirability of one's ends tend to correlate positively, whereas CLT explains why leaders with short time horizons would place more emphasis on the former set of considerations than the latter.

Alternative Explanations for Noncombat Efforts and Strategic Assessments

As already discussed, Johnson's domestic political concerns can partially explain his short time horizons and his attention to noncombat operations in 1964 and 1965. Likewise, the deteriorating security situation in the RVN made it difficult for officials to focus on the more distant future. The losses suffered by the ARVN and the vulnerability of the GVN did not, however, compel Johnson or others to abandon pacification and stabilization efforts so as to devote more attention to combat operations; contra the expectations of an opportunity costs framework, noncombat operations continued to feature heavily in administration deliberations and were even privileged as military plans advanced. What is more, and as detailed below, initial combat operations were consistently evaluated in terms of the political effects they would have in Saigon more than the effects they would have on the enemy. Contrary to fog-of-war arguments, civilians were just as ambivalent about the likely effectiveness of combat operations as they were about noncombat efforts. Looking through an organizational lens, one might suppose that if top military officials had been more integrated into the decision-making process there would have been greater pressure for a rapid transition to a U.S. combat role. While members of the JCS favored a more rapid military escalation than did top civilians in Washington, Westmoreland and the MACV did not eschew pacification or stabilization tasks for the greater use of force in the first half of 1965.

THE SECURITY ENVIRONMENT AND THE POLITICAL–MILITARY NEXUS

While the possibility of China or the Soviet Union intervening to support the DRV was not discounted, the prevailing attitude among U.S. officials in 1965 was that the United States could prevent the conflict in Southeast Asia from becoming globalized.[127] Decision makers considering whether to escalate U.S. involvement in the RVN focused a great deal more on whether, with assistance, the ARVN could effectively combat communist insurgents, and how American forces would fare in the fighting. Officials did not judge that U.S. power would dominate in either area. Given perceptions of a deteriorating security environment in the RVN, an opportunity costs framework predicts that policymakers would focus on the immediate future rather than more distant events, and devote little effort to assessing noncombat operations. While the unfavorable military situation did lead officials to adopt short time horizons, questions of Saigon's political durability were foremost in the minds of decision makers when military action was being considered. As has been shown, elaborate internal reforms were still being proposed for the South Vietnamese governing apparatus even after Rolling Thunder began. Largely because of Johnson's influence, administration discussions about a greater U.S. combat role were also heavily affected by considerations of potential political effects this would have in Saigon. Ultimately, the president and his advisers became focused on combat because they believed the GVN situation was so desperate that it could not withstand significant efforts at reform, nor would such reforms be sufficient to preserve a noncommunist South given the growing strength of the insurgency and Saigon's fears the Americans would abandon them.

Trends favoring the Vietcong were strong throughout the spring of 1964. In March McNamara reported that, with assistance from Hanoi, insurgents controlled approximately 40 percent of the RVN countryside. After his trip to the RVN in May, McNamara informed Johnson that the rate at which communist fighters were taking control of South Vietnamese villages was leveling off, but that the insurgents still held the initiative vis-à-vis the GVN.[128] Bundy was cautiously optimistic in September given Taylor's report that the military balance could hold "at least for the present" even though the "fabric of [Khanh's] Government is wearing thin." However, as the year drew to a close, Taylor summarized the state of affairs as one in which "the counterinsurgency program country-wide is bogged down and will require heroic treatment to assure revival." Due to the weakness of the GVN and the strength of the Vietcong, Taylor continued, "war weariness and hopelessness pervade South Vietnam."[129]

By March of 1965, the MACV estimated there were 40,000 regular Vietcong combatants operating in the RVN, while McCone believed the number was likely 50,000 or more. These estimates represented an increase of 15,000 to 20,000 from Defense Department estimates a year prior. The JCS projected that even with "the highest feasible mobilization" of ARVN forces, the South was incapable of effectively fighting the insurgency.[130] This assessment was reinforced by events starting in May 1965, in which concentrated Vietcong attacks devastated the RVN's military. As noted earlier, Westmoreland reported that the insurgents were destroying ARVN battalions faster than new ones could be raised.[131]

Contrary to the opportunity costs perspective, noncombat lines of operation not only overlapped with considerations of future combat, but were given greater weight as perceptions of the insurgency's strength grew. Concerns about the state of the GVN, and the effect it was having on the war effort, weighed heavily on the minds of top U.S. officials. In August 1964 Ambassador Taylor contacted the State Department with a list of priorities for the coming months. First was stabilizing Khanh's government and making it appear to the South Vietnamese that the GVN had long-term viability, which was linked to the next priority of maintaining morale in the RVN generally. Holding the Vietcong in check and making preparations for a possible "escalation of pressure" were Taylor's third and fourth priorities.[132] In line with these concerns, an escalated military campaign was seen to be as much about signaling the government in Saigon about U.S. intentions as it was to pressure Hanoi, in the hopes that a greater American commitment in Vietnam would strengthen the GVN's resolve and capability to govern. Telling the president he was unsure if Khanh could maintain political control in the South, Bundy said that U.S. military actions "would be more to heighten morale . . . than to accomplish anything specific in a military sense."[133]

Johnson was at first unwilling to countenance increased military involvement in the RVN, in part due to his focus on the upcoming 1964 election. Even the JCS, which opined that "strong military actions" would soon be necessary on the part of the United States, also recognized the GVN's insta-bility and held that "primarily political" solutions to this problem were "crit-ical to the eventual termination of the insurgency."[134] At the start of 1965 the scales finally tipped such that military courses of action began to outweigh noncombat operations, however. With the collapse of Saigon looming, Tay-lor informed the president that there was little the United States could do in-ternally to meaningfully impact GVN performance. Among the things the United States could not do were "change national characteristics [or] create leadership where it does not exist." The ability of Americans in the RVN to "stiffen" the government in Saigon by advisory means was, according to Taylor, "very limited."[135] Tapping into the president's preoccupation with the GVN's stability, Bundy and McNamara advised that a better government could not emerge in the absence of escalation because Saigon would remain unsure of the United States' commitment to its survival.[136]

Johnson at first appeared unwilling to commit to bombing the DRV. The same day Taylor had sent his message, the president informed his advisers he remained skeptical that escalation would improve morale in Saigon.[137] However, after hearing from Bundy and McNamara, Johnson seemed con-vinced the RVN could not be saved if the United States went along in its cur-rent, predominantly advisory, role. Though he had come to the position grudgingly, Johnson now averred that "stable government or no stable gov-ernment, we'll do what we have to do."[138] He also began to adopt the logic of his advisers, which emphasized the positive political impact U.S. military action would have in Saigon above the effects it would have on Hanoi. Af-ter authorizing air strikes in response to a Vietcong attack on Pleiku airfield on February 6, Johnson argued a failure to respond would have signaled both the DRV and RVN that the United States was abandoning the South. He told Taylor he was "impressed" by the argument that "the building of a mini-mum government will benefit by some private assurances from us to the highest levels that we do now intend to take continuing actions." On Febru-ary 17 he told Senator Everett Dirksen that instability in Saigon was intrac-table "because all of them are afraid we are going to pull out."[139] A day ear-lier Bundy recorded the president confiding with his top advisers that the use of force against the North was made necessary by the "desperate" con-dition of the GVN.[140]

In the cases of Iraq and Germany, policymakers resisted devoting resources to nonmilitary operations even though their advantage over the adversary was great or growing, in large part because it was assumed (despite a lack of evidence) that challenges facing stability and reconstruction efforts would be relatively simple to solve. Conversely, while the pressure to focus on a combat solution to the insurgency grew, a flurry of activity centered on the governmental capacity of Saigon commenced. Ironically, Taylor came to be-lieve that the United States was running a serious risk of overwhelming the

GVN with the density of its plans meant to improve the situation in Saigon. Ordering the cessation of the programs reflected the president's sensitivity to internal conditions in the RVN, not indifference.

THE FOG OF WAR: ADMINISTRATION BELIEFS ON THE USE OF FORCE

The first fog-of-war hypothesis, that leaders' strategic assessments depend on the accuracy and consistency of intelligence available to them, is supported in the Vietnam case. It is not clear, however, that the nature of intelligence regarding prospective combat operations was any better than that regarding noncombat tasks. Furthermore, officials were as ambivalent and pessimistic about the prospect of compelling the Vietcong and DRV into a favorable bargaining position via combat operations as they were about the chances of noncombat operations strengthening the RVN. Fredrik Logevall accurately characterizes pessimism within the Johnson administration as "endemic" in 1964, and doubts and negative prognostications greatly outweighed optimistic forecasts in 1965 as well.[141] The risks and potential costs of escalating the U.S. intervention were well grasped by those developing war plans. Even more "hawkish" senior U.S. officials worried about the chances of military victory and the tenacity of their opponent; in fact, the level of consensus among various members of the administration was substantial. Top policymakers were not confident that any new approach they took would produce a positive change quickly, and these doubts were aired with Johnson well prior to the initiation of sustained bombing against the DRV. The evidence does not support McNamara's later recollection that U.S. policymakers failed to evaluate how effective U.S. forces would be once committed, nor that decision makers ignored the likelihood of a stable GVN.[142] Military escalation could still be justified if policymakers believed the stakes were great enough, but as discussed, Johnson and his advisers' grasp of their ultimate objectives were shaky at best.

In October 1964 Ball wrote a sixty-seven-page memo to Bundy, Rusk, and McNamara evaluating the future of the RVN. He posed a staunch challenge to the idea that the fragile government in Saigon could be propped up if the United States only used greater force against the North. Ball foresaw that the DRV would be willing to absorb a great deal of physical punishment, and that the administration could not expect to control the extent of hostilities if direct action was taken against the DRV. Though Ball was the leading internal critic of administration plans, Johnson's others advisers expressed similar doubts. McGeorge Bundy told Ball he was aware things might go as his memo predicted, but that Ball had not presented compelling alternatives to escalation. In his nominal rebuttal of Ball's memo, William Bundy not only conceded that DT was flawed, but acknowledged that a bombing campaign against the DRV would not yield substantial results. Logevall observes that

Bundy's response to Ball's memo agreed with so many of the latter's arguments that "a reader could indeed be forgiven for thinking he too backed an early American extrication from the conflict."[143] Likewise, a Defense Department memo in March had stated that the decision to send in U.S. combat troops could produce a situation in which "our men may well be bogged down in a long war against numerically superior North Vietnamese and [Chinese Communist] forces," whereas CIA director McCone warned others in the administration that even if the GVN was strengthened, action against the North would carry with it "great" cost.[144]

On several occasions Johnson made comments indicating U.S. efforts would likely fail no matter what was tried. In May he told his advisers and congressional leaders that Saigon's prospects were not good, while McNamara himself felt the situation was bordering on "hopeless."[145] A few months later the Excom concluded that the RVN might "come apart" no matter what actions the United States took in Southeast Asia. Even if the DRV could be coerced into withdrawing support for the insurgency and escalated U.S. military involvement stabilized the GVN, the Excom consensus was that the United States would still face a long struggle against the Vietcong.[146] As 1964 drew to a close, Johnson proclaimed that he "never felt that this war will be won from the air" and said military planners would have to make greater use of Army Rangers and special operations forces to stiffen the resolve of the GVN. He admitted in February 1965 that he was "hoping out of hope" bombing the DRV would "draw people in Saigon together." Still, the president immediately acknowledged that this hope was most likely misplaced as far as coercing Hanoi. "Bombers won't bring them to their knees, unless we do something we wouldn't do," he remarked, making an implicit reference to targeting the North's population centers.[147] Upon receiving a letter from Bill Hosokawa, an associate of one of the president's friends, arguing that "the war in South Vietnam would continue for a long, long time even if we sealed that country off from the North," the president forwarded the letter to Bundy with the note "I very much agree with Hosokawa."[148] This echoed Johnson's arguments that internal conditions in the RVN were of greater concern than any external communist threat to Saigon.

Despite feeling the administration was getting into "a hell of a mess," McNamara recommended on July 1 to the president that 175,000 troops be sent to the RVN over a three-month period. At the same time he counseled that this might do no more than "demonstrate U.S. good faith," and predicted that increased casualties would strain domestic support while the Vietcong might go on fighting "almost indefinitely."[149] Though he had favored escalation, Bundy challenged McNamara's policy prescription, saying it would lead to the United States having total responsibility for South Vietnamese affairs, which he saw as "rash to the point of folly." Furthermore, he was skeptical that a ground war would have a significant effect in the "decisive field" of politics in the RVN.[150] These opinions echoed those of his brother, who believed "there is a point of sharply diminishing returns and adverse consequences that may lie somewhere between 70,000 and 100,000 US forces in total." Taylor had warned that the introduction of ground forces would lead to "serious losses" and "at the outset would probably not do too well in operations in strange terrain for which they have not been specifically and intensively trained."[151] Likewise, Bundy asserted that there was "no reason to suppose that the Viet Cong will accommodate us by fighting the kind of war we desire."[152] One of Ball's memos in July predicted that "humiliation would be more likely than the achievement of our objectives—even after we had paid terrible costs." Bundy forwarded Ball's memo to Johnson and attached a note suggesting the he be prepared to withdraw from the South if the GVN distanced itself from the United States.[153]

McNamara countered such assessments with relative optimism. He and General Wheeler estimated the United States could achieve victory in two to three years, though calling up military personnel would cost around $12 billion in 1965 and 1966. At the same time, Wheeler said he believed Ho Chi Minh's promise that he would go on fighting twenty years against the regime in Saigon.[154] McNamara acknowledged in a memo to Johnson that "casualties will increase and the war will continue for some time," estimating perhaps five hundred casualties a month by the end of 1965. McNaughton's draft report that July also noted that "even if [the outcome is] 'success,' it is not obvious how we will be able to disengage our forces from South Vietnam," and asserted that up to two U.S. divisions would have to remain in the country "for a period of years."[155]

ORGANIZATIONAL FACTORS AND CIVIL–MILITARY RELATIONS

The prosecution of the war in Vietnam has been described as the "triumph of the institutional culture" of the U.S. military. An "Army Concept" that wars could be won via conventional combat operations relying on high volumes of firepower allegedly encouraged a flawed warfighting strategy in which pacification and other noncombat operations were neglected.[156] Whether a less "conventional" military approach would have led to a different outcome in the Vietnam War is of less importance here than military leaders' assessments of noncombat operations. Did organizational culture blind General Westmoreland and others to the utility of noncombat operations? Researchers have paid less attention to the degree to which organizational factors impacted the assessments of the MACV under Westmoreland prior to July 1965. The evidence shows that along with civilians, Westmoreland attended to the political aspects of the intervention in 1964 and 1965.

Despite his reputation as a commander who favored pure firepower as a solution to the communist insurgency in the South, Westmoreland was not "utterly oblivious" to the political aspects of the war, as some have argued.[157] In February 1964, while still deputy commander of MACV, he received a communiqué from General William Yarborough, commander of the Army's Green Berets. Yarborough stressed that "the entire conflict in Southeast Asia is eighty percent in the realm of ideas and only twenty percent in the field of physical conflict. . . . The key to the beginning of the solution to Viet-Nam's travail now lies in a rising scale of population and resources control." The next day Westmoreland contacted David Nes, deputy chief of the Saigon Mission, to recommend the creation of a new "Nes Committee" that would focus on pacification efforts. The new committee would have more support staff than its predecessors, meet for longer periods of time, and assure coordination of efforts between civilians and the military.[158] Upon taking command of the MACV, Westmoreland showed awareness of the military's combat and pacification duties, declaring that U.S. advisers' foremost duties were to maintain "discipline, alertness, security, aggressiveness, fire and maneuver, emphasis on night operations, and always consideration of the civilian population. We must keep in mind that the campaign will be won at the province, district, village and hamlet levels where the battle is being waged for the hearts and minds of the people."[159]

In November 1964, Westmoreland expressed concerns that the pacification program was failing to show progress, mainly because RVN armed forces lacked understanding of civic affairs and were thus unmotivated to pursue them. He ordered that all advisers "devote their personal attention to this subject" and impress on their South Vietnamese counterparts its importance. There was a basis to Westmoreland's beliefs. GVN officials saw Operation Hop Tac, a major effort to pacify the provinces surrounding Saigon that had begun that summer, "only in terms of a military plan with a nebulous assist from the civilian agencies," according to one MACV officer. Another wrote that, given the intricacy of Hop Tac, the unstable GVN could not be expected to manage the necessary planning and coordination, especially in the face of an increasingly stronger insurgency.[160] MACV officer Major General Alden Sibly recorded that Khanh had told him RVN forces "must turn to the kind of conventional military operations which we understand and not continue to try to fight [the MACV's] kind of war which is new to us."[161] Though he felt U.S. personnel might have to exert more influence in Saigon to improve pacification efforts, Westmoreland was hesitant due to the overall effect new steps might have on the GVN. "If we agree to attempt this change and the GVN concurs (assuming we even ask them for their concurrence)," he asked, "can the present weak government withstand the resultant loss of prestige?" Westmoreland also questioned what the reaction of the RVN armed forces and Vietcong would be to greater U.S. control, whether interventions of U.S. personnel into more GVN matters would further slow its day-to-day operations, and whether GVN pacification efforts would deteriorate further if the United States adopted a greater "assumption of responsibility."[162]

Organizational theory predicts that military officers will advocate for combat operations prior to civilians as the security environment in a theater of operations is perceived to deteriorate, but it does not seem that Westmoreland was ahead of officials in Washington in this regard. Despite a deteriorating security situation, Westmoreland was not especially forceful in pushing for a greater U.S. combat role. In January 1965 the MACV asserted that if the advisory effort in the South was not working, "there is less reason to think that U.S. combat forces would have the desired effect."[163] Similarly, Westmoreland told Wheeler that an increased American military presence in the RVN would be insufficient to reverse the unfavorable trends officials in Washington were observing. "Unless there are reasonable prospects of a fairly effective governance in South Vietnam in the immediate offing," he stated, "no amount of offensive action by the U.S. either in or outside South Vietnam has any chance by itself of reversing the deterioration now underway." He also worried that the GVN would become convinced that U.S. support was unconditional, which would reduce any incentive the government might have to increase its effectiveness.[164]

In February Westmoreland appeared to reverse himself, saying that the United States had reached a point "where we can ill afford any longer to withhold available military means to support the GVN counterinsurgency campaign." Of course, in this regard the general's assertion was not unlike those of many top civilians in Washington in the early months of 1965. The apparent shift in Westmoreland's position, which clearly persisted after 1965, is also understandable given that U.S. forces were increasingly faced with both an unconventional insurgency and the threat of attacks by larger communist units.[165] Even given the security conditions in Vietnam, Westmoreland did not assert that combat operations would replace pacification efforts. He told CIA station chief Peer De Silva that month that there was "plenty of room" for RVN People's Action Teams and Popular Forces to work in rural areas of the provinces "at this critical juncture in the counterinsurgency."[166] In March, Westmoreland still believed the top U.S. priority should be an effective "central national authority" in the RVN, though he did not believe such a government was foreseeable in the short term.[167] Westmoreland arrived at a concept of operations which he felt would be "properly focussed [sic] upon the population—that is, upon the people. There is no doubt whatsoever that the insurgency in South Vietnam must eventually be defeated among the people in the hamlets and towns." He believed that the security situation must first be improved if success were to be had, however, which meant engaging U.S. troops in combat against communist forces.[168]

Officials in Washington did not perceive Westmoreland was rigidly focused on the use of force. Bundy's aide Michael Forrestal opined that the U.S. embassy and AID mission in the RVN were poorly coordinated and run in 1964, but "such coordination between U.S. agencies as there is takes place because of the efforts of General Westmoreland. He accomplishes this by taking the Deputy AID Director and the [U.S. Information Service] Chief with him on his trips to the provinces and using these occasions to discuss and coordinate specific actions under the pacification program."[169] In February 1965 Bundy wrote to Johnson that while Westmoreland and officers at the MACV "inevitably think first of military programs," it was also the case that "they have been imaginative and understanding about the importance of other aspects" of U.S. policy in Vietnam. Due to "the generous spirit and broad mind of General Westmoreland," Bundy thought the United States could rely on special operations forces under his command to strengthen the civil government and police in the RVN as well as assist with economic development programs.[170]

Conclusion

CLT helps to explain and integrate evidence from the Vietnam case that otherwise seems unrelated or incongruous. However, the effects of individual personality and idiosyncratic experience on assessment were apparent within the Johnson administration. For instance, one historian has noted that, among top officials in Washington, Ball was set apart by his tendency to ask "*why* among those who largely asked *how*," or in the language of CLT, to focus on high-level abstract ends rather than concrete means.[171] The evidence presented here provides no apparent reason why Ball should have differed from his colleagues in this respect. Ball's time horizons should not necessarily have been any longer or shorter than those of other officials. He had been assigned to play the role of devil's advocate, which may have encouraged him to highlight the ambiguous nature of administration goals. It is possible that he was generally prone to think abstractly. Whatever the reason, one cannot use time horizons, the key explanatory variable of CLT emphasized here, to explain Ball's assessments.

It might also be argued that Johnson's personal characteristics had a substantial effect on the nature of his assessments in Vietnam that confound the CLT explanation. White House press secretary George Reedy characterized the president as someone who could "devise ingenious schemes for achieving goals but not ponder the validity of the goals" and someone who had trouble recognizing when "the game might not be worth playing."[172] Likewise, Johnson's friend Abe Fortas stated that "Johnson was not a conceptualist. He hated to put ideas in broad conceptual terms."[173] These statements, by men familiar with the president, indicate that Johnson was chronically inclined to think about issues concretely rather than abstractly. If this were true, his time horizons perhaps augmented this personal attribute in 1964–1965, but were arguably not necessary to explain Johnson's assessments of Vietnam. However, others have characterized Johnson in polar-opposite terms. When it came to domestic affairs, for example, Rusk said that the president's "objectives were large and bold. He didn't think in small terms. He thought in the most far reaching terms."[174] This was not solely the case for domestic affairs. Bundy said that while Johnson could obsess over small details, "his control over big issues—everything in the Middle Eastern case [the Arab–Israeli War in 1967]—led to an extremely sound, basic policy." As Francis Bator argues, the depiction of Johnson as someone out of his depth when it came to foreign policy arises in large part from his involvement in the Vietnam "quagmire," and has been undone by recent work on his management of American relations with Europe during his presidency.[175] These accounts strongly indicate Johnson's tendency toward abstract or concrete thought was moderated by the context of specific cases, rather than solely being a function of his own personal attributes.

One of the notable similarities between the Vietnam War, the occupation of Germany, and the Iraq War is that military officers complained that they were unaware of the political aims being sought by their civilian superiors. This is paradoxical, because in comparison to the other two conflicts, the strategic assessments made by key decision makers in the Johnson administration in 1964 and 1965 were heavily skewed toward concrete reasoning. However, it is not hard to see how mirror-opposite imbalances between concrete and abstract thought can lead to similar outcomes via different mechanisms. In the transformative interventions studied here, American leaders with long time horizons were overly optimistic that they could achieve their aims. This optimism corresponded with a lack of willingness to consider the operational details of policies meant to secure their objectives, and a blunted capacity to engage with arguments regarding the feasibility of their goals. This general lack of engagement made it difficult for subordinates to divine their more senior officials' intentions regarding the late stages of interventions, and obscured which groups had responsibility for the various aspects of postwar affairs. In Vietnam, conversely, senior officials did not fail to engage with the production and analysis of concrete operations. However, they had trouble articulating to *themselves*, let alone others, exactly what ends their intervention was meant to achieve. Thus, there was a lack of understanding between the military and civilians in both types of interventions—transformative and maintenance—though the causal mechanisms in these cases diverge.

The behavior of key decision makers during the escalatory period of the Vietnam War contradicts most of the hypotheses laid forth to explain how leaders assess risks and costs of noncombat military operations. Johnson and his senior advisers paid close attention to military and political developments in the RVN, and perceived significant negative trends in both areas. They doubted the GVN could be preserved without heavy support from U.S. military forces. Despite the deteriorating security situations, they continued to devote considerable resources toward improving governance in the RVN and pacification efforts even after Rolling Thunder began in March 1965. This approach was adopted by both civilians and high-ranking military officers. Whatever organizational "inertia" that may have affected the Army's prosecution of the war after the summer of 1965 was checked by key field commanders beforehand.

It is striking that officials continued their efforts at maintaining the GVN via nonmilitary means while they were planning a major military campaign, given their pessimism about the effectiveness of bombing and ground combat units once deployed. But the unsteadiness of the GVN remained disconnected from broad questions of the U.S. national interest. Political aspects of the intervention, much like the military measures, were problems to be solved, and though administration members might recognize their intractability, they did not weigh these costs against the value of the ultimate ends being sought in Vietnam. For the most part objectives were unclear, and attempts by Ball and others to draw attention to high-level issues failed to gain traction. Previous works on the Vietnam War have puzzled over officials' capacity to recognize the costs of the conflict, including awareness that troops could not be easily extricated even if "victory" was achieved, and their corresponding inability to understand the goals they were pursuing. CLT is necessary to reconcile the seemingly odd juxtaposition of a fixation on operational details and neglect of high-level objectives.

Conclusion

Reviewing Theoretical and Policy Implications

Even ideally rational actors face significant challenges when assessing the costs of noncombat operations. The success of stability and reconstruction activities is often contingent on a preceding period of combat, the dynamics of which may be difficult to predict. Even if noncombat operations occur prior to major combat, these activities often necessitate the acquiescence or active cooperation of local populations if they are to be effective. Presuming such cooperation is forthcoming, there is still the potential for substantial levels of Clausewitzian friction. Command structures may change; new personnel may be transferred into an area of operations while other forces are redeployed; and coalition politics may create a demand for elaborate organizational machinery for command and control. According to U.S. Army doctrine existent at the time of the Iraq War, "transition between operations may be the most difficult follow-on operation to accomplish."[1]

The challenges outlined require top officials to assess whether the costs of consolidating and maintaining the political objectives of a military campaign will be prohibitively high. This calls for an understanding of how noncombat operations will advance high-level goals, as well as a clear idea of the objectives of an intervention itself. American presidents and their advisers have had trouble meeting these demands. The four administrations studied here either made overly optimistic assessments of the feasibility of noncombat tasks, had trouble seeing how these tasks would be affected by combat activities, or were uncertain of how these activities would advance the higher-level objectives of a military campaign. Officials often failed to grasp operational costs and details, or displayed an inability to think of noncombat operations as means to higher ends, rather than ends in and of themselves. Rarely, however, did they commit both types of errors in the same campaign. Officials who sought transformative ends exhibited concrete thinking in the short term and more abstract thought when considering the more distant future. Alternatively, the nature of assessments made by officials with maintenance goals was relatively concrete regardless of the stage of conflict under consideration.

To explain the foregoing observations, this book applies construal level theory (CLT) to the question of strategic assessment in military interventions. CLT does not assume that feasibility and desirability considerations are always equally salient to decision makers. Instead, the theory provides an explanation for when and why feasibility will be given greater weight relative to desirability and vice versa. Desirability considerations pertaining to high-level goals are abstract and largely unrelated to the processes by which those goals might be achieved. Conversely, feasibility considerations require concrete assessment of how actions will be carried out. In comparison to feasibility considerations, evaluations of desirability are simple and less contingent on contextual variation. Officials focused on a goal's desirability were less likely to attend to information about the costs of executing a set of operations, even if those operations were necessary to secure the objectives they sought. Privileging desirability over feasibility thus produced unwarranted optimism about future actions. Individuals who were more focused on the near term were primed to think concretely and thus more likely to avoid this bias when considering future actions and events. Understandably, however, individuals with short time horizons were not intrinsically motivated to think about the more distant future, and were also prone to endorse courses of action that could be feasibly executed but did not necessarily advance the higher purposes of the military campaign.

While the evidence examined here supported the core expectations of CLT, the causal importance of temporal construal appeared to be moderated by individual traits. The theory also has implications for the importance of nonpsychological factors that have been advanced to explain strategic assessment and performance. This chapter concludes with policy implications of the theory and areas for future research.

CLT and Its Alternatives

OPPORTUNITY COSTS AND THE FOG OF WAR

Explanations that rely on the fog of war and opportunity costs to explain strategic assessments share much in common. Both presume that decision makers are procedurally rational actors whose ability to plan ahead is limited only by the constraints placed on them by limited information and resources. What is more, the fog of war can affect perceptions of relative power disparities, as military opponents have an incentive to disguise their true capabilities and intentions from one another. Neither mechanism operated exactly as hypothesized in the cases examined.

The first opportunity costs hypothesis is that leaders' time horizons grow along with their military advantage over opponents. This was true of Franklin Roosevelt during World War II, who began to invest time and energy into postwar plans for Germany once an Allied victory looked likely in 1944. Likewise, Lyndon Johnson and his advisers focused on the immediate rather than more distant future in part due to the deteriorating security situation in Vietnam. Conversely, Harry Truman and his top advisers began to deliberate over the expansion of war aims before the United States clearly possessed the military advantage in Korea. Although the Bush administration's long time horizons corresponded with a large military advantage for the United States over Iraq, that advantage never changed substantially, making it difficult to evaluate the effect of military preponderance on time horizons in that case. While perceived power advantages may have lengthened time horizons, officials usually did not display a greater corresponding investment in the evaluation of noncombat operations. Contrary to the second opportunity costs hypothesis, officials pursuing the most ambitious goals were typically the most resistant to demands that more resources be allocated to planning for noncombat tasks even when the United States had large or growing military advantages. The most rigorous consideration of the costs of noncombat activities took place during the Korean and Vietnam Wars, wars in which U.S. officials saw their military advantages as either uncertain or deteriorating.

The findings just described are also inconsistent with the fog-of-war framework. The first hypothesis stemming from the fog-of-war literature is that officials' assessments depend on the accuracy and consistency of available intelligence, the quality of which would be better for combat rather than noncombat operations. This supposition did not stand in either the case of the Iraq War or the occupation of Germany, in which Presidents George W. Bush and Roosevelt largely ignored intelligence warnings about the nature of the postwar environment, even if they came from credible sources that had been trusted when other matters were being assessed. Their assessments were governed by the value they attached to their ends, and they seized on information consistent with those objectives and their established beliefs. Leaders' assessments in Vietnam and Korea did appear more contingent on available intelligence. However, Johnson and his advisers were comparatively better than Truman and company at understanding the implications of combat reports for the feasibility of planned noncombat activities, likely because combat and noncombat operations began to overlap in 1965. Conversely, Truman and those under him did not demonstrate an understanding of the impact China's entrance into the Korean War might have on plans to occupy territory north of the 38th parallel, even though the possibility of a Chinese invasion was taken seriously as it pertained to the ongoing offensive.

In no case but Iraq was the intelligence regarding combat operations noticeably more precise and consistent than those regarding noncombat tasks.

Whereas predictions about the costs of toppling Saddam Hussein were quite accurate, the predicted humanitarian crisis in Iraq that could occur during the invasion did not arise. While many sources predicted disorder and strife in Phase IV of the campaign, the scope of violence that emerged was greater than anticipated. Intelligence during World War II significantly overestimated the effect of Allied bombing against Germany, whereas reports from the frontlines from General Dwight Eisenhower's command as well as analysis by the Foreign Economic Administration correctly predicted that destruction in the Reich would be much greater than that countenanced by Washington policymakers. General Douglas MacArthur's and others' skewed estimates of how effective Chinese Communist Forces (CCF) would be against the United Nations (UN) coalition were certainly no better than projections about postwar reconstruction efforts. It is difficult to argue that the accuracy and consistency of intelligence reports on combat and noncombat activities in Vietnam were significantly different.

What is more, the two wars in which leaders adopted the most ambitious, transformative long-term aims were also those in which top policymakers were most sanguine about the costs and risks involved. This was reinforced by assumptions that were unsupported by intelligence but, if true, would greatly facilitate postwar operations and allow greater room for error in long-term planning. This directly contradicts the hypothesis that leaders will be most ambivalent or pessimistic about the chances of noncombat operations succeeding. The pattern of policymakers' assessments in the four cases makes more sense if one adopts the perspective of CLT: actors with highly valued long-term goals attached to a military intervention attend more to the desirability than feasibility of their aims when considering distant operations, while the reverse is true of those who lack such objectives.

ORGANIZATIONAL THEORY

Organizational theory predicts that the norms, principles, rules, and procedures governing action in organizations affect how group members make assessments and judge the value of different goals and outcomes. If there is variation between government organizations in this regard—if members of the State Department assess information differently than those in Defense, for example—then variation in the relative influence of organizational actors on senior decision makers should affect how leaders formulate their strategic assessments. The case studies here showed several ways in which organizations affected postwar outcomes, but not necessarily as the theory presented in the Chapter 1 would predict.

In many instances military actors behaved in ways congruent with organizational theory. Senior military officers seemed to acquiesce to the paucity of postconflict planning that took place prior to the 2003 invasion of Iraq and ignored how operations designed to topple Saddam's regime would make noncombat activities more difficult. This supports the hypothesis that the military is not inclined to invest resources in planning stabilization, reconstruction, and humanitarian operations. Likewise, General Eisenhower was intent on avoiding responsibility for the political and economic reconstruction of postwar Germany. General MacArthur, the military governor of Japan, clearly had experience with the activities Eisenhower avoided, though the effect his prior experiences with military government had on his command in Korea is less certain. Conversely, General Westmoreland emphasized the importance of pacification and noncombat operations in Vietnam. While Westmoreland supported the insertion of ground troops, he did not make the request for thirty-four U.S. battalions until June of 1965, months after civilian officials had begun to press for a greater combat role for American forces.

The military's resistance to noncombat tasks did not necessarily result in inaccurate assessments of the costs of those tasks. U.S. Central Command's plans for Phase IV in Iraq have in hindsight been judged to be at least as good, if not superior to, anything civilian planners produced.[2] War Department officials, Eisenhower, and other officers fighting through Europe near the end of World War II were more cognizant of the pressing need for postwar policy than were officials in Washington. However, per the second organizational hypothesis, the importance of military assessments of noncombat operations was contingent on the armed forces' autonomy and political power relative to civilians. In Germany, Vietnam, and Iraq, it appeared that the senior civilian leadership had a greater effect on the assessments and planning done by the military than vice versa. Top officials either encouraged obstructionist behavior by officers, as Roosevelt did in his dealings with the Working Security Committee, or rebuked officers who gave advice that did not accord with working assumptions, as General Eric Shinseki and others preparing for the Iraq invasion found. Johnson sidelined the Joint Chiefs of Staff, though he was more receptive to input from Westmoreland and officers in Saigon. While MacArthur's prestige certainly influenced the Truman administration's assessments of the UN offensive in Korea, it is less clear that the general's political influence impacted preparations for occupation. The White House did accept the Department of the Army's guidance on policy for postwar Korea rather than that put forth by State Department officials, but there is no evidence this was because of the relative political power of the two departments rather than the subjective quality of their proposals.

While the evidence from the cases conforms to organizational theory in many ways, the framework is not sufficient to explain the nature of civilian assessments of noncombat operations. The military did not have much influence over civilians' noncombat plans in Vietnam. Likewise, the quality of military input regarding the offensive in Korea in 1950 does not explain why civilians failed to grasp how a Chinese counterintervention would affect the institutional machinery they had established to manage noncombat operations. More strikingly, in the case of neither the Roosevelt nor Bush administrations can organizational factors explain why civilians effectively communicated and coordinated policy with general officers in regard to near-term combat operations but not regarding postconflict activities. CLT, however, predicts that actors will be more receptive to arguments that challenge assumptions about the feasibility of a given course of action that is most proximate in a sequence. Even if an organization is well outfitted to provide top civilians with advice on the late stages of interventions, leaders must be of the mind-set to receive that advice if it is to be translated into an executable plan. What is more, if leaders do not engage with the military on postconflict scenarios, officers may not perceive they have the political backing to proceed with long-term planning, as was the case in Germany, or be unclear over which parts of the government have responsibility during the late stages of an intervention, as occurred in Iraq.

CLT: Qualifications and Additional Implications

Leaders' future expectations have often been a crucial feature of much scholarship in international relations and security. The findings presented here challenge existing research, which has largely employed standard discounting models to explain policy decisions. They also have implications for work on analogous reasoning and learning in foreign policy, as well as research that has that has applied prospect theory to foreign policy analysis. First, however, this section reviews the ways in which temporal construal theory laid out in the Introduction and Chapter 1 should be qualified in light of the evidence from the cases investigated.

CLT AND THE IMPACT OF PERSONALITY

The personality traits of leaders, and the unique experiences different individuals bring with them to office, can have a major impact on how states conduct foreign policy.[3] Often, however, officials' predominant personality traits and leadership styles did not provide a helpful guide to understanding their behavior in wartime. In the case of Germany, it did not appear that Roosevelt's assessments or behavior in preparing for the postwar occupation represented his usual style of leadership, nor could they be attributed to his decaying health. Truman's leadership style has been described as uneven, and thus the contribution of that aspect of his personality toward policy in any given instance is questionable.[4] Johnson's preference for domestic politics was certainly evident in 1964–1965. At the same time, Johnson was not a foreign policy lightweight, and his domestic focus cannot account for an inability to envision ultimate ends or articulate definitions of success in Vietnam. Lastly, it has been asserted that Bush cared mainly about whether or not a given policy would work, not the details of how a policy would work.[5] This would suggest that Bush's assessments of post-Saddam Iraq were just a function of his stable personal attributes. However, the personality explanation cannot account for within-case variation in Bush's assessments of different phases of the war. Further, those who argue that Bush preferred to focus on the ends of policy rather than the means nevertheless acknowledge that the former president sometimes asked "hundreds of specific questions" of individuals with diverse viewpoints on various policy issues.[6]

On the whole, the factors highlighted by CLT better explained the assessments of government actors than did individual-specific traits, yet there were exceptions to this pattern. The beliefs exhibited by General MacArthur during the Korean War, and the corresponding actions he took on the battlefield, are more plausibly linked to his personality than any effects that might have resulted from temporal construal. Likewise, George Ball's unique focus on why, rather than how, the United States should or should not intervene in Vietnam may have been the result of a general proclivity to consider abstract questions. Condoleezza Rice's behavior appeared consistent with CLT in some instances and less so in others, which may be related to the relative difficulty of categorizing her in terms of her time horizons. In any event, it should be stressed that individuals' characteristics may affect the degree to which temporal construal, or any cognitive heuristic, impacts their strategic assessments.

Philip Tetlock's differentiation between "hedgehogs" and "foxes" may provide some insight in this regard. Hedgehogs are individuals who predominantly view political events through the lens of a single theory, whereas foxes are open to a multiplicity of theories about the way the world works. Tetlock finds that hedgehogs' predictions about political events are significantly less accurate than those of foxes. Furthermore, hedgehogs do even worse relative to foxes when both are asked to make predictions about increasingly distant future time periods. Hedgehogs are especially (and excessively) confident in their long-range projections.[7] This is plausibly related to their tendency to deduce outcomes from simple, preexisting theories, one of the mechanisms CLT expects to promote overconfidence. Thus, hedgehogs might be especially prone to the biases CLT highlights, particularly due to the deductive-reasoning mechanism, whereas foxes may be more resistant.

CLT can help explain why the appeal of a certain goal or course of action waxes or wanes over time: because actors are expected to feel more positively toward their objectives than the means by which valued ends are to be achieved, and the salience of ends relative to means increases with temporal distance, their goals appear less costly and thus more appealing when they are further removed in time. Importantly, however, CLT cannot account for the different objectives policymakers set out prior to military action. Once again, the importance of individuals, their life experiences, and associated worldviews must be taken into consideration. What explains why John Allison viewed an offensive into North Korea as a step toward rolling back communism in Asia, while John Foster Dulles viewed it mainly as a means of securing the U.S. position on the peninsula? One cannot answer such questions merely by examining the cognitive mechanisms by which people construe the future.

LEARNING, ANALOGOUS REASONING, AND CLT

Research drawing insights from constructivism, rational choice, and psychology have all employed the concept of learning as a crucial component of their explanations for foreign policy outcomes and strategic adjustment. It is striking that, despite the different foundations of these approaches to international relations, there is considerable agreement on several points. Learning is commonly defined as the acquisition of new ideas, a change of beliefs, or a shift in confidence in existing beliefs.[8] It is thought to require some noticeable event in one's environment, such as a change (or notable consistency) in an opponent's behavior, the failure or success of some policy endeavor, or an exogenous shock. Though not sufficient for learning, notable events are necessary to either provide political actors with new information or compel them to assess existing information in a new light.[9]

The evidence presented here has shown that learning sometimes takes place in the absence of any substantial signal from political leaders' environments. This was particularly apparent in the cases of Donald Rumsfeld and Bush in the lead-up to the Iraq War. Rumsfeld's beliefs about actions that would be necessary to secure the peace in Iraq changed dramatically in the early days of fighting. His estimates of potential postwar costs also appeared to increase. These changes happened prior to wide-scale looting or signs of an insurgency in and around Baghdad. If anything, one might have expected Rumsfeld to revise his estimates of the postwar environment in a more optimistic direction, given that initial information indicated the administration had overestimated the extent of the humanitarian crisis that could befall the Iraqi population during the invasion. Bush did not exhibit as striking a change as his defense secretary, but did come to accept a larger role for the UN before the scope of the burden of operating in post-Saddam Iraq became apparent.

It was not that Rumsfeld and Bush were exposed to new information; aside from the absence of clear environmental signals, various officials in the United States and the United Kingdom consistently warned about the aftermath of the Iraq invasion for months. Instead, it appears that existing arguments and "facts on the ground" in Iraq became reinterpreted as a result of shifting temporal frames, rather than pessimists in Washington and London altering the way they framed their arguments. Examples of shifting or vacillating beliefs in the absence of clear external signals were apparent in other cases as well. Dean Acheson came to realize that the United States could not keep North

Korea out of China's sphere of influence regardless of whether allied troops occupied the upper half of the peninsula. This realization, which echoed the earlier warnings of George Kennan, came three days before China's offensive on November 27, 1950, at a time when U.S. intelligence was uncertain as to the extent to which the CCF would be involved in the fighting.

Another proposed method of learning featured prominently in many accounts of foreign policy is that of analogous reasoning, in which contemporaneous events are understood using simplified analogies or interpretations of past events.[10] Schematically, the use of analogies to reason about upcoming events takes the form $AX:BX::AY:BY$; if situation A had attributes X and Y, and situation B has attribute X, it is inferred situation B will also have attribute Y.[11] Analogous reasoning is highly abstract, limiting the number of criteria considered when making a decision to a few prominent contextual details chosen on the basis of their resemblance to those of past events. CLT posits that individuals are increasingly prone to simplified, abstract thought as they focus on the more distant future. This indicates that policymakers will be more likely to use analogies to inform their assessments and choices when they have long time horizons and consider the later stages of an intervention, rather than when their attention is directed toward immediate events. From the perspective of CLT it is thus unsurprising that President Johnson and his advisers were disposed to concrete, context-driven reasoning when strategizing Vietnam policy. The theory expects that a short-term temporal focus of the sort found among Johnson and his advisers would work against the reliance on analogies or simple, general belief systems. In this case the extent to which historical analogies drawn from the Korean War and elsewhere drove administration policy decisions relative to contextual information and pressures was found to be overemphasized.[12]

CLT, however, predicts that senior officials preparing for the Iraq War would be more prone to use analogies to reason about the conditions facing U.S. forces in postwar Iraq. In that case it did appear that the general beliefs officials relied on were partially rooted in analogies drawn from distant events. Rumsfeld's opposition to nation building harkened to his interpretation of the U.S. experience of the 1990s in the Balkans. Conversely, Paul Wolfowitz and Douglas Feith seemed to discount communism's bloody aftermath in the former Yugoslavia. Instead, they focused on former Eastern Bloc states that had successfully integrated with the West to bolster their conclusion that a democratic Iraq would do the same.[13] The fact that Jay Garner, a commander in Operation Provide Comfort in 1991, was chosen to lead postwar efforts, along with the administration's belief that a short-term humanitarian crisis was the most likely postwar challenge, further suggests that Rumsfeld and other policymakers used the aftermath of the Gulf War as a template to determine what challenges would be present in Phase IV operations in 2003.

PROSPECT THEORY

Prospect theory has been the dominant psychological theory applied by students of international relations to questions of international security. The theory holds that people are risk-averse when presented with the opportunity to achieve gains, but risk-acceptant when attempting to avoid losses.[14] An oft-neglected point in regard to prospect theory is that it contains an explicit temporal dimension.[15] The theory predicts that an individual's perception of loss or gain, and thus propensity for risk, is dependent on their reference point, which can be the status quo, the status quo ante, or some future expectation level. Unlike CLT, prospect theory does not expect variations in distance to have an impact on cognition or preferences. CLT can thus be a complement to prospect theory, though at times it may also be a competing explanation.

Prospect theorists have observed that actors are slow to update their reference points after suffering a loss, remaining fixated on the past. This means that there should be considerable variance across actors in the amount of time separating the present from reference points focused on a loss. Sometimes this distance will be small, as when the United States intervened in Korea to restore its position in the Far East. In other instances it will be larger, as when Argentina invaded the Falkland Islands decades after losing them. Both invasions may have been risk-acceptant acts. However, CLT suggests that individuals who have suffered a recent loss will be more apt to think concretely about how they are going to reverse it, while those that have suffered a loss in the more distant past will be more absorbed by the desirability of regaining what was theirs. Thus, actors seeking to reverse recent losses can be expected to be more aware of the feasibility of different courses of action when planning a response, whereas interveners seeking to recover long-lost assets might have less realistic expectations.[16]

The above observation carries with it a corollary, namely that risk-acceptant behavior does not imply that an actor is either aware or oblivious to the feasibility of their actions. Prospect theory is a variant of expected utility theory, and thus assumes that individuals do take into account the likelihood of success.[17] Specifically, research has found that people tend to give probability estimates greater weight when the probability of an event is closer to zero compared to events with a moderate or high likelihood of occurrence.[18] Prospect theory might thus explain instances in which people take risky actions in pursuit gains, rather than losses, by establishing that a person overweighted a low probability of success. However, prospect theory cannot explain cases where actors pursue long-term gains and largely exclude probability considerations from their assessments, a pattern exhibited by many individuals studied in this book. This behavior can be explained if one assumes that the role of probability considerations in people's assessments varies as a function of time as well, as with CLT.

211

CLT: Policy Implications and Conclusion

As U.S. military officers have noted, officials have a tendency to think of interventions as being sequential in nature. This representation of war reinforces the tendency to perceive noncombat operations as more temporally distant than conventional combat by artificially defining them as something that comes last in a sequence, rather than overlapping with or having connections to preceding events. The commonly attached prefix "post"—"postconflict," "postcombat," "postwar"—indicates that noncombat operations are perceived as being distinct activities separated in time from combat actions. In transformative interventions, this will reinforce the psychological tendency to construe temporally distant events abstractly and bias actors' assessments toward optimism. What actions might counteract this tendency without creating a situation in which officials' assessments become overly concrete, leading them to have problems articulating and weighing competing priorities against one another?

A study of "post-major combat operations" in Iraq argued that military interventions should not be thought of as neatly divided phases. Instead, they are composed of an overlapping series of operations. For this reason the study recommended that in the future the U.S. government "conduct combat and stability planning in parallel" while engaging in "routine joint-interagency training" that would facilitate the execution of postconflict operations.[19] This is a promising start in that it would begin to counteract existing perceptions that stability operations are necessarily distinct activities at the end of a sequence, separate from all others. However, it is not clear such steps would effectively alleviate the types of harmful biases that CLT identifies regarding strategic assessment and military interventions. For instance, it is unclear how much interaction there would be between planners focused on "combat" and those considering "stability." If parallel planning means that both types of operations are considered at the same time, but separately by different groups, then postconflict plans might receive more resources than if they were delayed until combat planning was completed. Still, this would not necessarily mean that top decision makers would give equal attention to postconflict planning in comparison to combat operations. It must be remembered that the Roosevelt administration's postwar planning for Germany started early on during World War II, yet planners' work was given little attention by senior officials. Furthermore, there is no reason to think that parallel planning by separate groups would encourage individuals focused on postconflict operations to think of them as overlapping with combat (i.e., to adopt shorter time horizons), or motivate those charged with combat operations to contemplate how their plans would affect the prospects of success in other areas.

Regular interagency training might circumvent some of the problems just discussed. Previous presidential initiatives, specifically Bill Clinton's Presidential Decision Directive 56, sought in part to establish annual interagency training programs "in the development and implementation of pol-mil plans for complex contingency operations," but such efforts have not been sustained over time.[20] The Interagency Management System proposed under the Bush administration would only be used at the discretion of the National Security Council, cabinet, and deputy secretaries.[21] Aside from the sustainability of interagency collaboration, if it only occurs during the execution of noncombat operations, rather than prior to all operations in a proposed intervention taking place, it is unlikely that policymakers will give up artificially sequential framings of warfare. Even if collaboration is sustained well before the beginning of military operations, access to senior policymakers is crucial. In the case of the Iraq intervention, had more interagency training preceded the formation of the Office of Reconstruction and Humanitarian Assistance, Garner's team might have been better prepared to adapt to conditions in Baghdad and would have enjoyed greater clarity regarding its authority and relationship to the military command. Still, it would not have necessarily decreased the long-term optimism held by Bush and his senior advisers regarding the actual conditions that would prevail in Iraq after the invasion. In other words, better coordination between civilian and military entities might improve execution, but not address biased assessments that contribute to policymakers initiating prohibitively costly military campaigns.

To improve strategic assessment such that policymakers are aware of the potential long-term costs of military interventions, it is necessary that combat and noncombat operations are considered together, not merely parallel to one another. Returning to the example of World War II, it was not until State Department planners began deliberating with agencies charged with monitoring the day-to-day performance of the German war economy that overly optimistic presumptions about occupation plans began to be challenged. This suggests biases introduced by temporal construal could be dampened by institutional planning mechanisms. Government bodies composed of officials charged with thinking about the long-term policy aims of a proposed military intervention, as well as those concerned with the more immediate costs that would manifest in an armed conflict, might temper overly abstract and concrete assessments. Presenting intervention assessments in which stabilization and reconstruction considerations were incorporated with combat plans would more clearly define the temporal links and trade-offs between different lines of operation, as opposed to presenting separate plans at different times and allowing senior officials to try and draw out the links themselves. This would increase key decision makers' awareness of how concrete operations in the near and distant future related both to one another and high-level political goals, as well as expose different contingencies that might emerge from different courses of action.

Three additional caveats about collaborative bodies for integrating combat and noncombat plans are in order. First, their primary purpose should

not be understood as "red flagging" the plans of senior officials or representatives of other agencies. If a group's task is perceived to be challenging others' plans and assumptions, other officials are likely to perceive the criticism
as less diagnostic of potential flaws in their own reasoning.[22] It is thus necessary that the different actors in a mixed group are perceived to have actual
responsibility over policy so that their recommendations are seen to stem
from accuracy motivations and sincere preferences, rather than ritualized dis-
sent.

This brings up a second caveat regarding transaction costs. It is more difficult to reach consensus in groups composed of individuals with diverging
areas of responsibility and preferences than conditions in which group members' preferences and knowledge bases converge. Bringing in additional diverse perspectives to the planning process can lead to less efficiency in the
production of recommendations. Policymakers will find it difficult not to
forego or circumvent such procedures when they perceive they are in a crisis situation. This shortcoming can be addressed by promoting the regular
interaction of officials with expertise in combat and noncombat operations
so that they may consider approaches to potential crises, rather than forming such groups on a case-by-case basis after a conflict has started, so that
frameworks for action are already available when time pressure is great.

Senior officials can also exploit the inefficiency of diverse advisory groups
to create the impression that policy is being debated in a rigorous fashion,
when in fact the groups merely provide political cover for elite actors who
are unreceptive to their subordinates' advice. This was apparent in regard
to the Working Security Committee during World War II. Composed of both
civilians and military officials with the ability to veto one another's recommendations, the committee did not advise John G. Winant at the European
Advisory Committee in a timely manner. This inefficiency was sanctioned
by Roosevelt, not to promote intense deliberations over policy, but rather to
allow him more control over the postwar decision-making process. The in-
efficiencies that arise when diverse groups attempt to make coherent recommendations can be lessened by delegating an individual official authority
over the group. This leader might determine the primary questions to be addressed during the assessment process, assign responsibilities and tasks, and
establish a schedule directing when different elements of the group would
have to report. Rather than operating like the Working Security Committee,
in which various actors were given veto powers, such groups would perform more like the National Intelligence Council—though without having
to achieve a consensus opinion from sixteen different intelligence-gathering
bodies.

The existence of an entity designed to coordinate combat and noncombat
tasks could lead the United States to conduct fewer military interventions if
it made policymakers more aware of the potential difficulties in all stages of

a conflict, not just initial operations. At the same time, a coordinating body like the one described above could be used by top officials to create political cover for decisions, or as a useful target on to which blame could be deflected when interventions went poorly. Of course, the U.S. government already contains numerous intelligence-gathering bodies that politicians can point to when their policies produce undesirable consequences. Likewise, one could argue that the creation of an entity designed to increase the salience of noncombat operations would signal allies and domestic audiences that U.S. security strategy was becoming increasingly focused on the invasion, occupation, and reconstruction of states perceived to be threats. This could have significantly negative effects on American diplomacy, as was argued about the creation of a postwar planning office prior to the invasion of Iraq. Once again, however, the United States already conducts war-planning activities on a regular basis. The purpose of institutionalizing a body to incorporate noncombat requirements with combat plans would be to reduce the ad hoc nature by which stability operations might otherwise be taken into account.

Since 1945 the United States has engaged in more military interventions than any other country in the world. Given its relative capability to project force, along with the American state's historical tendency to see regime change and liberalization as advancing its interests, it would be somewhat surprising if the country did not continue to engage in military interventions of the transformative variety in the future. Furthermore, a large national security apparatus has emerged to manage American military interventions, a set of bureaucracies that are not easily reformed. Even with institutional change, the decisions of presidents and senior advisers can be substantially independent of the military and civilian organizations beneath them in times of war. For these reasons, the policy recommendations presented here might only exert effects on U.S. security strategy at the margins. If altering the perceived relationship of combat and noncombat activities did not reduce the frequency at which U.S. forces were deployed into combat, it might at least affect how personnel were used once deployed to a theater of operations.

Aside from institutional reform, a simpler imposition on the way leaders conduct military interventions may be to promote awareness of the cognitive constraints people face when trying to plan ahead. Awareness of such constraints will not eliminate them, but may nevertheless instill caution among policymakers thinking about taking their country to war. Policymakers as well as theorists would do well to remember that the subjective difficulty of all stages of military conflicts has implications for whether or not such endeavors should be initiated in the first place. Greater awareness of history can also demonstrate how the strategic assessment of noncombat operations in the midst of preparations for military intervention is a crucial but often neglected component of policy. Accurate assessments cannot guarantee an intervener's success, but can influence the length and cost of a military campaign. Winning the peace depends on planning for peace, and senior decision makers must carefully consider the plans of subordinates if they are to receive the political backing necessary for policies to be effectively implemented. This is especially demanding given the cognitive constraints that impinge on assessments of future events and transitions between complex combat and noncombat tasks.

Notes

Introduction. Ambitious Aims and Meager Plans

1. Harry L. Coles and Albert K. Weinberg, *Civil Affairs: Soldiers Become Governors* (Washington, DC: Center of Military History, U.S. Army, 2004).

2. John W. Dower, *Embracing Defeat: Japan in the Wake of World War II* (New York: W.W. Norton, 1999), 77–78, 213.

3. Ibid., 525.

4. Nadia Schadlow, "War and the Art of Governance," *Parameters* 33, no. 3 (2003): 86.

5. Aside from Schadlow, critics include James Dobbins et al., *America's Role in Nation-Building from Germany to Iraq* (Santa Monica, CA: RAND Corporation, 2003); Ray Salvatore Jennings, *The Road Ahead: Lessons in Nation Building from Japan, Germany, and Afghanistan for Postwar Iraq* (Washington, DC: U.S. Institute of Peace, 2003); Isaiah Wilson, *Thinking beyond War: Civil-Military Relations and Why America Fails to Win the Peace* (New York: Palgrave Macmillan, 2007).

6. Michael Moran, "Peacekeeping Revisited, Again: The 'P' Word Gets Another Look," *NBC-News.com*, Sep. 4, 2003, http://www.msnbc.msn.com/id/3070613/ (accessed Jun. 30, 2011).

7. Overviews include Yaacov Trope and Nira Liberman, "Temporal Construal," *Psychological Review* 110, no. 3 (2003): 403–421; Yaacov Trope and Nira Liberman, "Construal-Level Theory of Psychological Distance," *Psychological Review* 117, no. 2 (2010): 440–463.

8. Cited in U.S. Government Accountability Office, "Stabilization and Reconstruction: Actions Needed to Improve Government-Wide Planning and Capabilities for Future Operations," Oct. 2007, http://www.gao.gov/products/GAO-08-39 (accessed Jul. 10, 2014), 1.

9. Max Boot, *The Savage Wars of Peace: Small Wars and the Rise of American Power* (New York: Basic Books, 2002).

10. Nigel Lo, Barry Hashimoto, and Dan Reiter, "Ensuring Peace: Foreign-Imposed Regime Change and Postwar Peace Duration, 1914–2001," *International Organization* 62, no. 4 (2008): 717–736; Goran Peic and Dan Reiter, "Foreign-Imposed Regime Change, State Power and Civil War Onset, 1920–2004," *British Journal of Political Science* 41, no. 3 (2011): 453–475; Andrew J. Enterline and J. Michael Greig, "Beacons of Hope? The Impact of Imposed Democracy on Regional Peace, Democracy, and Prosperity," *Journal of Politics* 67, no. 4 (2005): 1075–1098.

11. On the multiplicity of factors that inhibit stable democracies taking root after military intervention see Andrew J. Enterline and J. Michael Greig, "The History of Imposed Democracy

and the Future of Iraq and Afghanistan," *Foreign Policy Analysis* 4, no. 4 (2008): 321–347. On the internationalization of civil wars see Patrick M. Regan, *Civil Wars and Foreign Wars: Outside Intervention in Intrastate Conflict* (Ann Arbor, MI: University of Michigan Press, 2000).

12. Department of Defense Directive 3000.05 and General Caldwell's assertion are found in U.S. Department of the Army, *Stability Operations* (Washington, DC: U.S. Department of the Army, 2008), vi.

13. Kathleen H. Hicks and Christine E. Wormuth, with Eric Ridge, *The Future of U.S. Civil Affairs Forces* (Washington, DC: Center for Strategic and International Studies, 2009), 21–23. The Office of Reconstruction and Stabilization was absorbed into the new Bureau of Conflict and Stabilization Operations under the administration of President Barack Obama.

14. Works in this time frame included James Dobbins, Seth G. Jones, Keith Crane, and Beth Cole DeGrasse, *The Beginner's Guide to Nation-Building* (Santa Monica, CA: RAND Corporation, 2007); Francis Fukayama, *State-Building: Governance and World Order in the 21st Century* (Ithaca, NY: Cornell University Press, 2004); Robert C. Orr, ed., *Winning the Peace: An American Strategy for Post-Conflict Reconstruction* (Washington, DC: CSIS Press, 2004); Roland Paris, *At War's End: Building Peace after Civil Conflict* (New York: Cambridge University Press, 2004).

15. David A. Lake, "Two Cheers for Bargaining Theory: Assessing Rationalist Explanations of the Iraq War," *International Security* 35, no. 3 (2010/11): 7–52.

16. Fred Iklé, *Every War Must End* (New York: Columbia University Press, 1991), 8.

17. Dominic D. P. Johnson, *Overconfidence and War: The Havoc and Glory of Positive Illusions* (Cambridge, MA: Harvard University Press, 2004).

18. David M. Edelstein, *Occupational Hazards: Success and Failure in Military Occupation* (Ithaca, NY: Cornell University Press, 2008), 26–27, 88–89.

19. Based on data from Patricia L. Sullivan and Michael Koch, "Military Interventions by Powerful States, 1945–2003," *Journal of Peace Research* 46, no. 5 (2009): 707–718; Edelstein, *Occupational Hazards*, 27.

20. Colin Dueck, *Reluctant Crusaders: Power, Culture, and Change in American Grand Strategy* (Princeton, NJ: Princeton University Press, 2006), 3; Jonathan Monten, "The Roots of the Bush Doctrine: Power, Nationalism, and Democracy Promotion in US Strategy," *International Security* 29, no. 4 (2005): 145; Dominic Tierney, *How We Fight: Crusades, Quagmires, and the American Way of War* (New York: Little, Brown, 2010), 7, 37.

21. George Bush and Brent Scowcroft, *A World Transformed* (New York: Alfred A. Knopf, 1998), 489.

22. Dueck, *Reluctant Crusaders*, 33.

23. Cheney's reversal is described in Barton Gellman, *Angler: The Cheney Vice Presidency* (New York: Penguin Press, 2008), 251.

24. John A. Nagl, *Learning to Eat Soup with a Knife: Counterinsurgency Lessons from Malaya and Vietnam* (Chicago: Chicago University Press, 2005), 200.

25. See, for example, Carl J. Friedrich, "Military Government and Democratization: A Central Issue of American Foreign Policy," in *American Experiences in Military Government in World War II*, ed. Carl J. Friedrich (New York: Rinehart, 1948), 211–237.

26. Lt. Col. Burt K. Thompson, "Nation-Building: A Bad Idea Whose Time Has Come?" in *A Nation at War in an Era of Strategic Change*, ed. Williamson Murray (Carlisle Barracks, PA: U.S. Army War College, 2004), 264.

27. In the American context, the classic work asserting officers' autonomy within the military sphere is Samuel P. Huntington, *The Soldier and the State: The Theory and Politics of Civil-Military Relations* (Cambridge, MA: Harvard University Press, 1957). Works challenging or refining this perspective include Eliot A. Cohen, *Supreme Command: Soldiers, Statesmen, and Leadership in Wartime* (New York: Simon & Schuster, 2002); Michael C. Desch, *Civilian Control of the Military: The Changing Security Environment* (Baltimore, MD: Johns Hopkins University Press, 1999); Peter D. Feaver, *Armed Servants: Agency, Oversight, and Civil-Military Relations* (Cambridge, MA: Harvard University Press, 2005).

28. Risa Brooks, *Shaping Strategy: The Civil-Military Politics of Strategic Assessment* (Princeton, NJ: Princeton University Press, 2008).

29. Alexander George, "The 'Operational Code': A Neglected Approach to the Study of Political Leaders and Decision-Making," *International Studies Quarterly* 13, no. 2 (1969): 214–215; Wilson, *Thinking Beyond War*, 16–17.

30. Daniel Kahneman and Amos Tversky, "Intuitive Prediction: Biases and Corrective Procedures," *TIMS Studies in Management Science*, 12 (1979): 313–327.

31. Roger Buehler, Dale Griffin, and Michael Ross, "Exploring the 'Planning Fallacy': Why People Underestimate Their Task Completion Times," *Journal of Personality and Social Psychology* 67, no. 3 (1994): 366–381.

32. Marjorie K. Shelley, "Gain/Loss Asymmetry in Risky Intertemporal Choice," *Organizational Behavior and Human Decision Processes* 59, no. 1 (1994): 124–159; Scott Highhouse, Susan Mohammed, and Jody R. Hoffman, "Temporal Discounting of Strategic Issues: Bold Forecasts for Opportunities and Threats," *Basic and Applied Social Psychology* 24, no. 1 (2002): 43–56.

33. Robin R. Vallacher and Daniel M. Wegner, *A Theory of Action Identification* (Hillsdale, NJ: Lawrence Erlbaum Associates, 1985).

34. Robin R. Vallacher and Daniel M. Wegner, "What Do People Think They're Doing? Action Identification and Human Behavior," *Psychological Review* 94, no. 1 (1987): 9.

35. For an overview of CLT's growing prominence see Ronald R. Krebs and Aaron Rapport, "International Relations and the Psychology of Time Horizons," *International Studies Quarterly* 56, no. 3 (2012): 531.

36. The first major study to demonstrate this prediction of CLT was Nira Liberman and Yaacov Trope, "The Role of Feasibility and Desirability Considerations in Near and Distant Future Decisions: A Test of Temporal Construal Theory," *Journal of Personality and Social Psychology* 75, no. 1 (1998): 5–18.

37. See Charles F. Hermann, "Changing Course: When Governments Choose to Redirect Foreign Policy," *International Studies Quarterly* 34, no. 1 (1990): 3–21, esp. 14–20.

1. Strategic Assessment and Noncombat Operations

1. A good review is Margaret G. Hermann, Thomas Preston, Baghat Korany, and Timothy M. Shaw, "Who Leads Matters: The Effects of Powerful Individuals," *International Studies Review* 3, no. 2 (2001): 83–131.

2. U.S. Department of the Army, *FM 3-0: Operations* (Washington, DC: U.S. Department of the Army, 2001). See specifically chaps. 7 and 8 on offensive and defensive operations.

3. Paul F. Diehl, Daniel Druckman, and James Wall, "International Peacekeeping and Conflict Resolution: A Taxonomic Analysis with Implications," *Journal of Conflict Resolution* 42, no. 1 (1998): 33–55; see also Paul F. Diehl, *Peace Operations* (Malden, MA: Polity Press, 2008), 15–16. Collective enforcement entails the military defeat of an aggressor state to defend populations threatened by aggression. Protective services are synonymous with the use of air and ground power to establish safe havens guarded by defenders prepared to use deadly force. Interventions in support of democracy rely primarily on the use of force to defend the democratically elected regime of a foreign state, or to depose a nondemocratically elected regime in favor of a future government of freely elected officials.

4. U.S. Department of the Army, *FM 3-07: Stability Operations* (Washington, DC: U.S. Department of the Army, 2008), I-15, V-2; Diehl et al., "Peacekeeping and Conflict Resolution," 39.

5. Mark Mazower, *Hitler's Empire: How the Nazis Ruled Europe* (New York: Penguin Press, 2008).

6. Virginia Page Fortna, "Interstate Peacekeeping: Causal Mechanisms and Empirical Effects," *World Politics* 56, no. 4 (2004): 481–519; Barbara F. Walter, "Designing Transitions from Civil War: Demobilization, Democratization, and Commitments to Peace," *International Security* 24, no. 1 (1999): 127–155.

7. Diehl et al., "Peacekeeping and Conflict Resolution," 39; U.S. Department of the Army, *FM 3-24: Counterinsurgency* (Washington, DC: U.S. Department of the Army, 2006), 2-12–2-13.

8. I follow the definition of Risa Brooks, *Shaping Strategy: The Civil-Military Politics of Strategic Assessment* (Princeton, NJ: Princeton University Press, 2008), 34. This definition is broader

than that of others who have defined strategic assessment as actors' perceptions of whether or not a given course of military action is yielding expected results; see Scott Sigmund Gartner, *Strategic Assessment in War* (New Haven, CT: Yale University Press, 1999).

9. Peter Liberman, *Does Conquest Pay? The Exploitation of Occupied Industrial Societies* (Princeton, NJ: Princeton University Press, 1996); David M. Edelstein, *Occupational Hazards: Success and Failure in Military Occupation* (Ithaca, NY: Cornell University Press, 2008).

10. Eric Carlton contends that an occupier's success depends on how effectively it socializes occupied populations to accept foreign governance, while Alexander Cooley argues the organizational structure of military government has a substantial impact on occupation dynamics. David Edelstein contends that the presence or absence of a shared threat between the occupier and occupied population determines whether cooperation or coercion is a more effective strategy. Carlton, *Occupation: The Policies and Practices of Military Conquerors* (Savage, MD: Routledge, 1992); Cooley, *Logics of Hierarchy: The Organization of Empires, States, and Military Occupations* (Ithaca, NY: Cornell University Press, 2005); Edelstein, *Occupational Hazards*, chap. 2.

11. This is true of both behavioral and emotional reactions; see Timothy D. Wilson and Suzanne J. LaFleur, "Knowing What You'll Do: Effects of Analyzing Reasons on Self-Prediction," *Journal of Personality and Social Psychology* 68, no. 1 (1995): 21–35; Timothy D. Wilson and Daniel T. Gilbert, "Affective Forecasting," *Advances in Experimental Social Psychology* 35 (2003): 345–411.

12. For a review of compensatory and noncompensatory strategies see Richard R. Lau, "Models of Decision-Making," in *The Oxford Handbook of Political Psychology*, ed. David O. Sears, Leonie Huddy, and Robert Jervis (New York: Oxford University Press, 2003), 19–59.

13. Good overviews of CLT are Nira Liberman and Yaacov Trope, "The Psychology of Transcending the Here and Now," *Science* 322, no. 5905 (Nov. 21, 2008): 1201–1205; Yaacov Trope and Nira Liberman, "Temporal Construal," *Psychological Review* 110, no. 3 (Jul. 2003): 403–421.

14. Daniel Kahneman and Amos Tversky, "Intuitive Prediction: Biases and Corrective Procedures," *TIMS Studies in Management Science* 12 (1979): 313–327.

15. Robert Jervis, *Perception and Misperception in International Politics* (Princeton, NJ: Princeton University Press, 1976), chap. 10.

16. Nira Liberman, Michael D. Sagristano, and Yaacov Trope, "The Effect of Temporal Distance on Level of Mental Construal," *Journal of Experimental and Social Psychology* 38, no. 6 (2002): 523–534.

17. Nira Liberman and Yaacov Trope, "The Role of Feasibility and Desirability Considerations in Near and Distant Future Decisions: A Test of Temporal Construal Theory," *Journal of Personality and Social Psychology* 75, no. 1 (1998): 6–7.

18. Dale W. Griffin, David Dunning, and Lee Ross, "The Role of Construal Processes in Overconfident Predictions about Self and Others," *Journal of Personality and Social Psychology* 59, no. 6 (1990): 1128–1139; Steven J. Sherman, "On the Self-Erasing Nature of Errors of Prediction," *Journal of Personality and Social Psychology* 39, no. 2 (1980): 211–221.

19. Jeffrey W. Taliaferro, "Power Politics and the Balance of Risks: Hypotheses on Great Power Intervention in the Periphery," *Political Psychology* 25, no. 2 (2004): 183.

20. Jack S. Levy, "Loss Aversion, Framing Effects, and International Conflict," in *Handbook of War Studies II*, ed. Manus I. Midlarsky (Ann Arbor, MI: University of Michigan Press, 2000), 198–199.

21. Liberman and Trope, "Feasibility and Desirability Considerations," 5–18.

22. Michael D. Sagristano, Yaacov Trope, and Nira Liberman, "Time Dependent Gambling: Odds Now, Money Later," *Journal of Experimental Psychology* 131, no. 3 (2002): 364–376; Marjorie K. Shelley, "Gain/Loss Asymmetry in Risky Intertemporal Choice," *Organizational Behavior and Human Decision Processes* 59, no. 1 (1994): 124–159; Scott Highhouse, Susan Mohammed, and Jody R. Hoffman, "Temporal Discounting of Strategic Issues: Bold Forecasts for Opportunities and Threats," *Basic and Applied Social Psychology* 24, no. 1 (2002): 43–56; Trope and Liberman, "Temporal Construal," 411.

23. Tal Eyal, Nira Liberman, Yaacov Trope, and Eva Walther, "The Pros and Cons of Temporally Near and Distant Action," *Journal of Personality and Social Psychology* 86, no. 6 (Jun. 2004): 781–783.

24. A good overview is Herbert Bless, "The Interplay of Affect and Cognition: The Mediating Role of General Knowledge Structures," in *Feeling and Thinking: The Role of Affect in Social Cognition*, ed. Joseph P. Forgas (New York: Cambridge University Press, 2000), 201–222. The opposite scenario, in which an action's concrete elements are evaluated more positively than its abstract elements, may also hold. For example, the abstract construal of "academic dishonesty" may be judged to be more negative than the concrete construal "peeking at my neighbor's answer on a test," and thus the act may be judged to be more unseemly when viewed from afar.

25. Frederick R. Leach and Jason E. Plaks, "Regret for Errors of Commission and Omission in the Distant Term versus Near Term: The Role of Level of Abstraction," *Personality and Social Psychology Bulletin* 35, no. 2 (2009): 221–229.

26. Joseph Cesario, Heidi Grant, and E. Tory Higgins, "Regulatory Fit and Persuasion: Transfer from 'Feeling Right,'" *Journal of Personality and Social Psychology* 86, no. 3 (2004): 388–404; Kentaro Fujita, Tal Eyal, Shelly Chaiken, Yaacov Trope, and Nira Liberman, "Influencing Attitudes toward Near and Distant Objects," *Journal of Experimental Social Psychology* 44, no. 3 (May 2008): 562–572; Richard E. Petty and Duane T. Wegener, "Matching vs. Mismatching Attitude Functions: Implications of Scrutiny of Persuasive Messages," *Personality and Social Psychology Bulletin* 24, no. 3 (1998): 227–240.

27. Hakkyun Kim, Akshay R. Rao, and Angela Y. Lee, "It's Time to Vote: The Effect of Matching Message Orientation and Temporal Frame on Political Persuasion," *Journal of Consumer Research* 35, no. 6 (2009): 877–889.

28. Cesario et al., "Regulatory Fit and Persuasion," 392–397.

29. Liberman and Trope, "Transcending the Here and Now," 1204.

30. On the effects of policymakers' prior beliefs on the interpretation of incoming information see Jervis, *Perception and Misperception*, chap. 4.

31. Jack S. Levy, "Learning and Foreign Policy: Sweeping a Conceptual Minefield," *International Organization* 48, no. 2 (1994): 279–312.

32. What follows expands on the definition in Ronald R. Krebs and Aaron Rapport, "International Relations and the Psychology of Time Horizons," *International Studies Quarterly* 56, no. 3 (2012): 530–531.

33. Miroslav Nincic, "Loss Aversion and the Domestic Context of Military Intervention," *Political Research Quarterly* 50, no. 1 (1997): 97–120; Elizabeth Saunders, *Leaders at War: How Presidents Shape Military Interventions* (Ithaca, NY: Cornell University Press, 2011).

34. Ibid.

35. Jonathan Mercer, *Reputation and International Politics* (Ithaca, NY: Cornell University Press, 1996); Daryl G. Press, *Calculating Credibility: How Leaders Assess Military Threats* (Ithaca, NY: Cornell University Press, 2005).

36. Elizabeth Saunders suggests that leaders who seek to transform the internal character of a targeted state "may have a longer time horizon, perhaps expecting that over time, a government with a favorable internal order will moderate any unacceptable foreign policies." Saunders, "Transformative Choices: Leaders and the Origins of Intervention Strategy," *International Security* 34, no. 2 (2009): 130–131.

37. Charles A. Kupchan, "Getting In: The Initial Stage of Military Intervention," in *Foreign Military Intervention: The Dynamics of Protracted Conflict*, ed. Ariel E. Levite, Bruce W. Jentleson, and Larry Berman (New York: Columbia University Press, 1992), 247, 251, 256–258.

38. Dominic D. P. Johnson, *Overconfidence and War: The Havoc and Glory of Positive Illusions* (Cambridge, MA: Harvard University Press, 2004), 41, 237.

39. Lau, "Models of Decision-Making," 31–32; Thomas C. Ormerod, "Planning and Ill-Defined Problems," in *The Cognitive Psychology of Planning*, ed. Robin Morris and Geoff Ward (New York: Psychology Press, 2005), 63.

40. Sagristano et al., "Time Dependent Gambling."

41. Antonio L. Freitas, Peter Gollwitzer, and Yaacov Trope, "The Influence of Abstract and Concrete Mindsets on Anticipating and Guiding Others' Self-Regulatory Effort," *Journal of*

Experimental Social Psychology 40, no. 6 (Nov. 2004): 739–752; Jens Förster, Ronald S. Friedman, and Nira Liberman, "Temporal Construal Effects on Abstract and Concrete Thinking: Consequences for Insight and Creative Cognition," *Journal of Personality and Social Psychology* 87, no. 2 (Aug. 2004): 177–189; Cheryl J. Wakslak, Yaacov Trope, Nira Liberman, and Rotem Alony, "Seeing the Forest When Entry is Unlikely: Probability and the Mental Representation of Events," *Journal of Experimental Psychology* 135, no. 4 (Nov. 2006): 641–653.

42. Based on data from Patricia L. Sullivan and Michael Koch, "Military Interventions by Powerful States, 1945–2003," *Journal of Peace Research* 46, no. 5 (2009): 707–718.

43. This may be related to other studies outside the CLT paradigm that have shown that altering the sequence in which events occur significantly affects people's preferences between options, even if the expected utility of the events is independent of the order in which they fall; Shane Frederick, George Loewenstein, and Ted O'Donoghue, "Time Discounting and Time Preference: A Critical Review," *Journal of Economic Literature* 40, no. 2 (2002): 363–364.

44. Anthony Cordesman, "Planning for a Self-Inflicted Wound: US Policy to Reshape a Post-Saddam Iraq," Washington, DC: Center for Strategic and International Studies, Dec. 31, 2002, http://www.comw.org/warreport/fulltext/0212cordesman.pdf (accessed Aug. 3, 2011). Similar arguments are found in Peter W. Chiarelli and Patrick R. Michaelis, "Winning the Peace: The Requirement for Full-Spectrum Operations," *Military Review* (Jul.–Aug. 2005): 4–17; Isaiah Wilson, *Thinking beyond War: Civil-Military Relations and Why America Fails to Win the Peace* (New York: Palgrave Macmillan, 2007), 16–17. Alexander George also argues that policymakers tend to evaluate risks sequentially; George, "The 'Operational Code': A Neglected Approach to the Study of Political Leaders and Decision-Making," *International Studies Quarterly* 13, no. 2 (1969): 214–215.

45. Robin R. Vallacher and Daniel M. Wegener, "Levels of Personal Agency: Individual Variation in Action Identification," *Journal of Personality and Social Psychology* 57, no. 4 (1989): 660–671.

46. Rachel Karniol and Michael Ross, "The Motivational Impact of Temporal Focus: Thinking about the Future and the Past," *Annual Review of Psychology* 47 (1996): 596.

47. Steven Peter Rosen, *War and Human Nature* (Princeton, NJ: Princeton University Press, 2005), 135–136.

48. Robert Powell, "Guns, Butter, and Anarchy," *American Political Science Review* 87, no. 1 (1993): 115–132; James D. Morrow, "Arms versus Allies: Trade-offs in the Search for Security," *International Organization* 47, no. 2 (1993): 207–233; Philip Arena and Scott Wolford, "Arms, Intelligence, and War," *International Studies Quarterly* 56, no. 2 (2012): 351–365.

49. Fred Iklé, *Every War Must End* (New York: Columbia University Press, 1991), 6, 8; Sarah E. Kreps, *Coalitions of Convenience: United States Military Interventions after the Cold War* (New York: Oxford University Press, 2011), 6–7, 30–31.

50. Stephen Krasner, *Defending the National Interest: Raw Materials Investments and U.S. Foreign Policy* (Princeton, NJ: Princeton University Press, 1978), 15; Kenneth N. Waltz, "Structural Realism after the Cold War," in *America Unrivaled: The Future of the Balance of Power*, ed. G. John Ikenberry (Ithaca, NY: Cornell University Press, 2002), 37.

51. John J. Mearsheimer, *The Tragedy of Great Power Politics* (New York: W.W. Norton, 2001), 141–143.

52. G. John Ikenberry, *After Victory: Institutions, Strategic Restraint, and the Rebuilding of Order after Major Wars* (Princeton, NJ: Princeton University Press, 2000), 57.

53. Kreps, *Coalitions of Convenience*, 6, 30.

54. On the importance of force employment see Stephen Biddle, *Military Power: Explaining Victory and Defeat in Modern Battle* (Princeton, NJ: Princeton University Press, 2004).

55. U.S. Army, *Stability Operations*, 2-2–2-3; U.S. Department of the Army, *FM 7-0: Training for Full Spectrum Operations* (Washington, DC: U.S. Department of the Army, 2008), 1–7.

56. Maxwell Taylor, U.S. ambassador in Saigon, told President Lyndon Johnson in January 1965 that the ability of Americans to advance U.S. policy in South Vietnam by advisory means was "very limited" and that "to take no positive action now is to accept defeat in the fairly near future." William Conrad Gibbons, *The U.S. Government and the Vietnam War: Executive and Legislative Roles and Relationships, Vol. 2* (Princeton, NJ: Princeton University Press, 1986), 387.

57. United Nations Security Council Resolution 794, http://daccess-dds-ny.un.org/doc/UNDOC/GEN/N92/772/11/PDF/N9277211.pdf?OpenElement (accessed Aug. 25, 2011).

58. Carl von Clausewitz, *On War*, ed. Michael Howard and Peter Paret (Princeton, NJ: Princeton University Press, 1989), 119–121.

59. Prominent examples of this logic include H.E. Goemans, *War and Punishment: The Causes of War Termination and the First World War* (Princeton, NJ: Princeton University Press, 2000); Robert Powell, "Bargaining and Learning while Fighting," *American Journal of Political Science* 48, no. 2 (2004): 344–361.

60. Thomas C. Schelling, *Arms and Influence* (New Haven, CT: Yale University Press, 1966); see also Alexander L. George, David K. Hall, and William E. Simons, *The Limits of Coercive Diplomacy: Laos, Cuba, Vietnam* (Boston, MA: Little, Brown, 1971).

61. Barry R. Posen, *The Sources of Military Doctrine: France, Britain, and Germany between the World Wars* (Ithaca, NY: Cornell University Press, 1984), 48–49.

62. Patricia L. Sullivan, *Who Wins? Predicting Strategic Success and Failure in Armed Conflict* (New York: Oxford University Press, 2012).

63. James G. March and Johan P. Olsen, "The Institutional Dynamics of International Political Orders," in *Exploration and Contestation in the Study of World Politics*, ed. Peter J. Katzenstein, Robert O. Keohane, and Stephen D. Krasner (Cambridge, MA: MIT Press, 1999), 308.

64. Gartner, *Strategic Assessment in War*.

65. Russell F. Weigley, *The American Way of War: A History of United States Military Strategy and Policy* (Bloomington, IN: Indiana University Press, 1973).

66. Andrew F. Krepinevich Jr., *The Army and Vietnam* (Baltimore, MD: Johns Hopkins University Press, 1986), 4–5; Andrew F. Krepinevich Jr., "How to Win in Iraq," *Foreign Affairs* 84, no. 5 (Sep.–Oct. 2005): 87–104; Isaiah Wilson, "America's Anabasis," in *War in Iraq: Planning and Execution*, ed. Thomas G. Mahnken and Thomas A. Keaney (New York: Routledge, 2007), 9–21.

67. Regarding Vietnam see Jonathan D. Caverley, "The Myth of Military Myopia: Democracy, Small Wars, and Vietnam," *International Security* 34, no. 3 (2010): 119–157; regarding Weigley's thesis see Brian M. Linn, "*The American Way of War* Revisited," *Journal of Military History* 66, no. 2 (2002): 501–530.

68. Harry L. Coles and Albert K. Weinberg, *Civil Affairs: Soldiers Become Governors* (Washington, DC: Center of Military History, U.S. Army, 2004), 98–101.

69. Michael D. Pearlman, *Truman and MacArthur: Policy, Politics, and the Hunger for Honor and Renown* (Bloomington, IN: Indiana University Press, 2008).

70. H. R. McMaster, *Dereliction of Duty: Lyndon Johnson, Robert McNamara, the Joint Chiefs of Staff, and the Lies That Led to Vietnam* (New York: HarperCollins, 1997).

71. Richard K. Betts, *Soldiers, Statesmen, and Cold War Crises*, 2nd ed. (New York: Columbia University Press, 1991).

72. Thomas E. Ricks, *The Generals: American Military Command from World War II to Today* (New York: Penguin, 2012).

73. The conceptual systemization here follows the recommendations of Gary Goertz, *Social Science Concepts: A User's Guide* (Princeton, NJ: Princeton University Press, 2006).

74. Alexander George and Andrew Bennett, *Case Studies and Theory Development in the Social Sciences* (Cambridge, MA: MIT Press, 2005), 153–160; Stephen Van Evera, *Guide to Methods for Students of Political Science* (Cambridge, MA: MIT Press, 1996), 37, 47.

75. Chaim D. Kaufmann, "Out of the Lab and into the Archives: A Method for Testing Psychological Explanations of Political Decision Making," *International Studies Quarterly* 38, no. 4 (1994): 561.

76. Moron H. Halperin, *Bureaucratic Politics and Foreign Policy* (Washington, DC: Brookings Institution, 1974), 24.

77. The term "intermediate mechanism" used here is synonymous with James Mahoney's less concise term "mechanism causal process observation." Mahoney, "After KKV: The New Methodology of Qualitative Research," *World Politics* 62, no. 1 (2010): 128–129.

78. Kaufmann, "Out of the Lab," 560.

79. Rose McDermott, *Presidential Leadership, Illness, and Decision Making* (New York: Cambridge University Press, 2008), chap. 4.

80. This has been especially true during and after the Cold War. Among others, see Walter McDougal, *Promised Land, Crusader State: The American Encounter with the World Since 1776* (New York: Mariner, 1998); Tony Smith, *America's Mission: The United States and the Worldwide Struggle for Democracy in the Twentieth Century* (Princeton, NJ: Princeton University Press, 1994); Karin von Hippel, *Democracy by Force: U.S. Military Intervention in the Post-Cold War World* (Cambridge, UK: Cambridge University Press, 2000).

81. Ian S. Lustick, "History, Historiography, and Political Science: Multiple Historical Records and the Problem of Selection Bias," *American Political Science Review* 90, no. 3 (1996): 605–618.

82. Even scholars who identify congressional checks on the executive branch acknowledge the information available to the president as a source of White House supremacy in security affairs; William G. Howell and Jon C. Pevehouse, *While Dangers Gather: Congressional Checks on Presidential War Powers* (Princeton, NJ: Princeton University Press, 2007), 6–10.

83. In the Vietnam case, as is true of all the cases, readers should not confuse officials' perceptions of the *local* balance of forces with perceptions of the *global* balance of power. Key members of the Johnson administration arguably believed the United States enjoyed a sizable military advantage globally vis-à-vis the Soviet Union and China. See Gareth Porter, *Perils of Dominance: Imbalance of Power and the Road to War in Vietnam* (Berkeley, CA: University of California Press, 2005).

2. The Occupation of Germany

1. Carl J. Friedrich, "Military Government and Democratization: A Central Issue of American Foreign Policy," and Dale Clark, "Conflicts over Planning at Staff Headquarters," in *American Experiences in Military Government in World War II*, ed. Carl J. Friedrich (New York: Rinehart, 1948), 21, 236–237.

2. Lucius D. Clay, "Proconsul of a People, by Another People, for Both Peoples," in *Americans as Proconsuls: United States Military Government in Germany and Japan, 1944–1952*, ed. Robert Wolfe (Carbondale, IL: Southern Illinois University Press, 1984), 104–105; John Gimbel, *The American Occupation of Germany: Politics and the Military, 1945–1949* (Stanford: Stanford University Press, 1968), 1.

3. Patrick J. Hearden, *Architects of Globalism: Building a New World Order during World War II* (Fayetteville, AR: University of Arkansas Press, 2002), 11–18.

4. A comprehensive review of the activities of these and similar bodies is Harley A. Notter, *Postwar Foreign Policy Preparation, 1939–1945* (Washington, DC: United States Department of State, 1950).

5. Carolyn W. Eisenberg, *Drawing the Line: The American Decision to Divide Germany* (New York: Cambridge University Press, 1996), 36; Henry L. Stimson and McGeorge Bundy, *On Active Service in Peace and War* (New York: Harper & Brothers, 1947), 570.

6. John Morton Blum, *From the Morgenthau Diaries: Years of War, 1941–1945* (Boston, MA: Houghton Mifflin, 1967), 340–342; Robert Dallek, *Franklin Roosevelt and American Foreign Policy, 1932–1945* (New York: Oxford University Press, 1979), 374.

7. Eisenberg, *Drawing the Line*, 14–15; Earl F. Ziemke, *The U.S. Army in the Occupation of Germany* (Washington, DC: Center of Military History, United States Army, 1975), 40–41; Paul Y. Hammond, "Directives for the Occupation of Germany: The Washington Controversy," in *American Civil Military Decisions*, ed. Harold Stein (Birmingham, AL: University of Alabama Press, 1963), 334.

8. United States Army, *Planning for the Occupation of Germany* (Frankfurt: Office of the Chief Historian, European Command, 1947), 9–16, 21.

9. The abbreviation "CCS" stood for Combined Chiefs of Staff, which gave final approval to the civil affairs document.

10. U.S. Army, *Planning for the Occupation*, 31, 44–46.

11. Ibid., 59–71.

12. Ibid., 84–91; Kenneth O. McCreedy, "Planning the Peace: Operation Eclipse and the Occupation of Germany," *Journal of Military History* 65, no. 3 (2001): 713–739.

13. Jean Edward Smith, ed., *The Papers of General Lucius D. Clay: Germany, 1945–1949* (Bloomington, IN: Indiana University Press, 1974), 66; see also McCreedy, "Planning the Peace," 719–720; U.S. Army, *Planning for the Occupation*, 5, 32; Earl F. Ziemke, "Improvising Stability and Change in Postwar Germany," in *Americans as Proconsuls*, 58.

14. Hearden, *Architects of Globalism*, 167; U.S. Army, *Planning for the Occupation*, 39, 57.

15. Roosevelt memorandum to the Secretary of State, Sept. 29, 1944, 1–2, Diplomatic Correspondence Germany: Jan.–Sep. 1944, box 31, Papers as President, President's Secretary's Files (hereafter "PSF"), Franklin D. Roosevelt Library, Hyde Park, New York (hereafter cited as "FDRL").

16. Warren F. Kimball, *Swords or Ploughshares? The Morgenthau Plan for Defeated Nazi Germany, 1943–1946* (Philadelphia, PA: J.B. Lippincott, 1976), 155.

17. John J. McCloy, "From Military Government to Self-Government," in *Americans as Proconsuls*, 119; U.S. Army, *Planning for Occupation*, 102–108; Carl J. Friedrich, "The Three Phases of Field Operations in Germany, 1945–1946," in *Military Government in World War II*, 257–258; Gimbel, *American Occupation of Germany*, 13.

18. Smith, *Lucius D. Clay*, 23.

19. Ziemke, *Occupation of Germany*, 445–446.

20. Francis L. Loewenheim, Harold D. Langley, and Manfred Jonas, eds., *Roosevelt and Churchill: Their Secret Wartime Correspondence* (New York: Saturday Review Press/E. P. Dutton, 1975), 41.

21. Warren F. Kimball, *Forged in War: Roosevelt, Churchill, and the Second World War* (New York: William Morrow, 1997), 243.

22. Franklin Roosevelt, "Annual Message to Congress on the State of the Union," Jan. 6, 1941, in *The American Presidency Project*, ed. John Woolley and Gerhard Peters, available online at http://www.presidency.ucsb.edu/ws/index.php?pid=16092&st=&st1= (accessed Jul. 11, 2014).

23. Willard Range, *Franklin D. Roosevelt's World Order* (Athens, GA: University of Georgia Press, 1959), 34.

24. A comprehensive review of the Welles trip is J. Simon Rofe, *Franklin Roosevelt's Foreign Policy and the Welles Mission* (New York: Palgrave Macmillan, 2007).

25. Gaddis Smith, *American Diplomacy during the Second World War, 1941–1945* (New York: Alfred A. Knopf, 1985), 43.

26. Roosevelt to Harry Hopkins, Adm. Ernst King, and Gen. George Marshall, Jul. 15, 1942, 2 (emphasis added), PSF (Safe Files), Harry Hopkins folder, box 3, FDRL.

27. Dallek, *Franklin Roosevelt*, 337, 338–342. Others who assert Roosevelt's offer was meant in part to protect liberal ideals enshrined in the charter include Smith, *American Diplomacy*, 45; John L. Gaddis, *The United States and the Origins of the Cold War, 1941–1947* (New York: Columbia University Press, 2000), 15; Lloyd C. Gardner, "FDR and Cooperation with the Soviet Union: A Policy of Procrastination," and Sumner Welles, "Political Cooperation During the War: A Lost Opportunity," in *Franklin D. Roosevelt and the World Crisis, 1937–1945*, ed. Warren F. Kimball (Lexington, MA: D.C. Heath, 1973), 128–129, 142.

28. Minutes, Subcommittee on Political Problems, Mar. 14, 1942, 2, 5, folder 6: Postwar Foreign Policy Files, 1940–1943, Subcommittee on Political Problems: minutes, box 190, Sumner Welles Papers (hereafter cited as "SWP"), FDRL.

29. Robert A. Divine, *Roosevelt and World War II* (Baltimore, MD: Johns Hopkins University Press, 1969), 85–91; James McAllister, *No Exit: America and the German Problem, 1943–1954* (Ithaca, NY: Cornell University Press, 2002), 33–36.

30. Hearden, *Architects of Globalism*, 149.

31. See discussions in Paul D. Mayle, *Eureka Summit: Agreement in Principle and the Big Three in Tehran, 1943* (Newark, DE: University of Delaware Press, 1987), 60–62, 65–66; Kimball, *Swords or Ploughshares*, 13; Smith, *American Diplomacy*, 74–75; Dallek, *Franklin Roosevelt*, 469, 473–474; McAllister, *No Exit*, 35–36.

32. Warren F. Kimball, *The Juggler: Franklin Roosevelt as Wartime Statesman* (Princeton, NJ: Princeton University Press, 1991), 99; Ziemke, *Occupation of Germany*, 80.

33. Steven Casey, *Cautious Crusade: Franklin D. Roosevelt, American Public Opinion, and the War against Nazi Germany* (New York: Oxford University Press, 2001), 132–141.

34. Ibid., 136; Joint Chiefs of Staff Memorandum for Information No. 180: Report on Political Conditions in Occupied Europe, Jan. 17, 1944, Naval Aide's Files: President's File P1–P21, box 171, Map Room Files (hereafter cited as "MRF"), FDRL.

35. McAllister, *No Exit*, 32.

36. Roosevelt memorandum for the Joint Chiefs of Staff, Apr. 1, 1944, folder 2, A/16: Warfare, Germany and German Occupied Countries, box 167, MRF, FDRL; Michael R. Beschloss, *The Conquerors: Roosevelt, Truman, and the Destruction of Hitler's Germany, 1941–1945* (New York: Simon & Schuster, 2002), 12.

37. Henry Morgenthau Jr., *Germany Is Our Problem* (New York: Harper & Brothers Publishers, 1945) 48–55; Kimball, *Forged in War*, 275; Friedrich, "Military Government and Democratization," 4 (fn. 2).

38. The Morgenthau Plan that was presented at the Quebec conference in September 1944 may be found in its entirety at the beginning of Morgenthau, *Germany Is Our Problem*, v–viii.

39. Memorandum by President Roosevelt to the Secretary of War, Aug. 26, 1944, 544, *Foreign Relations of the United States 1944, Vol. I* (Washington, DC: United States Government Printing Office, 1966). This volume is hereafter cited as *FRUS 1944*.

40. Hearden, *Architects of Globalism*, 148; Eisenberg, *Drawing the Line*, 17.

41. Subcommittee on Political Problems, "Tentative View of the Subcommittee on Political Problems," Aug. 12, 1942, 6, folder 8: Postwar Foreign Policy Files, 1940–1943, Subcommittee on Political Problems: Tentative Views, box 190; Subcommittee on Political Problems., P Document 125, Nov. 6, 1942, folder 6: Postwar Foreign Policy Files, 1940–1943, Subcommittee on Postwar Problems: Documents, P112–P140, box 193, SWP, FDRL.

42. On Welles's views on partition see McAllister, *No Exit*, 31–32, 51.

43. Memorandum on Official Statements of Post-War Policy, Jan. 3, 1942, chap. 9, 2, folder 2: Postwar Foreign Policy Files, 1940–1943, Official Statements of Postwar Policy, box 190, SWP, FDRL. On this theme in Hull's views and in the State Department more generally see Hearden, *Architects of Globalism*, 12–16; Kimball, *Swords or Ploughshares*, 5; Eisenberg, *Drawing the Line*, 17–19.

44. Memorandum by the Committee on Postwar Programs, May 31, 1944, 49–53, *Foreign Relations of the United States: The Conference at Quebec, 1944* (Washington, DC: United States Government Printing Office, 1972). This collection of documents is hereafter cited as *FRUS Quebec*.

45. Lubin, "Economic Policy with Respect to Germany," memorandum to Harry Hopkins, Se14, 1944, Book 9: Treatment of Germany (part 3 of folder 1), box 333, Henry Hopkins Papers (hereafter cited as "HHP"), FDRL.

46. Irwin L. Hunt, *American Military Government of Occupied Germany, 1918–1920* (Washington, DC: United States Government Printing Office, 1943). In a similar vein see Cassius M. Dowell, *Military Aid to the Civil Power*, ed. Igor I. Kavass and Adolf Sprudzs (Buffalo, NY: William S. Hein, 1972), originally published in 1925 by the United States Army Service School in Fort Leavenworth, Kansas.

47. Combined Civil Affairs Committee, "Directive for Military Government in Germany Prior to Defeat or Surrender," Apr. 29, 1944, appendix A, 3, folder 2, A/16: Warfare, Germany and German Occupied Countries, box 167; Combined Chiefs of Staff to Gen. Eisenhower, Aug. 19, 1944, folder 3: Germany Zones of Occupation, box 35, MRF, FDRL.

48. Roosevelt memorandum for the Joint Chiefs of Staff, Apr. 1, 1944, folder 2, A/16 Warfare-Germany and German Occupied Countries, box 167, MRF, FDRL.

49. For examples, see Margot Louria, *Triumph and Downfall: America's Pursuit of Peace and Prosperity, 1921–1933* (Westport, CT: Greenwood Press, 2001), 142; Henry L. Stimson, interview by Allen Nevins and Dean Albertson in *The Reminiscences of Henry L. Stimson* (New York: Trustees of Columbia University in the City, 1972), 6.

50. Stimson and Bundy, *On Active Service*, 565–568; Sean L. Malloy, *Atomic Tragedy: Henry L. Stimson and the Decision to Use the Bomb against Japan* (Ithaca, NY: Cornell University Press,

2008), 34, 47, 69, 81–82; David F. Schmitz, *Henry L. Stimson: The First Wise Man* (Wilmington, DE: Scholarly Resources, 2001), 165.

51. Elting E. Morison, *Turmoil and Tradition: A Study of the Life and Times of Henry L. Stimson* (Boston, MA: Houghton Mifflin, 1960), 604.

52. Stimson and Bundy, *On Active Service*, 553–557; see also Kimball, *Swords or Ploughshares*, 4.

53. Stimson and Bundy, *On Active Service*, 56; Schmitz, *Henry L. Stimson*, 165–166.

54. The Secretary of War (Stimson) to the President, Sep. 5, 1944, 99; Memorandum by the Secretary of War (Stimson), Sep. 9, 1944, 123, *FRUS Quebec*; Presidents of the American Society of Civil Engineers et al., "Program for Industrial Control of Postwar Germany," Oct. 2, 1944, Book 9: Treatment of Germany (part 1 of folder 1), box 333, HHP, FDRL.

55. Ziemke, *Occupation of Germany*, 102–103. These statements belie McCloy's recollection after the war that Roosevelt believed there would be a "great deal of unrest" in Germany due to hunger and other problems; McCloy, "Military Government to Self-Government," 116–117.

56. Foreign Economic Administration, "Civil Affairs Guide: Coal Production and Distribution in Germany," Jul. 1944, 1–3, Book 9: Treatment of Germany (Post War Germany), box 333, HHP, FDRL.

57. SHAEF Main Versailles, France, to War Department, Nov. 28, 1944, 2–3, folder 10: Surrender of Germany, 1944–1945, box 110, MRF, FDRL.

58. Alfred C. Mierzejewski, *The Collapse of the German War Economy, 1944–1945* (Chapel Hill, NC: University of North Carolina Press, 1988), 73, 76. See also Alan J. Levine, *The Strategic Bombing of Germany, 1940–1945* (Westport, CT: Praeger, 1992), 18–19, 91–92.

59. U.S. Joint Intelligence Committee (JIC), Weekly Summary No. 33, Aug. 25, 1943, 10, box 506, Henry Morgenthau Jr. Papers (hereafter cited as "HMP"), FDRL.

60. JIC, Weekly Summary No. 73, Jun. 1, 1944, 24, box 506, HMP, FDRL; see also Mierzejewski, *German War Economy*, 99.

61. Jorg Friedrich, *The Fire: The Bombing of Germany, 1940–1945* (New York: Columbia University Press, 2006), 89; Smith, *Lucius D. Clay*, 41.

62. Gimbel, *Occupation of Germany*, 20–22.

63. Eisenberg, *Drawing the Line*, 67–68.

64. Casey, *Cautious Crusade*, 177; McAllister, *No Exit*, 54; Kimball, *Swords or Ploughshares*, 40–41.

65. Morgenthau, *Germany Is Our Problem*, viii.

66. David Reynolds, *From World War to Cold War: Churchill, Roosevelt, and the International History of the 1940s* (New York: Oxford University Press, 2006), 239; Kimball, *Swords or Ploughshares*, 80.

67. Loewenheim et al., *Roosevelt and Churchill*, 602, 607.

68. SHAEF to War Department, Aug. 23, 1944, 2, folder 10: Surrender of Germany, 1944–1945, box 110, MRF, FDRL.

69. Roosevelt–Churchill Dinner Meeting, Sep. 13, 1944, 325–326; Roosevelt–Churchill Meeting, Sep. 15, 1944, 361, *FRUS Quebec*; Eisenberg, *Drawing the Line*, 43.

70. Roosevelt memorandum for the Acting Secretary of State, Feb. 21, 1944, 2, folder 2, A/16: Warfare, Germany and German Occupied Countries, box 167, MRF, FDRL.

71. Hammond, "Directives for the Occupation," 344.

72. Office of War Information's Bureau of Intelligence, "Special Intelligence Report: Attitudes toward Peace Planning," Mar. 6, 1943, I, OF 4351: Post War Problems, March 1943, box 2, Papers as President, Official File, FDRL.

73. Office of Public Opinion Research of Princeton University, "Presenting Post-War Planning to the Public,"1943, chart 11, Book 7: Post War Planning, 1943, box 328, HHP, FDRL. Gallup poll data from *Gallup Brain*, Gallup Poll 323, Jul. 18, 1944, http://brain.gallup.com/documents /questionnaire.aspx?STUDY=AIPO0323 (accessed Jul. 14, 2014).

74. See, for example, Barbara Farnham, *Roosevelt and the Munich Crisis: A Study of Political Decision-Making* (Princeton, NJ: Princeton University Press, 1997); Casey, *Cautious Crusade*.

75. Ibid., 159, 181–182.

76. Hugh R. Wilson, Memorandum on World Order, Jan. 22, 1940, 1 (emphasis added), folder 7: Postwar Foreign Policy Files, 1940–1943, Postwar: General, 1940–1941, box 191, SWP, FDRL.

77. See Department of State Division of Special Research, "Post-War Political Problems Preliminary Analysis," Feb. 19, 1942, 3–4, and "Problems of General Security Preliminary Analysis," Feb. 19, 1942, 1–2, folder 7: Postwar Foreign Policy Files, 1940–1943, Advisory Committee, Postwar: General 1942, box 190, SWP, FDRL.

78. Subcommittee on Political Problems, Minutes, P–5 Apr. 4, 1942, 4–5, folder 6: Postwar Foreign Policy Files, 1940–1943, Subcommittee on Political Problems: Minutes, box 190, SWP, FDRL.

79. Subcommittee on Postwar Problems, P Minutes 42, Jan. 23, 1943, 2–3, folder 3: Postwar Foreign Policy Files, 1940–1943, Subcommittee on Postwar Problems: Minutes 42–60, SWP, FDRL.

80. Eisenberg, *Drawing the Line*, 19–20.

81. Hammond, "Directives for the Occupation," 342–346; see also David W. Ellwood, *Rebuilding Europe: Western Europe, America, and Postwar Reconstruction* (New York: Longman, 1992), 53.

82. Hammond, "Directives for the Occupation," 341.

83. SHAEF to War Department, Aug. 23, 1944, 2 (emphasis added). See also Ziemke, *Occupation of Germany*, 87, 100–101; Memorandum by the Assistant to the President's Naval Aide (Elsey), n.d., 157–158, *FRUS Quebec*.

84. Hammond, "Directives for the Occupation," 341, 358.

85. Ziemke, *Occupation of Germany*, 40–41, 60–61.

86. Eisenberg, *Drawing the Line*, 29.

87. Smith, *Lucius D. Clay*, 8, 13, 23–24; see also Hammond, "Directives for the Occupation," 438.

88. Letter dated April 20, 1945 in Smith, *Lucius D. Clay*, 6 (emphasis added).

89. U.S. Group CC Staff Meeting, Minutes, May 19, 1945, 1; U.S. Group CC Staff Meeting, Minutes, May 13, 1945, 2, Staff Meetings: U.S. Military Government in Germany, May 12, 1945–January 22, 1946, box 68, Charles Fahy Papers, FDRL.

90. Kimball, *The Juggler*, 95, 101–102.

91. U.S. Army, *Planning for the Occupation*, 27; Kimball, *Swords or Ploughshares*, 41, 66, 80; Hearden, *Architects of Globalism*, 206; Stimson and Bundy, *On Active Service*, 576; Smith, *American Diplomacy*, 125; Dallek, *Franklin Roosevelt*, 461; Mayle, *Eureka Summit*, 87.

92. Elsey memorandum, n.d., 155; Loewenheim et al., *Roosevelt and Churchill*, 432.

93. McAllister, *No Exit*, 17, 28, 44.

94. Combined Chiefs of Staff Minutes, Dec. 4, 1943, 688, *Foreign Relations of the United States: The Conferences at Cairo and Tehran, 1943* (Washington, DC: United States Government Printing Office, 1961). This volume is hereafter cited as *FRUS Cairo/Tehran*.

95. Roosevelt memorandum for the Acting Secretary of State, Feb. 21, 1944, 1, folder 2, A/16: Warfare, Germany and German Occupied Countries, box 167, MRF, FDRL; Kimball, *Swords or Ploughshares*, 80.

96. Stettinius to the President, Aug. 2, 1944, 1; Roosevelt to Acting Secretary of State Stettinius, Aug. 3, 1944, folder 3: Germany, Zones of Occupation, box 35, MRF, FDRL.

97. Tripartite Dinner Meeting, Sep. 14, 1944, 350, *FRUS Quebec*.

98. Dallek, *Franklin Roosevelt*, 476; Roosevelt to Winant, Oct. 9, 1944, President-Winant 1944–1945, box 11, MRF, FDRL; see also McAllister, *No Exit*, 46–47.

99. Dallek, *Franklin Roosevelt*, 476–477.

100. James T. Postwarl, Memorandum on Possible Revision of German Units, Jul. 10, 1942, 1, folder 6: Postwar Foreign Policy Files, 1940–1943, Germany, Postwarl, James T., box 191, SWP, FDRL.

101. Kimball, *Swords or Ploughshares*, 4, 6; Loewenheim et al., *Roosevelt and Churchill*, 457; President Roosevelt to the British Prime Minister (Churchill), Feb. 29, 1944, 188, *FRUS 1944*.

102. Roosevelt to Hull, Oct. 20, 1944, Diplomatic Correspondence Germany: Oct. 1944–1945, box 32, PSF, FDRL; Ziemke, *Occupation of Germany*, 106; Hammond, "Directives for the Occupation," 398.

103. Dallek, *Franklin Roosevelt*, 390–391; McAllister, *No Exit*, 33–36, 38–39.

104. Gaddis, *Origins of the Cold War*, 13, 31, 96–97.

105. William D. Leahy for the Joint Chiefs of Staff, memorandum to the President, Nov. 18, 1943, folder 3: Germany, Zones of Occupation, box 35, MRF, FDRL; Dallek, *Franklin Roosevelt*, 147–148.

106. Memorandum by the Assistant to the Secretary of the Treasury (White), Aug. 13, 1944, 881–882, *FRUS Cairo/Tehran*.

107. Ziemke, *Occupation of Germany*, 102, 163–164; Eisenberg, *Drawing the Line*, 30; Elsey memorandum, n.d., 157.

108. Department of State Office of European Affairs, Division of Central European Affairs, "Status of Negotiations and Discussions on Germany," Aug. 22, 1944, 4, folder 2, A/16: Warfare, Germany and German Occupied Countries, box 167, MRF, FDRL; The Secretary of State to the President, Aug. 28, 1944, 48, *FRUS Quebec;* James Stettinius, Personal to the President, 2, Aug. 2, 1944, folder 3: Germany, Zones of Occupation, box 35, MRF, FDRL.

109. Roosevelt to Acting Secretary of State Stettinius, Aug. 3, 1944; Roosevelt., Memorandum for the Secretary of State, Sep. 29, 1944, 1, Diplomatic Correspondence Germany: Jan.–Sep. 1944, box 31, PSF, FDRL.

110. Ambassador Harriman to the President, Sep. 23, 1944, folder 9: Additional Roosevelt–Stalin Messages (Jul. 1944–Jan. 1945), box 35, MRF, FDRL.

111. Memorandum of Conversation between Mr. A. A. Sobolev, Minister-Counsellor of Soviet Embassy in London, Vice Chairman of Soviet Delegation to Dumbarton Oaks, and Mr. Leo Pasvolsky, Sept. 28, 1944, 1–2, Book 9: Treatment of Germany (part 1 of folder 1), box 333, HHP, FDRL; McAllister, *No Exit*, 55.

112. Joint Chiefs of Staff memorandum to Roosevelt, 1, Apr. 28, 1944, box 35, folder 3: Germany, Zones of Occupation, MRF, FDRL. Along these lines, Winant told Hull that the Soviets were well briefed on British plans and that if American policy was to be given its "due weight . . . it is necessary to circulate authoritative policy papers without further delay." The Ambassador in the United Kingdom (Winant) to the Secretary of State, Oct. 7, 1944, 348, *FRUS 1944*.

113. Memorandum by the Counselor to the United States Delegation to the European Advisory Commission (Kennan), Apr. 4, 1944, 209, *FRUS 1944*; Elsey memorandum, n.d., 155.

114. U.S. Army, *Occupation of Germany*, 27–28.

115. Richard Neustadt, *Presidential Power and the Modern Presidents* (New York: Free Press, 1990); James David Barber, *The Presidential Character: Predicting Performance in the White House* (Englewood Cliffs, NJ: Prentice Hall, 1977); Kimball, *Swords or Ploughshares*, 128.

116. Alexander L. George, *Presidential Decisionmaking in Foreign Policy: The Effective Use of Information and Advice* (Boulder, CO: Westview Press, 1980).

117. Stimson and Bundy, *Active Service*, 563; Kimball, *Swords or Ploughshares*, 44.

118. Eric Larrabee, *Commander in Chief: Franklin Delano Roosevelt, His Lieutenants, and Their War* (New York: Harper & Row, 1987), 2, 14; Dallek, *Franklin Roosevelt*, 532; Godfrey Hodgson, *The Colonel: The Life and Wars of Henry Stimson, 1867–1950* (New York: Alfred A. Knopf, 1990), 271.

119. These individuals' views are cited in Range, *Roosevelt's World Order*, 77. See Range's endnote 1, 208.

120. Cited in Neustadt, *Presidential Power*, 133.

121. Kimball, *Swords or Ploughshares*, 12, 15, 19.

122. Stimson's observations about Roosevelt's health are noted in Kimball, *Swords or Ploughshares*, 33. See also Rose McDermott, *Presidential Leadership, Illness, and Decision Making* (New York: Cambridge University Press, 2007), 83, 89, 103–104.

123. Kimball, *Swords or Ploughshares*, 12–13, 28; Smith, *American Diplomacy*, 121; Range, Roosevelt's World Order, 83–84; McAllister, *No Exit*, 28.

124. Hammond, "Directives for Occupation," 398.

125. Kimball, *Swords or Ploughshares*, 32.

126. Roosevelt–Churchill Dinner Meeting, 326, Sep. 13, 1944; Dallek, *Franklin Roosevelt*, 473–474.

127. Figures from the Composite Index of National Capabilities detailed by J. David Singer, "Reconstructing the Correlates of War Dataset on Material Capabilities of States, 1816–1985," *International Interactions* 14, no. 2 (1988): 115–132.

128. Board of Economic Warfare, "Trends in the German Economic Potential," Jan. 14, 1943, 1, folder 6: German Capabilities, box 110, MRF, FDRL.

129. JIC, "German Strategy in 1943," Dec. 3, 1942, 1, 3–4, folder 2, A/16, Warfare, Germany and German Occupied Countries, box 167, MRF, FDRL.

130. The Committee of Historians for the Commanding General of the Army Air Forces, "Germany's War Potential," Dec. 1943, 5–7, Naval Aide's Files: Axis War Potential A/16, box 164, MRF, FDRL. Though doubtful of a German collapse, the report also noted that while the "German military machine . . . is still a formidable fighting force" it could not "keep pace with the growth of Allied military power."

131. Franklin Roosevelt, "Annual Budget Message," Jan. 6, 1943; Franklin Roosevelt., "State of the Union Address," Jan. 7, 1943. Both documents from the *Presidency Project*.

132. Kimball, *Swords or Ploughshares*, 73.

133. Roosevelt, "Annual Budget Message," Jan. 10, 1944.

134. Hammond, "Directives for the Occupation," 410–411; Dallek, *Franklin Roosevelt*, 359.

135. Ziemke, *Occupation of Germany*, 3–7, 12–14, 21; Harry L. Coles and Albert K. Weinberg, *Civil Affairs: Soldiers Become Governors* (Washington, DC: Center of Military History, United States Army, 2004), 22, 98–101.

136. Ziemke, *Occupation of Germany*, 15–22; Coles and Weinberg, *Civil Affairs*, 108.

137. Merle Fainsod, "The Development of American Military Government Policy during World War II," in *Military Government in World War II*, 31, 34.

138. British General Frederick Morgan, the Chief of Staff for the Supreme Allied Commander, concluded in August of 1943 that if a German collapse occurred, combat forces would prove less useful than civil affairs officers. Morgan requested postwar directives from London and Washington, but his appeal would go wanting. Ziemke, *Occupation of Germany*, 26–31; Eisenberg, *Drawing the Line*, 30.

139. Roosevelt memorandum to the Secretary of War, Aug. 26, 1944, 544; U.S. Army, *Planning for the Occupation*, 75–76.

140. SHAEF Forward on Continent to War Department, Sept. 5, 1944, folder 10: Surrender of Germany, 1944–1945, box 110, MRF, FDRL.

141. Gaddis, *Origins of the Cold War*, 104, 107–108; Hammond, "Directives for the Occupation," 332–334.

142. H. Freeman Matthews to Harry Hopkins, Oct. 9, 1944, Book 9: Treatment of Germany (part 3 of folder 1), box 333, HHP, FDRL; see also Gaddis, *Origins of the Cold War*, 114.

143. McCreedy, "Planning the Peace."

144. Elmer Plischke, "Denazification in Germany: A Policy Analysis," in *Americans as Proconsuls*, 204, 222 (emphasis added).

145. Fainsod, "Military Government Policy," 51.

3. "Phase IV" and the Invasion of Iraq

1. Figures from Michael E. O'Hanlon and Ian Livingston, "Iraq Index: Tracking Variables of Reconstruction & Security in Post-Saddam Iraq," Brookings Institution, Jan. 31, 2011, 3, 7, http://www.brookings.edu/about/centers/saban/~/media/Centers/saban/iraq percent20 index/index20120131.PDF (accessed May 23, 2012).

2. David M. Edelstein, "Occupational Hazards: Why Military Occupations Succeed or Fail," *International Security* 29, no. 1 (2004): 49–91.

3. Special Inspector General for Iraq Reconstruction (SIGIR), *Hard Lessons: The Iraq Reconstruction Experience* (Washington, DC: United States Government Printing Office, 2009), 323–324.

4. Along with the SIGIR report see Nora Bensahel et al., *After Saddam: Prewar Planning and the Occupation of Iraq* (Santa Monica, CA: RAND Corporation, 2008), 234–239; David A. Lake, "Two Cheers for Bargaining Theory: Assessing Rationalist Explanations of the Iraq War," *International Security* 35, no. 3 (2010/11): 36–37; Michael R. Gordon and Bernard E. Trainor, *Cobra II: The Inside Story of the Invasion and Occupation of Iraq* (New York: Pantheon Books, 2006), 138–163;

George Packer, *The Assassin's Gate: America in Iraq* (New York: Farrar, Straus & Giroux, 2005); David L. Phillips, *Losing Iraq: Inside the Postwar Reconstruction Fiasco* (New York: Westview Press, 2005); Thomas E. Ricks, *Fiasco: The American Military Adventure in Iraq* (New York: Penguin, 2006). Perhaps the most prominent defense of the Bush administration's postwar planning is Douglas J. Feith, *War and Decision: Inside the Pentagon at the Dawn of the War on Terrorism* (New York: HarperCollins, 2008).

5. Donald Rumsfeld, memorandum on "Iraq: An Illustrative List of Potential Problems to be Considered and Addressed," Oct. 15, 2002, *The Rumsfeld Papers* (online library; hereafter cited as *RPL*), http://library.rumsfeld.com/doclib/sp/310/Re Parade of Horribles 10-15-2002 .pdf (accessed Jul. 21, 2011).

6. Condoleezza Rice, *No Higher Honor: A Memoir of My Years in Washington* (New York: Crown Publishers, 2011), 192.

7. Bob Woodward, *State of Denial* (New York: Simon & Schuster, 2006), 136; Gordon and Trainor, *Cobra II*, 161, provides a similar evaluation.

8. Bob Woodward, *Plan of Attack* (New York: Simon & Schuster, 2004), 276–278.

9. Transcript of Testimony of Jack Straw before the Iraq Inquiry Committee (Iraq Inquiry), Feb. 2, 2011, 115, http://www.iraqinquiry.org.uk/media/53031/Straw percent202011-02-02 percent20S1.pdf (accessed May 16, 2012); Statement by Major General Tim Cross to the Iraq Inquiry, "Post-Invasion Iraq: The Planning and the Reality after the Invasion from Mid-2002 to the End of August 2003," Dec. 2009, 9, http://www.iraqinquiry.org.uk/media/39160/timcross -statement.pdf (accessed May 24, 2012).

10. SIGIR, *Hard Lessons*, 9; Ricks, *Fiasco*, 78.

11. Gordon W. Rudd, *Reconstructing Iraq: Regime Change, Jay Garner, and the ORHA Story* (Lawrence, KS: University Press of Kansas, 2011), 34; Gordon and Trainor, *Cobra II*, 26–27.

12. Rudd, *Reconstructing Iraq*, 49–50.

13. Ibid., 53–56.

14. Gordon and Trainor, *Cobra II*, 143; Ricks, *Fiasco*, 80. A detailed description of the difficulties associated with the task force can be found in Bensahel et al., *After Saddam*, 46–50.

15. Ricks, *Fiasco*, 110. General Tommy Franks, top commander in OIF, also assumed a great deal of support by the Iraqi army in Phase IV; Tommy Franks, *American Soldier* (New York: Regan Books, 2004), 419.

16. Donald P. Wright and Timothy R. Reese, *On Point II: Transition to the New Campaign* (Fort Leavenworth, KS: Combat Studies Institute Press, 2008), 79; Gordon and Trainor, *Cobra II*, 145.

17. SIGIR, *Hard Lessons*, 7, 15–16; Rudd, *Reconstructing Iraq*, 130–131; Philips, *Losing Iraq*, 127.

18. SIGIR, *Hare Lessons*, 16; Feith, *War and Decision*, 376, 378; L. Paul Bremer, *My Year in Iraq: The Struggle to Build a Future of Hope* (New York: Simon & Schuster, 2006), 25; Gordon and Trainor, *Cobra II*, 159; Bensahel et al., *After Saddam*, 32; Ali A. Allawi, *The Occupation of Iraq: Winning the War, Losing the Peace* (New Haven, CT: Yale University Press, 2007), 83.

19. Transcript of Testimony of Carolyn Miller before the Iraq Inquiry, Jul. 21, 2010, 8, 10, http://www.iraqinquiry.org.uk/media/49663/20100721-miller-final.pdf (accessed May 21, 2012); Transcript of Testimony of Michael Boyce and Kevin Tebbit before the Iraq Inquiry, Dec. 3, 2009, 107, http://www.iraqinquiry.org.uk/media/40465/20091203-final.pdf (accessed May 22, 2012).

20. SIGIR, *Hard Lessons*, 7–8.

21. Ibid., 9–10.

22. Gordon and Trainor, *Cobra II*, 149–154.

23. Phillips, *Losing Iraq*, 131.

24. Transcript of Testimony of General Richard Dannatt before the Iraq Inquiry, Jul. 28, 2010, 76, http://www.iraqinquiry.org.uk/media/53218/Dannatt percent202010-07-28 percent20S1 .pdf (accessed May 20, 2012).

25. Lake, "Two Cheers," 15–16.

26. Wright and Reese, *On Point II*, 25–26, 142–143; Bensahel et al., *After Saddam*, 12; Gordon and Trainor, *Cobra II*, 145–146, 465.

27. Packer, *Assassin's Gate*, 132–133; SIGIR, *Hard Lessons*, 3.

28. SIGIR, *Hard Lessons*, 56–60; Bensahel et al., *After Saddam*, 84–89.

29. Rudd, *Reconstructing Iraq*, 247–248; James Dobbins, Seth G. Jones, Benjamin Runkle, and Siddharth Mohandas, *Occupying Iraq: A History of the Coalition Provisional Authority* (Santa Monica, CA: RAND Corporation, 2009), 8–9; SIGIR, *Hard Lessons*, 33–36, 63–64.

30. Rudd, *Reconstructing Iraq*, 313, 332; SIGIR, *Hard Lessons*, 74–75.

31. Wright and Reese, *On Point II*, 32.

32. Sarah E. Kreps, *Coalitions of Convenience: United States Interventions after the Cold War* (New York: Oxford University Press, 2011), 114–115, 126–130.

33. Cited in ibid., 128.

34. Feith, *War and Decision*, 317.

35. Packer, *Assassin's Gate*, 146; SIGIR, *Hard Lessons*, 12–13; Rudd, *Reconstructing Iraq*, 53.

36. My thanks to Ronald R. Krebs for this last point.

37. Nadia Schadlow, "War and the Art of Governance," *Parameters* 33, no. 3 (Autumn 2003): 85; see also Wright and Reese, *On Point II*, 66.

38. Feith, *War and Decision*, 275.

39. Woodward, *Plan of Attack*, 276.

40. Isaiah Wilson, "America's Anabasis," in *War in Iraq: Planning and Execution*, ed. Thomas G. Mahnken and Thomas A. Keaney (New York: Routledge, 2007), 12.

41. Gordon and Trainor, *Cobra II*, 166–167; Bensahel et al., *After Saddam*, 12.

42. Transcript of Testimony of Simon Webb before the Iraq Inquiry, Jun. 23, 2010, 30–31, http://www.iraqinquiry.org.uk/media/50159/webb20100623-declassified.pdf (accessed May 17, 2012).

43. Transcript of Testimony of Major General Tim Cross before the Iraq Inquiry, Dec. 7, 2009, 42, http://www.iraqinquiry.org.uk/media/40477/20091207pmcross-final.pdf (accessed May 24, 2012); Rudd, *Reconstructing Iraq*, 137, 157.

44. Franks, *American Soldier*, 441; SIGIR, *Hard Lessons*, 20.

45. Some examples in the secondary literature are Richard A. Clarke, *Against All Enemies: Inside America's War on Terror* (New York: Free Press, 2004), 265; Bradley Graham, *By His Own Rules: The Ambitions, Successes, and Ultimate Failures of Donald Rumsfeld* (New York: PublicAffairs, 2009), 67–68, 83–84; Alex Roberto Hybel and Justin M. Kaufman, *The Bush Administrations and Saddam Hussein: Deciding on Conflict* (New York: Palgrave MacMillan, 2006), 83–87, 127; Robert Jervis, *American Foreign Policy in a New Era* (New York: Routledge, 2005), 80–83; F. Gregory Gause III, "The Iraq War and American National Security Interests in the Middle East," in *Balance Sheet: The Iraq War and U.S. National Security*, ed. John S. Duffield and Peter J. Dombroski (Stanford, CA: Stanford University Press, 2009), 69–71.

46. Webb testimony, 23.

47. Steven R. Weisman, "Preemption: Idea with a Lineage Whose Time Has Come," *New York Times*, Mar. 23, 2003, B1.

48. Condoleezza Rice, "Promoting the National Interest," *Foreign Affairs* 79, no. 1 (Jan.–Feb. 2000): 45–62; see also Steven Metz, *Decisionmaking in Operation Iraqi Freedom: Removing Saddam Hussein by Force* (Carlisle, PA: Strategic Studies Institute, 2010), 10–11.

49. Transcript of Testimony of Jonathan Powell before the Iraq Inquiry, Jan. 18, 2010, 16, http://www.iraqinquiry.org.uk/media/44184/20100118pm-powell-final.pdf (accessed May 22, 2012); Clarke, *Against All Enemies*, 30–32.

50. Transcript of Testimony of David Manning before the Iraq Inquiry, Nov. 30, 2009, 24, http://www.iraqinquiry.org.uk/media/40459/20091130pm-final.pdf (accessed May 22, 2012); Transcript of Paul Wolfowitz interview with Sam Tannenhaus of *Vanity Fair*, May 9, 2003, http://www.defense.gov/transcripts/transcript.aspx?transcriptid=2594 (accessed May 25, 2012).

51. Transcript of Testimony of Edward Chaplin and Peter Ricketts before the Iraq Inquiry, Dec. 1, 2009, 54, http://www.iraqinquiry.org.uk/media/40462/20091201am-final.pdf (accessed May 22, 2012); Bob Woodward, *Bush at War* (New York: Simon & Schuster, 2002), 339–341; Woodward, *Plan of Attack*, 230, 259, 412, 428.

52. Transcript of Testimony of David Manning before the Iraq Inquiry, Jun. 24, 2010, 28–29, 42–43, 57, http://www.iraqinquiry.org.uk/media/50168/manning2010-06-24-declassified.pdf (accessed May 16, 2012); Webb testimony, 22.

53. Rice, *No Higher Honor*, 187.

54. George W. Bush, *Decision Points* (New York: Broadway, 2010), 232 (emphasis added).

55. Feith, *War and Decision*, 284; SIGIR, *Hard Lessons*, 21; Woodward, *Plan of Attack*, 154–155.

56. Transcript of Testimony of Christopher Meyer before the Iraq Inquiry, Nov. 26, 2009, 84–85, http://www.iraqinquiry.org.uk/media/40453/20091126am-final.pdf (accessed May 22, 2012).

57. Bill Keller, "Is it Good for the Jews?" *New York Times*, Mar. 8, 2003, A17.

58. Jeffrey Goldberg, "A Little Learning: What Douglas Feith Knew, and When He Knew It," *New Yorker*, May 9, 2005, 36.

59. Rudd, *Reconstructing Iraq*, 148.

60. Meyer testimony, 10, 21; Christopher Meyer, *DC Confidential: The Confidential Memoirs of Britain's Ambassador to the U.S. at the Time of 9/11 and the Iraq War* (London: Wiedenfeld and Nicolson, 2005), 235–236. Similar assessments of Wolfowitz and Feith's views can be found in Packer, *The Assassin's Gate*, 60; Metz, *Removing Saddam Hussein*, 13, 20, 24; James Fallows, *Blind into Baghdad: America's War in Iraq* (New York: Vintage Books, 2006), 43, 108–109.

61. Peter Slevin, "Bush to Cast War as Part of Regional Strategy," *Washington Post*, Feb. 26, 2003, A19.

62. Donald Rumsfeld, *Known and Unknown: A Memoir* (New York: Sentinel, 2011), 482, 498–499.

63. Donald Rumsfeld, memorandum to Gen. James Jones, Sep. 10, 2001, *RPL*, http://library.rumsfeld.com/doclib/sp/592/2001-09-10%20to%20General%20Jones%20re%20Iraq%20memo%20attachment.pdf (accessed Jul. 13, 2014). Donald Rumsfeld, notes on "Some Big Issues to Focus On," May 22, 2001, *RPL*, http://library.rumsfeld.com/doclib/sp/933/2001-05-22 re Some Big Issues To Focus On.pdf (accessed Jul. 19, 2011).

64. Donald Rumsfeld, untitled memorandum, May 31, 2001, *RPL*, http://library.rumsfeld.com/doclib/sp/2412/2001-05-31 Memo.pdf (accessed Jul. 19, 2011); Donald Rumsfeld, memorandum to Paul Wolfowitz, Jan. 4, 2002, *RPL*, http://library.rumsfeld.com/doclib/sp/734/2002-01-04%20To%20Paul%20Wolfowitz%20re%20Paper%20on%20Deterrence-%20Memo%20Attachment.pdf (accessed Jul. 13, 2014).

65. Quoted in Colin Dueck, *Reluctant Crusaders: Power, Culture, and Change in American Grand Strategy* (Princeton, NJ: Princeton University Press, 2006), 156.

66. Feith, *War and Decision*, 55–56; Ron Suskind, *The Price of Loyalty: George W. Bush, the White House, and the Education of Paul O'Neill* (New York: Simon & Schuster, 2004), 76–78, 85–86; Fallows, *Blind into Baghdad*, 40.

67. Feith, *War and Decision*, 82.

68. Ibid., 49, 64–66; Metz, *Removing Saddam Hussein*, 20; Graham, *By His Own Rules*, 288–289, 292–294.

69. Boyce and Tebbit testimony, 100.

70. Meyer testimony, 31.

71. Powell testimony, 70. See also Meyer testimony, 5–7; Karen DeYoung, *Soldier: The Life of Colin Powell* (New York: Alfred A. Knopf, 2006), 315–317; Gordon and Trainor, *Cobra II*, 14; Ricks, *Fiasco*, 27–28.

72. Feith, *War and Decision*, 51; Graham, *By His Own Rules*, 289; Metz, *Removing Saddam Hussein*, 13.

73. Powell testimony, 71.

74. Nick Ritchie and Paul Rogers, *The Political Road to War with Iraq: Bush, 9/11 and the Drive to Overthrow Saddam* (New York: Routledge, 2007), 62; Rice, "Promoting the National Interest," 61.

75. Ritchie and Rogers, *Political Road to War*, 157.

76. Condoleezza Rice, "Rethinking the National Interest," *Foreign Affairs* 87, no. 4 (Jul.–Aug. 2008): 3.

77. Richard B. Cheney, *In My Time: A Personal and Political Memoir* (New York: Threshold Editions, 2011), 387, 390; Barton Gellman, *Angler: The Cheney Vice Presidency* (New York: Penguin, 2008), 239, 250–251.

78. Gellman, *Angler*, 226, 231, 242, 253.

79. Excerpts from "In Cheney's Words: The Administration Case for Removing Saddam Hussein," *New York Times*, Aug. 27, 2002, A8.

80. Condoleezza Rice, memorandum to Richard Cheney et al. on "Iraq: Goals, Objectives, Strategy," Oct. 29, 2002, *RPL*, http://library.rumsfeld.com/doclib/sp/4136/2002-10-29%20From %20Condoleezza%20Rice%20re%20Principals<#213>%20Committee%20Review%20of%20Iraq %20Policy%20Paper.pdf (accessed Jul. 13, 2014).

81. Dobbins et al., *Occupying Iraq*, 1, 40.

82. Franks, *American Soldier*, 391–392. RAND's review accords with these views; Bensahel et al., *After Saddam*, 236–237.

83. Woodward, *Plan of Attack*, 109, 157–158; Wright and Reese, *On Point II*, 72; Risa A. Brooks, *Shaping Strategy: The Civil-Military Politics of Strategic Assessment* (Princeton, NJ: Princeton University Press, 2008), 235; Franks, *American Soldier*, 361–362.

84. Woodward, *Plan of Attack*, 149.

85. Ibid., 126, 147, 133, 174, 207–208.

86. Woodward, *Plan of Attack*, 97, 124, 147, 173, 205, 228, 323; Bush, *Decision Points*, 234–235; Cheney, *In My Time*, 399; Rice, *No Higher Honor*, 188.

87. On American worries about a humanitarian crisis see Ricks, *Fiasco*, 80; Gordon and Trainor, *Cobra II*, 138.

88. Woodward, *Plan of Attack*, 147.

89. Ibid., 276–278, 358–359.

90. See, for instance, Private Secretary of Richard Dearlove, letter to David Manning, Dec. 3, 2001, 7–8, http://www.iraqinquiry.org.uk/media/52012/2001-12-03-Dearlove-Private-Secretary-to-Manning-letter-and-attachments.pdf (accessed May 16, 2012); Transcript of Testimony of Tony Blair before the Iraq Inquiry, Jan. 29, 2010, 171, http://www.iraqinquiry.org.uk/media /45139/20100129-blair-final.pdf (accessed Jun. 1, 2012); Transcript of Testimony of Geoffrey Hoon before the Iraq Inquiry, Jan. 19, 2010, 106, http://www.iraqinquiry.org.uk/media/45042 /20100119-hoon-final.pdf (accessed Jun. 1, 2012).

91. Bensahel et al. state that "the war in Iraq did not generate a significant humanitarian emergency, largely because of the ways in which the war was fought"; *After Saddam*, 73.

92. SIGIR, *Hard Lessons*, 31. This asymmetry is also noted in Dobbins et al., *Occupying Iraq*, 107; Dominic D. P. Johnson, *Overconfidence and War: The Havoc and Glory of Positive Illusions* (Cambridge, MA: Harvard University Press, 2004), 193, 210.

93. Clare Short, memorandum to Tony Blair, Feb. 14, 2003, http://www.iraqinquiry.org.uk /media/44223/140203short-blair.pdf (accessed August 3, 2011).

94. Cross testimony, 18.

95. Feith, *War and Decision*, 362; author redacted, "Maintaining Public Order during Combat Operations in Iraq, Feb. 9, 2003," Department of Defense, Washington, DC, http:// www.waranddecision.com/docLib/20080403_MaintainingPublicOrder.pdf (accessed August 3, 2011).

96. Douglas Feith, Senate Foreign Relations Committee, *The Future of Iraq*, 108th Cong., 1st sess., February 11, 2003.

97. SIGIR, *Hard Lessons*, 11–12, 20–21; Nicholas Cannon, memorandum to Kara Owen, 1, Mar. 7, 2003, http://www.iraqinquiry.org.uk/media/50760/Cannon-to-Owen-Iraq-Post-Con flict-Issues-7March2003.pdf (accessed Jun. 1, 2012).

98. Rudd, *Reconstructing Iraq*, 68, 137.

99. Nora Bensahel, "Mission Not Accomplished," in *War in Iraq*, 137–138; Bensahel et al., *After Saddam*, 234–236.

100. Gordon and Trainor, *Cobra II*, 142, 150.

101. Donald Rumsfeld, Senate Armed Services Committee, *U.S. Policy toward Iraq*, 107th Cong., 2nd sess., Sep. 19, 2002; SIGIR, *Hard Lessons*, 12.

102. Feith, *War and Decision*, 370, 372, 375, 403, 448.

103. Gordon and Trainor, *Cobra II*, 20; Ricks, *Fiasco*, 23–24, 56–57, 104–105; Philips, *Losing Iraq*, 68; Rudd, *Reconstructing Iraq*, 142–143, 145, 149.

104. Feith, *War and Decision*, 403; Allawi, *The Occupation of Iraq*, 96.

105. Wright and Reese, *On Point II*, 142.

106. Ibid., 142–143.

107. Woodward, *Bush at War*, 332; Woodward, *Plan of Attack*, 149–150.

108. Woodward, *Plan of Attack*, 152; DeYoung, *Soldier*, 402.

109. DeYoung, *Soldier*, 430.

110. Dominick Chilcott, memorandum to Edward Chaplin, Jan. 17, 2003, 2, http://www.iraqinquiry.org.uk/media/51131/ChilcotttoChaplin-IraqDayAfterIssues-dated17January2003.pdf (accessed May 17, 2012).

111. Powell testimony, 28–29, 32.

112. Packer, *Assassin's Gate*, 96.

113. Powell testimony, 70.

114. Rice, "Promoting the National Interest," 53; Metz, *Removing Saddam Hussein*, 12.

115. Wright and Reese, *On Point II*, 67; Rudd, *Reconstructing Iraq*, 42.

116. Donald H. Rumsfeld, "Transforming the Military," *Foreign Affairs* 81, no. 3 (May–Jun. 2002): 20–32; Donald Rumsfeld, untitled memorandum, May 31, 2001, Donald Rumsfeld, memorandum to Chairman, Joint Chiefs of Staff; Commanders, Combatant Commands, Jun. 28, 2002, *RPL*, http://library.rumsfeld.com/doclib/sp/2536/2002-06-28%20to%20Joint%20Chiefs%20of%20Staff%20Commanders%20re%20Implementing%20Guidance%20%20for%20the%202002%20Contingency%20Planning.pdf (accessed Jul. 13, 2014).

117. Gordon and Trainor, *Cobra II*, 93–94; Gregory Fontenot, E.J. Degen, and David Tohn, *On Point: The United States Army in Operation Iraqi Freedom* (Annapolis, MD: Naval Institute Press, 2005), 406–407; Graham, *By His Own Rules*, 329.

118. Graham, *By His Own Rules*, 383–384.

119. Gordon and Trainor, *Cobra II*, 161; Woodward, *State of Denial*, 131–134; Packer, *Assassin's Gate*, 132–133.

120. Cross testimony, 40; Boyce and Tebbit testimony, 62; Rudd, *Reconstructing Iraq*, 108. See also Graham, *By His Own Rules*, 350, 381–382, 404–405.

121. Metz, *Removing Saddam Hussein*, 51; Fallows, *Blind into Baghdad*, 8, 61.

122. Philip Everts and Pierangelo Isernia, "Trends: The War in Iraq," *Public Opinion Quarterly* 69, no. 2 (2005): 268–269.

123. Ibid., 270–271.

124. Boyce and Tebbit testimony, 84.

125. Woodward, *State of Denial*, 91.

126. Fallows, *Blind into Baghdad*, 74; Dale R. Herspring, *Rumsfeld's Wars: The Arrogance of Power* (Lawrence, KS: University Press of Kansas, 2008), 71, 108; Packer, *Assassin's Gate*, 111–112.

127. Donald Rumsfeld, "Beyond Nation Building," remarks delivered at the 11th Annual Salute to Freedom, Intrepid Sea-Air-Space Museum, New York City, Feb. 14, 2003, http://www.defenselink.mil/speeches/speech.aspx?speechid=337 (accessed August 24, 2011).

128. Donald Rumsfeld, memorandum to Richard Cheney et al., Jul. 1, 2002, *RPL*, http://library.rumsfeld.com/doclib/sp/314/2002-07-01 to VP Cheney et al re Supporting the Iraqi Opposition.pdf (accessed Jul. 21, 2011). Interestingly, while Rumsfeld borrowed analogies from World War II to justify his position on postwar Iraq, it is unlikely that the intervention in Afghanistan shaped his thinking, as opposed to what some have asserted (e.g. SIGIR, *Hard Lessons*, 8; Metz, *Removing Saddam Hussein*, 45–46). Before the Iraq War, Rumsfeld said that "it is hard for me to imagine another Afghanistan. If you think about that situation, it is kind of distinctive . . . I don't think we're going to run around with a cookie mold and repeat this." Cited in Stephen Biddle, *Afghanistan and the Future of Warfare: Implications for Army and Defense Policy* (Carlisle, PA: Strategic Studies Institute, 2002), 4. Furthermore, he was unsatisfied with postinvasion progress in Afghanistan, and it seemed prewar debates about Iraq were informing his thinking about U.S. involvement there rather than vice versa. Rumsfeld asked Wolfowitz in September 2002, "If we should have a John McCoy for Iraq [*sic*; reference to commissioner of the U.S. occupation of Germany, John McCloy], why shouldn't we have one for Afghanistan? Someone is going to have to take that over and do it right, and it is not getting done right." Donald Rumsfeld, memorandum to Paul Wolfowitz, Sep. 14, 2002, *RPL*, http://library.rumsfeld.com/doclib/sp/1000/2002-09-14 to Paul Wolfowitz re (no subject).pdf (accessed Jul. 21, 2011).

129. Manning testimony, Jun. 24, 2010, 42–43, 57; Manning testimony, Nov. 30, 2009, 67–68.

130. Transcript of Testimony of Admiral Michael Boyce before the Iraq Inquiry, Jan. 27, 2011, 78, http://www.iraqinquiry.org.uk/media/51818/20110127-Boyce.pdf (accessed May 17, 2012).

131. Francis Fukuyama, *America at the Crossroads: Democracy, Power, and the Neoconservative Legacy* (New Haven, CT: Yale University Press, 2006), 52–53, 60–61, 132.

132. Packer, *Assassin's Gate*, 113; Fallows, *Blind into Baghdad*, 79; Graham, *By His Own Rules*, 351–352; Cross statement, 14.

133. See SIGIR, *Hard Lessons*, 3, 8, 16, 40; Woodward, *State of Denial*, 144–145, 150–151; Dobbins et al., *Occupying Iraq*, 35.

134. Donald Rumsfeld, memorandum to Douglas Feith, Mar. 17, 2003, 1, *RPL*, http://library.rumsfeld.com/doclib/sp/1640/2003-03-17 to Doug Feith re Currency.pdf; Donald Rumsfeld, memorandum to George W. Bush, Apr. 1, 2003, 1, *RPL*, http://library.rumsfeld.com/doclib/sp/321/2003-04-01 to President Bush re Iraqi Interim Authority.pdf; Donald Rumsfeld, memorandum to Colin Powell, Apr. 2, 2003, 1, *RPL*, http://library.rumsfeld.com/doclib/sp/1681/2003-04-02 to Colin Powell re Disaster Assistance Response Team and the Garner Group.pdf; Donald Rumsfeld, memorandum to Douglas Feith, Apr. 7, 2003, 1, *RPL*, http://library.rumsfeld.com/doclib/sp/1686/2003-04-07 to Doug Feith re Issues with Various Countries.pdf; Donald Rumsfeld, memorandum to Douglas Feith, Apr. 11, 2003, 1, *RPL*, http://library.rumsfeld.com/doclib/sp/1790/2003-04-11 to Doug Feith re Recruiting Arabic Speakers.pdf; Donald Rumsfeld, memorandum to Paul Wolfowitz, Apr. 23 2003, *RPL*, http://library.rumsfeld.com/doclib/sp/1696/2003-04-23%20to%20Paul%20Wolfowitz%20et%20al%20re%20Money%20Spent%20on%20Iraq.pdf (all accessed August 6, 2011).

135. SIGIR, *Hard Lessons*, 57.

136. Rumsfeld, *Known and Unknown*, 398.

137. Donald Rumsfeld, memorandum on "Principles for Iraq-Policy Guidelines," May 13, 2003, 1–4, *RPL*, http://library.rumsfeld.com/doclib/sp/331/2003-05-13%20re%20Principles%20for%20Iraq-Policy%20Guidelines.pdf (accessed Jul. 13, 2014).

138. Donald Rumsfeld, memorandum to Douglas Feith, May 21, 2003, 2, *RPL*, http://library.rumsfeld.com/doclib/sp/325/2003-05-21%20to%20Feith%20re%20Oil%20and%20Democracy.pdf (accessed Jul. 13, 2014).

139. Rice, "Iraq: Goals, Objectives, Strategy," 3.

140. Rudd, *Reconstructing Iraq*, 239.

141. Donald Rumsfeld, memorandum to L. Paul Bremer, Jun. 21, 2003, 1, *RPL*, http://library.rumsfeld.com/doclib/sp/335/2003-06-21%20to%20Paul%20Bremer%20re%20Forming%20the%20Interim%20Administration.pdf (accessed Jul. 13, 2014).

142. Donald Rumsfeld, memorandum to L. Paul Bremer, Jun. 24, 2003, 2, *RPL*, http://library.rumsfeld.com/doclib/sp/1740/2003-06-24%20to%20Jerry%20Bremer%20re%20Peacekeeping-%20Memo%20Attachment.pdf (accessed Jul. 13, 2014).

143. Rudd, *Reconstructing Iraq*, 160–161.

144. Bremer, *My Year in Iraq*, 43; Rudd, *Reconstructing Iraq*, 305–306.

145. Rudd, *Reconstructing Iraq*, 98, 100.

146. Rudd, *Reconstructing Iraq*, 95, 97.

147. SIGIR, *Hard Lessons*, 10, 12, 36; Rudd, *Reconstructing Iraq*, 95.

148. Bremer, *My Year in Iraq*, 26; Woodward, *State of Denial*, 123; Rudd, *Reconstructing Iraq*, 133, 146.

149. Bensahel et al., *After Saddam*, 38–39, 237–239; Packer, *Assassin's Gate*, 119–120, 122; Phillips, *Losing Iraq*, 138; Feith, *War and Decision*, 350; Gordon and Trainor, *Cobra II*, 152–156; Wright and Reese, *On Point II*, 77; Rudd, *Reconstructing Iraq*, 158.

150. Wright and Reese, *On Point II*, 76; Feith, *War and Decision*, 318, 349.

151. Woodward, *State of Denial*, 144–145; SIGIR, *Hard Lessons*, 39; Rudd, *Reconstructing Iraq*, 169–170.

152. John P. Burke, "The Bush Transition," in *Considering the Bush Presidency*, ed. Gary L. Gregg and Mark J. Rozell (New York: Oxford University Press, 2004), 21–36; Charles E. Walcott and Karen M. Hult, "The Bush Staff and Cabinet System," in *Considering the Bush Presidency*,

52–68; Karen M. Hult, "The Bush White House in Comparative Perspective," in *The George W. Bush Presidency: An Early Assessment*, ed. Fred I. Greenstein (Baltimore, MD: Johns Hopkins University Press, 2003), 76–77.

153. Brooks, *Shaping Strategy*, 236.

154. Kreps, *Coalitions of Convenience*.

155. For political reasons why the United States was motivated to pursue the UN route see Alexander Thompson, *Channels of Power: The UN Security Council and U.S. Statecraft in Iraq* (Ithaca, NY: Cornell University Press, 2009), chap. 5.

156. Kreps, *Coalitions of Convenience*, 130–134.

157. Transcript of Testimony of Tony Blair before the Iraq Inquiry, Jan. 21, 2011, 20, http://www.iraqinquiry.org.uk/media/50865/20110121-Blair.pdf (accessed May 18, 2012); Boyce and Tebbit testimony, 32.

158. Blair testimony, Jan. 21, 2011, 50.

159. Meyer testimony, 26, 49.

160. Manning testimony, Nov. 30, 2009, 23–25.

161. Boyce and Tebbit testimony, 37–38, 63; Rumsfeld's comments cited in Thompson, *Channels of Power*, 155.

162. Rice, "Iraq: Goals, Objectives, Strategy," 2.

163. Chaplin and Ricketts testimony, 34–35.

164. Ibid., 35–36.

165. Ibid., 56; Transcript of Testimony of Stephen Pattison before the Iraq Inquiry, Jan. 31, 2011, 83, http://www.iraqinquiry.org.uk/media/51900/20110131-pattison-final.pdf (accessed Jun. 4, 2012).

166. Transcript of Testimony of Andrew Turnbull before the Iraq Inquiry, Jan. 13, 2010, 35, http://www.iraqinquiry.org.uk/media/44181/20100113pm-turnbull-final.pdf (accessed Jun. 4, 2012).

167. Thompson, *Channels of Power*, 155, 197–198.

168. Chaplin and Ricketts testimony, 75–76; Boyce and Tebbit testimony, 113; Transcript of Testimony of Dominick Chilcott before the Iraq Inquiry, Dec. 8, 2009, 55–56, http://www.iraqinquiry.org.uk/media/40483/20091208chilcott-final.pdf (accessed Jun. 8, 2012).

169. Rice, "Iraq: Goals, Objectives, Strategy," 3; Manning testimony, Nov. 30, 2009, 97.

170. Manning testimony, Nov. 30, 2009, 97.

171. Transcript of Testimony of Kevin Tebbit before the Iraq Inquiry, May 6, 2010, 34–35, http://www.iraqinquiry.org.uk/media/50171/tebbit-20100506-declassified.pdf (accessed May 17, 2012); Rudd, *Reconstructing Iraq*, 132.

172. Interview of Jay Garner, *PBS Frontline: The Lost Year in Iraq*, Oct. 17, 2006, http://www.pbs.org/wgbh/pages/frontline/yeariniraq/interviews/garner.html (accessed Jun. 5, 2012); Manning testimony, Jun. 24, 2010, 108.

173. Rudd, *Reconstructing Iraq*, 127, 145–146.

174. Ibid., 308, 310.

175. Ibid., 312–313, 332.

176. Powell testimony, 128.

177. Rudd, *Reconstructing Iraq*, 204; Ricks, *Fiasco*, 154, 163–164.

178. Transcript of Testimony of Andy Bearpark before the Iraq Inquiry, Jul. 6, 2010, 82, http://www.iraqinquiry.org.uk/media/48580/20100706-bearpark-final.pdf (accessed May 21, 2012).

179. Blair testimony, Jan. 21, 2011, 123, 149–153. See also Miller testimony, 36; Pattison testimony, 80; Turnbull testimony, 35–37.

180. Boyce testimony, 68; Geoffrey Hoon, memorandum to Tony Blair, Mar. 22, 2002, 2, http://www.iraqinquiry.org.uk/media/51634/HoontoPrimeMinister-minute-Iraqdated-22March2002.pdf (accessed May 16 2012).

181. Simon Webb, memorandum to the PS/Secretary of State, Apr. 12, 2002, 2, http://www.iraqinquiry.org.uk/media/52573/webb-ps-sofs-bush-war-on-terrorism-2002-04-12.pdf (accessed May 17, 2012); Jack Straw, letter to Tony Blair, Jul. 8, 2002, 1–2, http://www.iraqinquiry.org.uk/media/50793/Straw-to-Blair-Iraq-Contingency-Planning-8July2002.pdf (accessed May 20,

2012); Jonathan Powell, memorandum to Tony Blair, Jul. 19, 2002, 2, http://www.iraqinquiry .org.uk/media/50772/Powell-to-Blair-19July2002-minute.pdf (accessed May 20, 2012).

182. Geoffrey Hoon, memorandum to Tony Blair, Oct. 15, 2002, 4, http://www.iraqinquiry .org.uk/media/51205/HoontoBlair-IraqUKMilitaryOptions-dated15October2002.pdf (accessed May 17, 2012); Matthew Rycroft, memorandum to Peter Watkins, Jan. 15, 2003, 1, http:// www.iraqinquiry.org.uk/media/51235/RycrofttoWatkins-IraqMilitaryPlanning-dated15January2003.pdf (accessed May 17, 2012).

183. Permanent Joint Headquarters record of Chief of Staff briefing to Prime Minister, Jan. 15, 2003, 2, 10, http://www.iraqinquiry.org.uk/media/51270/PJHQRecordofCOSBriefingtoPrimeMinister-dated15January2003.pdf (accessed May 17, 2012).

184. Jack Straw, memorandum to Tony Blair, Apr. 7, 2003, 1, http://www.iraqinquiry.org .uk/media/50796/Straw-to-Blair-Iraq-ORHA-7April2003.pdf (accessed May 20, 2012).

185. Blair testimony, Jan. 21, 2011, 124–125; see also Turnbull testimony, 73.

186. Manning testimony, Nov. 30, 2009, 27; Transcript of Testimony of Tom McKane before the Iraq Inquiry, Jan. 19, 2011, 67, http://www.iraqinquiry.org.uk/media/51684/20110119 -mcKane-final.pdf (accessed May 20, 2012).

187. Boyce and Tebbit testimony, 22, 43, 50–51, 92, 103.

188. McKane testimony, 61–62.

189. Suma Chakrabarti, memorandum to Andrew Turnbull, Apr. 1, 2003, 1–2, http:// www.iraqinquiry.org.uk/media/42184/2010-01-12-chakrabarti-turnbull2.pdf (accessed Jun. 8, 2012).

190. Chaplin and Ricketts testimony, 74.

191. Manning testimony, Nov. 30, 2009, 4–5; Chaplin and Ricketts testimony, 11–14.

192. Blair testimony, Jan. 29, 2010, 41.

193. Boyce and Tebbit testimony, 16–17; see also Chaplin and Ricketts testimony, 29.

194. For an overview see Thompson, *Channels of Power*, 138–139, 156, 190.

195. Tony Blair, memorandum to Jonathan Powell, Mar. 17, 2002, 1, http://www.iraqinquiry .org.uk/media/50751/Blair-to-Powell-17March2002-minute.pdf (accessed May 20, 2012); Blair testimony, Jan. 21, 2011, 29, 44, 129.

196. Transcript of Testimony of John Prescott before the Iraq Inquiry, Jul. 30, 2010, 96, http://www.iraqinquiry.org.uk/media/49704/20100730-prescott-final.pdf (accessed May 20, 2012); Powell testimony, 137.

197. Dearlove's Private Secretary, letter to David Manning, 4, 6.

198. Statement by Jack Straw to the Iraq Inquiry, Jan. 28, 2011, 6, http://www.iraqinquiry. org.uk/media/51681/Straw-statement-28-01-2011.pdf (accessed May 16, 2012).

199. Manning testimony, Nov. 30, 2009, 28; Chaplin and Ricketts testimony, 21; Transcript of Testimony of Desmond Bowen before the Iraq Inquiry, Dec. 7, 2009, 9, 36, http://www.iraqin quiry.org.uk/media/40474/20091207pmbowen-final.pdf (accessed Jun. 8, 2012).

200. See, for instance, Blair testimony, Jan. 21, 2011, 44–46; Turnbull testimony, 71–72; Manning testimony, Nov. 30, 2009, 51–52.

201. Gordon and Trainor, *Cobra II*, 146; David Johnson, memorandum to Martin Howard, Jul. 6, 2004, 5, http://www.iraqinquiry.org.uk/media/51137/JohnsontoHoward- percent20Op-TelicLessons-6July2004.pdf (accessed May 18, 2012).

202. Calculated using the Composite Index of National Capability; J. David Singer, "Reconstructing the Correlates of War Dataset on Material Capabilities of States, 1816–1985," *International Interactions* 14, no. 2 (1988): 115–132.

203. Stephen Biddle, "Victory Misunderstood: What the Gulf War Tells Us about the Future of Conflict," *International Security* 21, no. 2 (1996): 158–160.

204. Feith, *War and Decision*, 290. For a description of how potential biological and chemical attacks were dealt with during OIF, see Fontenot et al., *On Point*, 171–174.

205. Gordon and Trainor, *Cobra II*, 90; Fontenot et al., *On Point*, 69.

206. British Joint Intelligence Committee, "Southern Iraq: What's in Store?" Feb. 19, 2003, 1, http://www.iraqinquiry.org.uk/media/50766/JIC-Assessment-19February2003.pdf (accessed May 20, 2012); Dannatt testimony, 75.

207. Feith, *War and Decision*, 363.

208. Pattison testimony, 80; Transcript of Testimony of Stephen Pattison and John Buck before the Iraq Inquiry, Jan. 31, 2011, 15, http://www.iraqinquiry.org.uk/media/53016/Buck percent20Pattison percent202011-01-31 percent20S2.pdf (accessed May 17, 2012).

209. Brooks, *Shaping Strategy*, 230; Metz, *Removing Saddam Hussein*, 50.

210. A list of U.S. intelligence community assessments of postwar Iraq can be found in United States Senate Select Committee on Intelligence, *Report on Prewar Intelligence Assessments about Postwar Iraq, Together with Additional and Minority Views*, 110th Cong., 1st sess., S. Rpt. 110-76, 92–106. See also Packer, *Assassin's Gate*, 113; SIGIR, *Hard Lessons*, 3; Ricks, *Fiasco*, 72, 107–108; Johnson, *Overconfidence and War*, 196–197.

211. U.S. Senate, *Intelligence Assessments about Postwar Iraq*, 7.

212. Ibid., 8–10, 20, 29. Recipients included Stephen Hadley, Rice's chief assistant; I. Lewis Libby, Cheney's national security adviser; Wolfowitz; and Feith. The full listing of recipients is on 108–187.

213. Gordon and Trainor, *Cobra II*, 157; Packer, *Assassin's Gate*, 97.

214. Woodward, *Plan of Attack*, 229–230.

215. Ricks, *Fiasco*, 64–65; Michael Dobbs, "Concern Grows over U.S. Need for Allies," *Washington Post*, Jan. 27, 2003, A1.

216. Rudd, *Reconstructing Iraq*, 30–32.

217. Joint Center for Operational Analysis, "Transitions in Iraq: Changing Environment, Changing Organizations, Changing Leadership," Jul. 21, 2006, 16, http://www.fas.org/blog/secrecy/2010/03/transition_iraq.html (accessed Aug. 3, 2011); see also Wright and Reese, *On Point II*, 64–65, 80.

218. Rudd, *Reconstructing Iraq*, 165.

219. Cross testimony, 8; Boyce and Tebbit testimony, 114; Transcript of Testimony of General Mike Jackson before the Iraq Inquiry, Jul. 28, 2010, 4, http://www.iraqinquiry.org.uk/media/49380/20100728-jackson-final.pdf (accessed May 20, 2012).

220. Ricks, *Fiasco*, 110; Bensahel et al., *After Saddam*, xviii–xix; Wright and Reese, *On Point II*, 76.

221. Brooks, *Shaping Strategy*, 233–234.

222. Cross testimony, 7; Bensahel et al., *After Saddam*, 15–17, 60–63; Gordon and Trainor, *Cobra II*, 139–140; Ricks, *Fiasco*, 78.

223. Metz, *Removing Saddam Hussein*, 17–18; Graham, *By His Own Rules*, 385–386.

224. Brooks, *Shaping Strategy*, 4, 233–243.

225. Ibid., 245.

226. Bensahel et al., *After Saddam*, 17, 60–63.

4. An Occupation That Never Was: Korea, 1950–1951

1. Allan R. Millett, *Their War for Korea: American, Asian, and European Combatants and Civilians, 1945–1953* (Dulles, VA: Brassey's, 2002), 266.

2. U.S. leadership saw threats from communism as practically omnipresent by this point, making it unlikely they would categorize South Korea as uniquely vulnerable compared to other trouble spots across the globe. Roy E. Appleman, *South to the Naktong, North to the Yalu* (Washington, DC: Office of the Chief of Military History, Department of the Army, 1961), 37; James F. Schnabel, *United States Army in the Korean War, Policy and Direction: The First Year* (Washington, DC: Center of Military History, United States Army, 1992), 61–62; Burton I. Kaufman, *The Korean War: Challenges in Crisis, Credibility, and Command* (Philadelphia, PA: Temple University Press, 1986), 27–28.

3. Richard K. Betts, *Soldiers, Statesmen, and Cold War Crises* (Cambridge, MA: Harvard University Press, 1977), 154; Robert J. Donovan, *Tumultuous Years: The Presidency of Harry S. Truman, 1950–1953* (New York: W.W. Norton, 1982), 192.

4. The Ambassador in the Soviet Union (Kirk) to the Secretary of State, Jun. 25, 1950, 139; Intelligence Estimate Prepared by the Estimates Group, Office of Intelligence Research, Department of State, Jun. 25, 1950, 150, *Foreign Relations of the United States, 1950, Vol. 7: Korea* (Washington, DC: United States Government Printing Office, 1976). This volume is hereafter cited as *FRUS*.

5. The Secretary of State to the Embassy in the United Kingdom, Jun. 27, 1950, 187, *FRUS*.

6. Text of the resolutions can be found in Chi Young Pak, *Korea and the United Nations* (Boston, MA: Kluwer Law International, 2000), 212–213.

7. Pak, *Korea and the United Nations*, 78–79, 213.

8. Bruce Cumings, *The Origins of the Korean War, Volume II: The Roaring of the Cataract, 1947–1950* (Princeton, NJ: Princeton University Press, 1990), 655–660; Memorandum by the Executive Secretary of the National Security Council (Lay) to the National Security Council, Jul. 17, 1950, 410, *FRUS*.

9. Agreed Memorandum, Summary of United States–United Kingdom Discussions on the Present World Situation, Jul. 20–24, 463–465; Draft Memorandum Prepared in the Department of Defense, Jul. 31, 1950, 505–509, *FRUS*.

10. Pak, *Korea and the United Nations*, 213–215.

11. Schnabel, *The First Year*, 146–151, 153.

12. Department of State, OIR Report No. 5360.1: Significant Political and Economic Developments in Korea, Sep. 5–21, folder 13, box 6, Papers of Harry S. Truman: Staff Member and Office Files: Selected Record Relating to the Korean War (hereafter cited as "SMOF"), Harry S. Truman Library, Independence, Missouri (hereafter cited as "HSTL").

13. Memorandum by the Executive Secretary of the National Security Council (Lay) (hereafter "NSC 81/1"), Sep. 1, 1950, 687–690, *FRUS*.

14. Pak, *Korea and the United Nations*, 214.

15. The Acting Secretary of State to the United States Mission at the United States, Sep. 26, 1950, 781, *FRUS*.

16. The Secretary of Defense (Marshall) to the Commander in Chief, Far East (MacArthur), Sep. 29, 1950, 826, *FRUS*. Chief of Staff of the Army J. Lawton Collins supports this interpretation of Marshall's intent; Collins, *War in Peacetime: The History and Lessons of Korea* (Boston, MA: Houghton Mifflin, 1969), 148.

17. The United States Representative at the United Nations (Austin) to the Secretary of State, Nov. 3, 1950, 1036, *FRUS*.

18. The Joint Chiefs of Staff to the Commander in Chief, Far East (MacArthur), Nov. 6, 1950, 1075–1076, *FRUS*.

19. David S. McLellan and David C. Acheson, eds., *Among Friends: Personal Letters of Dean Acheson* (New York: Dodd, Mead, 1980), 103–104; Memorandum by Mr. John P. Davies of the Policy Planning Staff, Nov. 17, 1950, 1181–1182, *FRUS*.

20. The Joint Chiefs of Staff to the Commander in Chief, Far East (MacArthur), Nov. 8, 1950, 1097–1098, *FRUS*.

21. United Nations General Assembly Resolution 410 (V), Relief and Rehabilitation of Korea, Dec. 1, 1950, http://www.un.org/depts/dhl/resguide/r5.htm (accessed May 8, 2012); The Charge in Korea (Drumright) to the Secretary of State, Oct. 28, 1950, 1011, *FRUS*; Gene M. Lyons, "American Policy and the United Nations' Program for Korean Reconstruction," *International Organization* 12, no. 2 (1958): 180–192.

22. This point is made in works including Robert J. McMahon, *Dean Acheson and the Creation of an American World Order* (Washington, DC: Potomac Books, 2009), 96–98; William Stueck, *The Road to Confrontation: American Policy toward China and Korea, 1947–1950* (Chapel Hill, NC: University of North Carolina Press, 1981), 140–141, 146; David Halberstam, *The Coldest Winter: America and the Korean War* (New York: Hyperion, 2007), 187; Michael D. Pearlman, *Truman and MacArthur: Policy, Politics, and the Hunger for Honor and Renown* (Bloomington, IN: Indiana University Press, 2008), 30; Jeffrey W. Taliaferro, *Balancing Risks: Great Power Intervention in the Periphery* (Ithaca, NY: Cornell University Press, 2004), 134, 140.

23. Transcript, John H. Muccio, Oral History Interview, Dec. 7, 1973, by Richard D. McKenzie, 13, HSTL, http://www.trumanlibrary.org/oralhist/muccio3.htm (accessed Jul. 13, 2014).

24. Harry S. Truman, *Memoirs, Volume Two: Years of Trial and Hope* (Garden City, NY: Doubleday, 1956), 333–334, 341, 345–346; see also Lawrence S. Kaplan, "The Korean War and U.S. Foreign Relations: The Case of NATO," in *The Korean War: A 25-Year Perspective*, ed. Francis H. Heller (Lawrence, KS: Regents Press of Kansas, 1977), 42; Donovan, *Tumultuous Years*, 216; McLellan and Acheson, *Among Friends*, 100; Taliaferro, *Balancing Risks*, 133; Schnabel, *The First Year*, 67–68.

25. Monte M. Poen, ed., *Strictly Personal and Confidential: The Letters Harry Truman Never Mailed* (Boston, MA: Little, Brown, 1982), 53; see also D. Clayton James, *Refighting the Last War: Command and Crisis in Korea, 1950–1953* (New York: Free Press, 1993), 19–20; Truman, *Memoirs, Vol. 2*, 341.

26. Truman, *Memoirs, Vol. 2* 380–381.

27. Pearlman, *Truman and MacArthur*, 64; Kaufman, *Challenges in Crisis*, 38. Truman began using the term "police action" privately as well; see Poen, *Strictly Personal*, 23.

28. Donovan, *Tumultuous Years*, 212; see also Martin Lichterman, "To the Yalu and Back," in *American Civil Military Decisions*, ed. Harold Stein (Birmingham, AL: University of Alabama Press, 1963), 581.

29. Harry Truman, "Radio and Television Report to the American People on the Situation in Korea," Sept. 1, 1950, in *The American Presidency Project*, ed. John Woolley and Gerhard Peters, http://www.presidency.ucsb.edu/ws/index.php?pid=13604&st=&st1= (accessed Jul. 13, 2014). Prior to this, Acheson and Ambassador Warren F. Austin had made similar statements to the UN; William Stueck, *The Korean War: An International History* (Princeton, NJ: Princeton University Press, 1995), 63; James, *Refighting the Last War*, 181; Rosemary Foot, *The Wrong War: American Policy and the Dimensions of the Korean Conflict, 1950–1953* (Ithaca, NY: Cornell University Press, 1985), 69.

30. Transcript, Robert B. Landry, Oral History Interview, Feb. 28, 1974, by James R. Fuchs, 37–38, HSTL, http://www.trumanlibrary.org/oralhist/landryr.htm (accessed Jul. 13, 2014).

31. The Ambassador in Korea (Muccio) to the Secretary of State, Aug. 17, 1950, 595; Memorandum by Mr. Walter P. McConaughy, of the Staff of the Ambassador at Large (Jessup), Aug. 25, 1950, 651, *FRUS*.

32. Richard E. Neustadt, *Presidential Power and the Modern Presidents: The Politics of Leadership from Roosevelt to Reagan* (New York: Free Press, 1990), 106.

33. Truman, *Memoirs, Vol. 2*, 325; Betts, *Cold War Crises*, 17.

34. Stueck, *Road to Confrontation*, 156.

35. Memorandum by the Joint Chiefs of Staff to the Secretary of Defense (Johnson), Jul. 10, 1950, 346, *FRUS*; see also James, *Refighting the Last War*, 133–135.

36. Allen R. Millet, *War for Korea, 1945–1950: A House Burning* (Lawrence, KS: University Press of Kansas, 2005), 109–110; Foot, *The Wrong War*, 28–29, 57; Stueck, *Road to Confrontation*, 221; Stueck, *Rethinking the Korean War*, 80.

37. Stueck, *Rethinking the Korean War*, 78–80; Stueck, *The Korean War*, 25; Millet, *A House Burning*, 255.

38. Dean Acheson, House Committee on Foreign Affairs, *Korean Aid: Hearings on H.R. 5330*, 81st Cong., 1st sess. Jun. 23, 1949.

39. Dean Rusk, *As I Saw It* (New York: W.W. Norton, 1990), 165; Memorandum of Conversation, by Mr. Frederick E. Nolting, Special Assistant to the Deputy Under Secretary of State (Matthews), 258, *FRUS*.

40. The Secretary of State to the Embassy in the Soviet Union, Jun. 26, 1950, 176; The Secretary of State to the Embassy in the United Kingdom, Jul. 10, 1950, 347–351, *FRUS*.

41. Stueck, *The Korean War*, 54, 78; Foot, *The Wrong War*, 49.

42. Millet, *A House Burning*, 237.

43. Draft Memorandum Prepared by the Policy Planning Staff, Jul. 22, 1950, 450, 453, *FRUS*.

44. Stueck, *Rethinking the Cold War*, 96; Memorandum by the Director of the Office of Northeast Asian Affairs (Allison) to the Assistant Secretary of State for Far Eastern Affairs (Rusk), Jul. 1, 1950, 272, *FRUS*.

45. Memorandum by the Director of the Office of Northeast Asian Affairs (Allison) to the Director of the Policy Planning Staff (Nitze), Jul. 24, 1950, 461, *FRUS*.

46. Draft Memorandum Prepared by the Policy Planning Staff, Jul. 25, 1950, 472–473; Memorandum by the Director of the Office of Northeast Asian Affairs (Allison) to the Assistant Secretary of State for Far Eastern Affairs (Rusk), Jul. 27, 1950, 480–481, *FRUS*.

47. Stueck, *Road to Confrontation*, 188; see also James, *Refighting the Last War*, 34–35.

48. This conversation is recounted in Averell Harriman to Charles S. Murphy, 3, Jun. 8, 1951, MacArthur, Douglas: Memorandum of Conversations, Averell Harriman, box 111, President's

Secretary's Files (hereafter cited as "PSF"): General File, HSTL; Truman, *Memoirs, Vol. 2*, 351; see also Schnabel, *The First Year*, 107. On MacArthur's meeting with Chiang see Harry J. Middleton et al., "From Where I Stood: A Panel," in *The Korean War*, 25.

49. Appleman, *South to the Naktong*, 493; Cumings, *Origins of the Korean War*, 712; Douglas MacArthur, *Reminisces* (New York: McGraw Hill, 1964), 350.

50. Ibid., 370, 378. For a similar statement see MacArthur's testimony in *Military Situation in the Far East: Hearings before the Committee on Armed Services and the Committee on Foreign Relations*, 82nd Cong., 1st sess., 44 (hereafter cited as "MacArthur Hearings").

51. MacArthur Hearings, 245 (emphasis in original).

52. Taliaferro, *Balancing Risks*, 150; Memorandum by the Counselor (Kennan) to the Secretary of State, Aug. 14, 1950, 575; Memorandum by the Counselor (Kennan) to the Secretary of State, Aug. 21, 1950, 624, *FRUS*; Stanley Weintraub, *MacArthur's War: Korea and the Undoing of an American Hero* (New York: Touchstone, 2000), 205.

53. Dean Acheson letter to Paul Nitze, Jul. 12, 1950, 2, Jul. 1950 folder, box 67, Dean G. Acheson Papers (hereafter cited as "DAP"), HSTL.

54. Transcript, Paul Nitze, Oral History Interview, Aug. 5, 1975, by Richard D. McKinzie, 264–265, HSTL, http://www.trumanlibrary.org/oralhist/nitzeph3.htm#oh4 (accessed Jul. 13, 2014).

55. Draft Memorandum Prepared in the Department of Defense, Jul. 31, 1950, 503–504; Memorandum of Conversation, by Mr. James W. Barco, Special Assistant to the Ambassador at Large (Jessup), Aug. 25, 1950, 646–647, *FRUS*. On the administration's incredulity about the probability communists would honor commitments in Korea or elsewhere, see Dan Reiter, *How Wars End* (Princeton, NJ: Princeton University Press, 2009), 75–79.

56. Reiter, *How Wars End*, 75.

57. NSC 81/1, 688.

58. Draft Memorandum Prepared in the Department of State for National Security Council Staff Consideration Only, Aug. 30, 1950, 661; Draft Memorandum Prepared in the Department of State, Aug. 31, 1950, 673; NSC 81/1, 687–690, *FRUS*.

59. See, for instance, The Acting Secretary of State to the Embassy of India, Oct. 4, 1950, 875–876, *FRUS*.

60. The Joint Chiefs of Staff to the Commander in Chief, Far East (MacArthur), Oct. 9, 1950, 915, *FRUS*.

61. Memorandum by the Central Intelligence Agency (CIA), Oct. 12, 1950, 934; NSC 81/1, 687, *FRUS*.

62. The Consul General at Hong Kong (Wilkinson) to the Secretary of State, Oct. 31, 1950, 1019, *FRUS*.

63. Memorandum by the Director of the Office of Chinese Affairs (Clubb) to the Assistant Secretary of State for Far Eastern Affairs (Rusk), Nov. 1, 1950, 1023, *FRUS*.

64. Schnabel, *The First Year*, 223–225, 229; Appleman, *South to the Naktong*, 669.

65. Memorandum of Conversation: Situation in Korea, Nov. 21, 1950, 4, folder: Nov. 1950, box 68, DAP, HSTL.

66. Kennan to the Secretary of State, Aug. 21, 1950, 625; see also Draft Memorandum Prepared by the Policy Planning Staff, Aug. 21, 1950, 615, *FRUS*.

67. Memorandum for the President, Notes from the 73rd NSC Meeting, Nov. 24, 1950, 5, Memoranda for the President: Meeting Discussions, 1950, box 188, PSF: Subject File 1940–1953, HSTL.

68. Memorandum for the President, Jun. 28, 1951, 2, Memorandum for the President: Meeting Discussions, 1951, box 188, PSF: Subject File 1940–1953, HSTL.

69. Dean Acheson, *Present at the Creation: My Years in the State Department* (New York: W.W. Norton, 1969), 454.

70. Draft Memorandum by Messrs. John M. Allison and John K. Emmerson of the Office of Northeast Asian Affairs, Aug. 21, 1950, 620, *FRUS*.

71. Department of Defense, Jul. 31, 1950, 506, *FRUS*; Cumings, *Origins of the Korean War*, 711; Stueck, *Road to Confrontation*, 206. For Allison's draft memo see Draft Memorandum by the Director of the Office of Northeast Asian Affairs (Allison), Aug. 12, 1950, 567–573, *FRUS*.

72. Foot, *The Wrong War*, 34; Millet, *A House Burning*, 124–126; John Foster Dulles, *War or Peace* (New York: Macmillan, 1950).

73. Foot, *The Wrong War*, 72; Cumings, *Origins of the Korean War*, 713; Halberstam, *The Coldest Winter*, 327.

74. Lyons, "United Nations' Program for Korean Reconstruction," 182.

75. Truman, *Memoirs, Vol. 2*, 321–322, 325–326.

76. Minutes of the Twelfth Meeting of the United States Delegation to the United Nations General Assembly, Oct. 3, 1950, 845, *FRUS*.

77. Harry Truman, "Address in San Francisco at the War Memorial Opera House," Oct. 17, 1950, in *American Presidency Project*, http://www.presidency.ucsb.edu/ws/index.php?pid=13644&st=&st1= (accessed Jul. 13, 2014).

78. NSC 81/1, 692.

79. CIA, memorandum on the Daily Korean Summary, Oct. 30, 1950, 2, Daily Korean Summaries: Sep.–Oct., 1950, box 210, PSF: Intelligence File, 1946–1953, HSTL.

80. Edgar Johnson, Address before the United Nations Association of Maryland, Nov. 27, 1950, 8, Korea: addresses concerning subject of, box 1, Edgar A. J. Johnson Papers (hereafter cited as "EJP"), HSTL.

81. CIA, memorandum on the Daily Korean Summary, Nov. 30, 1950, 2, Daily Korean Summaries: Nov.–Dec., 1950, box 210, PSF: Intelligence File, 1946–1953, HSTL.

82. Dean Acheson, telegram to the U.S. Delegation at the UN (USUN), Jul. 25 1950, 1, folder 16 (1 of 2), box 6, SMOF, HSTL.

83. Economic Cooperation Administration, Budget Estimate: Assistance to the Republic of Korea, Fiscal Year 1951, Jan. 30, 1950, 1, Korea: ECA Budget Estimate for, Aid to—FY 1951, box 1, EJP, HSTL.

84. Memorandum by the Secretary of State to the President, Oct. 11, 1950, 927, *FRUS*; Dean Acheson, outgoing telegram (recipient unknown), Dec. 12, 1950, 1, folder 16 (2 of 2), box 7, SMOF, HSTL.

85. CIA, memorandum on the Daily Korean Summary, Nov. 7, 1950, 2, Daily Korean Summaries: Nov.–Dec., 1950, box 210, PSF: Intelligence File, 1946–1953, HSTL.

86. CIA, memorandum on the Korean Situation, Aug. 9, 1950, 2; CIA, memorandum on the Korean Situation, Aug. 28, 1950, 2, Daily Korean Summaries: Jun.–Aug., 1950; CIA, memorandum on the Korean Situation, Oct. 2 1950, 2; CIA, memorandum on the Korean Situation, Oct. 5, 1950, 2, Daily Korean Summaries: Sep.–Oct., 1950, box 210, PSF: Intelligence File, 1946–1953, HSTL.

87. Transcript, John J. Muccio, Oral History Interview, Feb. 18, 1971, by Jerry N. Hess, 81–82, HSTL, http://www.trumanlibrary.org/oralhist/muccio2.htm (accessed Jul. 13, 2014).

88. Edgar A. J. Johnson, Public Lecture at the University of California Korean Summer Program, Jun. 22, 1951, 11, Korea: addresses concerning subject of, box 1, EJP, HSTL.

89. Gregg Brazinsky, *Nation Building in South Korea: Koreans, Americans, and the Making of a Democracy* (Chapel Hill, NC: University of North Carolina Press, 2007), 32.

90. NSC 81/1, 692–693.

91. Secretary of State to the Embassy in Korea, Oct. 28, 1950, 1007, *FRUS*.

92. Truman, "Address in San Francisco," Oct. 17, 1950.

93. Dean Acheson, telegram to USUN, Aug. 3, 1950, 1, folder 16 (1 of 2), box 6, SMOF, HSTL.

94. Memorandum by the Ambassador at Large (Jessup) to the Deputy Under Secretary of State, Aug. 17, 1950, 593–595; Memorandum Prepared in the Department of State, Aug. 28, 1950, 653, *FRUS*.

95. James E. Webb, telegram to USUN, Sep. 27, 1950 1–2, folder 16 (1 of 2), box 6, SMOF, HSTL. Acheson had broached the topic of candidates for agent general with Truman a week prior to China's entrance into the war; Dean Acheson, notes on a meeting with the President, Nov. 20, 1950, 1, Nov. 1950, box 68, DAP, HSTL.

96. C. Darwin Stolzenbach and Henry A. Kissinger, *Civil Affairs in Korea, 1950–1951* (Chevy Chase, MD: Operations Research Office, Johns Hopkins University, 1952), 24.

97. Harry Truman, letter to the ECA on ECA's Responsibilities for Korean Relief and Rehabilitation, Oct. 6, 1950, 1–2, folder 16 (1 of 2), box 6, SMOF, HSTL.

98. Draft Memorandum by the Planning Adviser, Bureau of Far Eastern Affairs (Emmerson), Sep. 22, 1950, 756, 758–759, *FRUS*.

99. The Secretary of Defense (Marshall) to the Secretary of State, Oct. 8, 1950, 853, *FRUS*.

100. Minutes of the Seventh Meeting of the United States Delegation to the United Nations General Assembly, Sep. 26, 1950, 777, *FRUS*.

101. Draft Memorandum by the Planning Adviser, Bureau of Far Eastern Affairs (Emmerson), Oct. 2, 1950, 835–837; NSC 81/1, 692, *FRUS*.

102. Emmerson, Oct. 2, 1950, 836; Draft Paper Prepared in the Department of the Army, Oct. 3, 1950, 854–855, *FRUS*.

103. Ibid., 856.

104. Brazinsky, *Nation Building in South Korea*, 14–15.

105. Twelfth Meeting of the United States Delegation to the United Nations, Oct. 3, 1950, 846, *FRUS*.

106. Ibid., 839–840.

107. Secretary of State to the Embassy in Korea, Oct. 28, 1950, 1007–1010, *FRUS*; see also Schnabel, *The First Year*, 219.

108. Secretary of State to the Embassy in Korea, Oct. 28, 1950, 1009, *FRUS*.

109. Ibid.

110. Stanley Sandler, *Glad to See Them Come and Sorry to See Them Go: A History of U.S. Army Civil Affairs and Military Government, 1775–1991* (Ft. Bragg, NC: US Army Special Operations Command History and Archives Division, 1993), 335.

111. Stolzenbach and Kissinger, *Civil Affairs in Korea*, 17.

112. Brazinsky, *Nation Building in South Korea*, 16–18; Stueck, *The Korean War*, 29–30.

113. Brazinsky, *Nation Building in South Korea*, 28–29.

114. Millet, *A House Burning*, 121; Stueck, *The Korean War*, 27–30; Truman, *Memoirs, Vol. 2*, 329–330.

115. Transcript, John J. Muccio, Oral History Interview, Feb. 10, 1971, by Jerry N. Hess, 21–22, HSTL, http://www.trumanlibrary.org/oralhist/muccio1.htm (accessed Jul. 13, 2014).

116. Muccio, Oral History Interview, Dec. 7, 1973, 14–15.

117. Ibid., 15, 29.

118. Department of Defense, Jul. 31, 1950, 505–506, 508, *FRUS*; Twelfth Meeting of the United States Delegation to the United Nations, Oct. 3, 1950, 841, *FRUS*; Schnabel, *The First Year*, 194.

119. Dean Acheson, telegram to John Muccio, Oct. 12, 1950, 1, folder 22, box 7, SMOF: Selected Record Relating to the Korean War, HSTL.

120. Commander in Chief, Far East (MacArthur) to the President, Oct. 16, 1950, 963, *FRUS*.

121. The Secretary of State to the Embassy in Korea (214), Oct. 18, 1950, 978; The Secretary of State to the Embassy in Korea (215), Oct. 18, 1950, Oct. 18, 1950, 979, *FRUS*.

122. CIA, memorandum on the Daily Korean Summary, Oct. 18, 1950, 2; CIA, memorandum on the Daily Korean Summary, Oct. 23, 1950, 1–2, Daily Korean Summaries: Sep.–Oct. 1950, box 210, PSF: Intelligence File, 1946–1953, HSTL.

123. The Charge in Korea (Drumright) to the Secretary of State, Oct. 18, 1950, 941–942, *FRUS*.

124. Secretary of State to the Embassy in Korea, Oct. 18, 1950, 979, *FRUS*.

125. The Ambassador in Korea (Muccio) to the Secretary of State, Oct. 20, 1950, 985; The Secretary of State to the Embassy in Korea, Oct. 23, 1950, 994, *FRUS*.

126. NSC 81/1, 692.

127. CIA, memorandum on the Korean Situation, Sep. 28, 1950, 2, Daily Korean Summaries: Sep.–Oct., 1950, box 210, PSF: Intelligence File, 1946–1953, HSTL.

128. Joint Chiefs of Staff (JCS), telegram (92608) to CINCFE Tokyo, Japan, Sep. 26, 1950, 5, Korea: Messages (JCS and CINCFE: Aug.–Sept., 1950), box 14, SMOF: Naval Aide to the President Files, 1945–1953, HSTL.

129. Department of the Army, Oct. 3, 1950, 856–857, *FRUS*.

130. The Secretary of State to the United States Mission at the United Nations, Oct. 17, 1950, 975, *FRUS*.

131. MacArthur to the President, Oct. 16, 1950, 963, *FRUS*.

132. The Ambassador in the Netherlands (Chapin) to the Secretary of State, Oct. 13, 1950, 942, *FRUS*; Everett Drumright, telegram (261) to Acheson, Oct. 14, 1950, 1–2, folder 22, box 7, SMOF, HSTL.

133. The Charge in Korea (Drumright) to the Secretary of State, Oct. 30, 1950, 1017, *FRUS*.

134. The Secretary of State to the Embassy in Korea, Oct. 25, 1950, 997, *FRUS*.

135. Secretary of State to the Embassy in Korea, Oct. 28, 1950, 1007 (emphasis added), *FRUS*.

136. Substance of Statements Made at Wake Island Conference on Oct. 15, 1950, 953, *FRUS*.

137. CIA, memorandum on the Daily Korean Summary, Oct. 30, 1950, 2, Daily Korean Summaries: Sep.–Oct., 1950, box 210, PSF: Intelligence File, 1946–1953, HSTL.

138. CIA, Daily Korean Summary, Nov. 14, 1950, 1; CIA, Daily Korean Summary, Dec. 12, 1950, 2, Daily Korean Summaries: Nov.–Dec., 1950, box 210, PSF: Intelligence File, 1946–1953, HSTL.

139. Eighth United States Army Korea Command Report: Section III: Staff Section Reports: Book 12: Civil Assistance Headquarters, Dec. 1950, 3, Civil Assistance folder, box 22, U.S. Army Papers, HSTL.

140. See, for example, Memorandum on Formosa, by General of the Army Douglas MacArthur, Commander in Chief, Far East, and Supreme Commander, Allied Powers, Japan, Jun. 14, 1950, 161–165, *FRUS*.

141. Allison and Emmerson, Aug. 21, 1950, 622, *FRUS*.

142. Allison, Aug. 12, 1950, 568–569, *FRUS*.

143. Memorandum Prepared in the CIA, Aug. 18, 1950, 602, *FRUS*.

144. Memorandum by Mr. Frank Ragusa of the Division of Security Affairs to the Assistant Secretary of State for Far Eastern Affairs (Rusk), Sep. 29, 1950, 825, *FRUS*.

145. Minutes of the Fourth Meeting of the United States Delegation to the United Nations General Assembly, Sep. 21, 1950, 745–746, *FRUS*.

146. Twelfth Meeting of the United States Delegation to the United Nations, Oct. 3, 841, 845, *FRUS*.

147. Memorandum by Mr. John Foster Dulles, Consultant to the Secretary of State, to the Secretary of State, Sep. 22, 1950, 751, *FRUS*.

148. Dulles to the Secretary of State, Sep. 22, 1950, 752; Minutes of the Ninth Meeting of the United States Delegation to the United Nations General Assembly, Sep. 28, 1950, 800, *FRUS*.

149. Extracts of Memorandum of Conversations, by Mr. W. Averell Harriman, Special Assistant to the President, with General MacArthur in Tokyo on August 6 and 8, 1950, Aug. 20, 1950, 544, *FRUS*; Truman, *Memoirs, Vol. 2*, 351.

150. Memorandum of Conversation by the Political Adviser in Japan (Sebald), Nov. 14, 1950, 1149, *FRUS*; Foot, *The Wrong War*, 85; Cumings, *Origins of the Korean War*, 712.

151. Schnabel, *The First Year*, 153; Robert Debs Heinl, *Victory at High Tide: The Inchon-Seoul Campaign* (Philadelphia, PA: Lippincott, 1968), 42. See also Appleman, *South to the Naktong*, 493–495; Pearlman, *Truman and Macarthur*, 89; James, *Refighting the Last War*, 166.

152. On MacArthur's proclivity toward overconfidence see Stueck, *Rethinking the Korean War*, 112. For other accounts of MacArthur's custom of overstepping his bounds see Stueck, *Road to Confrontation*, 195; James, *Refighting the Last War*, 32–33, 207; Lichterman, "Yalu and Back," 587.

153. Reiter, *How Wars End*, 68–70.

154. James, *Refighting the Last War*, 137.

155. Schnabel, *The First Year*, 54–57.

156. Robert K. Sawyer, *Military Advisers in Korea: KMAG in Peace and War* (Washington, DC: Office of the Chief of Military History, Department of the Army, 1962), 134, 141; The Secretary of State to Certain Diplomatic and Consular Offices, Jul. 26, 1950, 477, *FRUS*.

157. The Ambassador in the Soviet Union (Kirk) to the Secretary of State, Jul. 6, 1950, 312–313; ibid., Jul. 6, 1950, 315–316; The Secretary of State to the Embassy in the United Kingdom, Jul. 7, 1950, 327, *FRUS*.

158. Report on the Position and Actions of the United States with Respect to Possible Further Soviet Moves in the Light of the Korean Situation, Aug. 22, 1950, 23, Meetings: 66: Aug. 24, 1950, box 181, PSF: Subject File, 1940–1953, HSTL.

159. Taliaferro, *Balancing Risks*, 134, 155; Foot, *The Wrong War*, 88.

160. Aside from Taliaferro, other works of political science that claim U.S. officials discounted what should have been clear signals of China's capabilities and resolve include Alexander L. George and Richard Smoke, *Deterrence in American Foreign Policy: Theory and Practice* (New York: Columbia University Press, 1974), chap. 7; Richard Ned Lebow, *Between Peace and War: The Nature of International Crisis* (Baltimore, MD: Johns Hopkins University Press, 1981), 149–164. For an excellent rebuttal of these arguments see Branislav Slantchev, *Military Threats: The Costs of Coercion and the Price of Peace* (New York: Cambridge University Press, 2011), chap. 6.

161. Treasury Secretary John Snyder felt that domestic politics were an important factor behind the decision. Halberstam, *The Coldest Winter*, 330–331; see also Lichterman, "Yalu and Back," 596–597; Donovan, *Tumultuous Years*, 276–277.

162. It has been argued that U.S. policymakers decided to cross the 38th parallel and continue the advance northward to make up for the costs they incurred by sending military forces to the peninsula; Taliaferro, *Balancing Risks*, 154–155.

163. For a formal depiction of this logic compared to that of sunk costs see James D. Fearon, "Signaling Foreign Policy Interests: Tying Hands versus Sinking Costs," *Journal of Conflict Resolution* 41, no. 1 (1997): 68–90.

164. Poll data from *Gallup Brain*, Gallup Poll 461, Sep. 15, 1950, http://brain.gallup.com/documents/questionnaire.aspx?STUDY=AIPO0461 (accessed Jul. 14, 2014). See also Foot, *The Wrong War*, 62–63, 95–96.

165. Donovan, *Tumultuous Years*, 271.

166. Memorandum for the President, Notes from the 71st NSC Meeting, Nov. 10, 1950, 4, Memoranda for the President: Meeting Discussions, 1950, box 188; Robert J. Smith, Memorandum to the Executive Secretary, National Security Council, Nov. 15, 1950, 3–5, Meetings: 72: Nov. 22, 1950, box 182, PSF: Subject File, 1940–1953, HSTL.

167. Halberstam, *The Coldest Winter*, 102, 105; see also Stueck, *Road to Confrontation*, 195.

168. Vorin E. Whan Jr., ed., *A Soldier Speaks: Public Papers and Speeches of General of the Army Douglas MacArthur* (New York: Frederick A. Praeger Publishers, 1965), 221.

169. Transcript, U. Alexis Johnson, Oral History Interview, Jun. 19, 1975, by Richard D. McKinzie, 50–51 (emphasis in original), HSTL, http://www.trumanlibrary.org/oralhist/johnsona.htm (accessed Jul. 14, 2014).

170. Foot, *The Wrong War*, 96; Millet, *A House Burning*, 236.

171. Memorandum for the President, Notes from the 73rd NSC Meeting, Nov. 24 1950, 5–6.

172. Nitze, Oral History Interview, Aug. 5, 1975, 266.

173. Lichterman, "Yalu and Back," 602 (similarly, see 611–612); The Commander in Chief, United Nations Command (MacArthur) to the Joint Chiefs of Staff, Nov. 25, 1950, 1231–1233, *FRUS*.

174. Dean Acheson, letter to Harold Stein, Jan. 30, 1957, 2, Martin Lichterman: Case Writer, box 9, Papers of Harold Stein, Civil-Military File, HSTL. See also Halberstam, *The Coldest Winter*, 331; Pearlman, *Truman and MacArthur*, 110–111.

175. Taliaferro, *Balancing Risks*, 147; Reiter, *How Wars End*, 86.

176. NSC 81/1, 687.

177. Memorandum of Conversation, by the Deputy Assistant Secretary of State for Far Eastern Affairs (Merchant), Sep. 27, 1950, 793–794, *FRUS*; Donovan, *Tumultuous Years*, 277–279. As H. Freeman Matthews wrote, there was some question "regarding the political sympathies and biases" of Panikkar; The Deputy Under Secretary of State (Matthews) to the Special Assistant to the Secretary of Defense for Foreign Military Affairs and Assistance (Burns), Oct. 19, 1950, 981, *FRUS*.

178. Memorandum of Conversation, by Mr. John M. Allison of the United States Delegation to the United Nations General Assembly, Oct. 4, 1950, 868, *FRUS*.

179. The British Embassy to the Department of State, undated, 814–815; Memorandum by the Planning Adviser, Bureau of Far Eastern Affairs (Emmerson), Oct. 16, 1950, 974, *FRUS*.

180. Stueck, *The Korean War*, 91, 98; Thomas J. Christensen, "Threats, Assurances, and the Last Chance for Peace: The Lessons of Mao's Korean War Telegrams," *International Security* 17, no. 1 (1992): 131–132.

181. Drumright to the Secretary of State, Oct. 30, 1950, 1014, *FRUS*. According to Appleman, there were approximately 120,000 Chinese soldiers in North Korea at the time of the Wake Island Conference; *South to the Naktong*, 767. James estimates as many as 228,000 of the CCF were across the Yalu by the end of October; *Refighting the Last War*, 188.

182. Walter B. Smith, memorandum to Harry Truman, Nov. 1, 1950, 1, Daily Korean Summaries: Nov.–Dec., 1950, box 210, PSF: Intelligence File, 1946–1953, HSTL.

183. The Charge in Korea (Drumright) to the Secretary of State, Nov. 11, 1950, 1129, *FRUS*; Appleman, *South to the Naktong*, 756–757, 761.

184. CIA, Daily Korean Summary, Nov. 20 1950, 2, Daily Korean Summaries: Nov–Dec. 1950, box 210, PSF: Intelligence File, 1946–1953; NSC 81/2: A Report to the National Security Council by the Executive Secretary on United States Courses of Action with Respect to Korea, Nov. 14, 1950, 1, Meetings: 72: Nov. 22, 1950, box 182, PSF: Subject File, 1940–1953, HSTL.

185. Memorandum by the CIA, Nov. 24, 1950, 1221, *FRUS*.

186. Memorandum of Conversation by Allison, Oct. 4, 1950, 868, *FRUS*. See also The Secretary of State to the Acting Secretary of State, Oct. 5, 1950, 884, *FRUS*.

187. The Commander in Chief, Far East (MacArthur) to the Joint Chiefs of Staff, Nov. 9, 1950, 1107–1109, *FRUS*.

188. Notes of Maj. Gen. John H. Hilldring cited in Sandler, *Glad to See Them Come*, 328.

189. Johnson added the ECA was "prepared to recommend a new version of one of the beatitudes; we think it should read 'blessed are the peace-makers for they shall surely catch hell!'" Edgar A. J. Johnson, undated memorandum, 1, Korea: addresses concerning subject of, box 1, EJP, HSTL.

190. Ibid., 1–2.

191. Ibid., 3–5.

192. Stolzenbach and Kissinger, *Civil Affairs in Korea*, 22, 30–33.

193. Ibid., 19, 22, 40.

194. Warren Austin, telegram (1090) to Dean Acheson, Jan. 30, 1951, 1; Dean Acheson, telegram (676) to USUN, Feb. 1, 1951, 1, folder 16 (2 of 2), box 7, SMOF, HSTL.

195. Ernest Gross, telegram (1285) to Dean Acheson, Mar. 15, 1951, 1; Dean Acheson, telegram (735) to J. Donald Kingsley, Mar. 28, 1951, 1–3, folder 16 (2 of 2), box 7, SMOF, HSTL.

5. State Building during Escalation in Vietnam

1. James M. Carter, *Inventing Vietnam: The United States and State Building, 1954–1968* (New York: Cambridge University Press, 2008), 79–81, 140–141.

2. Yuen Foong Khong, *Analogies at War: Korea, Munich, Dien Bien Phu, and the Vietnam Decisions of 1965* (Princeton, NJ: Princeton University Press, 1992); Elizabeth N. Saunders, *Leaders at War: How Presidents Shape Military Interventions* (Ithaca, NY: Cornell University Press, 2011), chap. 5.

3. Andrew F. Krepinevich Jr., *The Army and Vietnam* (Baltimore, MD: Johns Hopkins University Press, 1986); John A. Nagl, *Learning to Eat Soup with a Knife: Counterinsurgency Lessons from Malaya and Vietnam* (Chicago: Chicago University Press, 2005).

4. Daniel Ellsberg, "Cycles of Optimism and Pessimism," in *To Reason Why: The Debate about the Causes of U.S. Involvement in the Vietnam War*, ed. Jeffrey P. Kimball (New York: McGraw-Hill, 1990), 169.

5. NSAM-273, Nov. 26, 1963, 1–2, Papers of Lyndon Baines Johnson, Lyndon Baines Johnson Library and Museum, Austin, Texas (hereafter cited as "LBJL"), http://www.lbjlib.utexas .edu/Johnson/archives.hom/NSAMs/nsam273.asp (accessed Jul. 14, 2014).

6. NSAM-280, Feb. 14, 1964, 1–2, LBJL, http://www.lbjlib.utexas.edu/Johnson/archives .hom/NSAMs/nsam280.asp (accessed Jul. 14, 2014).

7. Memorandum from the Secretary of Defense (McNamara) to the President, Mar. 16, 1964, 154, *Foreign Relations of the United States, 1964–1968, Vol. I: Vietnam 1964* (Washington, DC: United States Government Printing Office, 1992). This volume is hereafter cited as *FRUS 1964*.

8. Memorandum from the President's Special Assistant for National Security Affairs (Bundy) to the President, May 22, 1964, 350; Draft Memorandum for the President Prepared by the Department of Defense, May 24, 1964, 363–368, *FRUS 1964*.

9. Summary Record of a Meeting, Honolulu, Jun. 1, 1964, 8:30 a.m–12:30 p.m., 412–413, *FRUS 1964*.

10. NSAM-314, Sep. 10, 1964, 1, LBJL, http://www.lbjlib.utexas.edu/Johnson/archives .hom/NSAMs/nsam314.asp (accessed Jul. 14, 2014).

11. Memorandum for the Record of a Meeting, Washington, White House, Nov. 19, 1964, 914–915; National Security Council Working Group, "Courses of Action in Southeast Asia," Nov. 21, 1964, 916–929, *FRUS 1964*. For sake of clarity, references to William Bundy will always include his first name.

12. Telegram from the Embassy in Vietnam to the Department of State, Jan. 6, 1965, 21; Telegram from the Embassy in Vietnam to the Joint Chiefs of Staff, Feb. 22, 1965, 347, *Foreign Relations of the United States, 1964–1968, Vol. II: Vietnam January–June 1965* (Washington, DC: United States Government Printing Office, 1996). This volume is hereafter cited as *FRUS 1965*.

13. Memorandum of Meeting, Feb. 8, 1965, 187; Summary Record of the 548th Meeting of the National Security Council, Feb. 10, 1965, 216–225, *FRUS 1965*.

14. Carter, *Inventing Vietnam*, 166; David Ekbladh, *The Great American Mission: Modernization and the Construction of an American World Order* (Princeton, NJ: Princeton University Press, 2010), 206–208; Lloyd C. Gardner, *Pay Any Price: Lyndon Johnson and the Wars for Vietnam* (Chicago: Ivan R. Dee, 1995), 193.

15. Carter, *Inventing Vietnam*, 126.

16. Administrative History, Agency for International Development, 377, Vol. 1, Part II: Chaps. 12–13, box 1, LBJL.

17. NSAM-328, Apr. 6, 1965, 2–3, LBJL, http://www.lbjlib.utexas.edu/johnson/archives .hom/NSAMs/nsam328.asp (accessed Jul. 14, 2014).

18. William Conrad Gibbons, *The U.S. Government and the Vietnam War: Executive and Legislative Roles and Relationships, Vol. 3* (Princeton, NJ: Princeton University Press, 1989), 277, 279, 317 (hereafter cited as "Gibbons, *Vol. 3*"); Memorandum for the Record, Jun. 8, 1965, 739–741, *FRUS 1965*.

19. Gibbons, *Vol. 3*, 320–326; Taylor to the Joint Chiefs of Staff, Feb. 22, 1965, 2, document 13a, Deployment of Major U.S. Forces to Vietnam, Jul. 1965 (Vol. 2; hereafter cited as "Deployment of Forces"): Tabs 61–87, box 40, National Security Files (hereafter cited as "NSF"), National Security Council History: Deployment of Major U.S. Forces to Vietnam, Jul. 1965 (hereafter cited as "NSCH"), LBJL.

20. Gibbons, *Vol. 3*, 330–331.

21. Ibid., 428.

22. This method of dissonance alleviation is based on the classic study of Elliot Aronson and Judson Mills, "The Effect of Severity of Initiation on Liking for a Group," *Journal of Abnormal and Social Psychology* 59, no. 2 (1959): 177–181.

23. Stanley Karnow, *Vietnam: A History* (New York: Penguin, 1984), 322–323.

24. Transcript, McGeorge Bundy, Oral History Interview II, Feb. 17, 1969, by Paige E. Mul hollan, 8, LBJL, http://www.lbjlib.utexas.edu/johnson/archives.hom/oralhistory.hom/Mc-GeorgeB/Bundy 2 web.pdf (accessed Jul. 14, 2014). See also Michael R. Beschloss, ed., *Taking Charge: The Johnson White House Tapes, 1963–1964* (New York: Simon & Schuster, 1997), 261; Gordon M. Goldstein, *Lessons in Disaster: McGeorge Bundy and the Path to War in Vietnam* (New York: Henry Holt, 2008), 97–98.

25. Transcript, Clark Clifford, Oral History Interview II, Jul. 2, 1969, by Paige E. Mulhollan, 2, LBJL, http://www.lbjlib.utexas.edu/johnson/archives.hom/oralhistory.hom/CliffordC /cliffor2.pdf (accessed Jul. 14, 2014); Transcript, George Ball, Oral History Interview I, Jul. 8, 1971, by Paige E. Mulhollan, 8, LBJL, http://www.lbjlib.utexas.edu/johnson/archives.hom /oralhistory.hom/Ball-G/Ball-g1.pdf (accessed Jul. 14, 2014).

26. William J. Jorden, "Foreign Policy Gaps in the 1964 Campaign," memorandum to McGeorge Bundy, Nov. 5, 1964, 1–3, document 1, President's Campaign 1964: Foreign Affairs, box 41, NSF, Subject File, LBJL. For more on the dominance of domestic over foreign policy con-

cerns in Johnson's White House in 1964 see Brian VanDeMark, *Into the Quagmire: Lyndon Johnson and the Escalation of the Vietnam War* (New York: Oxford University Press, 1991), 23, 54, 100; H. R. McMaster, *Dereliction of Duty: Lyndon Johnson, Robert McNamara, the Joint Chiefs of Staff, and the Lies That Led to Vietnam* (New York: HarperCollins, 1997), 117, 210; John P. Burke and Fred I. Greenstein, *How Presidents Test Reality: Decisions on Vietnam, 1954 and 1965* (New York: Russell Sage Foundation, 1989), 119; Karnow, *Vietnam: A History*, 322–323, 357; Doris Kearns, "Lyndon Johnson's Political Personality," *Political Science Quarterly* 91, no. 3 (1976): 390.

27. Gareth Porter, *Perils of Dominance: Imbalance of Power and the Road to War in Vietnam* (Berkeley: University of California Press, 2005), 183.

28. David Kaiser, *American Tragedy: Kennedy, Johnson, and the Origins of the Vietnam War* (Cambridge, MA: Harvard University Press, 2000), 319, 344–345; Fredrik Logevall, *Choosing War: The Lost Chance for Peace and the Escalation of the War in Vietnam* (Berkeley: University of California Press, 1999), 144–145.

29. Larry Berman, *Planning a Tragedy: The Americanization of the War in Vietnam* (New York: W.W. Norton, 1982). For a recent debate over this argument see Francis M. Bator, "No Good Choices: LBJ and the Vietnam/Great Society Connection," *Diplomatic History* 32, no. 3 (2008): 309–340, and responses to Bator in the same issue.

30. McNamara to the President, Mar. 16, 1964, 154, *FRUS 1964*; William Conrad Gibbons, *The U.S. Government and the Vietnam War: Executive and Legislative Roles and Relationships, Vol. 2* (Princeton, NJ: Princeton University Press, 1986), 209 (hereafter cited as "Gibbons, *Vol. 2*"); Logevall, *Choosing War*, 76–78.

31. Memorandum from the President's Special Assistant for National Security Affairs (Bundy) to the President, Jan. 9, 1964, 8, *FRUS 1964*; Memorandum from the President's Special Assistant for National Security Affairs (Bundy) to the President, Feb. 7, 1965, 184, *FRUS 1965*.

32. Memorandum of a Conversation between the Joint Chiefs of Staff and the President, Washington, Mar. 4, 1964, 129, *FRUS 1964*; Beschloss, *Taking Charge*, 263, 398.

33. Ibid., 266–267.

34. Letter from the Under Secretary of State (Ball) to the Secretary of State, May 31, 1964, 400, *FRUS 1964*; Beschloss, *Taking Charge*, 365; Mark Moyar, *Triumph Forsaken: The Vietnam War, 1954–1965* (New York: Cambridge University Press, 2006), 293.

35. Memorandum for the Record, Apr. 21, 1965, 580; Memorandum for the Record, Apr. 22, 1965, 599, *FRUS 1965*.

36. Data obtained using the Roper Center for Public Opinion Research's online iPoll database. On the ambiguity of the public's attitudes on Vietnam in late 1964 see Logevall, *Choosing War*, 287–288. While Logevall asserts Johnson could have carried public opinion with him whether he chose to escalate or withdraw in Vietnam, it is plain Johnson did not believe that to be the case.

37. Gibbons, *Vol. 3*, 293; VanDeMark, *Into the Quagmire*, 71, 161–163; Moyar, *Triumph Forsaken*, 293, 414; McMaster, *Dereliction of Duty*, 96, 179–180, 263, 296; Berman, *Planning a Tragedy*, 150.

38. Transcript, McGeorge Bundy, Oral History Interview I, Jan. 30, 1969, by Paige E. Mulhollan, 22–23, LBJL, http://www.lbjlib.utexas.edu/johnson/archives.hom/oralhistory.hom/McGeorgeB/Bundy 1 web.pdf (accessed Nov. 6, 2011). Bundy voiced largely the same opinion almost twenty-five years later, saying Johnson's attitude had been "I'll make peace with my left hand and I'll make war with my right hand, and everybody is with me. And I'm going to do it without calling up the reserves. I'm not going to alarm the American people." Transcript, McGeorge Bundy, Special Interview I, Mar. 30, 1993, by Robert Dallek, 20, LBJL, http://www.lbjlib.utexas.edu/johnson/archives.hom/oralhistory.hom/McGeorgeB/Bundy Dallek 1 web.pdf (accessed Nov. 6, 2011).

39. Logevall, *Choosing War*, 273; McGeorge Bundy memorandum to Lyndon Johnson, Feb. 16, 1965, 2, document 116, Deployment of Forces (Vol. 1): Tabs 11–41; Rusk to the American Embassy in Saigon, Mar. 3, 1965, document 38a, Deployment of U.S. Forces (Vol. 2): Tabs 88–119, box 40, NSF, NSCH, LBJL.

40. NSAM-328, 3.

41. Bator, "No Good Choices," 318; see also Berman, *Planning a Tragedy*, 146.

42. Gardner, *Pay Any Price*, 177; see also Leslie H. Gelb and Richard K. Betts, *The Irony of Vietnam: The System Worked* (Washington, DC: Brookings Institution, 1979), 109.

43. Michael R. Beschloss, ed., *Reaching for Glory: Lyndon Johnson's Secret White House Tapes, 1964–1965* (New York: Simon & Schuster, 2001), 381–382.

44. Bator, "No Good Choices," 318–319; Logevall, *Choosing War*, 297–298.

45. Transcript, McGeorge Bundy, Special Interview II, Nov. 10, 1993, by Robert Dallek, 17–18, 25, LBJL, http://www.lbjlib.utexas.edu/johnson/archives.hom/oralhistory.hom/McGeorgeB/Bundy Dallek 2 web.pdf (accessed Nov. 6, 2011).

46. Johnson told Lodge in March 1964 that they always had to be "knocking down the idea of neutralization wherever it rears its ugly head . . . by whatever means we can." See George McT. Kahin, *Intervention: How America Became Involved in Vietnam* (New York: Knopf, 1986), 208, 295; Logevall, *Choosing War*, 122.

47. Summary Record of a Meeting, Department of State, Washington, May 30, 1964, 10:30 a.m., 397–398, *FRUS 1964*.

48. Logevall, *Choosing War*, 147; Memorandum from Michael V. Forrestal of the National Security Council Staff to the President, May 29, 1964, 396–397, *FRUS 1964*.

49. Telegram from the Embassy in Vietnam to the Department of State, Aug. 10, 1964, 657; Telegram from the Embassy in Vietnam to the Department of State, Aug. 18, 1964, 690–692, *FRUS 1964*.

50. See, for instance, Memorandum from the Joint Chiefs of Staff to the Secretary of Defense (McNamara), Aug. 27, 1964, 714; Telegram from the Embassy in Vietnam to the Department of State, Sep. 6, 1964, 735, *FRUS 1964*; Logevall, *Choosing War*, 214, 218–220; VanDeMark, *Into the Quagmire*, 34.

51. McGeorge Bundy to Lyndon Johnson, Dec. 23, 1964, document 7, McGeorge Bundy, Vol. 7: 10/1-12/31/64 [1 of 2], box 2, NSF, Memos to the President: McGeorge Bundy (hereafter cited as "Bundy Memos") Vol. 5–8, LBJL.

52. Carter, *Inventing Vietnam*, 156; Gregory A. Daddis, *No Sure Victory: Measuring U.S. Army Effectiveness and Progress in the Vietnam War* (New York: Oxford University Press, 2011), 65.

53. Paper Prepared by the National Security Council Working Group, Nov. 21, 1964, 916, *FRUS 1964*; Memorandum from the Assistant Secretary of State for Far Eastern Affairs (Bundy) to Secretary of State Rusk, Jan. 6, 1965, 32, *FRUS 1965*; Maxwell Taylor to Lyndon Johnson, Jan. 6, 1965, 2, document 8, Deployment of Forces (Vol. 1): Tabs 1–10, box 40, NSF, NSCH, LBJL.

54. Memorandum from the President's Special Assistant for National Security Affairs (Bundy) to President Johnson, Feb. 7, 1965, 175, *FRUS 1965*.

55. Memorandum from the President's Special Assistant for National Security Affairs (Bundy) to President Johnson, Jan. 27, 1965, 95–97, *FRUS 1965*; Gibbons, *Vol. 3*, 47, 160–161.

56. Maxwell Taylor to Dean Rusk, Apr. 17, 1965, 1, document 42a, Deployment of Forces (Vol. 3): Tabs 170–199, box 41; Westmoreland, "Concept of Operations—Force Requirements and Deployments, South Vietnam," Jun. 14, 1965, 6, document 16a, Deployment of Forces (Vol. 5): Tabs 293–313, box 42, NSF, NSCH, LBJL.

57. Carter, *Inventing Vietnam*, 51.

58. Robert McNamara to Lyndon Johnson, Mar. 13, 1964, 1, document 28, McGeorge Bundy, Vol. 2: 3/1-31/64 [1 of 2], box 1; Position Paper on Southeast Asia, Dec. 2, 1964, document 53b, McGeorge Bundy, Vol. 7: 10/1-12/31/64 [2 of 2], box 2, NSF, Bundy Memos Vol. 1–4, LBJL.

59. US Options and Objectives in Vietnam, Jun. 10, 1965, 1, document 59a, Deployment of Forces (Vol. 4): Tabs 258–280, box 41, NSF, NSCH, LBJL.

60. Porter, *Perils of Dominance*, 244.

61. Saunders, "Transformative Choices," 150; Beschloss, *Taking Charge*, 74 (emphasis in original).

62. Dean Rusk, "Viet-Nam," Jul. 1, 1965, 1, document 24a, Deployment of Forces (Vol. 6): Tabs 341–356, box 43, NSF, NSCH, LBJL.

63. Memorandum from the President's Special Assistant for National Security Affairs (Bundy) to the President, Dec. 16, 1964, 1011, *FRUS 1964*. In April 1965 Bundy drafted a memo which stated that the GVN should release a statement regarding the eventual reunification of Vietnam. The memo read that this would need to be a "top order of business." However, it seems clear that Bundy saw this as crucial to countering communist propaganda. Making the GVN appear capable of leadership to the South Vietnamese was Bundy's top priority—reuniting the North and South was not taken seriously as a U.S. objective. Gibbons, *Vol. 3*, 236–237.

64. Berman, *Planning a Tragedy*, 102–103.
65. Ekbladh, *The Great American Mission*, 210. Additionally, see Carter, *Inventing Vietnam*, 167–168, 173–174; Gardner, *Pay Any Price*, 192; McMaster, *Dereliction of Duty*, 262; Goldstein, *Lessons in Disaster*, 170; Burke and Greenstein, *How Presidents Test Reality*, 188. For a dissenting opinion see Christopher T. Fisher, "The Illusion of Progress: CORDS and the Crisis of Modernization in South Vietnam, 1965–1968," *Pacific Historical Review* 75, no. 1 (2006): 34.
66. Chester L. Cooper, "Analysis of White House Mail on Vietnam: April 4 through April 12," 1–2, document 20a, Deployment of Forces (Vol. 3): Tabs 141–169, box 41, NSF, NSCH, LBJL.
67. NSAM-329, Apr. 9, 1965, 2, LBJL, http://www.lbjlib.utexas.edu/Johnson/archives.hom/NSAMs/nsam329.asp (accessed Jul. 14, 2014).
68. McGeorge Bundy, "Senator Mansfield's views on South Vietnam," memorandum to Lyndon Johnson, Jan. 6, 1964, document 43, McGeorge Bundy, Vol. 1: 11/63-2/64 [2 of 2]; Robert McNamara, "South Vietnam," memorandum to Lyndon Johnson, Mar. 13, 1964, 1, McGeorge Bundy, Vol. 2: 3/1-31/64 [1 of 2], box 1, NSF, Bundy Memos Vol. 1-4, LBJL.
69. Burke and Greenstein, *How Presidents Test Reality*, 180; Gibbons, *Vol. 3*, 180.
70. The metaphor was used in Paper Prepared by the Assistant Secretary of Defense for International Security Affairs (McNaughton), Mar. 10, 1965, 431, *FRUS 1965*.
71. McGeorge Bundy, Memorandum for the Record: Meeting on South Vietnam, Sep. 9, 1964, 4, document 23, McGeorge Bundy, Vol. 6: 7/1-9/30/64 [1 of 2], box 2, NSF, Bundy Memos Vol. 5-8.
72. Gibbons, *Vol. 3*, 157.
73. Beschloss, *Taking Charge*, 364.
74. Porter, *Perils of Dominance*, 249–250.
75. Paper Prepared by the National Security Council Working Group, Nov. 21, 1964, 918, *FRUS 1964*; Logevall, *Choosing War*, 246–247; for officials' doubts on the importance of Vietnam for containing China see ibid., 291–292.
76. Beschloss, *Reaching for Glory*, 350; Porter, *Perils of Dominance*, 251.
77. William Raborn to Lyndon Johnson, Jul. 20, 1965, 1–4, document 1a, Deployment of Forces (Vol. 7): Tabs 401–420, box 43, NSF, NSCH, LBJL.
78. McGeorge Bundy, "Senator Mansfield's Views on South Vietnam," memorandum to Lyndon Johnson, Jan. 6, 1964, document 43, McGeorge Bundy, Vol. 1: 11/63-2/64 [2 of 2]; Roger Hilsman, "South Viet-Nam," memorandum to Dean Rusk, Mar. 14, 1964, 2, 4 (emphasis in original), document 14c, McGeorge Bundy, Vol. 2: 3/1-31/64 [1 of 2], box 1, NSF, Bundy Memos Vol. 1-4, LBJL.
79. McGeorge Bundy, "Your 6 PM Meeting with Taylor, Johnson et al.," memorandum to Lyndon Johnson, Jun. 25, 1964, 1–2, document 10, McGeorge Bundy, Vol. 5: 6/1-30/64, box 2, NSF, Bundy Memos Vol. 5-8, LBJL.
80. McNamara to the President, Mar. 16, 1964, 161–164, *FRUS 1964*.
81. Memorandum from the President's Special Assistant for National Security Affairs (Bundy) to President Johnson, Mar. 6, 1965, 403, *FRUS 1965*.
82. Dean Rusk to Henry Cabot Lodge, May 5, 1964, 2, document 51h, McGeorge Bundy, Vol. 4: 5/1-27/64 [2 of 2], box 1, NSF, Bundy Memos Vol. 1-4, LBJL.
83. Saunders, *Leaders at War*, chap. 5.
84. Saunders, "Transformative Choices", 150–151, 153. Johnson had shown interest in political and economic development in South Vietnam as an answer to the communist challenge there since his trip there in 1961, though he also warned Kennedy that "if the Vietnamese government, backed by a three year liberal aid program cannot do this job, then we had better remember the experience of the French." Porter, *Perils of Dominance*, 181.
85. Memorandum from the President's Special Assistant for National Security Affairs (Bundy) to the President, May 22, 1964, 350; Draft Memorandum Prepared for the President by the Secretary of State's Special Assistant for Vietnam (Sullivan), May 24, 1964, 359–362, *FRUS 1964*; McGeorge Bundy, "The Honolulu Team Returns," memorandum to Lyndon Johnson, Jun. 3, 1964, document 53; McGeorge Bundy, "Our Current Work on Southeast Asia," memorandum to Lyndon Johnson, Jun. 10, 1964, document 39, McGeorge Bundy, Vol. 5: 6/1-30/64, bo x 2, NSF, Bundy Memos Vol. 5-8, LBJL.

86. Telegram from the Department of State to the Embassy in Vietnam, Jul. 25, 1964, 571–572; Telegram from the Embassy in Vietnam, Aug. 10, 1964, 657–659, *FRUS 1964*.

87. NSAM-314, 2.

88. Message from the Ambassador in Vietnam (Taylor) to the President, Sep. 30, 1964, 802–804, *FRUS 1964*, is the first of these assessments.

89. Message from the President to the Ambassador in Vietnam (Lodge), Jan. 7, 1964, 6, *FRUS 1964*; see also Kaiser, *American Tragedy*, 375; Kahin, *Intervention*, 238, on Johnson's attentiveness to the political situation in Saigon.

90. Memorandum of a Meeting, White House, Washington, Sep. 9, 1964, 11 a.m., 752, *FRUS 1964*; Gibbons, *Vol. 2*, 353; Logevall, *Choosing War*, 105–106; Gardner, *Pay Any Price*, 146.

91. Saunders, *Leaders at War*, chap. 5; Khong, *Analogies at War*, 138–145.

92. Johnson's colorful phrase was that he did not want to send a "widow woman to slap Jack Dempsey"; Notes on a Meeting, White House, Washington, Dec. 1, 1964, 11:30 a.m., 966–967, *FRUS 1964*.

93. Instructions from the President to the Ambassador to Vietnam (Taylor), Dec. 3, 1964, 975–976 (emphasis added), *FRUS 1964*; Gibbons, *Vol. 2*, 379.

94. Bundy to the President, Dec. 16, 1964, *FRUS 1964*, 1010; see also Kahin, *Intervention*, 252.

95. McGeorge Bundy to Johnson, 6, Feb. 7, 1965, 3–4, document 45, Deployment of Forces (Vol. 1): Tabs 11–41, box 40, NSF, NSCH, LBJL.

96. George Ball to Maxwell Taylor, Feb. 13, 1965, 1, document 100, Deployment of Forces (Vol. 1): Tabs 42–60; Dean Rusk, memorandum on Vietnam, Feb. 23, 1965, 1–2, document 22b, Deployment of Forces (Vol. 2): Tabs 61–87, box 40, NSF, NSCH, LBJL.

97. McGeorge Bundy, "Memorandum for Discussion," Mar. 16, 1965, 1, Deployment of Forces (Vol. 2): Tabs 88–119, box 40, NSF, NSCH, LBJL. For a more thorough outlining of the points of the proposed new noncombat effort see McGeorge Bundy, "Non-Military Actions in South Vietnam," memorandum to Lyndon Johnson, Mar. 24, 1965, document 175a, Vietnam Vol. 31, Memos (A) [1 of 3]: 3/12-31/65, box 15 [1 of 2], NSF, Country File: Vietnam, LBJL. These included establishing a U.S. Interagency Action Group with a civilian chief of staff to guide and coordinate pacification operations; assigning U.S. personnel full time to Vietnamese political and religious groups and key GVN official and ministries; improving the benefits available to U.S. personnel in South Vietnam to encourage extended tours and better people; and new programs for waging informational and psychological warfare. Less important programs included establishing a teaching hospital in Saigon; increasing humanitarian assistance at the village level; and organizing disaster teams to cope with war damage, floods, and emergency refugee problems. The GVN would be pressured to delegate more power to province chiefs and develop popular security forces and civic action programs based on villages and districts, requiring American personnel to make administrative and jurisdictional modifications. Saigon was also to develop its political base; institute economic warfare against Vietcong-held areas; and revitalize the Chu Hoi program for Vietcong defectors.

98. NSAM-328, 1; American Embassy Saigon to State and Defense Departments, Apr. 15, 1965, 1–3, document 25a, Deployment of Forces (Vol. 3): Tabs 141–169, box 41, NSF, NSCH, LBJL.

99. Telegram from the Embassy in Vietnam to the Department of State, Apr. 17, 1965, 563; Telegram from the Embassy in Vietnam to the Department of State, Apr. 17, 1965, 567, *FRUS 1965*; Maxwell Taylor to Dean Rusk and McGeorge Bundy, Apr. 16, 1965, document 35a, Deployment of Forces (Vol. 3): Tabs 170–199, box 41, NSF, NSCH, LBJL.

100. Telegram from the White House to the Embassy in Vietnam, Apr. 17, 1965, 571, *FRUS 1965*.

101. Robert McNamara, "Program of expanded military and political moves with respect to Vietnam," memorandum to Lyndon Johnson, Jun. 26, 1965, 5, document 13b, Deployment of Forces (Vol. 6): Tabs 341–356, box 43, NSF, NSCH, LBJL.

102. Carter, *Inventing Vietnam*, 157–158, 164.

103. Maxwell Taylor to Dean Rusk, Jul. 11, 1965, 3 (section 5 of 9), document 43a, Deployment of Forces (Vol. 6), Tabs 357–383, box 43, NSF, NSCH, LBJL.

104. Richard A. Hunt, *Pacification: The American Struggle for Vietnam's Hearts and Minds* (Boulder, CO: Westview Press, 1995), 35–36, 80.

105. Ibid., 70.

106. Paper Prepared by the Assistant Secretary of State for Far Eastern Affairs (Bundy), Feb. 23, 1966, 248–253, *Foreign Relations of the United States, 1964–1968, Vol. IV: Vietnam 1966* (Washington, DC: United States Government Printing Office, 1998).

107. Porter, *Perils of Dominance*, 230, 257.

108. Letter from the Under Secretary of State (Ball) to the Secretary of State, May 31, 1964, 401, *FRUS 1964*; Logevall, *Choosing War*, 174.

109. Gibbons, *Vol. 3*, 259, 261–262.

110. Rufus Phillips, *Why Vietnam Matters: An Eyewitness Account of Lessons Not Learned* (Annapolis, MD: Naval Institute Press, 2008), 250.

111. McGeorge Bundy, "Possible Successor to Lodge," memorandum to Lyndon Johnson, Jun. 6, 1964, document 47, box 2, McGeorge Bundy, Vol. 5: 6/1-30/64, NSF, Bundy Memos Vol. 1–4, LBJL.

112. Robert S. McNamara, *In Retrospect: The Tragedy and Lessons of Vietnam* (New York: Random House, 1995), 108.

113. Memorandum from the Joint Chiefs of Staff to the Secretary of Defense (McNamara), Jun. 2, 1964, 437, *FRUS 1964*; McMaster, *Dereliction of Duty*, 249–250.

114. McMaster, *Dereliction of Duty*, 191.

115. Gelb and Betts, *Irony of Vietnam*, 307; Gibbons, *Vol. 2*, 366.

116. McMaster, *Dereliction of Duty*, 248, 265–266, 272.

117. Gibbons, *Vol. 3*, 84; Goldstein, *Lessons in Disaster*, 226. This is also a theme in Palmer's book, *The 25-Year War: America's Military Role in Vietnam* (Lexington, KY: University Press of Kentucky, 1984).

118. Daddis, *No Sure Victory*, 47.

119. McGeorge Bundy to Johnson, Feb. 7, 1965, 4, document 45, Deployment of Forces (Vol. 1): Tabs 11–41, box 40, NSF, NSCH, LBJL.

120. McGeorge Bundy to Lyndon Johnson, Apr. 1, 1965, document 72a, Deployment of Forces (Vol. 2): Tabs 120–140, box 41, NSF, NSCH, LBJL.

121. McGeorge Bundy, Memorandum for Discussion, Mar. 16, 1965, 3, Deployment of Forces (Vol. 2): Tabs 88–119, box 40, NSF, NSCH, LBJL.

122. Gibbons, *Vol. 3*, 287.

123. Ellsberg, "Cycles of Optimism and Pessimism," 169.

124. VanDeMark, *Into the Quagmire*, 199, 203.

125. "Possible Items for Discussion" (author unknown), Jul. 22, 1965, document 10a, Deployment of Forces (Vol. 7): Tabs 401–420, box 43, NSF, NSCH, LBJL.

126. Gibbons, *Vol. 3*, 404; Burke and Greenstein, *How Presidents Test Reality*, 179.

127. See, for example, Notes of the Leadership Meeting, White House, Washington, Aug. 4, 1964, 6:45 p.m., 620, *FRUS 1964*; Memorandum from the Joint Chiefs of Staff to Secretary of Defense McNamara, Feb. 11, 1965, 241; Special National Intelligence Estimate, Feb. 18, 1965, 324, *FRUS 1965*; Kahin, *Intervention*, 338–339; Porter, *Perils of Dominance*, 186–188, 204.

128. McNamara to the President, Mar. 16, 1964, 155–157; Notes Prepared by the Secretary of Defense (McNamara) May 14, 1964, 323, *FRUS 1964*.

129. McGeorge Bundy to Lyndon Johnson, Sept. 24, 1964, document 3, McGeorge Bundy: Vol. 6, 7/1-9/30/64 [1 of 2], box 2, Papers of Lyndon Baines Johnson, President 1963–69, NSF, Bundy Memos Vol. 5–8, LBJL; Paper Prepared by the Ambassador in Vietnam (Taylor), n.d., 948–949, *FRUS 1964*. Khanh was the head of the military government in South Vietnam from January 1964 to February 1965.

130. Memorandum Prepared in the Department of Defense, Mar. 2, 1964, 119, *FRUS 1964*; Telegram from the Embassy in Vietnam to the Department of State, Mar. 2, 1965, 394; Memorandum for the Record, Mar. 18, 1965, 459, *FRUS 1965*.

131. Westmoreland, "Concept of Operations—Force Requirements and Deployments, South Vietnam," Jun. 14, 1965, 6, document 16a, Deployment of Forces (Vol. 5): Tabs 293–313, box 42, NSF, NSCH, LBJL.

132. Telegram from the Embassy in Vietnam to the Department of State, Aug. 18, 1964, 680–690, *FRUS 1964*.

133. Memorandum from the President's Special Assistant for National Security Affairs (Bundy) to the President, Aug. 31, 1964, 723, *FRUS 1964*.

134. Memorandum from the Joint Chiefs of Staff to the Secretary of Defense (McNamara), Oct. 27, 1964, 847, *FRUS 1964*.

135. Telegram from the Embassy in Vietnam, Jan. 6, 1965, 15, *FRUS 1965*.

136. Memorandum from the President's Special Assistant for National Security Affairs (Bundy) to the President, Jan. 27, 1965, 95–97, *FRUS 1965*. They also informed Johnson that Rusk did not disagree with their assessment of the situation in the RVN, but that the secretary of state thought escalation was too risky at the time.

137. Personal Notes of a Meeting with President Johnson, Jan. 6, 1965, 38, *FRUS 1965*.

138. Logevall, *Choosing War*, 318.

139. Memorandum of a Meeting, Feb. 8, 1965, 187–189, *FRUS 1965*; Porter, *Perils of Dominance*, 212; Beschloss, *Reaching for Glory*, 181.

140. Personal Notes of a Meeting with President Johnson, Feb. 16, 1965, 291, *FRUS 1965*.

141. Logevall, *Choosing War*, 109, 255. Similarly, Gibbons concluded that throughout 1964 "there was considerable doubt among U.S. officials about the outcome of the struggle in Vietnam." Gibbons, *Vol. 2*, 384.

142. Robert S. McNamara, James G. Blight, and Robert K. Brigham, *Argument without End: In Search of Answers to the Vietnam Tragedy* (New York: PublicAffairs, 1999), 388.

143. Gibbons, *Vol. 2*, 360–362; Logevall, *Choosing War*, 247–248.

144. Department of Defense, Mar. 2, 1964, 120; Memorandum Prepared by the Director of Central Intelligence (McCone), Mar. 3, 1964, 125, *FRUS 1964*.

145. Gibbons, *Vol. 2*, 384; Summary Record of the 532d Meeting of the National Security Council, Washington, May 15, 1964, Noon, 332; Summary Record of a Meeting, Honolulu, Jun. 1, 1964, 8:30 a.m.–12:30 p.m., 419, *FRUS 1964*.

146. Paper Prepared by the National Security Council Working Group, Nov. 21, 1964, 918; Memorandum of the Meeting of the Executive Committee, Washington, Nov. 24, 1964, 5 p.m., 943, *FRUS 1964*; see also Logevall, *Choosing War*, 259; Goldstein, *Lessons in Disaster*, 176–177.

147. Telegram from the President to the Ambassador in Vietnam (Taylor), Dec. 30, 1964, 1058–1059, *FRUS 1964*; Personal Notes, Feb. 16, 1965, 291, *FRUS 1965*.

148. VanDeMark, *Into the Quagmire*, 49.

149. Ibid., 154; Kahin, *Intervention*, 356.

150. VanDeMark, *Into the Quagmire*, 167–168; Gibbons, *Vol. 3*, 328.

151. William Bundy, "Holding on in South Vietnam," memorandum to Rusk et al., Jun. 30, 1965, 3, document 12a, Deployment of Forces (Vol. 6): Tabs 341–356, box 43, NSF, NSCH, LBJL; Telegram from the Embassy in Vietnam to the Department of State, Mar. 27, 1965, 488, *FRUS 1965*.

152. Gibbons, *Vol. 3*, 328; for similar concerns voiced by Bundy and Forrestal in March of the previous year see Memorandum for the Record of the White House Daily Staff Meeting, Washing, Mar. 30, 1964, 8 a.m., 198–199, *FRUS 1964*.

153. Gibbons, *Vol. 3*, 328; Porter, *Perils of Dominance*, 222.

154. VanDeMark, *Into the Quagmire*, 191, 194, 197.

155. Gibbons, *Vol. 3*, 332, 370.

156. Nagl, *Learning to Eat Soup with a Knife*, 115; Krepinevich, *The Army and Vietnam*, 5; see also Kaiser, *American Tragedy*, 309, 416.

157. Jeffrey Record, *Beating Goliath: Why Insurgencies Win* (Washington, DC: Potomac, 2007), 121.

158. Major General William P. Yarborough letter to Westmoreland, Feb. 26, 1964, 3–4, document 11; Westmoreland to David Nes, Feb. 27, 1964, 1–2, document 13; Nes to Westmoreland et al., Feb. 29, 1964, document 26, #3 (History Backup): 17 Feb. 64–30 Apr. 64 [I], box 1, Papers of William C. Westmoreland (hereafter cited as "WWP"), LBJL.

159. Westmoreland to USMACV, Jun. 20, 1964, #6 (History Backup): 1 Jun. 64–3 Aug. 1964 [I], box 2, WWP, LBJL.

160. Westmoreland "Civic Action in Vietnam," memorandum to USMACV, Oct. 1, 1964, document 109; #8 (History Backup): 1 Sep. 64–8 Oct. 64 [II]; Colonel Daniel A. Richards, "Orga-

nization of Hop Tac Council," memorandum to Westmoreland, Oct. 24, 1964, document 55; Lieutenant General J.L. Throckmorton, "Hop Tac Evaluation," memorandum to Maxwell Taylor, Oct. 24, 1964, document 58, #9 (History Backup): 9 Oct. 64–13 Nov. 64 [I], box 3, WWP, LBJL.

161. Major General Alden K. Sibley, memorandum for record, Aug. 14, 1964, document 72, #7 (History Backup): 27 Jul. 64–31 Aug. 64 [I], box 3, WWP, LBJL.

162. Westmoreland, "Assumption by U.S. of Operational Control of the Pacification Program in SVN," memorandum to Maxwell Taylor, Nov. 14, 1964, 1–2, document 40, #10 (History Backup): 14 Nov. 64–7 Dec. 64 [I], WWP, LBJL.

163. Telegram from the Embassy in Vietnam to the Department of State, Jan. 6, 1965, 28, *FRUS 1965*.

164. Telegram from the Commander, Military Assistance Command, Vietnam (Westmoreland) to the Chairman of the Joint Chiefs of Staff (Wheeler), Oct. 17, 1964, 838; Telegram from the Commander, Military Assistance Command, Vietnam (Westmoreland) to the Ambassador in Vietnam (Taylor), Oct. 31, 1964, 861–863, *FRUS 1964*.

165. Dale Andrade, "Westmoreland Was Right: Learning the Wrong Lessons from the Vietnam War," *Small Wars & Insurgencies* 19, no. 2 (2008): 145–181; John M. Carland, "Winning the Vietnam War: Westmoreland's Approach in Two Documents," *Journal of Military History* 68, no. 2 (2004): 553–574; Andrew J. Birtle, "PROVN, Westmoreland, and the Historians: A Reappraisal," *Journal of Military History* 72, no. 4 (2008): 1213–1247.

166. Westmoreland, "Doctrine of Pacification as It Applies to the Rural Population," memorandum to Mr. De Silva, Feb. 14, 1965, document 80, #13 (History Backup): 21 Jan. 65–28 Feb. 65 [I], box 5, WWP, LBJL.

167. Gibbons, *Vol. 3*, 159, 176.

168. Westmoreland, "Concept of Operations—Force Requirements and Deployments," 1–2.

169. Michael Forrestal memorandum, May 26, 1964, document 3a, McGeorge Bundy, Vol. 4: 5/1-27/64 [1 of 2], box 1, NSF, Bundy Memos Vol. 1–4, LBJL.

170. McGeorge Bundy to Johnson, Feb. 7, 1965, 6–7, document 45, Deployment of Forces (Vol. 1): Tabs 11–41, box 40, NSF, NSCH, LBJL.

171. VanDeMark, *Into the Quagmire*, 85 (emphasis in original).

172. Logevall, *Choosing War*, 79.

173. Burke and Greenstein, *How Presidents Test Reality*, 248.

174. Transcript, Dean Rusk, Oral History Interview I, Jul. 28, 1969, by Paige E. Mulhollan, 4, LBJL, http://www.lbjlib.utexas.edu/johnson/archives.hom/oralhistory.hom/rusk/rusk01 .pdf (accessed Jan. 5, 2012).

175. Bundy, Oral History Interview I, 35; Bator cites the scholarly reception of Thomas A. Schwartz, *Lyndon Johnson and Europe* (Cambridge, MA: Harvard University Press, 2003); see Bator, "No Good Choices," 310–313.

Conclusion. Reviewing Theoretical and Policy Implications

1. U.S. Army, *Field Manual 3-0: Operations* (Washington, DC: Department of the Army, 2001), para. 6-82.

2. Nora Bensahel et al., *After Saddam: Prewar Planning and the Occupation of Iraq* (Santa Monica, CA: RAND Corporation, 2008), 12–13; Donald P. Wright and Timothy R. Reese, *On Point II: Transition to the New Campaign* (Fort Leavenworth, KS: Combat Studies Institute Press, 2008), 77.

3. Margaret Hermann, Thomas Preston, Baghat Korany, and Timothy M. Shaw, "Who Leads Matters: The Effects of Powerful Individuals," *International Studies Review* 3, no. 2 (2001): 83–131.

4. Fred I. Greenstein, *The Presidential Difference: Leadership Style from FDR to Clinton* (New York: Free Press, 2000), chap. 3.

5. Stanley Allen Renshon, "The World According to George W Bush: Good Judgment or Cowboy Politics?" in *Good Judgment in Foreign Policy: Theory and Application*, ed. Stanley Allen Renshon and Deborah Welch Larson (Lanham, MD: Rowman & Littlefield, 2003), 294.

6. Ibid., 292–294.

7. Tetlock, *Expert Political Judgment: How Good Is It? How Can We Know?* (Princeton, NJ: Princeton University Press, 2005), 82.

8. Jack S. Levy, "Learning and Foreign Policy: Sweeping a Conceptual Minefield," *International Organization* 48, no. 2 (1994): 283.

9. Widely cited psychological, rationalist, and constructivist approaches employing this assumption include (respectively) Charles Hermann, "Changing Course: When Governments Choose to Redirect Foreign Policy," *International Studies Quarterly* 34, no. 1 (1990): 3–21; Andrew Kydd, *Trust and Mistrust in International Relations* (Princeton, NJ: Princeton University Press, 2005); Jeffrey Legro, *Rethinking the World: Great Power Strategies and International Order* (Ithaca, NY: Cornell University, 2007).

10. Yuen Foong Khong, *Analogies at War: Korea, Munich, Dien Bien Phu, and the Vietnam Decisions of 1965* (Princeton, NJ: Princeton University Press, 1992); Jeffrey Record, *Making War, Thinking History: Munich, Vietnam, and Presidential Uses of Force from Korea to Kosovo* (Annapolis, MD: Naval Institute Press, 2002); Richard E. Neustadt and Ernest R. May, *Thinking in Time: The Uses of History for Decisionmakers* (New York: Free Press, 1986).

11. Khong, *Analogies at War*, 7, 37.

12. On this point see Gavan Duffy, "Give Structure Its Due: Political Agency and the Vietnam Commitment Decisions," *Japanese Journal of Political Science* 2, no. 2 (2001): 161–175. Khong argues that Johnson and most of his top advisers ascribed to several lessons drawn from the Korean War: communist aggression must not be rewarded; the stakes in Vietnam were extremely high; force would successfully coerce North Vietnam; and the United States could not provoke a Chinese counterintervention. Khong, *Analogies at War*, 140.

13. Francis Fukuyama, *America at the Crossroads: Democracy, Power, and the Neoconservative Legacy* (New Haven, CT: Yale University Press, 2006), 52–53, 60–61, 132.

14. For overviews of prospect theory and its use in international relations see Jack S. Levy, "Loss Aversion, Framing Effects, and International Conflict: Perspectives from Prospect Theory," in *Handbook of War Studies II*, ed. Manus I. Midlarsky (Ann Arbor, MI: University of Michigan Press, 2000), 193–221; Jonathan Mercer, "Prospect Theory and Political Science," *Annual Review of Political Science* 8 (2005): 1–21.

15. An exception is Jack Levy, who notes that "trade-offs between immediate and future risks . . . raises a difficult theoretical problem and one which has not received much attention in the literature on prospect theory." Levy, "Prospect Theory and International Relations: Theoretical Applications and Analytical Problems," *Political Psychology* 13, no. 2 (1992): 301.

16. The Argentinean regime's assessments did appear to be heavily colored by mistaken general beliefs, analogies drawn from previous events, and abstract ideals such as justice, patterns CLT predicts will be associated with temporal distance. See David A. Welch, "Culture and Emotion as Obstacles to Good Judgment: The Case of Argentina's Invasion of the Falklands/Malvinas," in *Good Judgment in Foreign Policy*, 191–216.

17. Bruce Bueno de Mesquita and Rose McDermott, "Crossing No Man's Land: Cooperation from the Trenches," *Political Psychology* 25, no. 2 (2004): 271–288.

18. Levy, "Loss Aversion, Framing Effects, and International Conflict," 198–199 (figs.1 and 2). Gary Schaub Jr. notes that recent studies estimate the "inflection point" at which probabilities go from being over- to underweighted lies, on average, around 0.34. Schaub, "Deterrence, Compellence, and Prospect Theory," *Political Psychology* 25, no. 3 (2004): 399.

19. Joint Center for Operational Analysis, "Transitions in Iraq: Changing Environment, Changing Organizations, Changing Leadership," July 21, 2006, 12, 182–184, http://www.fas.org/blog/secrecy/2010/03/transition_iraq.html (accessed Aug. 3, 2011).

20. Clinton's directive may be found online at http://clinton2.nara.gov/WH/EOP/NSC/html/documents/NSCDoc2.html (accessed Aug. 8, 2012).

21. Kathleen H. Hicks and Christine E. Wormuth, with Eric Ridge, *The Future of U.S. Civil Affairs Forces* (Washington, DC: Center for Strategic and International Studies, 2009), 22; United States Government Accountability Office, "Stabilization and Reconstruction: Actions Needed to Improve Government-wide Planning and Capabilities for Future Operations," Oct. 2007, 6–7.

22. Both Irving Janis and Alexander George made this observation when recommending mechanisms to counteract biased decision making; Janis, *Groupthink: Psychological Studies of Policy Decisions and Fiascoes* (Boston, MA: Houghton Mifflin, 1982), 267–268; George, "The Case for Multiple Advocacy in Making Foreign Policy," *American Political Science Review* 66, no. 3 (1972): 773.

Index

Other Books by Liz Wilkey

In her *Poems from the Pew* series, written with a lively sense of imagination, Liz offers these additional Christian children's poetry books exclusively through Amazon:

1. Gus's Gum and Jenny's Penny: Parable Poems for Christian Children.

2. If Jesus Owned the Diner: And Other Faith-filled Thoughts for Christian Children.

3. He Lived Among Us: A Journey through The Gospel for Christian Children.

Made in the USA
Columbia, SC
30 March 2018